A Factotum in the Book Trade

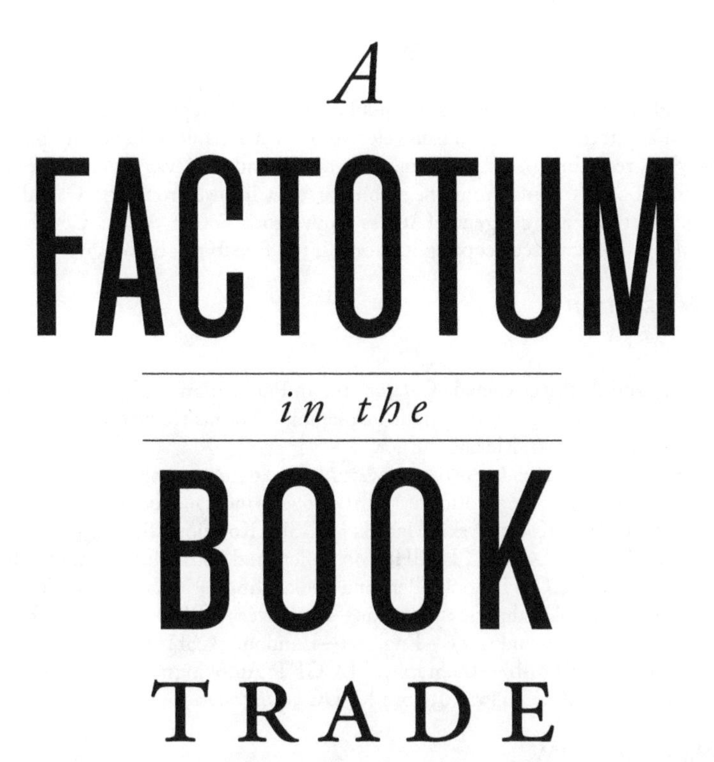

A Memoir

MARIUS
KOCIEJOWSKI

Biblioasis
Windsor, Ontario

FIRST EDITION
10 9 8 7 6 5 4

Library and Archives Canada Cataloguing in Publication
Title: A factotum in the book trade : a memoir / Marius Kociejowski.
Names: Kociejowski, Marius, author.
Identifiers: Canadiana (print) 20210354771 | Canadiana (ebook) 20210354798 | ISBN 9781771964562 (softcover) | ISBN 9781771964579 (ebook)
Subjects: LCSH: Kociejowski, Marius. | LCSH: Kociejowski, Marius—Childhood and youth. | LCSH: Booksellers and bookselling—England—Biography. | LCSH: Booksellers and bookselling—England—London. | LCSH: Book industries and trade—Employees—Biography. | LCSH: Book industries and trade—England—London. | CSH: Authors, Canadian (English)—Biography. | LCGFT: Autobiographies.
Classification: LCC Z280 .K63 2022 | DDC 381/.45002092—dc23

Edited by Daniel Wells
Copyedited by Chandra Wohleber
Text and cover designed by Michel Vrana

Published with the generous assistance of the Canada Council for the Arts, which last year invested $153 million to bring the arts to Canadians throughout the country, and the financial support of the Government of Canada. Biblioasis also acknowledges the support of the Ontario Arts Council (OAC), an agency of the Government of Ontario, which last year funded 1,709 individual artists and 1,078 organizations in 204 communities across Ontario, for a total of $52.1 million, and the contribution of the Government of Ontario through the Ontario Book Publishing Tax Credit and Ontario Creates.

PRINTED AND BOUND IN THE UNITED STATES

for Dan Wells
to do with as he likes

CONTENTS

Chapter One

A FLOATING WORLD

A SHADOW MOVES ACROSS MY PLATE. WHEN IT REACHES full eclipse, which will be in a few months' time, I will be out of the antiquarian book trade forever. Try as I might, I can't rinse the rancid taste of that word out of my mouth. What is *forever* when set against the universe? It's about the length of a sticking plaster. And that we should think ourselves indispensable. A necessary illusion, without it we'd surely lose our will to live. We seek, in whatever small way, to be recognised for what we achieve. The shop in Cecil Court, where I have worked for over a decade, will be closing although its proprietor, Peter Ellis, will continue to operate from home. I wish him well but, and I'm sure he will agree with me, the bookshop is, and will always be, the soul of the trade. What happens there does not happen elsewhere. The multifariousness of human nature is more on show there than anywhere else, and I think it's because of books, what they are, what they release in ourselves, and what they become when we make them magnets to our desires.

The world was made,' says Stéphane Mallarmé, 'in order to result in a beautiful book.' All else—the filling of an order, the cataloguing of a book—is mere procedure. A computer screen will take us further away from, not closer to, the Eleusinian mysteries. Anyway I thank Peter Ellis for the best years of my working life. I've had fewer problems with him than with anyone else. This may seem like a backhanded compliment, which it isn't. I've had my share of trouble. I've seen discord: I've seen one man take his own business and cheat it, lie to it, bleed it into tulip-shaped glasses, starve it to death over Michelin-starred dishes; I've seen a man whose mind dissolved at the bottom of a vodka bottle; I've seen another descend into madness. A grumbler Peter may be, quick to anger too, but compared to them, he has been straight as a die. Maybe it's because the book trade is so fragile—so susceptible to the world's turbulence, and to the vicissitudes of what is or is not in fashion—that it is so often an intemperate zone. This said, I've been lucky enough to be close to what I love. And yet what we love can bring out not only the best but also the worst in ourselves. When the day arrives, and the final turning of the key in the front door lock sounds louder than it's ever done before, it'll be all I can do to keep a stoic face. It is not so much a job I'll be leaving as a way of life.

I am not, in the fullest sense, a bookseller, which is to say an independent one, although the opportunities for me to become one did arise. The choice was between selling books and writing them. One would not allow for the other; put it down to some configuration in the brain. I am not so sure I can consider myself a bookshop assistant either and maybe this is because I am deluded enough to believe that a man clutching a rare volume is somehow, if only for seconds at a time, bestowed with a pedigree. It is not how one feels holding a box of cereal. It might be said one can sell them both. The book world is, however, a world in which one might keep one's face. There are less dignified ways to survive, some of them so ghastly the world of the bookseller is by comparison effete. I am, by choice, maybe temperament too, a factotum in the book trade. The tough business end of things has been for others to administrate. I envy them not. I have a phobia for window envelopes. Columns with numbers in them terrify me. Amazingly, over a passage of forty-five years, I have got away with being close to innumerate, which is something of an achievement in a world of sales. I can translate Roman numerals into Arabic, however, and I know which way up a book sits in the hand and on a good day I can even alphabetize. What more can anyone want to ask of me? I have always been at the service of other people, which, for those wanting a satellite reading of where I stand, is the position from whence these words come, the ticklish underbelly of the trade.

I have been invited to write a memoir of my working life from a crouching angle and not from some elevated place—the factotum as watcher, spook, chronicler of the mundane. I resisted, I pleaded. I said I would rather not produce a sedative. Many such books are. The dedicatee of this book, who may be its only reader—if so, it's plenty enough for me—after over half a decade of petitioning has finally worn me down. This book is his to do with as he likes.

So what am I to say of it all? What should my approach be? What at first I figured would be a breeze now weighs heavily on me. Can I remember anything or, more to the point, is what I remember reliable? We fabricate our own lives, which is not to say we falsify them, but that with respect to the present the past is always shaped by it, it's the mould in which the jelly's made. There again, I know things nobody else does, and so that raises the question of how much I should divulge of a world reputed for its tetchiness. The book trade is naturally secretive even when it pretends otherwise. What one might think is an open book is actually a closed one. The reason is simple: one does not want to reveal the identities of one's sources, one's customers or where the next big buy will be. As gossip is the bastard child of secrecy there's no end to the wagging of tongues. I've never known a bookseller whose ears do not perk up at news of a close neighbour's infelicities. Maybe it's because he knows he might be next in line. And yet try and get him to speak into a microphone he'll send you on a wild goose chase. The bookseller is a master of deflection. So I'm largely on my own with this one. I don't want to get bogged down in 'shop talk' or matters of points and issues or auction rings or a thousand other things that seem to fascinate other booksellers because they bore me silly and if the writer is bored chances are he will bore. There'll be no yeast in the prose.

A young woman I spoke to about this, who paints her face in all the primary colours, such that at the sight of her the traffic either brakes or accelerates, when I expressed my doubts about writing this book, she said to me, 'Go on, young people love reading about old white men selling books.' She's all sass, Natalie. She used to work for the children's bookshop next door and was ousted for thinking she is worth as much as she believes she is. I'm sure she's right, but she ought to have known her boss would care not a jot for her vision of how things should be. She ought to have known there are a hundred people waiting to fill her shoes. There is any number of willing human sacrifices. Anyhow Natalie rules the world with her rainbow face. Will she, though, ever rule herself? Yes, she will. She's got talent in abundance, which at present she is either loath or fearful to put into practice. She tells me she's working on a graphic novel, or what—Lynd Ward her point of reference—she prefers to call a 'visual story.'* It is based on Johannes Kepler's *Somnium* (*The Dream*, 1634) whose hero, Duracotus, works, as did the author himself, with Tycho Brahe.† Also, with its voyage to the moon, it is a candidate for the earliest science fiction. Will she do it? I'm sure she's got what it takes.

I wonder sometimes whether the trade is not taking leave of me. This may sound as if the sun circles the world and that I've

* The American artist and storyteller Lynd Ward is best known for his 'wordless novel' *Gods' Man* (1929), the Faustian tale of a man who signs away his soul for a magic paintbrush, an interesting choice of medium given that the story is told entirely in wood engravings. Many cataloguers place the apostrophe of the book's title in the wrong place.

† In 1572, Tycho Brahe discovered a new supernova in the constellation Cassiopeia. What excites the modern imagination is that it was the 'same yond star that's westward from the pole' in Shakespeare's *Hamlet*. With respect to more earthly matters, Natalie Kay-Thatcher's chapbook *How to Start a Feynman* (2011), though small, is hugely worthy of our respective magnifying glasses.

put myself at the centre of the universe. *Where's everybody gone?* Secondhand bookshops, once a feature of almost every borough, town and village, continue to close, even in supposedly bookish places like Oxford and Cambridge. When I first settled in London, in 1974, I could walk from my bedsit in Earls Court Square and within a half hour be at one of six or seven bookshops. My favourite bookseller was Sheila Ramage, the kindliest face in the trade, who ran Notting Hill Books. She died on January 24, 2020. At least I had a chance to tell her what her shop meant to me and that it was a place in which I made numerous discoveries. It was always there that I'd find the book I didn't know I wanted. The shop closed down in 2012. Now they've all gone.

So what brought things to this impasse? It is almost too easy to blame outside forces although it wouldn't be a mistake to do so. Town and city are no longer the organic growths they once were. They have begun to operate on a purely functional level that has little to do with what actually brings grace into our lives. You eviscerate a habitat of its culture and the species it supports will find it increasingly difficult to survive or else they'll mutate into something else. Greed is behind much of this, landlords squeezing as much as they can out of small businesses while governments of whatever hue increase rates. There has been an overall failure of imagination, an inability to see consequences. Small wonder Peter Ellis has had it up to here. With the collapse of individual enterprises, and with people finding their solution on the internet it has got so that one area of London looks much like any other, the same wretched chains. Will somebody write the book that'll describe how the internet has changed the cityscape? I could also say the trade at its most rarefied is collapsing from inside, by which I mean there is something that has gone integrally wrong with the trade itself. My compatriots will not appreciate me saying this: the antiquarian book trade is slowly but surely destroying the antiquarian book trade.

If twenty years ago someone told me there wouldn't be a single classical music shop left in London I would have guffawed because, after all, there will always be classical music aficionados just as there would always be readers of good literature. Who, just a couple of decades ago, would have thought it possible? There's nowhere I can go now for a musical fix or where I may abandon myself to happenstance. So many of one's best discoveries are made while having a browse. A slack word gathers force: William Hazlitt, in his essay "On the Conversation of Authors" in *The Plain Speaker* (1826), speaks of the human bookworm who 'browses on the husks and leaves of books, as the young fawn browses on the bark and leaves of trees.' We browse on our culture, drawing from it things upon which we may, if we so choose, concentrate and maybe even add to. The computer has shot the idea of the browse out of our skies. We go directly to the thing we require and look to neither side of it. Such discoveries as we do make are accidental and not quite the fruit of a good browse. There may be infinitely more choice, but to be spoiled for choice extinguishes desire.

My favourite record dealer was Sally Rettig, a big woman with a small space between her front teeth who could strike terror into those who blundered into one of her many prejudices. I went into her shop once, seeking out, in all innocence, some recordings of Elisabeth Schwarzkopf singing Schubert lieder. She bellowed at me, 'We don't sell blonde Nazi singers!' The other customers, browsers, were quite unfazed. This was England before it got *sleek*, when so much was still allowable. Character is the greater part of any small business touching on arts and literature. Sally's in music heaven, bless her, and I don't know what happened to her business partner, Colin Butler, who always produced a wry smile as she launched into yet another of her tirades. What joy they brought into people's lives. A world more amenable would have seen to it their shop became an institution that survived them, but sadly it predeceased Sally and when it did a light went out forever. Walk all over London, you will not find its like.

If I deviate, my purpose is to demonstrate how the character of a city is measurable through its smaller enterprises. I posit the unthinkable. Will the day come where there are no more secondhand bookshops? I think not, but of this I can't be absolutely sure. The driving out of or rather the failure to encourage such enterprises will be seen as yet another chapter in the already over-long history of human stupidity. London is fast becoming a cultural catastrophe. My favourite bookshops are closing one by one. At this rate very soon there will be nowhere left for me to browse. I won't step into any of those jumped-up bookshops that masquerade as art galleries with nice little walnut tables where you sit down and pay three times the price for the privilege. They are the province of hedge fund managers and cocaine addicts, often both one and the same. American dealers with their so-called book galleries started that trend and now, as with so much else, it has crept over here. I want dirt; I want chaos; I want, above all, mystery. I want to be able to step into a place and have the sense that there I'll find a book, as yet unknown to me, which to some degree will change my life.

Books can, books do.

The other week I was in a bookshop near to where I live, idly perusing the literary criticism section, which rarely affords me pleasure, and there I spotted a book I'd never seen before, *King Lear: The Space of Tragedy* (1977) by the Russian film director Grigori Kozintsev. I hadn't been aware that while filming Shakespeare's play he kept a journal. It was years since I'd seen the film. I leafed through it and there was barely a page that didn't contain at least one line that immediately detached itself from the surrounding text and astonished me. 'And then the devil receives his compensation from the poet,' Kozintsev writes. 'It is the devil's hour of death, and perhaps even a whole day's holiday. He can snore in the poet's blood with the sleep of the dead.' It's not easy to isolate his lines because standing alone they seem at times a bit purple, and yet this is prose wrung from the blood and not the stuff of dead-eyed literary theorists. I bought it and in preparation watched the film again. Although flawed in places, in one instance grievously so, the film is just short of a masterpiece. The book, on the other hand, and despite its somewhat drab title, is wholly one. I am now close to the end of it, reading it slowly because of the joy it affords me. It is a treasure not only of Shakespeare criticism, which it is, or of filmmaking, which it also is, but at its most profound level it is an examination of the soul. Already it has become one of my 'secret' texts with the alchemical properties such books contain. It cost me £2.50. I sell books for a hundred times that price, which yield in absolute terms a hundred times less. This is why bookshops are magic places: somewhere, in one of their nooks and crannies, there awaits a book that will ever so subtly alter one's existence. And with every shop that closes so, too, goes still more of the serendipity which feeds the human spirit.

As for my own small part in the trade, I will have had a decent run of it. Already I'm past retirement age. What else could I have done? Smoked haddock, prayer cushions, green shoelaces, there are any number of things one can sell but very few things one can sell with panache. I found myself in the unemployment office once, being interviewed for what is now called 'Jobseeker's Allowance.' The man interrogating me asked what I did for a living. I told him I sold books. (I kept it simple.) 'Well, then,' he said, 'you can sell shoes.' 'It wouldn't be the same,' I protested. 'How so?' he replied. 'They were old books,' I answered, 'some of them valuable, and the selling of them requires knowledge.' I felt him looking at me as if through the wrong end of a telescope. A few days later, I got a phone call from Joanna Herald of Ulysses Bookshop and I was back in the swim. The book trade is a floating world for people of intelligence unsuited for anything else, a statement that may not be welcomed by fee-paying members of the Antiquarian Booksellers' Association, but I am thinking more of the people who work in it rather than those who run it, and as such, and assuming I'm possessed of a pinch of intelligence, it has kept me afloat for over four decades.

One's daily work is no easy thing to describe. One may produce a thriller, the higher the body count the better, but to speak of what falls within the mundane requires far more than imagination provides. Will somebody please throw me a line? Ah, and here it comes, just in time. Not long ago, I read J. L. Carr's *A Month in the Country* (1980) which, because it is so popular and, worse still, a runner-up for the Booker Prize, I had dismissed. I'm such a snob sometimes. A close friend of mine gave it to me.

What could I do? I had to read it. Near the beginning of this small gem of a book, a first edition of which, by the way, fetches as much as £475, which is quite a lot for only 111 pages—yes, but *what* pages—the following sentence leapt out at me: 'Our jobs are our private fantasies, our disguises, the cloak we can creep inside to hide.' I read this several times, trying to grasp its meaning although it is clear enough. Absolute clarity is of itself a mystery almost impossible to probe. It's why I could never quite 'get' Edward Thomas's "Adlestrop" although it is one of the most simple, most transparent, poems in the English language. *Our jobs are our private fantasies, our disguises, the cloak we can creep inside to hide.* Carr is right: we who work and do so in full view of the mercantile world must necessarily hide ourselves, and the greater the skill we bring to the making of a camouflage, the more room we allow for our imaginative faculties.

Certainly I've seen the best and the worst of it, the rise and fall of a number of bookshops, but first I'll have to locate the gland that one day soon will make me pine for a particular dimension of my existence, a zone in which there's no saying from one day to the next who or what will enter it.

* * *

Yesterday it was a fiddler from Milwaukee or, rather, a violinist when playing early English baroque, his area of expertise, and a fiddler when playing country and western. The latter one might call a divertissement. I've been a bit confused by the distinctions made between violin and fiddle, violinist and fiddler, and now, researching the matter, I discover words that feel just right to me: 'You don't spill beer on a violin.' The C&W side of things is a recent, somewhat troubling, development, he told me, at least for his wife who said to him that had she suspected as much she would never have married him. I am at too great a distance to be able to give their marriage a call, but I suspect things are not all that bad, certainly not enough to warrant mariticide or uxoricide, but musically it would be a shame if the one makes him lose sight of the other.

A bit to my surprise, he purchased Patrick Leigh Fermor's *The Broken Road* (2013), the third and final volume of the author's youthful memories of his walk from the Hook of Holland to Constantinople. I say 'surprise' because in my experience not many Americans go for Fermor. There may be just a bit too much Harris Tweed in his style. *The Broken Road* was cobbled together by the author's literary executors from his journals, incomplete drafts and notes. Constantinople itself comprises no more than a couple of pages of brief sketches of little consequence. If Fermor was unable to complete the trilogy I suspect, although this may be putting a romantic spin on things, it's because to have done so would have been tantamount to bidding farewell to life. On the whole I think the writing in *The Broken Road* is often better than the overwrought prose of the second volume, *Between the Woods and the Water* (1986), which betrays an occasional weakness for the purple. For all its rough edges *The Broken Road* has the ring of direct as opposed to remembered experience.

One of my sweetest memories from my years of working for the firm of Bertram Rota Booksellers is when I catalogued Fermor's correspondence with the actress and socialite Lady Diana Cooper. A beauty of a kind that barely makes sense outside the 1930s, she put most of the men she encountered into a trance. Some fell in their traces, Maurice Baring, for example. I catalogued his letters to her as well, a sad business given that he had by then succumbed to Parkinson's disease and visually stuttered all over the page. They were the confused jottings of a mere mortal faced with a goddess. Similarly wowed, but very much in control of himself, Fermor, in his letters to her, was brought to the exquisite and rendered incapable of describing a walk across a field without making of it a brilliant literary exercise. As it turned out, the letters had to be returned to Diana Cooper's son, John Julius Norwich, because he realised in the nick of time that they had slipped by mistake into the bigger archive. Patrick Leigh Fermor was still alive. As for the indecency of putting a living person's correspondence into the public domain very few people nowadays have any such scruples. There was a time when this simply wasn't done, when to do so was considered *bad form*. I was glad, though, to have had my time wasted in such a pleasurable way.

Boyish exuberance followed Fermor into old age. I saw him once in the London Library being cautioned for making a racket in the reading room. I suspected he had had a wet lunch and was giddy with ebullience. I informed my customer that he had a treat in store, a wonderful description of a Balkan folk dance.

When I asked him his name he told me it was Jonathan Brodie, 'Brodie as in "Deacon Brodie",' which was an impressive bit of referencing given that the historical figure was the inspiration for Robert Louis Stevenson's *Strange Case of Dr Jekyll and Mr Hyde* (1886). A few years earlier, together with W. E. Henley, Stevenson wrote a play called *Deacon Brodie or The Double Life* (1880), which is widely considered an artistic failure. It is very rare, a book any serious collector of Stevenson with a deep enough pocket will own but almost certainly will not have read. Deacon Brodie: Was this some kind of lure? Was there something in my face that betrayed a passion for the writer I would most like to have at my table?

'Are you a Stevensonian *too*?' I asked.

There are certain authors who in their readership create a kind of brotherhood, one of the conditions for this being that although the writer in question may be highly visible he has been critically undervalued or else, as in the case of Stevenson, marooned in a specific genre. A few years ago, I revisited *Treasure Island* (1883) and gained from it nothing other than a pleasant glow from an ancient fire. This is not because I consider it anything less than one of the masterworks of juvenile literature, which it certainly is, but because it was already so deeply etched in my mind that everything was precisely as I had left it sixty years before. Blind Pew tapping his way down the dark path to Jim Hawkins's home held no surprises for me. It is now the *other* Stevenson that claims me, and on this Brodie and I were agreed, the Stevenson of the essays and travel narratives.

With one dance already in the ether, I spoke to Brodie of my favourite passage from the posthumously published *In the South Seas* (1900) in which Stevenson describes a dance he witnessed in Butaritari, one of the Gilbert Islands in the South Pacific: 'The *hula*,' he writes, 'as it may be viewed by the speedy globetrotter in Honolulu, is surely the most dull of man's inventions, and the spectator yawns under its length as at a college lecture or a parliamentary debate. But the Gilbert Island dance leads on the mind; it thrills, rouses, subjugates.' And now follow words that stand in for a thousand books of criticism and which I partly italicise because what they impart goes straight to the heart of all artistic creation: 'it has the essence of all art, *an unexplored imminent significance*.'

I am presently taken back to my friendship with the poet Christopher Middleton who, by the way, was quite the most wonderful man with whom to go book-hunting for his was a mind that journeyed down the more dimly lit avenues of literature. What I owe him is incalculable. Who else would have put me on to Marmaduke Pickthall? Dmitri Merezhkovsky? And, yes, Rose Macaulay? Now there's another highly visible, highly undervalued author who gave us one of the best opening lines in all literature: '"Take my camel, dear," said my aunt Dot, as she climbed down from this animal on her return from High Mass.' What joy it is to discover a few lines later that the camel is domiciled in a Sussex village. The world seems not to have fully twigged to her genius and I advise collectors to obtain *The Towers of Trebizond* (1956), a first edition of which can still be had for the price of a new book. They will be rewarded for the whole of their cognisant lives.

It was not a one-way traffic between Middleton and myself. I put him onto Bruno Schulz some years before the anglophone world began to clamour for him: *Cinnamon Shops* (1963), scarce because when it failed to sell it was remaindered and when the remainder failed to move it was pulped and after it was pulped it would be quite a few years before it was reissued as *The Street of Crocodiles* (1977). Schulz was, and still is, an obsession of mine, and it was William Hoffer, the notorious Vancouver bookseller, who sold me a pristine copy of the original *Cinnamon Shops*.* Bill Hoffer deserves, and will have, a chapter of his own.

---

* It was three years before I was able to locate a copy of *Cinnamon Shops* (MacGibbon & Kee, 1963). I remember asking the proprietors of Skoob Books,

Christopher Middleton was the first to bring the Swiss writer Robert Walser across the language divide; *The Walk and other stories* (1957) was published while the reclusive author was still alive. When told of it, Walser, never a very loquacious man, was said to have remarked from the mental asylum where he chose to live, '*So, so*,' which is the German for '*My, my*.' Why, in all these years, has nobody ever asked me for a copy of the first English edition? It is the poet Denise Riley's favourite book, which ought to be a strong enough recommendation. Why does it not fetch as high a price as Christopher Isherwood's *Sally Bowles* (1937), a book of roughly the same dimensions? This is a nonsense, I know, but at the end of my career I find myself in many ways as perplexed as I was at the beginning of it. Why does Ian Fleming's *Casino Royale* (1953) command a much higher figure than T. S. Eliot's *The Waste Land* (1923)? When Christopher and I visited bookshops he would eye the duodecimo, clothbound editions such as those J. M. Dent produced early in the century, muttering small endearments to them. Very few publishers nowadays take so much care in the production of the classics of literature. Anyway, to get back to Stevenson, I am not a little proud to have introduced Christopher to *In the South Seas*. As for the passage I've just quoted, he said of it: 'So it is always on the brink and leaving something to the reader or to the listener, which is not just a secret and not just a mystery but is the sense of being on the verge of something. That's what I suppose resonance and suggestion are all about.'*

I brought into work a spare copy I had as a gift for Patti Smith. Where is she? And if she comes in, where did I put the book? She

---

when they were still working in the basement of Joseph Poole on Charing Cross Road, to watch out for a copy. One day I got a call from them, saying they'd found one. I almost ran all the way there. It turned out to be a pulp fiction, Bruno Schwarz's *Dames Are Dynamite* with a lurid cover showing a woman in a revealing red dress flogging a man, which, when one thinks about it, is not all that far removed from Bruno Schulz's masochistic drawings of men kneeling in submission at women's bare feet.

* *Palavers: Christopher Middleton in Conversation with Marius Kociejowski* (Shearsman Books, 2004).

had been in several times before, always without fanfare or security people in tow, this time humming a tune. I wondered whether she was working out an idea for a song. I did not, of course, make anything of her presence. Such people you let be. She spent quite a while looking at the books and suddenly I heard her gasp, 'Oh, my favourite author!' Who could it be? There was very little Beat poetry in stock and I knew we didn't have any Rimbaud or, for that matter, Verlaine. I could see the Blake volumes from where I was sitting. Who was it, then? I asked this knowing full well that such verdicts vary from day to day, depending on what preoccupies one at the time. A small shift of perspective, a change of mood, and Byron falls victim to Shelley, Dostoevsky to Tolstoy, and Graham Greene to Henry Green. When she came to the desk with her newly found treasure I almost leapt with joy to see it was Robert Louis Stevenson. It was a copy of *Memories* (1923) with Jessie M. King's artwork on the cover. I got her engaged on the matter of Stevenson and when I mentioned *In the South Seas* she had not heard of it. The book awaits her. And that magical phrase, surely she'd fall upon it, maybe even slip it into one of her songs.

An unexplored imminent significance. Maybe, too, those words can be extended to the blossoming of friendship because I think my conversation with Jonathan Brodie clinched it for us both. We'll be meeting again, I'm sure. There have been a number of such friendships whose beginnings I owe to the trade. I'll be speaking of them from time to time because for me the antiquarian book trade has always been about books and people. I can't emphasise this enough. I firmly believe the fact of being surrounded by books has a great deal to do with flushing to the surface the inner lives of people. All those books—the good, the bad, the mediocre—when banded together act upon the slumbering mind with invisible spores. What we receive from them may not relate to anything inside the books themselves but altogether they constitute *intelligence.* And if intelligence is a form of enthusiasm and enthusiasm the engine that drives the universe, then surely there is some law of electromagnetism to explain what happens between people when in the midst of books, lots of them. This may include saying nothing at all. Almost every Saturday morning a man comes into the shop looking for titles issued in the Oxford English Novel series, which tend to be the most accurate editions available, and although we have never spoken I get a powerful sense of an inner life, which talk would only serve to dispel.

If books are conducive to conversation some people are distinctly uncomfortable with them. I have known people who stepped into my home and, after glancing at my books and remarking on their sheer volume, clearly felt oppressed by them. As for the shop there is a breed of *Homo sapiens* that will walk inside, take a deep breath, and say, 'Mmm, I just love the smell of old books.' They are to be got rid of as quickly as possible, with whatever violence it takes. I have heard the line a thousand times and never, never have I sold a book to any one of those people. Also one must be ruthless with those who ask, 'What is the most expensive book you've got here?' Often it is the male of the species trying to impress the female. There is an even more objectionable subspecies who with their mobile phones like to photograph each other holding an open book although very rarely are their eyes ever fixed on the page. The punishment for them cannot be too severe. The very worst of all, however, are the pumped-up booksellers who come in saying, 'You got any high spots?'

'Yes,' is my standard response, 'all of them.' This is a matter I will return to with extreme prejudice.

As I plan to write about people as well as books and about my role as marriage broker between the two, be warned that the diversions will be many. Anyway I abhor the straight line. My hope is that these words may go some way towards explaining what it is exactly that I'll be taking leave of much too soon in my life. Meanwhile, Mr Brodie, wherever you may be, rosin your bow.

* * *

Suddenly a ghost moves across the page. There will be plenty more. I have reached a point in my life when of my acquaintances the dead have begun to outnumber the living. Ghosts are ghosts only until we join them. The people I knew from my early days in the trade are mostly gone and with them a set of attitudes with respect to books and collecting that is fast becoming difficult to appreciate. Where is he now, the rather dapper man in the bow tie, of a species I term 'hickory American,'* the gentleman from Philadelphia who collected Emily Dickinson? I wish I knew because I would dearly like to find out more about him. What was his name, for God's sake? I remember he was involved with a small collection of Dickinson manuscripts, which by now may have joined the main collection at the Houghton Library in Harvard. Whenever he came into the shop we'd talk of her as if she were a common, though distant, relative.

It's a curious business collecting Emily Dickinson because textually the early editions are wrong, their editors having sanitized the author's many grammatical tics and expurgated all those dashes that give such a sense of urgency to the poems. She was all nerve—there was not time enough for her to punctuate. The manuscripts bear this out with the words often spilling over the edge of the page onto the table. An American bookseller of some repute once boasted to me he had a signed first edition Dickinson. I should have told him I'd pay him ten, no, a *hundred* times, his asking price. The only poem she published during her lifetime was in an anthology, *A Masque of Poets* (1878), and even then it is not attributed to her. What was this man saying to me? A *signed* Dickinson? Away with him, vamoose. I have a slight ethical problem when it comes to selling her books. If it is a collector determined to have every edition of Dickinson no matter how inaccurate, that's fine, and indeed I wouldn't mind having a copy of *Poems* (1890) whose floral design on the cover feels true to what's inside. But when an innocent comes in looking for a collection of Dickinson's poems I begin to falter. At the very least it should be the one-volume edition edited by Thomas H. Johnson, which first appeared in 1955 in three volumes.

---

* The 'hickory American' is an old school democrat in the widest sense of the word, as close to an aesthete as the country will tolerate. They've become rare.

My arithmetic, poor though it is, leads me to a grassy plot, for my hickory American must have been in his early eighties when I last saw him. And that was almost twenty years ago. We *talked Emily* and we agreed on how she had been taken up by any number of dubious causes, such that she is claimed by some to have been a proto-feminist and even a lesbian. She wrote passionately to women, of course, but it's strange how the deep, often physical affection between women of earlier times has been cast in modern parlance, or, worse still, betrayed by women themselves. The revisionist is, more often than not, the enemy of literature. In Terence Davies's biographical film *A Quiet Passion* she is oddly addressed as "Ms. Dickinson." A postman delivering her mail would have been confused by the honorific. My ghost in a bow tie told me of when he paid a visit to Dickinson's grave at Amherst. 'I got down on one knee,' he said, 'and I muttered, "O Emily, what *are* they doing to you?"'

* * *

Several years ago, some fool in one of the dailies wrote that booksellers don't read.

The very next day, an even bigger fool came into the shop and, speaking as if the idea had just occurred to him, announced, 'It is well known that booksellers don't read.'

'Yes,' I replied, 'I read the same article.'

I examined his face for signs of embarrassment but there were none. Sadly, though, it is often true. There are booksellers who might just as well be selling pears and apples. One of the best-known of them had no more than a couple of shelves of books in his house and those were merely for show. There's another who comes to mind, who was not really such a bad fellow, and, in any case, he had already stopped selling books for something more lucrative, either cars or houses. I met him in the street one day, close to where I live, and invited him back for a coffee. I went off to grind the coffee and when I came back I found him almost as if in a fever, pulling volume after volume from my bookshelves, turning to the copyright pages, and then shoving them back. I'm not sure

I ever saw anyone move at such speed through so many books and indeed I feared that he might do some damage to them.

'But they are not for sale,' I said.

I thought, mistakenly, I caught some apology in his features.

'What, really!' he cried. 'You've got some valuable books here.'

I told him he was mistaken, that they were worth *absolutely nothing*.

'Absolutely nothing?' He laughed.

'Absolutely nothing,' I repeated. 'As long as these books remain on my shelves, which is exactly where I want them to be, they are of no monetary value whatsoever. If I decide to sell them, which is highly unlikely, only then will they be worth anything.'

I couldn't have put it more simply, but my words bounced off him. He quickly drank his coffee and left, clearly thinking I had a screw loose. It is not often, though, that a bookseller is also a book collector. I will write about one who was, with near-fatal consequences. Selling and collecting becomes a bridging exercise difficult to maintain and it may be one of the reasons why I never became a bookseller in the full sense of the word.

* * *

Somehow I'd pictured myself shuffling into old age and becoming one of those cranky figures I remember from when I first haunted Cecil Court in the 1970s, who couldn't give a fig whether or not they sold a book. Such places could be found all over London. One could step into even the smallest shop and there was always the sense of an inner sanctum to which only the elect had admittance. This is important to note. At that point, and it would still be the case later, a bookseller was deeply ensconced in a culture of secrecy. One simply did not speak of the inner workings of the trade. Now, of course, the guts are all over the place. One may poke through them at one's leisure. One speaks openly, shamelessly, of one's gains and one's losses. I contradict myself. There are still plenty of secrets, especially when one's own survival depends on keeping them. Anyway, to go back to those little bookshops and their secret zones, all the books one desired were in those cubbyholes, just beyond one's reach, or so one imagined. Money was not the key to them nor could a smile move the misanthropic hearts of those crotchety old men in their small dark shops. (What man of feeling, though, would not choose the misanthrope over the indiscriminate lover of his own species?) Selling a book was never uppermost in their thoughts, and indeed there was much pleasure to be had in *not* selling a book to someone thought undeserving of it. It was a great shame when booksellers began to have to sell books in order to survive.

Some of them were blissfully rude, especially in Cecil Court. A sign in Bob Chris's shop read: 'Do not mistake courtesy on my part as an invitation to stay all day.' I remember trying to buy a book from him once, the Spring 1941 issue of the clothbound *Folios of New Writing* which contained "Mr. Jonas," an uncollected story by Henry Green based on his experiences in the Auxiliary Fire Service,* the beauty of its prose complementing the terrible beauty of fire. When I asked him whether he had one, he grunted and said no. Just then, my eye alighted on a copy on the shelf behind his desk.

'There's one!' I said.

He turned slowly as if this were the biggest demand that had been made on him all week. 'So there is,' he muttered.

After weighing the matter for a moment, he said, 'It's not for sale.'

---

* Green or Greene? I still think time will tell who the better writer is. This said, Henry Green is one of those authors whose reputation needs to be revived every ten years, Green's genius was in making the ordinary miraculous. There are only nine novels, which actually is enough, but the range of his voice was such that each of the books is completely different. 'Prose is not to be read aloud,' he wrote, 'but to oneself alone at night, and it is not quick as poetry but rather *a gathering web of insinuations*.' What poetic quickness there is in that phrase! 'Prose should be,' he continues, 'a direct intimacy between strangers with no appeal to what both may have known. It should slowly appeal to fears unexpressed, it should in the end draw tears out of the stone.' What a shame alcohol stilled his voice. What he achieved, though, was enough.

The times were kinder to them, of course, the rents lower, the populace more literate in the wider sense of the word. The days are long gone when, figuratively speaking, booksellers were carried out of their shops in coffins. And now I've had to cancel my order for one. The future prospects for the antiquarian book trade are bleak or should I say for the bookseller as species, as clubbable misanthrope?

Chapter Two

THE ROAD I'D LATER TAKE

SO WHAT BROUGHT ME HERE? WHERE'S THE BEGINNING OF it all, the origin of the species I would later become? What am I to my grandchildren who on occasion come into the shop or who at home stare wide-eyed at all the books, so many of them surely there is only so much one can handle? Maybe I'm some white-haired figure out of an unimaginably distant past when, with respect to the written word, the typewriter was the highest technological advance since the invention of the printing press. *What is a typewriter?* I can hear them ask. It is not quite how I see myself, of course. I got to where I am in a few brisk strides. The question is how do I account for those strides and of what, when making them, was I made?

There were other paths open to me, some of them more profitable, though none that I'd ever seriously contemplate. Academe would have killed me, arts administration came close. The trajectory of my working life when seen from this vantage point barely makes sense. Who was that callow youth pushing a mail trolley inside a government Crown Office, who was forced to resign because of his allegedly immoral activities? (I couldn't believe the information they had gathered on my private life and this was well before the computer age.) Who was the short-order cook who dipped week-old pre-cooked spaghetti into boiling water for two minutes so that even now I can recognise its slithery texture anywhere? When I was still living in Canada I must have had a dozen jobs in the space of only three or four years. I became a picture framer in a small gallery in Ottawa where from time to time I was also involved in sales, my greatest achievement being the sale of a seascape, sight unseen, over the telephone. Mainly, though, I framed. My low point was when I tripped and put my foot through a large nineteenth-century gouache. It was a ghastly thing anyway and not to be venerated for its age. I got a job selling guitars, which lasted only a week. When I told the owner he was being duped by the manufacturers, that virtually all the instruments had faults of one kind or another, he sacked me immediately. I was uncommonly naïve.

My briefest employment was painting a flagpole. It lasted all of two days, the first spent in contemplation as to how it might be feasible, the second applying the paint. The sensible thing would have been to take down the flagpole and paint it at ground level, but it was firmly fixed in place. Another solution would have been to construct scaffolding around it, but there was no budget available for such an extravagance. Oddly enough, I can't remember how we did it although it did involve a certain amount of shimmying up and down the flagpole. What I do remember is that my boss did a runner on me. I was so stung by this that I made it my mission to find him, which eventually I did, although I received only half the money owed me.

At some point after the flagpole and before the art gallery I became sales assistant in a shop that sold wicker baskets and bamboo furniture. I was known to my friends as "The Wicker King." The manageress, who was in her thirties, who had as many syllables in her name as mine, would describe to me, in detail, her sexual escapades. She did so, I think, only because she was bored. I think the wicker, so much of it, finally got into the middle of her psyche. A single match, the place would have gone up in flames. She was perfectly capable of it. She was a diplomat's mistress, in an affair going nowhere, and I was her confidant. I got to learn in more detail than I wished what diplomats liked to do with their mistresses. She'd ask me if I thought it was abnormal behaviour. Whatever feels good, I muttered, for such was the wisdom of the times. At the close of each week, our pay in hand, away from the shop owner's eyes, we would demolish a basket, usually by placing it upside down on the floor and jumping or, more riskily, sitting down hard on it, she one week, me the next. She put a run through her nylon stocking once. She raised her skirt to show me. There was a very thin, rather delectable, streak of cruelty in her. It was around this time I discovered the Grove Press edition of the Marquis de Sade. Our weekly activity was a quick cure for *tædium vitæ* and, besides, there's nothing sweeter than the smell of a newly smashed basket. At first we giggled maniacally, but then high jinks evolved into solemn ritual and we became priestly in our countenance.

A year later, I worked in a light bulb warehouse. (All this took place after I dropped out of college and before I went to university, a period during which I floated aimlessly, as is often the case with young men who are lost to themselves.) The foreman was a man called Wilf who had in him the sly wit of the uneducated and could transfix me with a story which although inconsequential in itself temporarily plugged the holes that boredom drilled through our daily existence. Wilf's genius lay in his ability to keep his listener hanging for just a brief moment before the punch line, a pause that allowed one to consider, as if from a very high place, the absurdities of human nature. Such people have always been teachers to me. God willing, I ferry a bit of Wilf into my prose. He, too, had a weekly ritual not dissimilar to my earlier one, which was to take a G40 light bulb with a circumference roughly that of a grapefruit and, cigarette in mouth—like Sir Winston Churchill with cigars, he was a master of not letting the ash fall from it—he'd toss it backwards over his shoulder. *Pwoff.* There's no sound sweeter than the explosion of a plump light bulb upon concrete. The privilege, though, was his alone. Maybe, had I stuck it out, I'd be doing the same today, I'd have my apprentice and he, too, would have to wait until I've gone.

Pwoff.

* * *

Many years later, in the country I've made mine, I got to know of a couple of booksellers who would take a volume of some author loathsome to them both and use it to play a game of "bounce," the object of the exercise being not so different from skipping stones or what here, in England, is most charmingly called ducks and drakes. Such are the ways by which straitened humanity finds release. Barbaric I know, quite inexcusable, and so says John Milton in his *Areopagitica* (1644): 'Who kills a man kills a reasonable creature, God's image; but he who destroys a good book, kills reason itself, kills the image of God, as it were, in the eye.' Does he not say 'a *good* book'? I must confess—actually, no, confession does not come into this—I recently took a first edition, a signed one at that, which contained a passage that so offended me I tore it in two, down the middle of the spine. The book as physical object gave no resistance. This was not, I hasten to add, at the bookshop. So why present instances that are in themselves morally objectionable? It's to do with work, I suppose, not just its ritual absurdities, so often incomprehensible to people on the outside, but also the daily struggle to get through to the other side of it, the long hours we endure for a mere bubble of free time.

These are just a few of the many jobs I had before I crossed the Atlantic. My first employment in London was as a library assistant in the reference section of Kensington & Chelsea Library. I will never know why, when I didn't even know the Dewey Decimal System, I was given a job over the heads of junior librarians who waited for years to be in that position. The England of 1974 was more eccentric than it is now, and freer. When the head librarian Miss Ensing showed me the shelf number for weather, I asked her if it changes when the climate does.

'Oh,' came the reply, 'I hadn't thought of that.'

The slight curl in her voice suggested she took what I said as a lame attempt at a joke. At least I was in my element, among books, although I began to suspect that most librarians actually hate them. I watched with horror as they gleefully perforated the pages, rubber-stamped the pages and edges, the joy of the kill in their eyes. And then I came in for a shock. In the basement there was a skip virtually full of books, many of them excellent titles, which were scheduled for destruction. They were the books donated to the library in the belief they'd be provided with a good home. The librarians, in their wisdom, considered the books superfluous to their needs. The staff were not permitted to rescue any of them. When I protested, asked why the books weren't given to any of the local charity shops the excuse was that they might be spotted by their previous owners. And so it was that in one of the best public libraries in London *reason itself* was killed.

The first book I bought in England was *Crow* (1970) by Ted Hughes. I had left behind my modest library in Canada. I placed *Crow* on the marble mantelpiece of a rented room in Earls Court Square and told myself I would buy only as many books as it would take to fill the length of that space. Several thousand volumes later, I don't know what became of that promise. During my lunch breaks I would wander over to Kensington Church Walk where Bernard Stone had his Turret Book Shop. I could not have guessed then that one day he'd be my nemesis, but for a young man new to London it was the ideal of what a bookshop should be. Poetry was its specialty and the shop was in a vicinity once favourable to poets. Just around the corner from there, in an upstairs bedsit at 10 Kensington Church Walk, between 1909 and 1914, years which spanned both Imagism and Vorticism, lived Ezra Pound. D. H. Lawrence, Ford Madox Ford and the sculptor Henri Gaudier-Brzeska visited him there. The poet Hilda Doolittle lived at number 6, and Richard Aldington at number 8. And a ten-minute walk from there, at 3 Kensington Court Gardens, lived T. S. Eliot from 1957 until he died. On January 4, 1975, my birthday, the tenth anniversary of Eliot's death, my wife and I strolled into St Stephen's Church on Gloucester Road where he had been church warden.

We were invited to take seats and at the end of the service people shook hands. I had not realised I was sitting beside Eliot's widow, Valerie, who I'd meet again when she came into Bertram Rota, occasionally buying books to fill the gaps in her late husband's collection. Strange though it might seem, this was not such a rare thing, women buying books for their deceased husbands.

And then came my two years (or was it closer to three?) at the Poetry Society in Earls Court Square. What can I say of my time there? Why write about it at all? Quite simply, it was about staying on the line of my life, which, however indirectly, still had to do with books. My mistake was to think there could be a viable connection between books and the world of arts administration. The only way the latter can operate is to subscribe to the lowest common denominator. Woke culture, cancel culture, political correctness, positive discrimination, diversity (for some), sloganizing and idle thinking have all served to make arts administration easier than ever. There are no goals higher than keeping the machine well-oiled. Forget Parnassus. Forget Mnemosyne.

It wasn't that I actively sought employment there. It was more like rolling out of bed one day and finding myself behind a big wooden desk, plying myself with cups of instant coffee. (One still had to travel to central London for an espresso.) My wife was already working for the Poetry Society, her role being the administration of the verse-speaking examinations which brought in, after the annual Arts Council grant, the biggest revenue. I became her assistant, which is not exactly a recipe for domestic bliss. We carried into the building the moods we each woke into. My task was to slip verse-speaking medals into small plastic pouches. The complicated bit was counting them. My wife and I began our London existence in the annex of the fabled White House Hotel, a residential hotel of the kind the playwright Terence Rattigan wrote about, a fading palace of blighted lives. The Poetry Society was diagonally opposite the annex. During the time I worked at Kensington & Chelsea Library it never occurred to me to step inside the place. The very idea of a poetry society struck me then as the most unnatural of growths. Poets are not particularly clubbable.

Can one imagine William Blake paying his annual Poetry Society subscription? Lord Byron would have lampooned the place with an apt rhyme. I came to realise just how right my initial view of it was. Not once, in any of the committee meetings I attended, did I ever hear a serious conversation with respect to poetry and its future. The talk was always of admin and budgets. My advice to anyone who genuinely loves the arts—whether it be visual, music or literature—is to avoid any organisation that purports to be serving their furtherance. One's very best ideals are almost immediately surrendered to bureaucracy and compromise, then impotence, and, ultimately, corruption.

This said, my spell at the Poetry Society, which began in 1976, was a good introduction to the British poetry scene. As such it would also serve as an ideal excuse to escape the British poetry scene. I became, from the very first, a watcher: I watched, I noted, I withdrew. The spectacle of poets rushing towards some imaginary finishing line was unpleasant to observe. Never had I seen so many knives in so many backs although in a way this was a natural outcome of an unnatural process. Poetry is the most solitary of the arts. What can be said in the Society's favour, however, is that at its 21 Earls Court Square location there was a marvellous programme of weekly poetry readings. There was a spacious reading room in which one could listen to the likes of Basil Bunting, Ted Hughes, George Barker, Amy Clampitt, Roy Fisher, Tony Harrison, David Gascoyne, Sorley MacLean, Geoffrey Hill, W. S. Graham and Robert Creeley. One could rub shoulders with them afterwards. Even during its worst period—the so-called Battle of Earls Court—the readings remained catholic in their inclusiveness. A few more women might have been included, but in truth their voices were yet to be heard. There is nowhere in London where one can now go for such a literary feast, which, given the city's size and population, is something of a national disgrace. This is not a country that sufficiently honours its literature. Maybe this is because there is so much of it. You will not find such events at the current Covent Garden address unless, of course, one considers open mic evenings of aesthetic value. There ought to be a law against poets expressing themselves all over the place; there's no mop large enough to absorb the mess they make. The Poetry Society continues to be, as it has been for most of its history, at best an irrelevance, at worst an indelible stain on art's tabernacle. The fact it is of no consequence is in a way a measure of its success. Admin has triumphed over purpose. What higher goal than a smoothly run bureaucracy? I'll give it that. The Poetry Society runs smoothly nowhere. The move to Covent Garden was itself a kind of betrayal because the Earls Court premises was sold to the Society at an absurdly low price on condition that it would continue to operate there. It was, in other words, a gift made on a principle of trust. Maybe, though, nobody else remembers this.

When I started Kit Wright was the Education Secretary, an amiable figure who worked one level below the General Secretary, another amiable figure called Michael Mackenzie. They were, together, the very epitome of what was still a very English muddle. I rather ache for those times, when the gifted amateur was leagues ahead of the professional and when things were make-do. This is when the English are at their best. All this would soon change with the Thatcherite notion of value for money. When seen in those terms, the arts have no value. The Poetry Society was also home to a weekly poetry workshop called Poetry Round, which I attended, whose members would read a poem and then hold it up for criticism after which they would walk away limping or else full of themselves. It was where one learned that one might call one's fellow a complete swine, but never, never criticise, at least not too severely, his or her verses. Poetry Round would have been fit material for a satirical play. As far as I know, James Sutherland-Smith and I have been only people sufficiently weak of mind to continue the literary journey. Madge Herron made a great splash and died, refusing to submit her poems to the tyranny of the page, otherwise one hears only distant rumours of the other people.

After my wife left the Poetry Society I became Examinations Secretary and after Kit Wright's departure, I was made Education Secretary. I was put in overall charge of the Society's verse-speaking examinations and the Poets in Schools scheme, which at that point was subsidised by the booksellers WHSmith. At the time I looked upon the verse-speaking examinations as an anachronism, precious in the extreme, a ghastly exercise of *the voice proper*, but over the years I've come to see how wrong I was. Maybe it was only after going to numerous stultifying poetry readings, always praying for, and sometimes getting, the glowing exception, that I realised most poets could do with a shot of voice training. As for the Poets in Schools scheme, the results were variable. I was slow to realise that very few poets are up to the task. The most able of them was Kit Wright who knew how to communicate with, and draw the very best out of, children.

At this juncture I would like to pay tribute to the American poet Bill Butler who moved to England in the 1960s. I hope his shade doesn't mind if I am half a century late in doing so. Butler was very much a part of the sixties counterculture. After managing Better Books in Charing Cross Road, he moved to Brighton where, with his partner Mike, he ran the now-legendary Unicorn Bookshop. In 1968, the police raided the shop and removed several offensive titles, including copies of J. G. Ballard's *Why I Want to Fuck Ronald Reagan*, which Butler had published under the Unicorn imprint. (There were fifty signed copies and one is currently available from a UK bookseller for £2,250.) Bill was found guilty and the fine imposed was beyond his financial means. It also meant the demise of the bookshop. I am not saying he was a particularly good poet, but occasionally he wrote good poems, and he had a swagger about him that was attractive. I think he might have been a better poet had he not succumbed to exotic fumes. So little work of that decade is good. I didn't know at the time he was gay, but there was an unmistakable streak of the feminine in him coupled with 1950s movie star manliness. This might have made him the deeply troubled figure he was, his woes much exacerbated by his earlier brush with justice.

I arranged for him to visit a school for behavioural problems in the East End of London, attended by some of the most violent and troubled boys in the area. It was a risky business sending a poet there. I accompanied Butler as an onlooker. At first I thought I'd made a mistake. The boys looked as though they had been dragged there. Almost immediately, though, he captured their attention, speaking of oral poetic traditions among Native American tribes. As he spoke, I observed a lad of about sixteen sitting in the front row with a Stanley knife in his hand, pushing the blade in and out, in and out. After the session, I raised the issue with one of the teachers.

'He is fine as long as he has the knife,' he told me. 'It's when you take it away that he can be serious trouble.'

A sharp blade as comforter, this was a world away from the private girls' school in Tunbridge Wells I had visited a couple of weeks earlier. The teacher was thrilled by Butler's performance. The boys, too. They had been introduced to a world normally denied them. Although I often despise the notion of 'relevance' this was one case where it could be applied. Moreover, Butler himself was happy and spoke excitedly of the following week's session. The day before it was due, on October 20, 1977, I received a phone call. Bill Butler had committed suicide. Later, there were other reports that he had died of an accidental drug overdose. I am going only by what I was told at the time. I was so shocked that I failed to ask who the caller was. The following day, I went to the school to tell the boys their poet had died. There was an outpouring of sorrow. If only Butler could have guessed at what he meant to them, he might still be alive. It was the most successful Poets in Schools session ever and I trust it remains in the memories of the now middle-aged men, some of them probably gangsters, some of them reformed, who were there.

I was at the Poetry Society throughout the so-called poetry wars, which made the front pages of the newspapers. Some years later, an entire book was devoted to the subject. As an insider I have to say I think it is mostly invented history fuelled by the paranoia of a small core of poets inside a bigger movement they called the British Poetry Revival. Its emergence has been hailed as a critical point in twentieth-century British literature, a clash between the new and the old. There are now young book collectors who, pining for a world that never was, buy their cheaply mimeographed productions at vastly inflated prices. Were it true, that it really was a literary revolution, I might have been pleased to be at the centre of such a squabble. It was something rather less than that, however, a plain and simple bid for power. At the head of this group within a group was the sound and concrete poet Bob Cobbing, who I saw on a daily basis. There was something of the malevolent elf about him, but he could also be generous in promoting the people he admired. As with so many artists and writers who position themselves at the spearhead of a minority art, he developed a siege mentality that was quickly transmitted to his cohorts, most of whom were without any discernible talent, the most brilliant exception being Bill Griffiths who might have been even more brilliant had he not pledged his allegiance to people unequal to his own abilities. Their figure of veneration was the critic and lecturer Eric Mottram, who was then editor of *The Poetry Review*, the literary organ of the Poetry Society. The change Mottram brought was a welcome one in that what had been a rather staid magazine was opened wide to other kinds of voices, maybe too many Americans for my taste, but still it signalled a certain amount of vitality. Some of the Poetry Society membership were appalled by the magazine's radical new face. They cancelled their subscriptions, which was worrying because their annual fees were an important source of income.

The Poetry Society was funded in the main by the Arts Council of Great Britain whose literature director, a complete hack by the name of Charles Osborne, was hostile towards the Society. He pushed for and got an enquiry into the Society's affairs. It did not help matters when during an emergency session of the council, attended by Osborne himself, the volatile gay communist poet Eddie Linden stood up and accused Osborne of liking little boys. It was tantamount to handing the enemy a gift. During the compiling of the Witt Report virtually everyone working for the Society was interrogated, right down to the housekeeper and even a volunteer who served drinks during the poetry reading intervals, virtually everyone that is ... except me. My department was the one which brought in the most substantial revenue after the Arts

Council grant and so was ripe for investigation. I spent a few weeks waiting for a call that never came. Why I was never summoned is a mystery I've not been able to solve. Meanwhile, Bob Cobbing and his henchmen were looking for 'spies.' As a member of Poetry Round I was suspect. Things get rather tangled here. One of the Poetry Round group was David Lovibond who was noted for the volume of his poetic delivery, a classic instance of sound over matter, and his trenchant political views. James Sutherland-Smith later produced a wonderful parody of one of Lovibond's booming verses. It needs to be read with a stentorian voice:

> She took her clothes off by Durdle Door.
> She said one pic, but I wanted more.
> Then we walked to Kimmeridge Bay
> And on the seaweed I had my way.

Sutherland-Smith describes Lovibond's poetry as 'amateur rural nostalgia,' which, if true, does rather put one off nature. My wife and I went to dinner at Lovibond's place once. When we sat down at the table he brought out a black volume—the Holy Bible?—and proceeded to read passages from *Mein Kampf*. This was not, he claimed, necessarily an expression of his own political beliefs but an acknowledgement of the Führer's masterly prose. I understood then from where he derived his rhetorical style. Soon his voice would be heard well beyond the walls of the room where Poetry Round had its weekly meetings. James Sutherland-Smith is the best source for what happened next.* After Poetry Round some of the members went downstairs for a drink and there found themselves in the company of Bob Cobbing, Lawrence Upton and Jeremy Adler. A quarrel ensued. Lovibond, who never missed an opportunity to be provocative, gave voice to his infatuation with

* Sutherland-Smith's "The War of Lawrence Upton's Ear," an account of the conflict between Poetry Round and Bob Cobbing and his cohorts, can be found in his weblog for July 2011 on http://jamessutherlandsmith.co.uk. What it contains is too detailed to reproduce here.

Hitler: 'Fuck you,' he shouted, 'I follow the Führer!' It was an extraordinary thing to say in the presence of Jeremy Adler whose father, the author H. G. Adler, was a Holocaust survivor. (Some years later, Lovibond tried to enter politics as prospective Conservative candidate against Lord Alfred Dubs, then a Labour MP, a Jewish Czech Holocaust survivor rescued by Nicholas Winton, by which point he was cautioned by a former member of Poetry Round that were he to proceed in his folly his 'history' would be made known. Lovibond quickly pulled out of the race.) Bob Cobbing, aglow with the spectre of a literary stormtrooper in the Poetry Society, seized his chance. Lovibond was for him a gift from Valhalla. It followed that other members of Poetry Round were also of the same political stripe. They should have protected themselves more. They should have weeded out the weediest of weeds in their midst. Poetry Round was served notice and it fought back by calling for an Extraordinary General Meeting of the Society's membership. It was not the best of moves. So persuasive was Bob Cobbing's account of rising fascism in Poetry Round that the poet Michael Hamburger, who as a child in Berlin had witnessed the beginnings of Nazi Germany, got up and gave a short but impassioned speech on the dangers of totalitarianism. The reputation of Poetry Round was now unjustly smeared and it was forced to leave. As a member of it, I was put in a hard place. My efforts at some kind of reconciliation between both sides resulted in my becoming a suspect in the eyes of all. Quite simply, I failed, but then I was never much good at politics.

Meanwhile the poetry wars continued and just when it seemed that Cobbing and his crew were in the ascendant, at the next council meeting he and members of the British Poetry Revival stood up and walked out, declaring they were finished with the Society. This was, and remains, inexplicable. Among the departees were people who I'm sure never quite grasped the reason for their departure. I put it down to petulance. The General Secretary of the time, Robert Vas Dias, had tried to appease both sides only to be clobbered by both. Soon, weary with the whole business, he resigned and the Poetry Society, now supposedly at peace, and having survived the Witt Report, entered its darkest phase. What follows is forgotten, or, rather, suppressed history.

The council in its wisdom (which is to say the lack of it) decided that the new General Secretary should be a businessman, preferably with as little knowledge of poetry as possible. This would ensure non-partisanship. They hired a man whose only proven business experience was in the sale of women's sanitary products. The head of the council, the novelist Paddy Kitchen, giddy with the rightness of the cause, told the new General Secretary that physically he resembled E. M. Forster. He beamed. All I saw was a snake oil merchant. It was not long before we found ourselves on unfriendly terms. I struggle to remember why, but maybe it was simply my animal disgust with what crept rather than strode. Maybe it was because from his side I was the final barrier to the creation of a new streamlined version of the Society. I soon found myself in difficulties. Criticisms began to be made of my work performance, never directly, but in whispers and echoes. There was work I had failed to do, letters that had gone unanswered. My assistant, close to tears, informed me that letters addressed to me had been removed from my in-box by, yes, *him*. So yes, I had not done my job.

I tried to establish a series of talks, Poets on Poets, and I had it in mind to open with Geoffrey Hill on Robert Southwell. It was probably the best single plan I'd come up with, which would cost very little to put into motion and which in any case would have been mostly covered by the entrance fee. My proposal was mysteriously vetoed. Soon it reached the point where I and the General Secretary walked past each other in the same building without a single word being exchanged. There were three months of cold silence. I knew the danger I was in although in truth I was ambivalent with respect to my fate. I was already thoroughly disillusioned.

Then I noticed the disappearance of a number of antiques, including a sculpted bust of Tennyson, also a handsome set of old brass scales. I was informed they were being sold in order to raise funds. Why, then, were the proceeds from their sale not logged in the accounts book? And why were we in such a bad financial state? It was always difficult, but not *that* difficult. The decisions being taken during that period were Cromwellian in their philistinism. It was decided that the one thing the Poetry Society did not require was a poetry library and so many thousands of volumes, some of them rare and valuable, were sold off to a university library for a pittance. When I suggested that Jonathan Barker at the superbly run Arts Council Poetry Library be given a chance to see what books might be lacking in their collection, this, too, was vetoed. (Mind you, there had been an earlier pillaging by Bob Cobbing and his friends, a sale of books from the library in order to fund printing costs for their publications. What particularly irked me was the sale of rare, irreplaceable, volumes of gypsy verse. I couldn't bring myself to buy what were essentially stolen goods.)

The final straw was when I discovered large sums of money were being issued on a regular basis for the repair and maintenance of 'a Poetry Society car' that none of us had ever seen. The invoices were issued from a car repair in Sussex, which, upon further investigation, did not exist. The cheques were signed by the Honourable [sic] Treasurer with whom the General Secretary was conducting a rather poorly concealed affair. She also signed cheques for 'miscellaneous expenses'—hotel rooms, dinners and the like. I was faced with a major predicament because were this to be put in the public eye the Arts Council would almost certainly withdraw its grant and my colleagues would be out of a job. By now I had little thought of my own future, but I had to devise a way of getting the General Secretary removed. I resorted to the tactic of inference. There wasn't enough time for me to build a case against him. At the next council meeting, my foe was at one end of the long walnut table listing his achievements of the past couple of months. The members of the council sat on either side of the table, scribbling notes or else dozing off. I was at the other end of the table, at what I thought was a sufficient distance, and whispered to one of my colleagues, 'Bullshit.'

'Marius, do you have something to add to the proceedings?'

This was the first time he'd spoken to me in months.

'Well, yes, actually I do. You are a liar. And that is just the tip of the iceberg.'

I glanced at the two rows of heads all of which were now focussed on the table. There was total silence. I knew then that with the cowardice or unwillingness of the council members to pick up the bone I had just tossed them I was done for. I announced I would be handing in my notice and left the room. I went up to my office, placed a stencil in the typewriter—these being pre-computer days—and began to compose a resignation letter copies of which would be distributed to all members of the council. At least this might goad one of them into action. I had just begun to type when the Honourable Treasurer burst into my office.

'What are you doing?' she screamed.

'I am typing my resignation letter,' I replied.

'You can't do that, you've already resigned.'

'Would you kindly get out of my office.'

What happened next belongs to a Marx Brothers film. She flew at the typewriter and tore the stencil out of it. I chased after her and we got involved in a strange physical duel which involved her pushing on one side of the door while I pushed in the opposite direction. She, being a woman of rather greater bulk than me, sent me flying. It was a humiliating defeat. She then ran downstairs to inform the other council members that I was dangerous and had to be removed from the building immediately. I would not be allowed to serve my month's notice. The sad fact is that she clearly thought I was going to expose the affair between her and the General Secretary. Although it was true, and it was probably the chief reason for the theft of Poetry Society monies, it is not in my nature to expose sexual frailties. The council would have to figure out for itself what was happening. Paddy Kitchen, who I always considered a misled innocent, came upstairs to tell me I was to be out of the building within an hour, otherwise the police would be called to remove me. I then made the biggest mistake of my professional life. Why, for God's sake, didn't I stay put? Why didn't I let them carry me out, a human sacrifice to the Muse? A few months later, after the council finally came to its senses, the

General Secretary and Honourable Treasurer were quietly, *very* quietly, removed, no charges ever brought against them. And now, looking for their traces, it is almost as if they'd never existed. I did receive two letters from council members, words to the effect they should have listened to me.

I then became a freelance gardener. There are, so I was made to understand, subtle differences between plants and weeds, which strikes me as a form of botanical prejudice. Gardening was not meant for me. A few months later, I took a bag of books for purposes of sale into one of London's most prestigious bookshops. This small act would determine the course of my working life.

* * *

The above does not quite answer the question of *why books?* I must dig deeper.

I grew up in a farmhouse in rural Ontario. A Polish father and an English mother, a deeply sad couple, for them reading was one of their consolations, maybe the only one. When, owing to the vicissitudes of history, they went to Canada in 1948, my mother, in advance of the move, shipped several cartons of books from England and, thinking the greater number of her books would be easily replaceable, gave the rest away. She was sorely mistaken. Where they settled, which, depending on how one views these things, was either sixty or sixty thousand miles from Ottawa, there were no bookshops to be found anywhere. They had to fall back on what they already had because such was their poverty it would be a few years before they could afford even a radio. Apart from the Edmund Dulac illustrated edition of *Arabian Nights* (1907) my mother's books (for obvious reasons my father's books were left behind in pre-war Poland) were of no monetary value whatsoever and yet they were their greatest treasure in a country in which neither was ever truly able to settle. While those books were a buffer between them and a hostile world, for me they represented another kind of escape.

I squeeze myself inside the child that I once was, lying on the floor rummaging through my parents' books. They were mostly cheap paperbacks. A good many of them, such as the Signet Books edition of George Orwell's *Nineteen Eighty-Four*, had lurid covers promising what would never be delivered inside, in this instance a woman in the act of laying bricks, her uniform a blue dress with a plunging cleavage, a red sash that emphasises her narrow waist, not quite suitable gear for the job, and despite wearing an Anti-Sex League badge she has come-hither eyes. Ava Gardner would be perfect for the role. Maybe 1984 would not be such a bad year after all. She is standing back-to-back with a man who is rugged and virile—Gregory Peck could play him—the two of them caught in the act of being human by a ghastly troll in a tight-fitting black helmet who bore a striking resemblance to James Mason.

On the other hand, plain covers yielded shocks within that were still beyond the reach of my comprehension, for example, the very innocuous-looking *Tropic of Cancer.* I must have been about ten or eleven when I read some of its pages and although I knew little and puzzled over some of the riper passages I knew enough to place the book back on the shelf precisely where it was because it clearly belonged to a forbidden zone. And then there was Oscar Williams's *A Little Treasury of Modern Poetry: English and American* (1950) which contained F. R. Higgins's "Song for the Clatter-Bones" with its opening lines:

> God rest that Jewy woman,
> Queen Jezebel, the bitch
> Who peeled the clothes from her shoulder-bones
> Down to her spent teats

They sent a palpable shock through me. I do not think the poem anti-Semitic and yet I wish the thin volume in which it first appeared, *The Gap of Brightness*, had not been published in 1940. Such matters were then largely beyond my grasp although there was a volume in black cloth that contained photographs of hideous atrocities in Poland, images I've never been able to shed. Another species of horror, infinitely preferable, I found in a book of paintings by Hieronymus Bosch, which I'd study for hours on end, losing myself in their intricacies. When recently, in Vienna, I came across the real thing it was like re-entering childhood. And then there were the historical novels I so loved as a child, in particular Harold Lamb, his *Tamerlane: Conqueror of the Earth*, *Genghis Khan: Emperor of all Men*, and, best of all, *Suleiman the Magnificent: Sultan of the East*. I would stare at the upper cover of the Cardinal Edition paperback of Emil Ludwig's *Napoleon* and the subject at the centre, dark and swarthy, terrified me. What was it that so disturbed me about the American soldier on the cover of the Signet Giant paperback of Curzio Malaparte's *The Skin*? Was I the small boy in the image, cowering at his feet? Little could I have imagined that one day I would write a book about the city where it is set, Naples.

Also brought over from England, a case of taking coals to Newcastle, was Ernest Thompson Seton's *Wild Animals I Have Known* (1898). I found the small drawings in the margins of the pages frightening. Why? The fears of childhood are quite often inexplicable. And then, by the writer I mistakenly called Rhubarb Kipling, *The Jungle Book*, a gilt cobra on the cover of the second volume. Another title was the three-volume *A History of Everyday Things in England* by Marjorie and C.H.B. Quennell. (I never knew there was a fourth volume, which took *Things* to the fateful year of 1948 when my parents boarded a ship to the New World.)

Over the years the books became increasingly fragile, the covers of many of them held together with Sellotape. Central heating made things worse. My father died in 2003, my mother fourteen years later. The most terrible thing I had to face was the disposal of their books, many of which had by then completely fallen apart, their pages brittle and musty with age. My parents admonish me from their grave. Why didn't I take their books into my care? I took a few but as for the rest I invited people to take what they like. That accounted for very little. There was nothing in fit enough condition for the two bookshops in town, two more than there were in my childhood but neither of which had much to entice the adult mind. Standard practice in those parts nowadays is to take books to the dump. The high school library where I took refuge suffered that fate when superior minds determined that a library was not high in importance. Computers would fill the physical gap but not the gap between the ears of those smug self-congratulatory fools who determine what is best for young people. My parents' books finally went to a youth club charity sale. Even so, I knew the dump would be the destination for most of them, but at least it would not be by my hand. I packed them as quickly as possible so as to take some of the sting out of doing so.

One book arrested me. Something prevented me in just the nick of time from packing it with the others. Some books are, as it were, magnets tugging at something deep within ourselves. You go to them because you have to, because maybe they contain a message. This was a ragged copy of *Grimms' Fairy Tales*, printed by the Readers Library Publishing Company, in London, circa 1930, in paper-covered boards. The cover, by Zamar, depicts a Mozartian prince doffing his tricorn before a girl in a shabby dress, a broom beside her, her feet in red shoes decorously placed on a tasselled cushion. On the back cover is an ad for Nestlé's chocolate at 2p a bar. The book is held together by old cloth tape such as was once used to cover electrical wiring. The pages have browned over time and are extremely brittle. The book has virtually no value. The likelihood of anyone rescuing such a shabby mongrel from an outside bookstall is remote. And probably the book wouldn't have been put out there in the first place. There is a gift inscription in a rather elegant hand on the front free endpaper which reads: 'To Melody with v best love from Peter for a happy Birthday Jan: 19, 1932.' My mother, addressed by the name she later chose not to use, was six years old exactly.

What follows here illustrates the cruelty that is the hallmark of English families of a certain class and time, where the greatest damage was done not through actions but with words and sometimes not even words alone but the tone in which they were delivered. There is no race on earth with such a withering capacity to diminish another human being with simple language. I am not suggesting such things no longer happen or that we are more enlightened now, but that the way we speak is not as important as it once was, even if its purpose is to maim. Peter was my mother's half-brother, from what few things my mother told me a deeply sensitive boy, exceedingly bright and with a passion for literature. My grandmother, although kind to me at a distance—many of the books of my childhood she sent to me from England, a country which in my child's mind had become synonymous with books, good tea and chocolate—had little time for her own children who she sent off to boarding schools so that they would not interfere with her own, often amorous, pursuits. As for my grandfather, he was separated from his wife and was believed dead until one day my mother discovered he wasn't. The closest she ever came to meeting him was when he was pointed out to her at a distance.

Peter went to Winchester College, one of the finest schools in the country. Nobody will ever know what terrible shift took place in his mind there, but he wrote a desperate letter to his mother begging her to come and see him. His plea unanswered, he took his own life. Some months later, his half-sister, my mother, asked her mother why Peter hadn't been to visit and the reply came, 'Oh Peter's dead, darling, we don't talk about him anymore.' He was secretly buried somewhere in the West Country, nobody knows where, and with not even his parents in attendance. There survives not a single photograph of him, Peter, the boy who almost never was, whose erasure from the human race would have been complete were it not for a single piece of evidence, a battered copy of *Grimms' Fairy Tales*. A bookseller, were he to catalogue this book, which, because of its condition, would be highly improbable, would be duty-bound to mention the inscription on the front free endpaper, nothing more, certainly not the wording. Some people are fussy about such things and indeed, with books of worth, ownership and gift inscription affect if not the value then the book's saleability. This may strike the uninitiated as complete madness and in a way it is. Collectors now want their books without history and if there is one it had better be of significance. There are instances, however, when a very ordinary dedication in a very ordinary book can shift the universe

* * *

When I was a child I'd go to the village jumble sale and buy books for a pittance, not for what they were but for their tactile qualities. The only boy who spent his pocket money on books, so no competitors, I would merrily lug them home, W. J. Ghent's *The Road to Oregon* (1929), a missionary tract on how it is our Christian duty to clothe savages, a Will Durant history, which made me look smarter than I was, and I can't remember what else, but almost certainly nothing that would raise my body temperature now. I found one treasure, the burgundy pebbled-leather edition of *The Poetical Works of Mrs Hemans* with the immortal "Casabianca" whose opening lines 'The boy stood on the burning deck, / Whence all but he had fled' launched a thousand cruel parodies. It might have been the only book of poetry in the village or, conversely, if there was a single book of poetry to be found in the village it could only have been Mrs Hemans. I may have rescued her from a soggy fate. There was a certain gravitas in those musty volumes, the first book purchases I ever made, and they taught me one thing: *always* judge a book by the cover. If reading is a matter of depth, of reaching into the unknown and coming back with either a coal or a diamond, it's a peculiar aspect of our human condition that we place so much value upon surfaces.

Otherwise it was my parents' books or books that my parents specially ordered for me via the Hopkins' Drugstore in Kemptville, Ontario, or titles in the rather splendid Landmark Books issued by Random House, a history series for children, that one subscribed to, and which came in the post. And then there were the books my grandmother in England sent me, which seemed to have a special aroma of their own and were imbued with the message that one day I'd go there, to the land of books and chocolates. One of those treasures she sent me was Giovanni Guareschi's *The Little World of Don Camillo* (1951), which was another place I wanted to be. Such was my desire to be Italian I changed my name to Mario and remained so, even in my school records, until the age of eighteen.

A kindly woman in the town library let me go into the basement and take what I liked from the deaccessioned books and made sure I took away an encyclopaedia that was taking up space. I can't remember what edition it was, other than it comprised a dozen bulky volumes. I took special pleasure in the folding maps which, shame on me, I removed to make my own atlas. According to them, the Austro-Hungarian Empire still existed, Newfoundland was a British dominion* and one could locate African countries with now forgotten names, whose postage stamps were often in the shape of triangles. I was a young philatelist too.

When I was in my late teens I hitchhiked to Ottawa where I wandered into Shirley Leishman Books in its earliest manifestation, when it was at the corner of Gilmour and Elgin. The proprietor at that time, William Roberts, could not have imagined the effect he would have on me, for at the entrance of the shop was a rack of books that would alter the direction of my life. They were all published by New Directions and among the titles were Rimbaud's *Illuminations* and *A Season in Hell*, Baudelaire's *The Flowers of Evil*, Ferlinghetti's *A Coney Island of the Mind*, and *Selected Poems of Federico García Lorca*. With their slightly sinister, black-and-white photographic covers they comprised for me forbidden territory. It was there, too, I first caught sight of Ottawa's one and only Beat poet, hell raiser, the piratical-looking Bill Hawkins with his drooping moustache and circular wire-frame glasses, who, a few years later, in the grim environs of the Chateau Lafayette bar,† stood before my table and glared at me as if to say, *Who in the hell are you, brat.* I was by then writing bad poems and making a bit of a noise with them. Maybe I should have offered him a drink. Shirley Leishman filed for bankruptcy in 2013, but by then it was not even a ghost of the original shop that stole my young soul; it was just another air-conditioned bookshop.

When I was living in Ottawa in the late 1960s and early 70s and, as often was the case then, in difficult straits, I found a box of

---

* Which reminds me: there is a poem by John Ashbery that opens with a wonderfully droll line, 'Newfoundland is, or was, full of interesting people.'

† "The Laff," to give it a familiarity it scarcely deserves, founded in 1849, is the oldest bar in Ottawa.

books dumped by the side of the road for rubbish collection. There was nothing much to entice me, but I wondered if somehow the books could be converted into ready cash, so I lugged them to a young bookseller called Patrick McGahern who at that point had three small rooms in the old brick Medical Dental Building at the corner of Laurier and Metcalfe, and who has since become one of the foremost booksellers in Canada, one might even say a grandee. It is just over fifty years since he walked into the bank, seeking a loan for $2,400, his only collateral an old Pontiac and traces of an Irish accent that had somehow weathered three generations in exile. When the bank manager learned that the money sought was in order to buy a bookshop he quite rightly, in the face of such a ludicrous notion, frog-marched McGahern out the front door and onto the street where such pipe dreams curl up and die. There must have been something of the tough woodsman in McGahern though. Somebody else put in an offer for the shop and he was given until noon to secure the requisite figure. He went back to the bank and found a different person working there, clearly weak of spirit, quite possibly literate, who granted him the loan, and at ten minutes to twelve McGahern ran all the way to the shop which was where I found him three years later, still out of breath but very much alive. A man of feeling, he gave me a tenner for the books, which surely was a generous figure, but declined to take one which he thought *might* be of value, the Gallimard first edition of Ève Curie's biography of her mother, *Madame Curie* (1938). As a child I saw on television the 1943 movie made from it with Greer Garson in the title role; I would never forget the scene in which Pierre Curie, played by Walter Pidgeon, is run over by a horse and cart just as he was on the cusp of a major scientific breakthrough, which greatly appealed to my fledgling sense of doom. Something about that book radiated significance. My command of French was insufficient to the task of reading it, but it seemed to me just then the heirloom of a lost time. As I now discover, it is worth very little, but McGahern is to be commended for his sense of justice. Also it was the first time I understood that first editions of books could have a value. That for me was the first step in my decline, appreciating the monetary value that may accompany, or maybe even sometimes exceed, a book's intrinsic value. There are people with whom one can sit down and for the rest of one's life fail to explain why a first printing should be worth more than a second one. My mother, a voracious reader, was such a one. She suspected me of betraying literature. She was in a way right or at least as right as she was wrong. An old book bound in leather might make passable furniture or even become that most objectionable of words, a 'collectible,' which, when I become dictator, I will have expunged from the language, but why should a relatively modern book command a high price? And even McGahern tells me people now chase after trophies rather than books. After over forty years in the book trade, and now on the way to doubtful pastures, I'm not quite ready to answer my own question. Who was it who said a ninth printing is much rarer than a first? It makes absolutely no sense, yet it's to senselessness that I have devoted over four decades of my existence. It may be that to some degree Patrick McGahern is to blame for the road I'd later take.

Chapter Three

A GIRAFFE IN EDINBURGH ZOO

A LUNCH AT THE ZANZIBAR ON LONG ACRE WITH GEORGE Lawson, one of the directors of Bertram Rota, sealed my fate. I don't think it occurred to me that I was being sized up for a future in the book trade. Certainly I had given a dubious account of myself, sufficiently so, I would have thought, to warn anybody off me but, there again, there is no accounting for the naturally perverse in people. What was it George saw in me? 'Well,' he'd tell me four decades later, 'I thought you'd make a good bookseller.' It may be that with all my talk of mayhem and slaughter at the Poetry Society I'd unwittingly recommended myself for inclusion in the floating world of the book trade. When George said he expected me to report for duty the following morning I was already well into my cups. Also I needed a job. I was a criminally irresponsible gardener. My sense of chronology is not good, but I think I must have started work in the summer or early autumn of 1978, shortly before Karol Wojtyła became Pope John Paul II. Why I remember this is because George paused in front of my desk and in his sternest Presbyterian voice said that if a Pole could get into Bertram Rota then it should be easy enough for one to get into the Vatican.

If I may for a moment peer into the gene pool from which George comes perhaps it would suffice to say that he had an uncle who left money to a giraffe in Edinburgh Zoo because it reminded him of his late wife who was tall. Also he has the most delicate hands I'd ever seen on a male, one of his fingers bearing, so he told me, a ring that belonged to Mary, Queen of Scots. (It will be for the forensic scientist to determine the truth of this.) On occasion he would apply all or most of those fingers to the clavichord he kept in his office. I've heard him play it just once. Scarlatti or Buxtehude? Whichever, the instrument seems a perfect metaphor for his existence. A piano, by comparison, would make of his life too strident a prose.

Although many readers will be unfamiliar with the name of George Lawson they may already have encountered him in David Hockney's unfinished double portrait, painted between 1972 and 1975, in which he is paired with his partner of the time, the dancer Wayne Sleep. The painting captures him whole. What might seem formal attire was in fact his everyday clothes. Never once, in all the years I worked for Bertram Rota, did I see him minus a bow tie. Only recently I discovered he has hundreds of them. In the painting George is sitting sideways at his clavichord, not the ideal position in which to play the instrument and although his right hand is on the keyboard it was not, as previously reported, an A flat note he plays but a G which in his mind more perfectly catches the atmosphere. 'There's a quietude, a stillness about it,' he said recently at the launch of Hockney's *Double Portraits* exhibition at the Tate Modern. 'I think the painting is about stillness, the sound of that note, concentrating on a sound and listening.'

I had already met him on several occasions, once in 1975, at a dinner at Jane Kasmin's to which he invited me, and where for the first time I encountered the extraordinary Romanian singer Magdalena Buznea, who deserves her own biography although sadly she is now self-exiled from the woman she once was. I don't think there'll be any winging her back there. I did write a biographical sketch of her, but it had to be suppressed on account of what might have been true once no longer being so. Sometimes, though, the stories by which we live in the mind are truer than the ones we actually live. We adjust our lives to their shape. There are any number of artists who have done just that, who would not be what they were had they followed the straight line. The hungriest person at the table, Magdalena had just recently returned from Paris where she met the *chansonnier* and songwriter Charles Dumont, most famous for having composed Edith Piaf's "*Non, je ne regrette rien*." She had gone there, with an ardour only saints and fools have, to ask whether he might write a song for her. When years later, I asked her to recount the visit, she cited Socrates, with respect to his ideas on the 'chain of events' in which she found, appropriately enough, a philosophical illustration for her own existence. I wonder if she was aware of the aphorism attributed to him: *Ο ἐλαχίτων δεόμενος ἔγγιστα θεῶν* ('He who has the smallest wants approaches the gods most nearly'). She described how before meeting Dumont she sat in her hotel room, polishing her fingernails and toes. If Dumont did not actually write a song for Magdalena he gave her permission to use one that he had not performed himself, "*Un dimanche après la fin du monde*" and it was a verse from this she sang that night at Jane Kasmin's dinner table.

Un dimanche après la fin du monde
Si jamais tu pensais à moi
Un dimanche après la fin du monde
Dis-toi bien que je serais là
S'il ne reste rien de cette ville
Qu'un silence déprimant et hostile
*N'ai pas peur tu n'as qu'à m'appeler.**

* *Trans.* 'One Sunday after the end of the world / If you ever thought of me / One Sunday after the end of the world / Tell yourself I'll be there. / If there's nothing left of this city / Only a depressing and hostile silence / Don't be afraid, just call me.'

One Sunday after the end of the world when all that is left is a voice floating amid the ruins, which is how the song goes: its whiff of the apocalyptic played sweetly on my nerves. A stage actress of some repute in her native Romania, after she escaped the Ceaușescu regime she came to London where she was reduced to singing on the streets and scrubbing other people's floors while waiting for occasional TV bit roles, one of them, I seem to remember, as a poor refugee scrubbing other people's floors. An incredible sequence of events, which I hope one day will be allowed voice, resulted in her giving a performance at the London Palladium. George Lawson was there. What he told me is that someone in the audience lit a cigarette and in a fit of pique Magdalena strutted off the stage and out of what might have been a new chapter in her life. The story is a good one although for reasons she now firmly denies. The reason I dwell on this is because it is a song and not a book that takes me back to that period in my life, also because Magdalena told me she adores George's mind although we both agreed it is quite inscrutable.

As inscrutable, say, as that of the wily courtier in an Elizabethan play? Yes, I think so, which is not to cast George in a poor light because a certain wiliness with respect to how books and antiquities are made to move through time and space is absolutely requisite. Another occasion which brought him into my orbit was when he and Peter Schlesinger came to a reading I gave together with the New York poet Nathan Whiting at the Poetry Society in Earls Court Square. They both got a fit of the giggles, which I can well sympathise with because I, too, am a chronic giggler at poetry readings and indeed, not so long ago, trying to suppress my merriment, I burst a blood vessel in my nose. (The declaimer of verses, a humourless Dane, was not pleased with me, nor was the event organiser who said to me, 'I hope never to see you again.') I am not saying I was not the cause of their mirth, but I think Nathan might have been the surer candidate, his appearance being that of a Confucian sage in a baseball cap, and the fact, too, that he ran every page of *The London A to Z* and wrote a poem for each one.

I went to see George in Brighton where, several years into retirement, he lives in a flat overlooking the sea, from the window of which he studies the gradation of greys into blues. A blustery day, struggling to keep my hat on, I walked to his place along the empty pebble beach, and, with James Joyce already in my thoughts, I recalled the passage in *Ulysses* (1922) where, no idle reference this, Stephen Dedalus walks along another seashore.

Confined now to a wheelchair, although majestically so, George suffers from multiple system atrophy.

'It is wonderfully fatal,' he told me, 'degenerative and incurable.'

'Oh George!' I cried.

'No, no, no, it is *lovely*, three in one!'

As he reached for his pills he remarked the condition of the sea, directing my attention from the gunmetal grey of the choppy waves to the hallway of his flat which recently he had painted Yves Klein blue.

'I'm obsessed by blue,' he explained. 'I find it a sexy colour.'

George swallowed a blue pill for more, I think, than its brilliant hue.

When I worked under him he seemed to dwell so much inside the moment that I never got around to finding out anything about his previous existence. On a grey day in Brighton, I was to be pleasantly taken by surprise.

'I grew up in Edinburgh and when I was eighteen left for the west of Ireland,' he began. 'I thought I'd go to Trinity College, Dublin, which is the university I would most of all have liked to have gone to, although how I thought I was going to get in I don't know. I'd never passed a single exam in my life. I kept going west, first to Galway and then further into the Atlantic, where the Aran Islands are. I went to Kilronan in Inishmore.'

I perked up at the mention of the Aran Islands. I have the scarce Lilliput Press edition of Tim Robinson's *Stones of Aran: Pilgrimage* (1968). A masterpiece of its genre, no stone in it is left unturned. 'Cosmologists now say that Time began ten or fifteen thousand years ago,' it begins, 'and that the horizon of the visible universe is therefore the same number of light-years distant from us.' There's nothing like a shot of infinitude to make one feel the *now* of the stone upon which one perches. I never got to meet the author, there having been some sort of muddle in our respective itineraries, but he very kindly left me a bag of his books inscribed to me. At the time of writing, my copy of *Stones of Aran* has become even more of a treasure although I wish it were for reasons other. A few days ago, Tim Robinson, aged eighty-five, died of the pandemic that has kept the world in a state of siege.

'At that point they were the most primitive places left in Europe,' George continued, 'particularly the middle island, Inis Meáin, where they would still thresh corn or whatever it was, barley or wheat, over a stone. I kept thinking of Homer and the winnowing fan.* When I arrived by boat I saw a man being taken off the island in a straitjacket. I later discovered he was the Clerk of Works. I was abandoned there. The boat didn't come back, because of bad weather. One of the islanders remarked, "The captain is not a very courageous man."† Well, I took to living there. One day they said to me, "Can you read and write?" I *confessed.* "Ah, well then, you can be the new Clerk of Works because we have been given £40,000 by Dublin to put in a water supply scheme." The stipulation was that we take running water, of which there was none on the island, to the garden gates of the cottages and then their occupants would have to pay for taking it from the garden gates into their houses. This was a problem on account of the island being made of limestone. There is no soil to speak of and no trees because it is so windy. The logical

* Now this really is remarkable because that very morning, on the train to Brighton, I had been reading Adam Nicolson's *The Mighty Dead: Why Homer Matters* (2014), which, although wilfully eccentric at times, is one of the best books I've read on the subject. One of the most mysterious passages in all of Homer is where Tiresias tells Odysseus that after he returns to Ithaca he must make one more journey, taking with him a broad-bladed oar and to walk with it until he arrives at a place whose inhabitants know nothing of the sea, who do not excite their food with salt, and there he will meet a stranger, another traveller, who'll mistake the oar for a winnowing fan. Odysseus must then drive his oar into the ground and make a sacrifice to Poseidon. Tiresias, looking still deeper into Odysseus's future, says, in Robert Fitzgerald's translation, 'a seaborne death soft as this land of mist will come upon you when you are wearied out with rich old age.' May death be, when it comes, soft and gentle.

† George put on some sort of dour island accent here.

thing to do was put a tank at the top of the hill, pump water up into it, and then run pipes down. The problem with Aran is that on account of there being too little soil in which to bury a pipe in the ground you had to blow up the rock in order to make trenches. As explosives were not allowed on ordinary boats we had to smuggle them in. We constructed a tank on top of the hill and then blew up trenches by the side of the road to take the water down the hill in pipes. Well, nobody told me that when a pipe changes level it has to have a valve to let the air out. I didn't know that. I didn't know anything about water, but I learned. Of course the Irish were very anxious to get injured by the explosions. They rushed towards the flying rocks so they could claim compensation.'

'And did you do your bit for Ireland, George?'

'Yes, yes,' he said gleefully. 'I injured quite a few of them. Most were merely maimed. The long and the short of it is that after I had stayed for two years on the island the new water system was reasonably ready. I left before it was tested, but the denouement was that the islanders didn't *want* running water. They preferred to go in the morning and meet their friends at the well and have a gossip, so none of them took up the offer of water from the gate to the front doors of their cottages. It was a waste of money and time. So very Irish, I thought. We had a hurricane once. There was an anemometer on the roof of the lifeboat station and it registered 165 miles an hour and then it blew away. *I like that!* Curiously enough, I was there at the time of the Great Debate as to whether Guinness tasted better in wooden or metal barrels. They were just changing from wood to metal. It was then that Brendan Behan was asked to write a slogan for Guinness. I heard him speak a beautiful Irish when he visited the island and made a speech on the pier. When asked to write the slogan he replied, "Well, I will need to taste the stuff." So they sent him a crate of Guinness. He drank that and at the end of the next day said he hadn't thought of anything, so they sent him another crate and another and another. After a week he was quite sozzled. He said, "I have come up with something." "Oh, what is it?" they asked. "It's this," he replied. "Guinness gets you drunk."'

'So you could have been a great man in waterworks had you so decided.'

'Well, I'm afraid I have no knowledge of hydraulics.'

'Which surely is why you were ideally suited for the job.'

'Yes, I was perfectly alright.'

'So how do we get from Aran to bookselling?'

'I went back to Edinburgh where I got a job at Grant's Bookshop. There were two booksellers at that time, Grant's was the grand one, James Thin the more academic. I was given the keys of the Greyfriars Bobby bookstall on George IV Bridge, which had trays of books outside, clicked on to the railing. They were tuppence, sixpence, a shilling, two shillings, a crown and five bob. My, did we rejoice if we sold a five-bob book. They were mostly stolen by clergymen who had special coats designed with book-stealing pockets in them. Goodness knows why they wanted them. The shop was opposite, across the road. Greyfriars Bobby was a terrier dog and there is a statue of him there. His master died and he sat on the gravestone for fourteen years, so it is a sort of Robert Louis Stevenson tale. It was forever raining and I'd have to take books in again. After that I got a job here in Brighton, at Bredon's antiquarian bookshop in the Lanes. Curiously the first Mrs Bertram Rota worked there. It was run by Raymond Smith who was an eccentric, but a very good bookseller and it was he who taught me the generalities of bookselling. I had to know the best book on golf, the best book on butterflies and so forth. He had a cloth length cut from his suit whenever he had a suit made so his cap would match it. Also he taught me to polish books. "Use your fingers, it is the softest leather you can ever find." Raymond Smith then retired, and I went over to Glover & Daughter, which was the bookshop in Eastbourne. Glover & Daughter, it was the first time I had ever come across that situation. Poor Miss Glover, I called her "Miss Glover."'

George paused for a moment, clearly caught up by some puzzle.

'*Miss* Glover. So how could she have had a daughter?'

George puzzled a bit more.

'She went blind,' he continued. 'She also had books outside and she was the victim of people who would take the books from her trays and sell them to her. She never knew where they came from, poor thing.'

'Were you drawn to books because you had literary aspirations?'

'No, no, I'll tell you what it was. At my prep school I started a library. At the big school, the Royal High School in Edinburgh where Walter Scott went, which is the seventeenth oldest school in the world, founded in 1128, I used to hide in the library. It was wonderful. There were Holinshed Chronicles that made the best airplanes. If I had known more about it then I'm sure there were Shakespeare folios or Walter Scott manuscripts. I grew fond of books because I was always surrounded by them. And then I became a bookseller *not* a book reader.'

'But you've always had a vast knowledge of literature.'

'Well, that was fake.' He laughed. 'It's a knack. If one is friendly to books they often fall open at the node of the argument.'

A striking use of the word *node*: 'I will not here dissolue the node, ne yet maye not, but referring the same to the great masters of these mysteryes, I will partely declare my simple iudgement therein.' So says John Bossewell in his *Armorie* (1572). I wasn't having any of it though, node or no node, because for a man who doesn't read, many are the snippets of verse George quotes from memory. 'Beware the risen people that have harried and held,' he suddenly dropped like a shiny pebble into the middle of our conversation.

'What was that, George?'

'It was written in blood on the wall by Pádraig Pearse, Kilmainham Gaol, in Dublin, Easter Uprising, 1916.'

This is an interesting instance of how memory works or indeed how myth is made because the line is in fact a contraction of several from Pearse's poem "The Rebel" and it appears as a painted graffiti across the archway leading to the so-called 1916 Corridor of the prison. There's no blood in it, nor is it in Pearse's hand. Still, that George should have remembered it at all is impressive. Also I noticed he had a copy of Curzio Malaparte's *La Pelle* (*The Skin*, 1949), in the original Italian. It was not a book a man who doesn't read owns. I remember him, too, translating aloud, from the Latin and Greek, the epigraph to Eliot's "The Waste Land," the words spoken by Sibyl at Cumae. Well, there he may have faked it a little. I've been to Cumae. It's the place George most wants to see before he dies. A half hour's drive north of Naples: God willing, I'll take him there.

'I remember your enthusiasm for Basil Bunting,' I said, trying to keep him on the literary lane.

That was because I liked his voice. Pound and Bunting, and to a certain extent Robert Creeley, used to speak in the same way. I don't know whether Pound imitated Bunting or Bunting imitated him, but their voices were remarkably similar. I set eyes on Pound when he came to Eliot's funeral. Bunting, on the other hand, I owe my acquaintance to D. G. Bridson who was a chum of Bunting.* Bridson said to me, "The *i* is long, George, as in *Christ*." He and his very nice wife, Joyce, lived in Highgate and used to have me to dinner when I was just starting out at Rota. They were very kind to me.'

'And so you moved from Brighton to London?

'I applied for a job at Foyles because they paid the train fares for interviewees. I came to in the middle of an interview, this man saying to me, "I heard you are cut out to be store detective." I confess I couldn't answer. I then turned myself into an expert in modern European philology, which is why I got a job at E. J. Brill.† "Would you catalogue these books?" they asked me. "I would be delighted to," I replied. We had to do our catalogues in Dutch and so, not speaking a word of Dutch—I mean not even the *Dutch* speak Dutch!—I proceeded. I was there for about six months and then the opportunity came to go to Bertram Rota where at least I could understand the language. This was in Bodley House, Vigo

* Douglas Geoffrey Bridson was a BBC radio producer, the author of several radio plays, including *Aaron's Field* (1943) and a friend of Wyndham Lewis about whom he wrote a book, *The Filibuster* (1972).

† E. J. Brill, or Koninklijke Brill, is a major Dutch academic publisher founded in 1683 in Leiden. For some years it had a London office. Among its many achievements was the publication of the *First Encyclopaedia of Islam* (1913–1936), scholarship so impressive it was later translated into Arabic.

Street. Bertram was on a sort of mezzanine, drinking Beaujolais, which he claimed to have introduced to Britain. Bodley House was bombed severely during the war. Bertram Rota was in the RAF and put to examining aerial photographs to see what was in them and he had a colleague called Bonham-Carter, I'm not sure which one she was, and together they invented the exploding elephant pat for jungle warfare.'

A sudden memory set George laughing

'I remember someone saying to him, "You remember Miss Jones, don't you, Mr Bertram?" (Miss Jones had been his secretary for twenty years.) "Ah yes, I remember her well. Now tell me, she had *one of something*. Was it one eye or one leg?"'

Miss Jones was an amputee.

We talked music, George and I, something we never did in the past. Among his memories of life at Bertram Rota was Igor Stravinsky coming into the shop.

'I thought that when he died he would stop ordering books from us.'

Then followed what one might call "the Lawson pause."

'Well, he didn't.'

Another Lawson pause.

'Robert Craft would continue ordering books on his behalf for Madame Stravinsky.'*

* * *

One of my first tasks was going with George Lawson to a West London address to collect approximately six hundred books, very few of them rare, mostly the nondescript volumes one might pick up in the basement or on outside shelves of any general secondhand bookshop. A lover of intrigue, George gave me no indication as to what they were, and as I loaded them into the car I wondered to myself, *why these?* They were a ragged bunch. My job for the next week or so was to insert slips of paper into the books wherever I

* Robert Craft, American conductor and musicologist, was a close friend of the Stravinskys.

found dots in the margins of the pages. The original owner of these books, so I was told, whenever he spotted a phrase he liked would prick the margin with the tip of a finely sharpened pencil. I was not to miss one. There was one title in particular, again of no value in itself, J. G. Wood's *Common Objects of the Seashore* (1912) … *dot, dot, dot* … the lines beside them containing phrases which later I discovered the dotter had lifted almost wholesale for his own purposes. Plagiarism? No, not quite. What one finds on the beach is for one to take. There weren't really that many dots overall, maybe enough to fill the circumference of the pencil that made them, but those dots sold for many thousands of pounds. Complete manuscripts, often entire archives, sold for considerably less.

What gave these books value is that most of them were rubber-stamped J.J. on the front pastedowns and, incredibly, had been kept together ever since their original owner made use of them in Trieste while working on the early stages of a novel called *Ulysses*. When he left for Paris in June 1920 he left most of the books behind. There were, as one might expect, books touching on Homeric themes, among them a translation of the Danish author Jens Peter Jacobsen's *Siren Voices* (*Niels Lyhne*, 1896) which Joyce so admired he learned Danish so that he might read it in the original. Other titles in the library include Alexander Haig's *Uric Acid: An Epitome of the Subject* (1904) which, given that uric acid causes gout and "Gouty" was Joyce's nickname for Goethe, must have excited easily excitable academic circles; Brillat-Savarin's *Physiologie du goût ou Méditations de gastronomie transcendante*; P. Garnier's *Onanisme seul et à deux sous toutes ses formes et leurs conséquences* which would launch a thousand scholars in the direction of the masturbatory in *Ulysses*; a textbook of Euclid's Elements, which provided the geometrical allusions in the "Ithaca" chapter of *Ulysses*; N. J. Murphy's *The Prophecies of St. Malachy Concerning the Successors of St. Peter to the General Judgment, and the Destiny of Ireland*, now believed to be of spurious authorship, which will be good news for Pope Francis who, so goes one of the predictions, will be the last pontiff, but never mind that, it's what gave Malachi "Buck" Mulligan his name; and then there's H. P. Kelly's *Irish Bulls and Puns*, so befitting of the writer described by a late friend of mine as 'the lordliest punster of all time'; an Italian edition of the *Arabian Nights* whose Sinbad appears several times, once with his 'roc's auk's egg in the night of the bed of all the auks of the rocs' although I have not the Italian for that; several books by Marco Praga, a Milanese playwright of whom Joyce thought very highly indeed, whose recurring theme of adultery was to be a great influence on the writing of *Ulysses*; Leopold von Sacher-Masoch's *Grausame Frauen* (Cruel Women) and whose author's name gave rise to the term masochism, plenty of that in *Ulysses*; several volumes by or about Shakespeare, another key title being Georg Brandes's 1898 study of him, a book Joyce so revered he sent all his books to the Danish author; Tommaso Campanella's *La Città del sole* from which Joyce developed his ideas of mnemonics; Giacomo Leopardi's *Poesie* ('Leopardi changes not his spots') and then books by or about Balzac, Conrad, Flaubert, Ibsen, Kipling, George Moore, Shaw, Synge, Wagner, Wilde, Turgenev and Tolstoy. It was my memory of J. G. Wood's *Common Objects of the Seashore* that had earlier put me in a Stephen Dedalus frame of mind when walking along the shore to George's Brighton home. The Trieste library went to the Harry Ransom Humanities Research Center at the University of Texas.

'Did you believe the theory about the dots?' George asked me.

I found the question slightly disconcerting because I'd thought all along it had been an established fact. Was it a ruse then?

'I was convinced by them,' he continued, 'because there are passages quoted verbatim. We speculated Joyce's eyesight might have been such that for him the dots were enormous and so this was his way of marking passages he wanted to read again. Whether anyone has taken this further I don't know.'

Well, it was, or, rather, it had already been: Thomas J. Kenny wrote an essay "James Joyce's System of Marginal Markings in the Books of his Personal Library" published in *Journal of Modern Literature* 6.2 (1977). What Kenny describes is the dot system which Joyce had developed to even greater effect when writing *Finnegans Wake* (1939). The books he looked at were the ones in Joyce's Paris library. What he hadn't seen was the Trieste library with Joyce's earlier, slightly more primitive, dot system. What I most wanted to find out when I went to visit George in Brighton was how the books came to Bertram Rota in the first place and how it was that they'd been kept together for all those years. After Joyce left Trieste, his brother Stanislaus Joyce, who also lived there, took possession of them. After Stanislaus died the books went to his wife, Nelly, who then left them to her son, another James Joyce. What George remembers best was how *this* James Joyce physically resembled his uncle.

A few years later, I handled Joyce's diagonally striped blue-and-white tie, which he had presented to the printer of *Ulysses*, telling him he would like the covers done in the same Greek-flag blue. Also there was a porcelain lion, a punning gift that Joyce gave to Paul Léon whose collection this was. A good friend to Joyce, Léon also worked as his unpaid secretary. A skilled linguist who spoke seven languages he, together with Philippe Soupault and the author, assisted with the French translation of *Anna Livia Plurabelle*. On August 21, 1941, Paul Léon was taken to the Drancy internment camp in Paris and in 1942 was sent to Auschwitz where he died on the road between there and Birkenau death camp, which at that point was being built by slave labour. Sick and exhausted, Léon fell behind on the march and was shot.

George met Paul Léon's son, Alexis, in Paris.

'I remember him saying to me, "Mr Lawson, I don't know why you are so fascinated by *this* particular genocide." I thought it was a very odd remark to make about the genocide in which his father died.'

The collection narrowly escaped the clutches of an SS officer who knocked at the door of Léon's apartment on rue Casimir-Périer in Paris. He asked Lucie Noël Léon where her husband was and she told him he was in a rather better position to tell her. (She was a gentile and so escaped her husband's fate.) The SS officer was a keen Joyce collector and aware of the likelihood that Léon would have treasures. The Léons had had the foresight to hide the entire collection and it was this which I helped unpack from the boxes newly arrived from Paris. In addition to the silk tie and the lion, the collection included first editions of Joyce's works, the page proofs for *Finnegans Wake* (1939), rare photographs, correspondence relating to Joyce, and other memorabilia. They are now housed in the McFarlin Library at the University of Tulsa. What a strange place for them to end up. Scarcity and value have never intrigued me as much as the improbable directions things go.

Chapter Four

THE POPE OF LONG ACRE

BERTRAM ROTA WAS ONE OF THE LAST OLD ESTABLISHments, dynastic and oxygenless, with a hierarchy that could be more or less described as Victorian. No history of the book trade can be written without reference to it. It not only sold books but was also the most important agent in the English-speaking world for the sale of modern literary archives. When I joined the firm in 1978, its helmsman, Anthony Rota, was secure in the knowledge that the firm was a permanent fixture. This made him oblivious to what was happening on the street outside, which was already teeming with barbarians, the Young Turks of the book trade, who'd soon break up the empire. I never knew his father, Bertram Rota, who was one of the most revered booksellers in the country, often credited with having initiated the idea of 'modern first editions' although this rather begs the question at what point, exactly, a book may be considered an object of desire. After all, most books are first editions, a fact I glumly note whenever I study my royalty statements. There is no easy dividing line, but generally speaking the trade in modern first editions begins with the writers of the 1890s and ends with fairly recent publications that sell for more, sometimes ridiculously so, than their original asking price. There came a point in the mid-1980s when books only just out of print were going for silly prices. D. M. Thomas's *The White Hotel* (1981) is a perfect example of a 'flavour of the month' book for which interest would soon wane, not least because it is a load of tosh, Freudian gobbledygook and dismal sex. A copy could be had for between £100 and £150, sometimes more, whereas now the same book can be found for less than half that price and if one takes inflation into account then it is at least four times less. There are some long faces when people, thinking they had invested in a treasure, are offered £20 or £30 for a copy. What never ceases to surprise me is the degree to which some collectors willingly deceive themselves, but then they tend to be the ones who stop collecting altogether.

All that one hears or reads of Bertram points to a great bookman. Starting out in the Charing Cross Road in 1923, he eventually took over the old premises of the Bodley Head on Vigo Street and then there was a further move to the nearby, though less aesthetically pleasing address in Savile Row, which is where I first visited the shop in the mid-1970s. When quite unexpectedly Bertram died in 1966, his son Anthony took over. In 1977 the shop moved to the handsome building, the front of which was newly designed by John Prizeman, at 30 Long Acre. It was built in the 1870s as a carriage manufactory and at some point was a banana warehouse. It was also rumoured to have been built above a plague pit.

The first book I ever sold was on the first morning of my employment, a first edition of Darwin's *On the Origin of Species* (1859) priced at £2,000. Why do I remember this and forget so much else? I was complimented on my selling abilities, but in truth all I did was to remove it from the locked cabinet, put it into the customer's hands and take payment for it. As assistant to John Byrne, who was in charge of the fine press department and literary archives, I was first put to work cataloguing fine press books, which was akin to jumping in at the deep end because with fine press books in particular it is essential that one's descriptions of them be absolutely accurate. A single blemish was enough to make some of those books unsaleable. Quite frankly, I found them a bit jejune, as objects more in love with themselves than with their contents. There are exceptions, of course, such as the Nonesuch Press edition of Bernard de Fontenelle's *A Plurality of Worlds* (1929) where there is a perfect balance between content and appearance. Another production I like, for its simplicity, is Coleridge's *The Rime of the Ancient Mariner* (1930) designed by Bruce Rogers for the printing John Johnson did for Oxford University Press. It is not only a book one can look at but also listen to with pleasure, the lovely crackle it makes as one turns the pages. And while we're at it why not include, although really it is an illustrated as opposed to fine press book, Arthur Rimbaud's *A Season in Hell* (1949) illustrated with lithographs by Keith Vaughan? As for the Kelmscott Press Chaucer (1896), one of the most esteemed of all fine press books, I would not want to have it on my shelf; I like my books to be readable.

Squint a little, you might mistake him for Ronald Firbank, not just in the physiognomy but also something febrile in the eyes. As is the case with Firbank, one looks to John Byrne not for the plot but for the dialogue. 'The most dangerous bookseller in London': it's all he can do not to blush at the epithet. Certainly one would not wish to be at the receiving end of his sharp tongue or even at the end of what he does not say but implies. A sharp wit is often a mask for delicacy, however, and he is reliable and, more important than that, gifted (or burdened) with an innate sense of justice. He taught me more than anyone else in the trade.

Four decades later, we sat on a bench in Holland Park, the sound of a helicopter above, its propeller slicing the words on the recording I made of our conversation. Time was both with and against us.

'I have been thinking about time lately with that blithering M. Proust,' he announced. 'I think about overdue deaths and that wretched woman whose name I don't want to see on the page again, Albertine. I would have shoved her into the country and pushed her off a horse five hundred pages earlier.'

Dante, in Sisson's translation, got short shrift as well.

'The thing I found very difficult to detect is the poetry, but there is a moment at the end of *Il Paradiso* when time is completely suspended because for God it is always *now*. Well, good on you, God. I was reminded of something. I have no formal scientific education whatsoever. I wasn't required to take exams in physics, chemistry or biology. I watched from the outside, amused. I was very entertained when the Hubble telescope sent back information suggesting that our universe contains stars that are older than itself. Of course almost the entire scientific establishment closed ranks and said the data must be wrong. What they could never say is perhaps they have not altogether understood, because if there is anything they are most likely to get wrong it is time.'

A bench in Holland Park was as good a place as any in which to locate Dante's Empyrean. A couple of men, surprised by age, sought to reclaim time.

Gradually, maybe because I failed to empathise with fine press books, I moved into working with modern first editions, which by comparison were fairly straightforward to catalogue. Happily, though, and again with thanks to John Byrne, this was punctuated with the cataloguing of literary archives. This accounts for the most pleasurable work I did at Rota. All archives are unique. They are, in each instance, representative of the workings of the authorial mind. I am close to homicidal when I pick up a bookseller's catalogue and see an entry for four or five letters from an author described as 'an important archive.' This is just one more instance of a decline in bookselling practice. An archive is an archive, substantial, which is to say *of substance*. Ideally it will comprise the entirety of a writer's manuscripts and so much the better if it is accompanied by correspondence to him.

Among the tasks that were pushed my way were the cataloguing of the PEN International archive, in which I found a letter from Valerie Eliot to the committee of PEN, blaming them for taxing her husband with work that helped bring about his early demise; the archive of the administrator and musicologist Eric Walter White, which included superb letters to him from David Jones, Ted Hughes, the composer Michael Tippett and the film director and pioneer of silhouette animation, Lotte Reiniger; and, although my memory is in conflict with John Byrne's, maybe because I *wish* I'd catalogued them, the letters the novelist Henry Green wrote to the scholar and translator of Chaucer, Nevill Coghill, which, together with Patrick Leigh Fermor's letters to Lady Diana Cooper, were probably the best I have seen in my time. One passage that particularly struck me, which brings into play the fact that after leaving Oxford without a degree in 1926 Henry Green went to work in his father's factory in Birmingham: 'I keep on being incredibly grateful that I ever knew you. What seems to me the marvellous thing in life is the things one can't define, like when I see a sparrow flying among the noisy machinery at the works or seeing one of the huge factories lit up at night,—I'm talking of feelings of course, which must be the only substantial things,—and that's why it is so marvellous that two people should be incredibly happy in thinking of each other and why one keeps on thinking of your marriage almost as if one was in a blue sky. I keep on thinking of your children as the curves birds make against that sky. It's as if one were the wind itself, rustling along and enjoying it all.' *As the curves birds make against that sky*: such were the moments that made it all worthwhile, as if I were engaged in a kind of abstract archaeology or the discovery of lost worlds.

I catalogued the archive of a British philosopher whose work I so detested that at lunch breaks I'd go to the National Gallery and stand in front of Piero della Francesca's *The Nativity* just in order to recover my mental composure. The author was someone who combined elements of art criticism with heavy lashings of Sigmund Freud, the latter being of such anathema to me that I wonder if I did not cast a hex on the archive, for it was one of the very few we failed to sell and this was at a time when archives were comparatively easy to place. Sometimes when dealing with archives one must wash not only one's hands but also one's soul. There is a curious psychology in writers of a certain breed in that they *allow* themselves to include something of a deeply private and objectionable nature in their archives, almost as if it were a deliberate attempt at self-exposure. This happens too often for it to be untrue. Sometimes it takes the form of pornographic photographs of a writer's conquests, colour Polaroids of men's bottoms once, but we'll stop there. This archive provided one such ugly instance, a small black notebook containing a cold, extremely clinical, account of his sexual conquests and failures, more of the latter than the former although the women were always to blame for their inadequacies. I might have felt differently, maybe even gratitude, had there been a presence of the erotic, but no, this was the equivalent of a quick tumble in a tray of dead fish. I found myself wondering whether for the sake of the women named the notebook ought not to be destroyed. There could be no comparing this with what one imagines Lord Byron's journals were like. One day the solution presented itself. The great philosopher came into shop while I was cataloguing his archive. His beady little eyes lit up at the sight of his own oeuvre spread over my table. The notebook was there. Picking it up by the corners between my thumb and index finger, I returned it to him, saying I was sure he had put it in among his papers by mistake. 'Oh'—he chuckled—'so indeed, so indeed. I hadn't meant to.'

I catalogued Basil Bunting's library and papers, or, rather, as much as he allowed to survive, for he burned the letters Eliot, Pound and many others had written him, and he destroyed his manuscripts too. What did survive, because he'd left it at the poet Tom Pickard's home, was a small notebook containing his early drafts and notes towards his most famous poem *Briggflatts* (1966). Bunting's personal library comprised approximately a thousand volumes, many of them annotated by him, the most striking being a copy of Ezra Pound's *ABC of Economics* (1933), the extensive marginal notes within solid proof that Bunting was not one of Pound's uncritical disciples. As I had become the resident Bunting expert, I was later sent up to Haltwhistle near Newcastle upon Tyne to investigate a 'manuscript' Bunting had willed to his estranged wife, Sima Alladadian, who he met and married in 1948 while he was working for British Intelligence in Persia. He said of it that it would 'see her through.'

It was not a manuscript at all but a typescript of a history of the Corsairs. There was virtually nothing to indicate Bunting had a hand in it and I began to wonder if this was not one of the practical jokes for which he was famous. This was the man who placed a bet with T. S. Eliot that he could stop the traffic on Russell Square. He won. He tied a red ribbon across the road, from tree to tree, and the cars all stopped. If the 'manuscript' was a practical joke, it was a rather cruel one. I asked Sima if there was anything else. When she replied there were some bits and pieces of no consequence I asked whether I might see them. They filled no more than a plastic carrier bag but among them was a fair copy, in his hand, of Bunting's adaptation of the fourteenth-century satirical Persian poem *Mush u Gurba* (Mouse and Cat) by Obaid-e Zakani, which in Bunting's version becomes *The Pious Cat.**

'Anything else?' I asked Sima.

She said there were six bags of 'rubbish' removed from Bunting's desk and she had already disposed of them. Sima was not, I'm afraid, of literary bent and indeed she complained bitterly of her late husband's 'long-hair friends.'

Another enjoyable aspect of my job was when on occasion I went out buying books. One of the most sweetly melancholy experiences I had was when I went with Ronald Taylor to purchase the library of Sir Roger Chance, who lost an arm in the Great War and who had now gone blind. As brave in old age as he had been in youth, he was philosophically reconciled to the loss of his books because he knew they would be passed on to others who appreciated them. With each volume we selected he would ask what the title was and I'd tell him, and, depending on what it was, he would say a word or two about the book. This was his way of saying goodbye to them. He was a philosopher in manner, and I discovered he was also a philosopher in fact, having published *Until Philosophers Are Kings: A Study of the Political Theory of Plato and Aristotle in Relation*

* *The Pious Cat* (1986) was published by Bertram Rota in a limited edition of two hundred copies printed by Martino Mardersteig at the Stamperia Valdonega in Verona. It contains, in addition to the printed poem, a facsimile of Bunting's manuscript and, tucked into a pocket a facsimile of the Persian pamphlet he used. At the end of the book is a short essay I wrote, "From Kirman to Haltwhistle".

to the Modern State (1928) and *The End of Man* (1974). I acquired for myself, from his library, an 1881 edition of *La Divina Commedia* with a vellum spine and a leather title label, which although of no value in itself has value for me. Loosely inserted in the book is a letter addressed from an M. G. Jeffreys at the Villa Aschiezi to Lady Chance, commenting on a passage in the *Purgatorio* and closing, 'I will expect you here on Wednesday after you have seen off Miss Strachey.' A couple of months later, my mother, visiting from Canada, almost as if guided by some compass within her, walked over to my bookcase, took the volume down and seeing the name of the addressee on the letter asked me in a slightly shaky voice where I got the book. It transpired the Chances were childhood neighbours of hers in Rottingdean. She had played with their children, maybe in front of the shelf that contained the very book she singled out on mine. If, as is claimed, all that we see and experience is stored somewhere in the brain might it not be that the spine of that book triggered a childhood memory?

I was employed once in a secret mission of such magnitude that I can conclude that in some small measure I contributed to world peace. I was sent to purchase from the Dickens specialist Jarndyce in Great Russell Street a copy of *Great Expectations*, not the first 1861 edition in three volumes, but a beautifully bound one-volume edition, which would be suitable for presentation purposes. I was not to reveal to anyone, not even my colleagues, the nature of my mission. I think it is safe to say at this distance that the order for it originated at 10 Downing Street and that this was the copy presented to Mikhail Gorbachev at the Reykjavik Summit in 1986.

There is another instance when I found myself at the interstice of world history. In July 1991, the rather jovial American Under Secretary of State for Political Affairs came into the shop. 'Shhh,' he whispered, 'don't tell anyone I'm here. I'm supposed to be at the G7 meeting.' It was a particularly critical summit because Russia was on the cusp of economic and political collapse and it remained to be seen what America's stand would be in such an event. The customer was that rarest of creatures, a John Galsworthy collector. After he made a purchase, I asked him how things were going to fan out with Russia. He told me that in the next couple of weeks there was going to be a coup d'état in Russia, its object to have Gorbachev removed. As it turned out there was one, but the attempt failed.

* * *

Over the years I have often been asked who the Colonel Blimp figure on the main shop floor was, who always answered queries in the most perfunctory of voices, 'Yes, sir,' 'No, sir,' 'I'll make sure he gets the message, sir.'* The responses were always pitched in such a way that one was never sure whether he was being polite or impolite. The inevitable consequence was that some people thought he was terrible, others wonderful; I found him perfectly affable. Peter T. Scott—any omission of the *T* is a cardinal sin—did indeed come across as a military man with a military moustache to match the military voice. And even the blue-and-white striped mug in which he took his coffee had a Dad's Army aspect to it. I remember it broke once; he got another. When I worked with him it seemed that the whole of his private life was taken up with research on the Great War and indeed he had become so expert in it, in every facet, from Arras to zeppelins, that he was often consulted by professional writers and filmmakers. When I met up with him recently I reminded him of something he said years ago. Whatever provoked our conversation I can't remember—it might have been the mess in the Balkans—but I had suggested the world would be coming to an end soon and he said that for him it had already ended in 1918. This, so I thought, was the man stripped bare.

'It is no longer true,' he replied, 'I've reached 1941 in my researches.'

'Still you seem to hunger for another England, another time.'

'I know only too well from what I have read that the last place I'd ever want to be is somewhere other than where I am now. I do

* Actually, although it continues to be misused, the analogy is not right. The David Low 'Colonel Blimp' creation is jingoistic in the extreme, a pompous bore, and sports a walrus moustache.

not want to be in 1918, certainly not 1945. What I find interesting is that I can sit down, enter my own time machine with a book or an archive and travel back in time. I can visit, make notes, take photographs, and when I shut the book or close the file I am transported back into the present day. And I can go home, think about it, write about it and carry on with it the next day. It is to nobody's benefit other than my own and sometimes I wonder if it's of any benefit to me.'

My hope is that what he knows, which is immense, is somehow preserved. I had written to him earlier, asking for details of an interesting copy of Robert Graves's World War One memoir *Goodbye to All That* (1929) that passed through the shop. Admittedly I was seeking support for my own prejudices with respect to Graves's literary approach to factual matters, which all too often resulted in distortions if not outright falsehoods.

'The copy you recall,' Peter replied, 'belonged to Dr J. C. Dunn, the M.O. [Medical Officer] of the 2nd Battalion Royal Welch Fusiliers, the unit in which both Graves and Sassoon served. Dunn went on to write *The War the Infantry Knew* (1938), in my estimation the best first-hand account of the experiences of the British infantry on the Western Front. Dunn's copy of *Good-Bye* was to have appeared in our Great War catalogue, but Keith Simpson (who wrote the introduction to the catalogue and edited the new edition of Dunn's book) fell in love with it and happily accepted it in lieu of a fee. Oddly, it was this copy that confirmed my own distrust of Graves's account and this was doubly confirmed when I was preparing the notes for my edition of *Nothing of Importance* by Bernard Adams, who had also served in 2/RWF, and therefore had cause to check the Battalion War Diary. Here I found that Graves's service at the front was very much shorter than his own account would have had us believe from *Good-Bye*. Also, he was not above using the anecdotes of others from a time before he joined the battalion and transposing them to his own period of service and sector of the line. Sadly, this was a point I made much, much too subtly in my notes!' And now there's a fine instance of exactitude! In an introductory note to one of the firm's catalogues

Peter describes a youthful memory from his early days at Bertram Rota: 'One day I looked up to see a cloaked figure silhouetted in the doorway. As well as the cloak he was wearing a flat-crowned, broad-brimmed black hat; it was as if the familiar trade-mark figure from a bottle of Sandeman port had come to life in Vigo Street. He stepped forward, swept off his hat and he didn't need to identify himself: Robert Graves had come to call.'

When I asked him what it was like for him on that final day, when the shop had been reduced to four rooms on the second floor above what had been the most elegant bookshop in London, he told me he taped a message onto the mantelpiece: 'My name is Ozymandias, king of kings: / Look on my works, ye Mighty, and despair!'

'There wasn't a stick of furniture left. I started working for Bertram Rota on September 9, 1964, when I was seventeen, and left Friday, September 13, 2013, the thirteenth day of the thirteenth year of the new century. It was quite appropriate.'

We got onto the subject of Mr Howlett

* * *

A strange dream, I'll tell it before it fades. Mr Howlett was in it, which is no great surprise given that I knew I'd want to include his story here. Mr Howlett was a book runner and for those unacquainted with the term a book runner is someone who will buy a book for such and such a price in one place and then resell it at a higher price elsewhere. A book runner is only as good as the knowledge he possesses, and the best will make a moderate living from it while the lesser falls by the wayside. Mr Howlett was a proficient enough runner, occasionally striking gold, but happy enough to operate at a modest level making five pounds here, ten pounds there, although I remember being told that if he were to write a thousand-pound cheque it would be perfectly bona fide. He was the immaculate old tramp one might find in a children's story by Walter de la Mare, a figure emblematic of an England that had already begun to disappear, and whose elegance was not some fiction produced by a sentimental imagination. There were such people once, impoverished but proud, never less than gentlemen and ladies. When I last saw him, in the early 1980s, he was in his late seventies, so by my reckoning in the dream, which took place in the present day, he would have been about one hundred and twenty years old. I sought him out because I wanted to fill the holes in his story.

What was surprising about the dream was that he'd hardly aged in appearance and in fact he was quite nimble and more loquacious than I ever knew him to be. This I put down to his being happy to see someone from old times. I found him living in a dark subterranean place with an earthen floor, the only light being that which came through the open entrance. The only furnishings were a table and chair and a mattress on the floor. It was only the day after, when I related the dream to my wife, that I realised this was very much like one of the hovels of the poor I have been reading about in Ann Cornelisen's book *Torregreca* (1969), the fictional name she gives to the small town of Tricarico in the impoverished region of Southern Italy called Basilicata, and somehow the author's description of one particularly dismal abode slipped into my dream of Mr Howlett.

What I hadn't quite bargained for was that his story would overtake mine. I began to ask him about his life and he spoke with tremendous fluency of his childhood memories of the Great War and then of his own part in the Second World War when he was taken prisoner in North Africa. All this I recorded on a bulky cream-coloured tape recorder, a vintage model with double spools such as I remember from the 1950s. Also I was surprised to see a pamphlet in grey covers, which resembled those reports printed by the H.M.S.O. in the 1920s or '30s, only this was not so much an official as an autobiographical sketch, and on the cover of it I saw for the first time Mr Howlett's Christian name. When I knew him he chose not to reveal it, which was why he was always "Mr Howlett." Anthony Rota in his memoir says it was A. W. Howlett, but even he had no idea what the initials stood for. All I'll say is that it was not what I thought it would be. As he produced more and more details of his life I began to lose interest in my own book and wanted rather to faithfully transcribe his, which had a very specific rhythm and signature. I had no idea he could be such a gifted storyteller. I had the makings of a small vernacular masterpiece, which would put my own work in the shade.

At one point he clung to me as would a child to his mother, which was one of the dream's odder features. As his story grew more and more incredible, such that it began to feel like a dream within a dream, I was all the more relieved that it was being recorded because it was not something I'd ever be able to reconstruct from memory. After what seemed like several hours I asked him whether we might not take a recess and he suggested we go to his habitual eatery because there, he said, they had the best bean stew. While we ate I asked him whether I might photograph the pages of the grey pamphlet, but then I realised I'd forgotten to bring my camera. This, of course, was typical of the anxieties I feel when I go out gathering stories. I am always fearful of a battery running out or my mini-recorder failing to record. We finished our stew, which was as good as he said it was, and made ready to leave when I discovered the vintage tape recorder was gone. It had been stolen. I looked into his rheumy eyes and I knew then that he too would be unable to recapitulate his tale, because certain things in life offer themselves only once. I woke up, filled with desperation for what in my dream had been irretrievably lost. I remembered not a word of his story.

'He never divulged his first name,' Peter told me, 'and I considered that it would be rude to ask. Before the war he was a bookseller somewhere in or around Bromley, dealing in new books with a small commercial, subscription library on the side, mostly detective fiction, romances and westerns. I cannot now remember if he was captured in North Africa or Italy, but he was certainly in a POW camp in Italy until the Italians "changed sides" and then the Wehrmacht moved him and his fellow prisoners up to Austria where they were put to work on forestry and in a timber yard. When he was repatriated he swore never to work within four walls ever again and stuck to his promise until the end. He wore an old, battered, greasy brown trilby all the year round, an aged raincoat in summer and a threadbare overcoat (two sizes too large) in winter. He carried his "stock" in a series of cardboard boxes, each of which grew steadily more dilapidated until it fell apart and simply had to be replaced. I'd swear that the sisal twine he used as a handle never changed throughout the entire time I knew him. He always said he made much more money from selling stamps than he ever did from book dealing. There was a stamp shop on Vigo Street a few doors away from Bodley House and he always called in there first with his latest philatelic finds and then came to us to make a few more pounds on his stock of books.'

There is a story which Anthony Rota includes in his memoir with respect to one of Howlett's finds, a bright copy of George Orwell's *Keep the Aspidistra Flying* (1936). 'On occasions when Howlett thought his asking price was high,' he relates, 'he inadvertently signalled the fact by breaking into a quiet but perfectly audible hum. All he said was "It's a mint copy. Pity someone has written his name on the title-page."' And that someone had indeed scribbled his name, whoever that foolish Eric Blair was.* It is good to learn that Mr Howlett was given double his asking price although I can't help but wonder what that asking price was. It drives me to distraction to remember him one day bringing a fine copy in dustwrapper of Robert Byron's *The Road to Oxiana* (1937) for which he asked a mere £25. I knew then the book was worth a great deal more and I wish I'd pounced on one of the very few copies I've seen in its dustwrapper.

And speaking of Robert Byron I shall now memorialise one of the richest friendships to have come out of my time working for Bertram Rota. Setitia Butler, as she was then known (she later married the bookseller Anthony Simmonds), had worked for Heywood Hill, and was Robert Byron's niece. It was hard not to smile at her frequent mentions of "Uncle Robert," who died before she was born, but then she was rightly proud of the connection with the man whose great work, Paul Fussell says, a bit slackly to my mind, 'is to the travel book what *Ulysses* is to the novel between the wars,

* "George Orwell" was the pseudonym for Eric Blair.

and what *The Waste Land* is to poetry.' If the analogy doesn't quite work for me, there can be little doubting the book's importance. Its influence on later travel writers is incalculable. When I first read it, I felt the author had not strayed sufficiently far from the smokiness of the gentleman's club, but a second reading could not have been more ideally timed. I took it with me to Iran and yes, of course, he was right in declaring the Lutfullah Mosque in Isfahan far superior to the neighbouring Blue Mosque. What is important is not that I agreed with him but that he made me *understand* the difference. And he captured the atmosphere of repression although the regime I saw wore rather different clothes.

In manner and appearance, Setitia might have sprung from another age. The clothes she wore, the way she did her hair and especially, so I fancied, her manner of speech sprang out of the 1930s. This is not to suggest she adopted an artificial stance, far from it, for she was living proof of the old adage that style is character. She was not uppity with it either. A woman driven by curiosity, she looked in the places other people ignore, and with what she took from her experiences she might well have called Byron 'uncle.' Nothing mattered to her more than truth and justice. She knew the weight of those words both of which have become almost meaningless through constant misuse. She had a penchant for the ridiculous and as such ridiculousness was the hallmark of our friendship. I won her heart with my imitation of a henhouse at night, perhaps the closest I've ever come to creating a Zen-like experience. I switched off the lights in the basement of Bertram Rota to demonstrate it when Anthony Rota came down the steps, switched on the lights and stared at us in bewilderment, Setitia with her tight smile, and me still kicking up invisible straw. Our favourite place for lunch was a little Italian hole-in-the-wall on the street behind us where we never ceased to wonder how it was possible for an Italian to *not* know how to cook Italian food. *Lasagne, lasagne,* we sang to the tune of the drinking chorus in *La Traviata.*

'What's so funny?' Setitia would say after making one of her utterances.

When she worked at Heywood Hill, Setitia was one of the last people to see Lord Lucan before his disappearance. Just before the accidental murder of his nanny ('accidental' because almost certainly the intended target was his wife) he came to see Setitia in order to settle his outstanding bills. As Lucan had made a note in his diary to see her, the Savile Row police station sent someone to interview her. She did not notice anything out of the ordinary. She was sure that Lucan must have committed suicide because by her reckoning he was such 'a distinctive type, an Edwardian gentleman.' One reason this comes to mind is that not long ago, at Peter Ellis, I fell into conversation with an ex-policeman who had been the first to arrive at the Lucan residence. I would like to have asked him whether Lady Lucan was still flushed from having made love with Lord Lucan *after* the murder.

Setitia, who died too soon, knew what to hate and what to love.

* * *

There is one figure still missing from this picture and that, of course, is *the man himself*—"The Pope of Long Acre," which was how that old reprobate Anthony Newnham dubbed him.* Quite by accident, some years after I left the firm, I found myself at the memorial service for Anthony Rota at St James's Church, Piccadilly. I'd been working at the London Library nearby and was heading for a bowl of soup at the café attached to the church and there, at the main entrance, were my old colleagues Peter T. Scott and Jaqi Clayton.

'What really?' I said. 'Are you sure?'

At their bidding I joined them although I was keenly aware I had not been formally invited. There had always been a protocol surrounding the Rotas, of which it seemed only they knew the

* Anthony Newnham was a junior director under Bertram Rota in the 1950s, then went to America where he worked first for the Brick Row Book Shop in Austin, Texas, then joined another bookseller who went bankrupt, and finally became a carpenter and built houses for rock stars including Leon Russell for whom he also worked as a roadie.

rules. Anyone who'd quit their orbit was made to feel *persona non grata*. At first I misunderstood, thinking it was the actual funeral, and so I kept watching for a coffin and there was none. A private funeral had already taken place. The service was a peculiar jumble of Young Conservative nostalgia and evangelical happy-clappiness of a kind I'd never have associated with the man. Michael Meredith, the librarian at Eton, gave an eloquent address. It concluded with "Soul Limbo," which, fair enough, was the original BBC test match cricket theme.

At the reception, at BAFTA—film was another of Anthony Rota's enthusiasms—I walked over to his widow to express my condolences. She forestalled me.

'You are not wearing a tie.'

When I began to explain I was there only by chance, she interrupted me.

'Your hair has gone white.'

And it came back to me. Both of them, husband and wife, never forgot a slight. John Byrne provides one such example. There was a reception of some kind at the shop where champagne was being served, the initials on the bottle *L.P.C.* [Layton's Private Cuvée]. 'Oh I see,' he quipped, "Lowly-Priced Champagne."' It was stored up for years. Yes, that had to be it, my terrible blunder of a couple of decades before. The first time I met Jean Rota was when she walked through the shop door with what looked to me like a dust ball at the end of a leash. I leaned over my desk and muttered in my best Rodolfo Acosta voice, 'You call that a dawg?'* A withering look from the other end of the leash reduced me to toy dog size. Small wonder that during my years of penance my hair had gone white. And now, all these years later, white *and* contrite, I should have said to her, *I don't know what came over me. And I love dogs too, Mrs Rota, I really do.* Only this wasn't the time or place to say so. As I tend to do in situations where I'm uncomfortable,

* Rodolfo Acosta was the Mexican outlaw in countless Hollywood westerns. My wife has spent decades trying to explain to me that not everybody appreciates my sense of humour.

and with my condolences squeezed like a wet paper ball inside my trouser pocket, I knocked back another and then another glass of champagne. Suddenly I remembered my papers were still on the desk in the reading room of the London Library, only a few minutes to go before closing time. I fled the scene.

Why, so close to the end of this particular chapter of my life, am I having such trouble constructing a portrait of Anthony Rota? Maybe it's because of a fugitive aspect of his existence. Even when he was standing perfectly still there was this sense of him being on the run.

I need to adjust my oxygen to be able to re-enter that somewhat airless zone.

Was he mean? Was this not the man who phoned the police when the Beatles gave their last ever performance on the roof of the neighbouring Apple headquarters when it was on Savile Row? Actually the police were already there, but the fact he did so does point to a cast-iron mentality. Meanness is more difficult to write about than malevolence. My hesitation in saying anything at all about him may be due to my not wishing to pronounce judgement on someone who brought a tremendous amount to the trade and whose image in the minds of many continues unimpeachable. As president of the ABA and ILAB (International League of Antiquarian Booksellers) he did a great deal to bring into the trade a code of ethics, particularly with respect to bookselling etiquette and perhaps his most valuable contribution was the suppression of "The Ring," not Wagner's opera cycle, but the illegal practice of conniving to thwart the open market in auction.* Although morally unacceptable, "The Ring" was never quite in contravention of the law, which reminds me of what a sneak thief called Alf once told

* Anthony Rota writes, 'A ring is a clique of bidders, usually trade buyers, who make an informal agreement not to bid against one another at a public auction in the justifiable hope that their *ad hoc* syndicate will thus be able to make purchases at artificially depressed prices. They then hold a second auction among themselves (the knockout) and divide between them the difference between the prices realized in the public sale room and the higher total obtained in the secret auction.'—*Books in the Blood* (2002).

me: 'For every law sez you can't do it, there's another sez you can, only it's harder to find.' There was something of the handshaking politico in Anthony Rota and to further his cause he kept a small notebook in which he recorded small personal details of the more important of his customers—the names of their children, the college into which one of them hoped to gain admittance, details about their wives—and when a couple of years later he asked his client whether Timmy got into Princeton who could not marvel at the prodigious memory of the man and yes, of course, I'll have that very important association copy of W. Somerset Maugham's first book, overpriced though it is. Okay, say it was shrewd business tactics, but it should come as no surprise that his projected image often failed to tally with the one seen closer to home.

The stinginess of the man was sometimes, and most complicatedly, coupled with generosity. The move from Long Acre to Langley Court, the shifting of hundreds of heavy boxes, did a lifetime's worth of damage to my spine. We all had to take part in the move. It was cheaper than bringing in hired muscles. Months later, I was still having weekly treatments at rather more than I could afford. One day Anthony Rota summoned me to his office.

'Take a pew,' he said.

He spoke of having observed the pain I was in and then offered to help pay my chiropractor's fees. I was deeply touched, but my pride would not allow for it, so I asked him whether instead he could purchase my Wyndham Lewis collection. Yes, he would. When I brought it into work he shook his head, saying that nobody collected him anymore and that he could only offer me a paltry figure. As I was badly in need of money, I reluctantly agreed. The very same day he contacted the singer Bryan Ferry who had earlier expressed an interest in Wyndham Lewis. Ferry came to the shop and I was called upon to guide him through the books. He seemed a gentleman to me, which only slightly took the edge off the discovery that he bought the collection for close to four times what I was paid for it. I was too stunned to protest. The ethical practice Anthony Rota had so vociferously pushed at the captains of the trade was not extended to the galley slaves.

And now comes one of those curious corollaries, which are so much a feature of life in the book trade. A couple of weeks later, I stepped into Any Amount of Books on Charing Cross Road and there I saw a copy of the limited signed edition of Wyndham Lewis's *The Wild Body* (1927). I noticed a small mark on the lower cover. It was my copy! I saw another Lewis title; it, too, was mine. Why would Bryan Ferry, having just bought the books, sell them again so quickly and at considerably less than he'd paid for them? I went home, the question gnawing at me. The next day I phoned him. There was a moment's silence. And then came sorrow in his voice. 'Oh, I see it now,' he said. The books had been stolen from him by one of his assistants. 'I know he's had a hard time,' he said, 'shaking a drug habit. I'd like to give him a second chance. I'll ask him to buy back the books he stole and return them to me.' What I first saw in Bryan Ferry was true.

I have just reread Anthony Rota's memoir *Books in the Blood* (2002), its dustwrapper blood-red just so one gets the drift. An entertaining book, witty and urbane, it stands as a valuable record of bookselling over a particular period of time, although at times it feels like an official version of things as opposed to what they actually were. There is not a casualty in sight, not a single discrepancy between fact and appearance. All in all, it's a good book. So why the dissenting note? Well, it's this: I don't think books were ever in his blood, which is not quite the same as saying he was not a proficient seller of them or, for that matter, a smart committee man. What was missing in him, or at least in my periscopic view of the matter, was a genuine passion for books and literature, and indeed I think he was rather afraid of them for what deficiencies they might reveal in himself. A man in such a position tends to hide as much as he discloses and in his case I think he hid, though not very successfully because it was there for all to see, behind the façade of social ambition. What he enjoyed most was what the trade conferred upon him, a social status he might not have achieved elsewhere, which is fair enough, but where he deluded himself was in thinking his trade was not actually a trade. Very rarely would he step into an

English bookshop whereas he would do so with American shops, where he was quite happy to be called "Tony," which at home he would not tolerate. The very idea of dirtying his shoes at the PBFA (Provincial Book Fair Association) was unthinkable. One morning Ronald Taylor who was in charge of the antiquarian section suggested I accompany him to have a poke around the PBFA book fair at the Russell Hotel. Maybe, he said, I'd find something worthwhile. Almost immediately—somehow it had been missed by the other dealers—I spotted a fine copy in fine dustwrapper of Arthur Koestler's *Darkness at Noon* (1940), a legendarily scarce title, probably because in its year of publication several publishers' warehouses were destroyed by enemy action. It was priced at £200 which, after a trade discount, came to £180 (10 per cent was still the trade discount then.) A few hours later, the book was sold to an American institution for £650. I was summoned to Anthony Rota's office. I was expecting a word of gratitude.

'You are never to do that again.'

I was startled.

'We do not deal with *the trade*.'

What were we then?

I think sometimes he never properly understood who his real enemies were, while at the same time he failed to realise his real allies were close to hand, ready to be called upon, if only he could *see* them. I watched him shower praise on people who as soon as they were out of the front door ratted on him, American dealers in particular, whose allegiances he thought were exclusive to himself. They bought most of their books elsewhere. Who can blame them? They bought from anyone who had what they were looking for, at the right prices, but I think they might have been more careful of what they said because gossip moves quicker through the London book trade than anywhere else. This would suggest Anthony Rota was a poor judge of character. Well, yes, he was. We watched helplessly as even one of his closest associates swindled him, a bookseller who, announcing his 'retirement,' sold him his stock, sight unseen, which turned out to be the dregs or what in the trade are often called 'the evergreens,' the *unsaleable*.* The best he kept for himself for private trade.

The story I'd always heard was that the occupation of bookseller was never one Anthony Rota sought for himself but which he had thrust upon him. Apparently he wanted to be a farmer or if not a farmer then a dendrochronologist, which, for those untutored in the study of trees, is someone who determines a tree's age by counting the annual growth rings. This is normally achieved by means of an increment borer that removes a sample of the core with minimum damage to the tree. Years ago, I saw in the newspaper a story that could have been one of Aesop's fables. It concerned a dendrochronologist working in the Arctic tundra where trees a hundred years old grow no more than a foot in height. As might be expected, their wood is adamantine. This dendrochronologist struggled to obtain a sample and after several attempts, each of which ended in dismal failure, he grabbed a chainsaw and cut the tree down. I wonder whether one might not find in this an analogy for "the Fall of the House of Rota."

The saddest aspect of all this was the loyalty he engendered in his staff. We all did our absolute best for him although this was rarely acknowledged. We accepted as true what we knew not to be. We willingly took our measly salaries on the excuse it was the best he could do while at the same time, when he told us about them, we applauded his culinary exploits whether they were at a table in London, New York City or Tokyo. We applauded his ethical stance with respect to trade practice while those same ethics were not extended to ourselves. We would never dare sell a book of our own to another bookseller because it was forbidden to do so and although what he offered us would be maybe less than half of what he would offer a stranger coming in off the street with the same book we were grateful all the same. We accepted it all because we fell into a dream of hierarchy. It was, of course, already obsolete but we pretended otherwise, and one pretends because it gets one

* It is one of those bibliographical mysteries that books bound in green cloth are often the most difficult to sell.

through the day at the far end of which is something we like to think of as our real lives. *Our jobs are our private fantasies, our disguises, the cloak we can creep inside to hide.* With no give at the joins it is small wonder the mighty edifice came crashing down.

I was fortunate enough to be out of there before it happened. It is not my place to comment on what came after my time, but I'd been there long enough, fourteen years, to know it ought not to have happened. Also I was there long enough to know that what did happen was inevitable. Should I pick over the bones when the bones had already been stripped bare? The question is this: how was it possible that the foremost dealer of modern first editions, agent for many of the most important twentieth-century archives, the bookseller with the most solid clientele, and some of the best connections to institutions both here and in America, could have fallen so quickly? When I put this to Peter T. Scott, he replied, 'Actually it wasn't that short a time and can be best summed up by the North Country saying, "Clogs to clogs in three generations."'* And now, thinking on it, I see he was right. It had long begun to slide when I was there.

The main cause for the downfall was, I believe, a failure of imagination. There was nobody working there who did not have expertise in one area or another: Ronald Taylor was in charge of, although only rarely given the freedom to develop, the antiquarian section; George Lawson was, among other things, an expert in James Joyce and could work his charm with some of the most important librarians; Peter T. Scott was unquestionably the country's leading expert on books relating to World War One; John Byrne was expert not only in the cataloguing of literary archives but also one of the most knowledgeable people on fine printing;

* Said to be a Lancashire proverb, late nineteenth century: clogs were worn by manual workers in the north of England. The implication is that the energy and ability required to raise a person's material status from poverty is often not continued to the third generation, and that the success is therefore not sustained. A similar idea is found in Dryden's *Fables Ancient and Modern* (1700), 'Seldom three descents continue good.'—*The Oxford Dictionary of Phrase and Fable* (2000).

Arthur Uphill, Gertrude Stein his first amour, was supreme in his knowledge of the Americans in Paris; Martin Battey was an expert in science fiction although I never could understand why people would want to read about rubbery blobs with funny names; Robert Mayall of beloved memory, who not long ago died in a freak accident, was Robert Mayall, which was enough; and I like to think of myself as knowledgeable in the areas of modern poetry and foreign literature. It ought to have worked and again my answer as to why it didn't was a failure of imagination, an inability on the part of Anthony Rota to harness the not inconsiderable resources of his own staff and to give them the freedom to expand in their areas of expertise. There were other reasons too, the running of a new books library supply section that could never really pay for itself, an expansion in precisely the wrong direction. The biggest problem of all, however, was that instead of patiently studying the ring growths the would-be dendrochronologist took a saw to his own tree. It is the old story of a man who believes his own stories, who will cut shady deals with himself and then pretend to be surprised by the outcome. Anthony Rota's end was truly lamentable.

Peter T. Scott told me he had the impression I hated my job at Bertram Rota. It was never that, it was not the job itself but the purblindness it engendered in me. And yet we need it too, the mundane being a precious soil from which all sorts of things grow, although often they too are mundane. Most of the people who worked there hit upon hard times. One can say, of course, people choose their own paths. Who goes into books for riches? As for my own fortunes a surprising phone call would change things for me, but whether towards hell or paradise is another story.

Chapter Five

A PARAGON OF SEEDY EXACTITUDE

A BOOKSHOP SELLING MODERN FIRST EDITIONS OF LITERATURE attracts literary people. Should one write about them or not? The professional side of me says no, the other side, which enjoys anecdotes, yes. So I'll take the plunge. Philip Larkin in his capacity as librarian at Hull University came into Bertram Rota, looking for copies of his own early books for the university collections. This struck me as a self-flagellatory exercise. Surely he had a slave. If sometimes I label him "The Bard of Impotence" this is not to say he was not a good poet, a paragon of seedy exactitude, but that his oeuvre exudes impotence, whether it be his own, this country's, or both together. Despair becomes its own comfort zone, which may explain his immense appeal to the happily depressed masses. When I offered him a copy of his first book, *The North Ship* (1945), for £200 he balked at the price, saying, 'What, for *that* piece of rubbish!' The librarian left with his satchel empty. The poet, on the other hand, would he have thought the book less rubbishy had it been a tenth of the price?

A taller man than I'd imagined, certainly ruddier, Graham Greene stood in his beige mac at the entrance in a frozen stare, not at me but at the shop as a whole, as if it were a panorama into which he'd now set loose his demons. I sat silently at my desk, thinking it best not to interfere with his mental processes. I'd just been on a Graham Greene reading binge, *The Heart of the Matter* (1948) the book of his I liked most. And here he was, the man himself, icy with rage. Where was Greene the comic, who'd made me laugh out loud with his passage on Maltesers in *The Human Factor* (1978)? As abruptly as he entered, he turned on his heels and left. So what was all *that* about? I think I've discovered the answer in a festschrift presented to Anthony Rota on February 24, 2002, to mark the occasion of his seventieth birthday. A former employee, Richard Budd ("Billy Budd," his nickname), in his contribution relates what happened a decade earlier when a tall man came into the shop, asking to see Anthony Rota. 'Yes sir,' said Billy Budd. 'What name shall I say?' Budd continues: 'He drew himself up still higher and looked down on me with such disgust and disdain I was quite taken aback, and said with a sigh "Graham Greene." I got my own back though, I called Ann Brownson on the intercom and said "There's a Mr Greene to see Mr Anthony." Unfortunately there was a sequel. To my great embarrassment I had to go to Greene's flat in Albany to collect books Anthony had bought. The great man was there, he glowered at me while I packed the boxes and didn't say a word.' What I saw was, I think, the radioactive fallout from that earlier debacle.

One day I went into work with my jaw inflamed from an abscess in my tooth. I'd been unable to get an emergency appointment until the following morning and as it was getting worse by the minute I was about to ask to go home when Anthony Rota instructed me to go to north London and collect some Samuel Beckett correspondence from Dame Peggy Ashcroft. Goodness, Peggy Ashcroft. I had seen her as Winnie in the 1975 Peter Hall production of Beckett's *Happy Days* at the National Theatre, when she made it impossible for anyone to ever fill her shoes, and then, more recently, in the television drama series *The Jewel in the Crown* where she played the role of Barbie Batchelor. Poor Barbie, who could ever forget her bafflement when she gets news of the bomb dropped on Hiroshima foreshadowing, only minutes later, her own death 'in sudden sunshine, her shadow burnt into the wall behind her as if by some distant but terrible fire.'* It may be the single greatest instance of acting I've ever seen. I was terrified at the prospect of meeting her because I'm clumsy in the presence of people I greatly admire. I say stupid things or, rather, stupider than usual. And yet how could I not go? It would amount to no more than a hello and a handing over of a wad of letters, but for it to be with Peggy Ashcroft was just too irresistible.

'No, no, no,' she insisted, 'you must visit for a while.'

She positioned me in a chair opposite her and schoolgirlishly put her hands together on her lap and said, 'Now, I want to know *everything* about you. You look to me like a poet. I'm sure you are.'

She blinked like a startled bird at my every utterance and I understood then why it was that men fell madly in love with her. The pain in my jaw was gone. It was enough to make me believe in healing presences. So what shall I convey here with respect to the greatest of actresses? Actually, nothing. There was something very charming about her home although now I'm hard put to say what it was. Were there flowers everywhere? It feels now as if there were. I seem to remember a lovely natural light or maybe it was just the light surrounding her. What remains with me is a picture of luminescence transported into old age. She spoke of her son who ran a theatre group in Canada. I don't remember any more of what was said and it hardly matters, for what I realised later is that she had found out a great deal about me and that I'd found out absolutely nothing about her.

Elizabeth Jennings was another benign presence. Many were the writers whose archives we handled and she was the one I got to know best. She would arrive with plastic shopping bags full of spiral-bound notebooks such as schoolchildren use and which

* Paul Scott, *The Towers of Silence* (1971). *The Jewel in the Crown* is the first volume of his *Raj Quartet* and the line I just quoted is from the third in the series.

probably were the least expensive. I knew of her circumstances, that she lived very much on the edge, was subject to terrible depressions and had been incarcerated inside mental asylums, which probably accounted for her sad eyes. The tabloid 'bag lady' depictions of her were despicable. I never found her anything less than kindly, perfectly sane and quietly passionate. Her method of writing was unique. When she felt a book coming on she would compose hundreds of poems at a time, filling notebook after notebook, the majority of them in rhyme, some of them publishable. They were what she called her 'warming-up exercises' after which she would concentrate only on the poems that would go into her next collection. And even those had hardly any revisions to them although I think it's fair to say of her published work that she allowed too much to slip through the net. She spoke out of her deep sorrow, the only release from it, she told me several times, being her Catholic faith which prevented her from a fate worse than she already had to endure. I saw no reason to disbelieve her nor was she ever uppity with it, there being nothing cloying in her manner such as one sometimes gets with religious people, and certainly no dumping upon others the heaviness that is so often the keynote of the chronically depressed. She gave me an inscribed copy of *Growing-Points* (1975) which may be her best single collection: 'Your whispered world is not / Yours any longer. It's not there you grow.' She wore white ankle socks. She was a mystic in the truest sense.

The first time I saw John Ashbery was at the 1975 Cambridge Poetry Festival. Staying at my B&B was a poet my age, John Birtwhistle, who was brisk in manner, confident in the way of those who lack confidence and wore his hair somewhat like that of a mediaeval pageboy. I met him years later, his locks trimmed, when he related the following anecdote concerning that April day in Cambridge. He had gone to a café for a coffee and found himself sitting beside a rather dapper American. They began to talk and when talk turned to the subject of the poetry festival Birtwhistle asked him, 'Are you a poet then?' and the dapper American drawled, 'Well, you know how it is.' At the reading when the crow-faced, studiously miserable Charles Tomlinson took to the podium Ashbery was heard to say in a high-pitched voice, 'Mm, he looks like *fun*.' As yet I had no measure of Ashbery as a poet, but I was caught somewhere between scorn and admiration when from "The Skaters" he read the line, 'Any more golfing hints, Charlie?' This was a man who raised boredom to the level of brilliance. Some years later, Ashbery came into Bertram Rota with his English publisher, Michael Schmidt. When on a shelf behind me he spied a copy of Algernon Blackwood's *A Prisoner of Fairyland* (1913) he said in his campest voice, 'Hmm, I wonder what *this* is about.' It was too good an opportunity to miss: I jumped up and said, 'Oh, you know' and then sang to him, to the tune of the hit song from *Kismet*, 'Take my hand, I'm a prisoner in fairyland.' I'm glad to say he never forgot this, for not long before his death he mentioned it to another poet of my acquaintance.

* * *

My desk at Bertram Rota was at the entrance to the shop, where I sat beneath an indoor tree that occasionally shed leaves on me. A number of lasting friendships were made there, in that sacred arboreal space of mine, where, observed but unheard, I might dawdle a while. I could chat with people about things other than books. When Christopher Ricks came into the shop we talked Bob Dylan. When Fräulein Buch came into the shop we talked opera. Also, there being something of the flâneur in me, I liked to watch the passers-by. One day, a couple of attractive girls in bright summer dresses clickety-clacked down Long Acre, one of whom shouted at me on the other side of the glass, 'Don't just sit there, *do* something!' This greatly amused John Byrne for whom it became a catchphrase any time he caught me idling.

Another time, less happily, some youths tapped at the window, taunting me. After a few minutes of this, I stepped outside to ask them to move on when one of them pulled a gun from inside his jacket and at a distance of a couple of feet fired it directly at me. I heard the discharge. It was rather odd being shot at because I was unsure whether I was still alive or simply hadn't yet caught up with the fact of my own demise. They laughed and fled. Were it not a blank that was fired they'd be writing this book, not me. Another curious incident involved a drunken Gurkha who stood in front of my desk, threatening me. My guess was that he was a soldier, maybe decommissioned, and if so then it would be inadvisable of me to tell him to shut his face. I didn't see a *khukuri*, but as his rage grew he spoke of using one on me. At this point it occurred to me he might be as good as his word and so I reached for my last line of defence.

'Amar Singh Thapa wouldn't like to see you behaving like this.'

The Gurkha looked at me with something like disbelief in his features, mumbled something in Nepalese and fled. Whatever his murderous instincts, I'm sure I would have sympathised with them, but why *me*? This time, history was on my side. An ancestor on my mother's side, Sir David Ochterlony, during the Anglo-Nepalese war of 1814–16 confronted Amar Singh Thapa on the battlefield and such was the respect between the two men that halts would be called in the middle of battle to allow each side to gather their dead and wounded. Are there gentlemanly wars? One of the greatest people in the country's history, Amar Singh Thapa, "The Living Lion of Nepal," had come to my rescue.

This was my special place, alone at the front of the bookshop, and I would defend it at any cost. There was one instance of transgression that would subtly change my life. It may be argued that all people who come into a bookshop are interrupters of one shade or another. All would be well, I've heard booksellers say, were it not for the customers. Between 1983 and 1985, a handsome young man, Mediterranean in looks, dressed in navy blue or what the Spanish call *azul marino*, so dark a blue that in the artificial light it looked black to me, would come in and with all the arrogance of a bullfighter glare at me as he strode past my desk. At least that was how I perceived it at the time. Sometimes, for just an instant, he would stop there, as if challenging me, and I, from behind the Alhambra of my huge manual typewriter, would glare back at him. It was a bit like two gunfighters in a western taking each other's measure, one walking metaphorical circles around the other. This has very little to do with actual dislike and probably a great deal to do with forces of male attraction. There is a scene in the movie *Shane* (1953) where the hero and the villain, played respectively by Alan Ladd and Jack Palance, encounter each other in the dark beside a well and drink water from the same ladle, which strikes me as Homeric in its intimate magnitude. I felt something of this with my imaginary foe. We never, as far as I can remember, actually spoke although he remembers differently and tells me he tried to sell me a book once, but for now I'll stand by this slippery memory of mine. A story wrongly remembered is of itself another kind of story, one that may be false, but for what it effects in the soul true all the same.

I would notice the books he purchased and for the life of me I could not get an angle on his literary tastes. A bookseller can usually do so and act upon that knowledge but not in this case. Clearly he was going down some of literature's more obscure avenues. At one point he was buying the works of John Gawsworth, 'an excessively minor poet' according to the critic John Sutherland, whose biggest wave of success, if he ever had one, was in the 1930s, after which it trickled through the 1940s and then, drop by drop, into the oblivion of the basement rooms of secondhand bookshops in the provinces. Death comes in varying degrees.

I would like to contemplate for just a moment the obverse of the book trade with its graveyards of forgotten titles. Somebody should make a literary pilgrimage through one of those musty basements, selecting not just any old books but, say, a dozen that would seem to be of substance and in which the writing is more than passable, and then he should make it his business to find out who their authors were, what *their* stories were, and how their lives were refracted through the words they wrote, and consider the fact that for just a wink in time they sipped of the sweet nectar of immortality. Or so they believed. There are few births that are not celebrated and when I hold such a volume in my hands I think not just of the effort that went into its writing, but also of the sheer joy the author must have felt on receiving a publisher's letter of acceptance. One can almost hear the ghostly popping of champagne bottles that greeted the arrival of each new title, all the hopes that were launched for a brighter future. An alternative history might be constructed from this vast bibliography of the forgotten. What I am about to illustrate is someone who did just that, who for his own purposes took an obscure writer and raised him Lazarus-like from the necropolis of the unremembered.

John Gawsworth was a friend of, and, later, literary executor for, the fantasy writer M. P. Shiel. As well as being the author of *The Purple Cloud* (1901), a book much revered for its weirdness,* Shiel was also the first king of Redonda, which, as we shall see, is a matter of some importance. It is said that after Shiel's death Gawsworth kept his ashes in a biscuit tin on his mantelpiece, which he would sprinkle as a condiment over the meals he served to his more distinguished guests. Surely, at some point, the seating plan would have included his friend Lawrence Durrell, but whether this makes Durrell a cannibal I'm not sure, I haven't looked deeply into the matter, but I should imagine cannibals eat the flesh and chuck the bone, and so, technically speaking, he would be cleared of any such charge. Otherwise, in all other respects, Durrell did feed upon other people's lives, certainly his wife's and daughter's. In later life Gawsworth became a familiar figure at Bertram Rota when it was on Vigo Street and probably benefited more than was his due from Mr Bertram's generous nature.

This is where Fräulein Therese Buch enters the picture. She was rumoured to have been Gawsworth's lover. When I met her it was at Long Acre and Gawsworth was already several years in the grave. A woman in her seventies, German, possibly Jewish, rotund but not fat, a whitish mop of short hair, she resembled a panda bear with a cane. She was a woman of mysteries such as one would not dare intrude upon. I never mentioned Gawsworth, but recently I found a photograph of him with a woman at his side that could be a younger, slimmer, darker, zippier her. She was not well-to-do and would bring in the odd book to sell and whatever she

* As the story of a death-bringing cloud, it is not, at the time of writing, the summer of 2020, without relevance.

offered I bought, once or twice out of my own pocket. As a mark of gratitude she took me to an afternoon rehearsal of Verdi's *Don Carlos* when it was still in Visconti's gorgeous staging, at the Royal Opera House. Another time I met her when she was close to tears on the other side of the barrier at Pimlico tube station where the attendant refused to open the gate reserved for the disabled. She was apparently not lame enough to warrant a few seconds of his trouble. Much to the horror of my young daughters who were with me, I informed him in measured cadences that unless he opened the gate I would personally hurl him down the escalator and feel no remorse for any injuries he might sustain. I think Fräulein Buch enjoyed the operatic spectacle. The gate was opened and she waddled through, the attendant smiled weakly and my frightened daughters breathed again. I knew she had a story, but if she were alive, which I doubt, I'd still observe her silences.

As 'King Juan I of Redonda' Gawsworth inherited his crown from M. P. Shiel ('King Felipe'). The mythical kingdom does in fact have a physical presence, Redonda being an uninhabited pile of rock in the Leeward Islands. The first European to see it was Christopher Columbus who gave it its name. If any two countries were ever to have gone to war to over it, it would be only for the guano that covers it, guano being a composite of bat and bird shit, a fertiliser once highly regarded for its effectiveness but with the coming of artificial fertilisers it was no longer sought after. Curiously enough, I have been in correspondence with a Canadian writer called Michael Hingston who has produced a three-hundred-page history of the kingdom.* I fear for his sanity because he took his researches as far as actually flying over and then visiting the island at some physical risk to himself. There's nothing there, other than guano and stone. As for my collector of Gawsworthiana, here was somebody for whom literary fashion was of absolutely no consequence. As a customer he was, and still is, wholly inscrutable.

---

* *The Kingdom of Redonda* (Biblioasis, 2022).

One day he came up to me and spoke. I was mortified. What was I to do? Where were my trusty defences? He told me he had been living in England for the past two years, at Oxford, lecturing in Spanish literature and translation, and was now returning to Spain and that he did not want to leave without saying goodbye to me. I was, of course, totally disarmed. What's more, I liked him immediately. So, sometimes, first impressions badly misfire. I had no idea Javier Marías was a writer, for he had yet to make an impact on the anglophone literary scene. When he was seventeen he published his first novel in Spain, *Los dominios del lobo* (*The Dominions of the Wolf*, 1971) and, as if this weren't precocious enough, when he was fourteen he wrote "The Life and Death of Marcelino Iturriaga," one of the short stories collected in *While the Women Are Sleeping* (2010). I knew none of this, of course. It was only later, while glancing through a newly published anthology that I chanced upon a short story of his, "An Epigram of Fealty" in which Gawsworth and the Kingdom of Redonda make their first appearance. And in the story, although he is given the name of "James Lawson," the main character is definitely me, or, rather, my fictional double with 'cold, blue, unfriendly eyes' sitting at the front desk of a not entirely fictional shop called Bertram Rota. It was curious that he should have hit upon the name "Lawson." I have come to suspect Javier Marías of espionage. The characters in his novels are not so much observed as spied upon. In "An Epigram of Fealty" three beggars are standing outside the shop, one of whom later turns out to be Gawsworth. They are looking at a highly improbable window display which includes the original typescript of Samuel Beckett's *Watt* (1953), priced at £50,000, and a copy of Dylan Thomas's scarce pamphlet *Two Epigrams of Fealty* ([1953]), 'printed privately for the members of the Court of the Kingdom of Redonda.'* An author can do whatever he likes, but he will never be entirely free of our judgement: it would be a foolhardy bookseller who would put such expensive items in a shop window and in any case Bertram Rota did

* Dylan Thomas was made "Duke of Gweno" in 1947 in a Soho restaurant where Gawsworth was holding court.

not have window displays. It has to be said in the author's defence that "James Lawson" questions the wisdom of putting such rarities on show, but doing so provides him with a pretext to go onto the street and shoo the beggars away. This is a fiction, however, and Javier Marías has a knack for importing real names and situations into his stories. What he does with them afterwards is a matter of some amusement for those who find themselves there. It is not a particularly flattering sketch of me, but then I was delighted to be cast in a villain's role. Also it means I was not entirely alone in thinking there had been animal tensions between us.

Some years later, I read his first novel to be published here, *All Souls* (1992; *Todas las Almas*, 1989), set in Oxford, of course, and which has as one of its characters the very real John Gawsworth whose death mask, reproduced in the text, is taken from the cover of the posthumously published pamphlet *Some Poems* (1971) which I remembered the author buying several years before at Bertram Rota. Why does this sit so clearly in the memory? Well, it was such an improbable purchase for an interesting figure from another country to make. Clearly he spotted something of potential in the graveyard of the forgotten. All the while, then, he had been moving in a direction whose goal he himself could never have anticipated. Serendipity had plans for him. Shortly before he died, Gawsworth passed his title to Jon Wynne-Tyson ("King Juan II"), a publisher, animal rights campaigner, vegetarian and occasional author whose books touched on matters of, yes, animal rights and vegetarianism. After reading *All Souls* he abdicated his throne in favour of Javier Marías. The author had in a sense now become his own fiction. I should add here that there are pretenders to the throne, one of whom is a certain "King Bob" who at one point was chartering boat tours to Redonda. I offered to have him assassinated, but the dignified "King Javier" would prefer to rule in peace.

All these remarkable twists of fate comprise the theme of his next fascinating novel, *Dark Back of Time* (2001; *Negra espalda del tiempo*, 1998) in which he takes yet further the figure of Gawsworth. And this is where the reader himself becomes a fiction. I was reading the book on the tube, relishing his Chaplinesque description of entering Titles Bookshop in Oxford and of not knowing where to put his seeping bag of grapes. (I am happy to think the author might be as impractical as me. A plastic bag would have solved the problem.) The proprietor of the bookshop, a rather flinty Mrs Stone, suggests he place the grapes in the umbrella stand where, it being a sunny day, they will be perfectly safe. Ten pages later, a friend whom the author had previously arranged to meet there, 'Freud's granddaughter,"*—walks into the shop and plunges her dry umbrella down through the soggy bag. I was hugely enjoying this passage when a massive black woman sitting next to me on the tube bit into her green apple and a spray of juice flew from the side of her mouth across the left-hand page of my book. Quickly I applied the sleeve of my sweater, mopping up the fluid before the ink on the page began to bleed. I was quite prepared to disembowel my neighbour right there and then, but realised in time that such an action might be construed as having a racial motive whereas in reality it would have been a bibliomaniacal one. The apple exploded several times more. She was quite oblivious to my murderous glares. Soon I found myself adopting an absurd physical posture, leaning almost into the lap of the neighbour to the other side of me, my cupped hand shielding the book from further pluvial salvoes. I wonder, though, about these odd intersections where meet a Spaniard and a Pole, a dead poet and a living one, Redonda *y Londres*, apples and grapes.

I did say this happy transgression would effect a subtle change in my life and so it was that I became a fiction for a third time. In 1999, Javier Marías appointed me Poet Laureate in the English Tongue to the Court of Redonda, "Skelton" my *nom de guerre*. I am not required to fulfil any royal duties and he does not discharge any, which is probably just as well given that poet laureates do tend to

* Now let me guess. Sophie Freud, psychologist, born in Vienna, on a day trip from America where she lectures? Eva Freud? But no, poor thing, she died in 1944, in the South of France, aged just twenty. Or could he have been referring to one of Lucian Freud's 127 wives?

make a terrible hash of things when called upon to produce verses, but he did invite me to compile a list of the ten greatest poems in the language. As I felt a shade awkward about listing ten of my own poems I offered him instead Richard Stanyhurst's translation of the first four books of Virgil's Æneid (1582), considered by one critic 'a *monstrum horrendum* unparalleled in the annals of translation' and by others in words even less generous. Stanyhurst I owe to my ex-colleague at Bertram Rota, Arthur Uphill, who delighted in such literary aberrations. Amanda McKittrick Ros was another of his passions, his favourite book being *Irene Iddesleigh* (1897), described by Mark Twain as 'one of the greatest unintentionally humorous novels of all time.' Arthur Uphill was the only person I know who really did explode with laughter, but usually only if the object of his mirth was sufficiently small, say a misprint or a bad line of verse. His face would go all crimson, then came a guffaw like a rhinoceros's sneeze, followed by a virtual shower of spittle. Of all the people I worked with at Bertram Rota he was the most inscrutable. As for Javier Marías, he and I remain on good terms. Some fictional being bearing my name has appeared in a couple of his novels, these being the fourth and fifth occasions on which I have become a fiction, firstly on page 275 of his masterpiece *Your Face Tomorrow 1: Spear and Fever* (2005, *Tu rostro mañana 1: Fiebre y lanza*, 2002) where I, or, rather, my fictional double, appears with Keith Richards, Francis Bacon, Mrs Thatcher and other notables, and secondly, in *Thus Bad Begins* (2016, *Así empieza lo malo*, 2014) where in Madrid, on the office door of a building on Plaza del Marqués de Salamanca can be found a small metal plaque bearing the legend 'Marius Kociejowski: Middle East Travel' although, according to the narrator 'he was not, I presumed, a mere travel agent' and how right he was. The author, if he knew, would have been horrified.

* * *

It is time for a musical interlude. One day a woman with very short hair and a gentle Scots lilt came into the shop, asking me for a copy of Edith Sitwell's poetry collection *Gold Coast Customs*

(1929), which she told me she wanted to set to music. We had a copy, which she happily purchased. As of late Edith Sitwell has once more come into her own, the singer Morrissey an advocate of hers and so, too, the poet Jeremy Reed, whereas at that point she was impossible to sell. There is, by the way, a remarkable facial similarity between her and George Lawson. (I'm not sure how he'd take this.) I asked the customer if she were a musician and she said yes and then I asked her if she had a band and she said yes and finally I told her how I, too, once tried my hand at music but never made the grade and so I knew how hard it was. She agreed. I wished her all the luck with her great project and asked her to let me know how she got on. She thanked me, saying she would. When she left, my colleague Martin Battey turned to me, a look of horror in his eyes.

'Didn't you realise who that was?'

I confessed I didn't.

'It was Annie Lennox.'

I hope she remembers this, wherever she is. I have not found any evidence that she set *Gold Coast Customs*, a snappy title, to music. Speaking of women with cropped hair, one day I looked up from my typewriter to see a young woman, her hair roughly shorn, not stylishly as in the case of Miss Lennox, but in what I took to be a statement of independence. She asked me for the women's room and because I knew that as a euphemism "the ladies" had recently fallen into disfavour because, after all, what a terrible word it is, suggestive of country houses and women dressed in lace, I took her downstairs, told her to go to the end of the aisle, turn left and she'd find it there. I went back to my desk and forgot all about her. A few minutes, Anthony Rota went downstairs and returned with a red face.

'What have you done?' he said.

'What have I done *what*?' I replied.

'There's a woman downstairs in a rage. She came in looking for a copy of Marilyn French's *The Women's Room* and you showed her the way to the toilet.'

And so it was that I'd dealt a lethal blow to women's suffrage.

* * *

Bruce Chatwin lived in one of the flats above the shop. I'd see and talk to him quite often. A while back, I read an article by Blake Morrison which begins, 'Does anyone read Chatwin these days?' It is a question that only a few years earlier would have been inconceivable, for he appeared to be as secure in his position of travel writer as Robert Byron was in his. Also he wrote fiction and from there moved into a mode that falls somewhere between fact and fiction. When he died in 1989, aged forty-eight, he was considered one of the most important writers of his generation. Nicholas Shakespeare's massive biography of him, unintentionally perhaps, did more to weaken than to enhance his reputation. What it revealed was that what we took to be true was much too often the opposite. When I first met him I had no idea who he was. We chatted a while and he made vague references to some book he was working on. When I asked him if he wrote, he ran upstairs and a few minutes later returned and slapped a paperback copy of *In Patagonia* on my desk. I read the book and greatly enjoyed it. At that point it never entered my mind that I myself would one day write in that most perilous of genres. *In Patagonia* was applauded for its brilliance and rightly so, but when years later I read Shakespeare's book and discovered that many of the most vivid passages, in particular those recounting his meetings with people, were concocted I felt a little cheated. Presumably the reason Chatwin deviated from the truth was in order to give the book a certain, shall we say, panache.

George Lawson knew him well and winces a little at the memory of him. 'Bruce calls me "a mulatto hunchback" in one of his books.* I remember going to stay with him, wherever it was he lived, and there was nothing to eat so we had to send for the Hodgkins who came over with a picnic.† Elizabeth, Bruce's wife, had a pet sheep which she tied in front of the house, which was

* *The Viceroy of Ouidah* (1980).

† The painter Howard Hodgkin and his wife, Julia.

constantly run over. I didn't believe he had ever been to Patagonia. I never believed in *any of it*. I think he wrote it all in Long Acre.'

Well, we do know he went to Patagonia, but then a lot of people go to many different countries. What matters is what they take away from those places. If they happen to be writers, it matters all the more. There lingers some superstitious belief in the primacy of the word printed on a page. It is why quite a few people still buy books. They believe them. A couple of years ago, I sat tight-lipped at a dinner party where I listened to a rather pompous man recounting his trip to Aleppo and the nearby ruins of the Church of Saint Simeon. I knew one of the people he mentioned having met in the souq, although, given that he owned one of the more touristy carpet shops and was a bit of a hustler, this was no great surprise. There was, however, a note of dismissal in this man's account of him. What he said is that Arabs tell you their little stories in order to sell their wares, which is a common enough trope. Sometimes it's true, but this Arab really did have a story and it was not one the man at the table knew. Openly homosexual, the carpet seller was arrested on some minor pretext and then locked naked inside a wooden box for a month. There is no call for me here to enlarge on the various humiliations he had to endure. Shaking all over, he told me this with tears in his eyes. I will not say he was likeable, he wasn't, but his mind had been irreparably damaged. So much for selling one's wares. I began to find my dinner companion irksome. When he spoke about Saint Simeon he got most things right, but not all and when I picked him up on a couple of points he was clearly irritated and asked me whether I'd been there. It gave me malicious pleasure to be able to tell him I'd written the book on which he based his observations. My reason for relating the story is not in order to sell copies of my book, although I wouldn't mind especially now that Syria has ceased to be a destination, but to state that it is absolutely incumbent on a writer dealing with what's real to tell the truth or at least what he believes it to be. Chatwin was an excellent writer and raconteur, but he was not above inventing things in order to keep the reader's interest alive and in doing so he put into motion a worrisome trend in travel literature. It is hardly surprising that many readers have come to mistrust it as a genre.

Chatwin was at least two people and never did they meet in my presence. One was the boyish adventurer, the adrenalin rushing through his veins as he spoke of his ideas for projects. One day he came downstairs and announced he was going to write on the dwarf-kidnapping trade in the Middle East, which was probably true. Dwarves are highly prized by extremely bored and wealthy Saudis in particular. Also I was in a Damascus restaurant where the novelty was a dwarf, the smallest I've ever seen, carrying trays of sweets or whatever to the clientele. I mean no disrespect to the Syrian people, just some of them. The most excited I had ever seen Chatwin was when he came down to say he had just spoken to Nadezhda Mandelstam on the telephone, saying he didn't realise one could simply look up her number in the Moscow directory. Modern life does have its advantages. Chatwin had a habit, when he spoke like this, enthusiastically, of hammering his knees with his fist. When he was writing *On the Black Hill* (1982) he came down to ask me if I could think of any snippets of poetry on the theme of friendship and I gave him the lines from Ezra Pound's translation from the Chinese of Li Po: 'What is the use of talking, and there is no end to talking, / There is no end of things in the heart.' They appear towards the end of the novel.

This was the Chatwin I liked.

The other Chatwin was insufferable—the social climber, the snobby aesthete—and it was because of this side that I knew he could never be anything more than an acquaintance. When he came into the shop with the likes of David Hockney or Stephen Spender I became invisible, with never a sideward glance from his direction. The boyish adventurer had been displaced by someone who altered even the way he walked and spoke. At the end of his life, when he was dying of AIDS, he went through bouts of complete madness. Confined to a wheelchair, he would go up and down Old Bond Street, buying paintings and antiques, sometimes spending millions at a single go, while behind him, at a discreet distance, George Lawson's friend Eugene Lamb would follow and undo his purchases. But it is also the period during which he wrote a jewel of a book, the very sound of its title suggestive of lustre, *Utz* (1988). In it, *enfin*, the aesthete rules supreme, justifiably so. When it was shortlisted for the Man Booker Prize I saw a brief television interview with Chatwin. It shocked me. *Utz* did not win, but it was an extraordinary work for a skeleton, which is what he had become by this time, to write.

At this point he was no longer living upstairs. One day he phoned and told me he had some rare books he wished to sell and that he was about to put them in a cab. A cardboard box arrived, and I looked inside to see a random selection of books, mostly review copies, of absolutely no value. I phoned him.

'Well,' he asked excitedly, 'what do you think?'

I took a wild gamble. I told him that I very much hoped he would not be disappointed in my offer of a million pounds. Chatwin mulled it over for a minute, said, 'Fine!' and nothing more was heard of it.

At the time his entire archive had been deposited with Bertram Rota, which included all his travel notebooks and correspondence. We all knew he had not much time left and it was assumed that we would have the handling of his archive.

When recently I raised the matter with George Lawson, he was dismissive.

'He thought there were wonderful things in those notebooks he bought in Paris, but I don't think so. He certainly made a great fuss of them.'

One day, on what would be the last occasion we ever spoke, Chatwin phoned me to say he was wrapping up a collection of essays, the one that would be posthumously published as *What Am I Doing Here* (1989), and that he would like access to his papers. I could tell he was having one of his increasingly rare periods of perfect lucidity. I found myself in a bit of a quandary because I knew perfectly well the firm's hopes for the future handling of the archive. It was not that the archive was not his to do with as he liked, but I had absolutely no say in such matters, which made me wonder why he was asking me rather than George Lawson. Suddenly I twigged. One writer was addressing another on matters of a writerly nature.

'Send a cab,' I told him, 'I'll help load it up.'

It was the last we ever saw of the archive. The reprimand I felt sure would come, never came. Three decades later, George Lawson, this time with annoyance in his voice, said, 'Well, if he had come to us and said he wanted the manuscripts we would have given them.'

This was true, of course. We agreed that perhaps Chatwin had arranged for the return of his archive to be in as conspiratorial a manner as possible so as to juice up the story a little. Which story? The story of his final days. There had to be an air of suspense in whatever he did, especially now that he had so little time left to him. A few months later, Chatwin, arguably the greatest prose stylist of his generation, though not unduly handicapped by a desire for truth, was dead.

* * *

I wonder if the man who made the greatest impression on me, although he himself would not have realised it, was not the cellist Edmund Kurtz. Very few people seem to know about him, not even my friend the composer David Hackbridge Johnson, who seems to know everything there is to know about classical music, and yet Kurtz's contribution to music was immense, not least his transcriptions of Bach's Cello Suites from the original Anna Magdalena Bach manuscript, which incredibly nobody had done. A tall Russian Jew, immense, beautiful in the way certain male Russian Jews are, musicians in particular, I could imagine him picking up the cello as if it were a violin.

'Young man,' he said, 'you seem serious about music. Allow me to give you a lesson.' Kurtz's eyes twinkled with merriment at the prospect. If I read his wife's smile correctly I was about to be subjected to an old routine.

'Aspirin and penicillin,' he announced.

I was left to ponder those words dangling in space.

'Aspirin and penicillin,' he continued, 'the first makes you feel better for a while, whereas the second, the second is a miracle cure.'

Where was this going, I wondered.

'Music,' he said, 'the music which truly matters, can be divided into aspirin and penicillin, the music that brings temporary relief and the music that cures. So let us begin.'

I wish I could remember into which camps he put the composers he named. Was Mozart aspirin or penicillin? Haydn, penicillin or aspirin? Beethoven and Schubert, which was which? What I do remember, however, was when he worked his way into the twentieth century.

'Stravinsky, aspirin.'

This was getting interesting. And then he breathed in deeply, such that his chest expanded and as if in possession of an earth-shaking truth he declared.

'Prokofiev, *penicillin*.'

There was triumph in his voice.

'You knew Prokofiev?'

'Young man, come and visit me some time,' he answered, 'I'll tell you many stories.'

Why didn't I take him up on his offer? Over the years I have asked myself this question many times. Edmund Kurtz died, aged ninety-four, in 2004. Born in St Petersburg, then known as Petrograd, what memories, if any, did he have of the October Revolution? Surely, some. After all, he was nine at the time and must have felt through the mattress history's rumble. It was soon after that he fled with his family to Germany, a country at war, and there began to play the cello. Imagine this: aged sixteen, he made his debut recital in Rome; during the late 1920s he was personal cellist to Anna Pavlova when she danced Saint-Saëns's "Dying Swan" choreographed by Mikhail Fokine, her most famous role; and Kurtz was the first to record Prokofiev's Cello Sonata in C Major; and then, of course, there was his intimacy with the greatest of all cello suites. Of course I knew none of this at the time, so why had he alone made such a huge impression on me? After all, we barely spoke. I think it was because I had the overwhelming sense of what I would call a complete artist and by extension so, too, the life he lived must have been complete. It is not as if any of this was ever voiced and I have yet to hear a recording of him playing the cello. (After a certain point in his career he wouldn't record anymore, which is often the case with the very best artists in that to do so would be to muddy the azure.) It must have been something I could read in his deeply intelligent features, which were the expression of not just culture but also life in its infinite variety. It was a glimpse of what I should aspire to. I'd been marking time.

Chapter Six

HAWKS AND MAGPIES

MY JOB AT BERTRAM ROTA INTRODUCED ME TO A NEW human subspecies, book collectors. Such conclusions as can be made about them include the following: they are mostly to be avoided or else kept at a prophylactic distance; they tend to lack social graces and have alarming food regimes; their clothes are oddly tailored, sometimes resembling the square suits of illegitimate regimes. Often they will be minutes late in ordering a book from a catalogue and there is virtually no compensation for the loss of what was never theirs in the first place, this being an abstract matter for which there is no resolution in the soul, and so with words failing them they produce an eerie whine unlike anything heard elsewhere in the animal kingdom. There's no telling what they will do to obtain their object of desire.

I have not yet come upon any instances of homicide over rare books although it is a common enough theme in crime fiction. I have, on the other hand, seen murder in people's eyes. Where books are involved feelings run high. There is the interesting case of Sergey Savitsky who, while working on a remote station in Antarctica, stabbed his colleague Oleg Beloguzov in the chest with a kitchen knife. Beloguzov kept revealing the endings of books from the station library before Savitsky had a chance to read them, but this has more to do with reading etiquette than actual bibliomania. Also there is the recent case of an Oxford academic and bookseller murdered for a copy of Kenneth Grahame's *The Wind in the Willows* (1908) in the extremely rare dustwrapper, which he'd priced at £50,000, but this heinous act was fuelled by greed and not a love of books. Stupid man, the killer took the book home and immediately put it on eBay at a 'knockdown price' of £2,000. There is also the story of a nineteenth-century Catalan monk turned bookseller called Don Vincente who killed for books, which caused something of a stir in the press, but which was then discovered to have been a literary hoax perpetuated by Charles Nodier, master of the *conte fantastique*. Slightly less easy to dismiss is that Nodier himself was rumoured to have killed a fellow bibliophile who outbid him at a book auction. But this, too, may be a *conte fantastique*.

Whatever happened to Ron Shead, avid collector of the artist and writer Wyndham Lewis? As with so many devotees of that author, he moved with an air of intellectual menace. Lewisites* try their damnedest not to be affable. They wear black hats with wide brims and get caught up by minutiae in their man's works and have meetings in order to discuss them, which often end in disharmony. Although they wish it were not so, they tend to be likeable. Although he was prickly, I couldn't help but like Shead. I, myself, took the plunge with Lewis, thinking maybe he was the literary equivalent of putting on long trousers. I read several of his books and did not warm to him, but then surely one is not supposed to warm to him. Maybe, though, I read him more with my blood than with my intellect and such doubts as I have find their opposite in another Lewis collector, Peter Caracciolo, who

* The singular of which I now discover is a chemical warfare agent, a fact that might appeal to detractors of the author whom they consider to be a racist, fascist and misogynist.

has devoted many hours of scholarship in determining what is actually, as opposed to what is rumoured to be, the evolution of the author's mind.

Ron Shead used to carry a billy club, ostensibly for purposes of defence. I saw him once, running along the pavement, on the scent of a book he'd just heard was available, the top of his billy poking through the opening of his coat. One can easily imagine what Freud would have made of this image. The violence with which Shead might have applied his billy was as nothing compared to the violence he brought to the English language, a syntax as tortured as Wyndham Lewis's and then some. He also collected modern European literature in translation, which, unfortunately, was largely due to my encouragement. What it meant was that he would grab books before I had a chance to. We went together once to see one of the most mysterious of book dealers, R. W. Malynowsky, who let us have first crack at his catalogue of Russian literature in translation.

Strange how certain people, whose lives were once marginal to one's existence, as ghosts gradually move into, and begin to colonise, centre stage in one's thoughts. I may be said to have full olfactory function, which means that not only do certain smells revive memory but I can also summon those smells mentally and let them transport me. I could get all Proustian about this, but I haven't got the time he had in which to measure how much of it is lost, quite a bit judging by the sprawl of his magnum opus. Smell, apparently the strongest of memories, a recollected whiff of rolled tobacco, and there he is, Mr Malynowsky in his flat cap, wearing the ironic smile of one who had seen it all, although what that *all* might have included he would not divulge. A secretive man, shy and gentle, any questions about his past were always met with polite obstacles. He smoked his cigarettes down till they almost singed his lips.

I have come to believe human physiology is at least to some extent shaped by the times in which people reach majority, which is probably unprovable, but with Malynowsky what I saw in him was the Old Europe, which is instantly recognisable but almost impossible to describe. I think of high ceilings, I think of small tears in the seams of velvet-covered sofas, I think of heavy doors with triple locks, I think of the smell of boiled cabbage, I think of people who import smatterings of French into their conversation. I saw the last of Old Europe in those who took it as far as their years took them. They've mostly gone now. Some were family members of mine. Say then, Malynowsky breathed a different oxygen from that which we breathe.

I first met him when he had got hold of the remaining stock of the then very scarce first Ukrainian edition of George Orwell's *Animal Farm* (1945; *Kolgosp Tavrin*, 1947).* Collectors, although unable to read Ukrainian, will still want the book because it contains a special introduction by the author, translated into Ukrainian, in which Orwell describes not only his experiences in the Spanish Civil War but also the genesis of the book. This appears nowhere else in his writings. 'On my return from Spain,' he writes, 'I thought of exposing the Soviet myth in a story that could easily be understood by almost anyone and which could be easily translated into other languages ... I saw a little boy, perhaps ten years old, driving a huge cart-horse along a narrow path, whipping it whenever it tried to turn. It struck me that if only such animals became aware of their strength we should have no power over them, and that men exploit animals in much the same way as the rich exploit the proletariat. I proceeded to analyse Marx's theory from the animals' point of view.' The book was printed by a Ukrainian émigré press in Munich for refugees in the DP (displaced persons) camps. So who should have seized the copies of *Kolgosp Tavrin* as being seditious material if not the American military government in Munich who, acting in accordance to Law No. 191 and Control Regulation No.1 of whatever set of rules it was that forbade the circulation of publications discrediting any of the

* The Ukrainian title has been somewhat changed from Orwell's to *Collective Farm of Animals* in order to capture more fully the flavour of the Communist regime. Orwell's introduction, the original of which is lost, was translated back into English by Gillian Fenwick, Orwell's bibliographer.

"Four Powers," dutifully passed the edition to the Soviet authorities. Can one satirise what is already satire? Malynowsky, who obtained the copies through an unnamed source in an unnamed country, came and showed me a copy and after we agreed on a figure he released them one by one to Bertram Rota at £15 each for resale at £30. Our price was a shade unambitious for it is now a book that sells for between £800 and £1,200. I think it is accurate to say that most of the copies currently in circulation originally came from a gentle soul in a flat cap, a twinkle in his eyes, the rolled cigarette in his mouth a permanent fixture.

I now go looking for traces of him and what comes up is an unclaimed estate, an official form giving the dates of his birth, March 3, 1922, and his death, January 13, 1998, although I wonder how they can know this for sure, also the fact that he was a bachelor and died in Bloomsbury. As to when he came to England, the date of his naturalisation, kinship and other matters, one reads 'N/A' scattered throughout the columns as if those two letters divided by a stroke wipe away all that had once informed his existence. His full name is given as Roman Wolodymyr Malynowsky ('Wolodymyr' is the Ukrainian variant of 'Vladimir,' the Polish being 'Włodzimierz,' which would suggest that he and his family had their origins in what was once the Polish Ukraine). My father was born into, and as a small child fled, that sorrowful zone. I think it's safe to say that anyone from there will have been subject to many of history's most bitter episodes. *The London Gazette*, for February 15, 1955, lists Malynowsky, with a variant *j* at the end of his surname, his stated country of origin, Poland, his job, clerk. That word *clerk* contains multitudes. What it suggests, however, is that he had not yet settled on a life in the book trade.

I visited him once where he lived in spartan conditions in a small flat in the vaguely pyramidal, brutalist Brunswick Centre before it was given a makeover, when it was still a beehive of lost souls. A sense of abandonment was everywhere. Old newspapers tumbled through its central quadrangle and the shops beneath the dwellings were mostly empty or else struggling to survive. It is there that Jack Nicholson catches first sight of Maria Schneider in Michelangelo Antonioni's film *The Passenger* (1975). While the flat with its single bed and small kitchen provided Malynowsky with the bare necessities, actual life was elsewhere, a basement in Doughty Street where the only way to gain admittance was to strike the iron railings outside with a stick he'd left there for that purpose. This way only those he knew were granted admittance. A doorbell might signal catastrophe.

Strangely Malynowsky has become a fiction.

A witch, or, as she prefers to call herself, an "esotericist," Kala Trobe has made him the central character of her fictional opus *The Magick Bookshop Trilogy: Stories of the Occult* (2019), in which he becomes the Qabalistic owner of an occult bookshop.* The narrator is one Kala Trobe, and R. W. Malynowsky is one R. W. Malynowsky, which allows for a curious interface between fiction and reality. The real Kala Trobe, which is a pen name, worked in a bookshop in Bloomsbury called Unsworth, Rice & Coe, which is where I remember seeing her in the early 1990s. She was witch-like then. She was, perhaps, at that fledgling stage, a neophyte or sorcerer's apprentice. I would see her again, some years later, seated in the window of the esoteric bookshop Watkins Books, in Cecil Court, reading tarot, directly opposite where I work. Malynowsky frequented Unsworth, Rice & Coe and because he was greatly liked by everyone he was the only person allowed to smoke on the premises. A smoker himself, not even Charlie Unsworth smoked indoors. Kala speaks of Malynowsky as having had 'a shedload of rolling tobacco,' and copious amounts of vodka too. Over time, he and Kala became friends, each serving as the other's confidant, and, after she quit that scene for another, they kept up a steady, old-fashioned, handwritten correspondence. Theirs may be one of the last paper trails in existence. Also they supply the only clues to his earlier life. It must have been as much a matter of considerable grace for Malynowsky to have had a young woman interested in his life as

---

* She is also the author of *The Witch's Guide to Life* (2003). According to the book's synopsis, 'Some days it is not easy being a witch especially with the challenge of practising your craft in a world of nine-to-five mortals.'

it was for her to have, as she describes him, 'an honorary Grandpa.' I can vouch for her kindness in helping me. When I wrote to her, asking after the mystery that was R. W. Malynowsky, she was able to fill me in on what I had already divined, that he *might* have been Jewish and had seen trouble. What Polish Jew of his generation was spared that? There was more to come, however, which would at least partially open the floodgate. She kindly shared with me some of the letters he wrote her, from which one may delineate the ends and beginnings of a number of stories, although the threads between them are few and even those barely discernible.

'A very level-headed fellow,' which is how he describes himself and which is how I remember him, in those letters he recounts various supernatural experiences, most of which occurred at the most dangerous moments in his life. They served as his watchman's rattle. Some things are merely alluded to, a ghost in a vicarage in Podolye;* others are more detailed although even then only fleetingly, as if more would have been too much self-exposure. One day, when he was a student in Vienna, he saw two men and read their thoughts, the substance of which made him mentally and physically ill. The following morning he was arrested by the Gestapo on a charge of political resistance and he discovered that the two men had been to his house the day before, making enquiries. There is no explanation as to how, after two months in prison, he made his escape, especially if he were Jewish.† And there is

* A region in the Ukraine, called "Podolia" when it was under Polish rule, it was where pogroms frequently took place and where later the Nazi *Einsatzgruppen* were at their most demonic. I assume it was Malynowsky's ancestral home. 'The Podolian plain was swaddled in faith,' writes Joseph Roth in his essay "Furlough in Jablonovka" collected in *The Hotel Years* (2015). 'God was in Podolia, and Bethlehem was a hop and a skip away.'

† 'Some Eastern European Jews managed to survive the war by concealing their identity,' my friend Jarosław Anders writes me. 'That usually involved assuming a new "Christian" name, ideally supported by fabricated documents—a birth certificate, a certificate of baptism, etc. It also required relocating to a place where nobody knew your family. In many cases, people kept those wartime monikers after the war as their new legal names. I suspect something like that must have happened to the person known as "Roman

nothing to indicate how he got from Vienna to wartime London where one evening, taking a stroll down an unfamiliar street, he passed a telephone box when suddenly he heard a ringing inside. He felt compelled to answer it. At the other end of the line, over a thousand miles away, he heard his father's voice telling him he'd been recently murdered by the Gestapo. And then he speaks of poltergeists, which he describes as the manifestation of troubled spirits, whose purpose had been to warn him of danger ahead, while humorously adding that one can take out insurance against any damage they cause. Also he speaks of hearing, when not working or concentrating on something, continual music in his head, 'a varied and melodious programme … like the background on a painting.' It seems not to have unduly troubled him, maybe the opposite. He wonders where the melodies come from and who sends them. Somewhat wistfully, Malynowsky tells Kala his name means 'the place where the raspberries grow,' but that it was not a place he could ever go back to. (The Polish for raspberries is *maliny*, but this reading of his own name may be a shade fanciful.)

The character Kala made him into is not without foundation for he had revealed to her a side of which I knew nothing, but it is a commonly neglected fact of human nature that a man will reveal to a woman what he will never reveal to other men. I'm not qualified to speak of the paranormal not because I disbelieve but because I have yet to believe, but I know that often it is concomitant with extremity in a person's life and to be a Jew in Poland

---

Wolodymyr Malynowsky." His "legend" must have been pretty good if it survived an encounter with the Gestapo! If he came from the part of Ukraine that before 1919 was ruled by Austria, his family, like Bruno Schulz's, might have spoken German quite well. He even might have sought residence in Austria as a "former Austrian citizen." Paradoxically, it was often easier to survive in a country allied with Nazi Germany, like Italy, Hungary, Norway, even Vichy France, than in an occupied territory. Such stratagems were invariably difficult and accompanied by a sense of guilt, which would explain his reluctance to talk about them.' I find Jarosław's argument compelling. Also it would explain Malynowsky's reticence when it came to speaking of his Polish background. There again, maybe he was not Jewish at all.

during the Nazi occupation was as extreme as extreme gets and indeed being anyone at all was to be perpetually under sentence. Malynowsky was destined to have a sad and lonely death. Kala was in Indonesia when she experienced what Malynowsky called "brain radio." This is what she wrote me: 'I was writing him a postcard when I distinctly heard his voice saying in a kindly manner: "Save your money on the stamp, I won't be there to receive the postcard," along with the psychic implication that he had read its contents as I wrote/thought it. I remarked sadly to my companion that I was pretty sure Mr Malynowsky had passed on. I decided to send it anyway. When Charlie later went into his flat he found my postcard amid his pile of unread, posthumous mail … It wasn't until I returned several months later that I was officially informed of his death. Of course, one might argue that he isn't really gone, and I have on occasion, such as Samhain (Oct 31st or the full moon closest to it) burned or even smoked rolling tobacco for him, and dedicated a tipple of vodka to his memory.' When Charlie Unsworth, in the company of a council official, went to the flat he found Kala's letters to Malynowsky bound together with a ribbon. Also, beside the bed was a tin containing twenty rolled cigarettes, which Malynowsky, a most meticulous man, had got ready for the following day. It must have been the last thing he ever did.

What Unsworth did not find was a Will. Roman Wolodymyr Malynowsky died intestate. Advertisements in various papers, asking anyone who had known him to come forward, produced no results. All that his neighbours knew of him was that he lived next to them. All the landlord at Doughty Street knew was that he dealt in books. There was no trace of family. Whoever it was he knew on the continent and supplied him with the stock of *Kolgosp Tavrin* made no enquiries after him. Malynowsky had asked Charlie and myself to be his executors, but as a Will could not be found what he wanted left to the sheep then residing in Coram's Fields close to the Brunswick Centre went to the Crown instead. The proceeds would have come from the sale of his books. What a joy it would have been to inform them. I can easily imagine him peering through the railings at them, with that same ironic smile.

The day Ron Shead and I struck Malynowsky's iron railings, we struck gold beyond them. I managed to obtain from his catalogue inexpensive copies of scarce books by the Russian Symbolist Feodor Sologub, *The Old House and other tales* (1916) and *The Little Demon* (1916), as a well as a lovely copy in dustwrapper of Ivan Goncharov's *Oblomov* (1929) in Natalie Duddington's translation. Shead was rather more promiscuous than me, for he bought a whole stack of titles. Where is he, for God's sake? Well, actually therein lies the answer: God displaced Wyndham Lewis in Shead's affections. God displaced even foreign literature in translation. This is no scoffing matter. A Catholic convert, suddenly he became highly articulate, his syntax intelligible. The billy had metaphorically become firewood. Thus transfigured, repentant of the ways literature took him away from the divine, he sold me the whole of his book collection, including the Wyndham Lewis, which later Bryan Ferry bought, and replaced it with serious bulky tomes of religious commentary. Such books amassed bring a dark complexion to one's shelves. Last I heard he was about to put on a cowl. It is an easy enough image for me to conjure, Ron Shead with his bald head and blond goatee. I'm happily sandwiched in my reveries between a witch and a monk.

* * *

Where is the American collector who wore a miner's lamp on his forehead so as to enable him to penetrate the darker cavities of the bookshops he visited? Where is the man who collected Stefan and Franciszka Themerson's Gaberbocchus Press titles? Where is the man who came in asking not for books but the old bus and tram tickets often found inside them? Where is the man who collected virtually every edition of *The Natural History of Selborne* by Reverend Gilbert White? Where is *everybody*? Am I deluding myself in thinking collectors are no longer as colourful as they once were? I am wary of those who speak of how things used to be and yet when it comes to speaking of the clientele I cannot help but feel something has gone out of the life of the trade. There are very few collectors left who are driven by their own instincts, who delve into the nooks and crannies of literature. They tend to collect what most other people collect, which is to say the usual suspects. When they get bored with and decide to sell their books they feel they've been burned. There are some people, albeit not that many, with invaluable libraries and for whom collecting has become little more than a rich man's game. There is little pleasure to be derived from selling a book to them. Joyless, they are the ones who quibble the most over matters of condition and price. And then, at the other extreme, are those in whom a genuine love of books, books of any description, place them in a circle of hell from which there can be no escape.

As for the former who collect what they think they ought to collect, I won't waste too much breath. I'll take their money before shunting them into the furthest reaches of my gratitude. They comprise a minority, however. Most book collectors are serious people collecting books seriously albeit with varying degrees of pleasure. (The reader may now feel free to ignore my opening gambit, a cheap stunt put there in order to grab attention, admittedly irresponsible behaviour for someone of my years, but then these are desperate times.) Some of the most dedicated collectors are downright miserable, happy for only as long as it takes to wind the spool that brings home their silvery prize. Already they're keening for the next object of desire.

The most interesting customers are invariably those who shun fashion's dictates and follow their own paths whether they be for books on Hunnic tribes—yes, I have one such collector—or on the exact science of manhole covers, there being one collector of my acquaintance who lives in desolate hope. (Oh, and by the way, I detest the word *punter* unless it refers to a *John* in search of a prostitute and wish ill on all who say it although they are not quite as objectionable as those who talk about 'collectibles' and for whom there ought to be devised a particularly savage punishment.) As there are so many authors and subjects it would be a pointless exercise to speak of the multifariousness of collectors, but among those I met early on and have befriended there is the tammy-wearing professor from Toronto, William Blissett, who was an intimate of the poet David Jones* and carries with him a list of the books in the latter's library, which he is trying to replicate. There are collectors who want to recreate as closely as possible the reading matter of their favourite authors and it is, I suppose, a pleasant enough delusion of closeness. At least Professor Blissett earned his stripes, for he wrote a fine book about his friendship with Jones called *The Long Conversation* (1981), a copy of which he gave me, with an inscription that incorporates words from one of the poet's letters to him: '*Benedith arnoch* [blessing on you], in the tongue of the Cymry.' Aged one hundred, he is currently working on four books, one of which is about Wagner's influence on twentieth-century literature.

There is Peter Caracciolo who returns here not as a Lewisite but as editor of *The Arabian Nights in English Literature* (1988). An arresting passage in Wilkie Collins's *The Moonstone* (1868), where Miss Drusilla Clack intervenes with a comic allusion to *The Thousand and One Nights*, opened up a whole new literary universe for him, which he has been exploring now for close to four decades. When I asked him why, on occasion, he pays good money for first editions he produced, most appropriately, something in the nature of an arabesque. We had moved on to the Arabian Nights side of things, although I think that for him there is no 'side' because so much of Western literature is either directly or indirectly influenced by the Eastern tales that comprise that densely woven and often zestfully obscene work. Showing me his somewhat battered

---

* My own copy of the first edition of *The Anathemata* (Faber and Faber, 1952) with the publisher's compliments slip still inside it—might it have been sent on the instructions of T. S. Eliot?—came from the library of John Betjeman which I helped clear at 29 Radnor Walk in Chelsea. Obviously the ghost of Betjeman was unhappy at seeing his books removed because I cut my hand on the curved rail of the automatic stairlift, the scar still faintly visible. I can't imagine Jones's work was to Betjeman's taste, but they were on friendly terms. My other Jones treasure, which I also purchased when I worked for Bertram Rota, is copy number one of fifteen signed wood engravings of "The Oblation of Noe" which was included in *The Chester Play of the Deluge* (Golden Cockerel Press, 1927).

copy of the first volume of the Library Edition of Richard Burton's translation of *The Book of a Thousand Nights and a Night* (1894), which has a handsome ornate gilt design on the cover, I could see Caracciolo was about to give a masterclass in exegesis, and, being a scholar of the old school, he was not about to let theory obliterate his calling. He teaches by example, which would be no great thing in itself were it not supported by immense knowledge.

'Where will the young scholars of the future learn their trade?' he said before he proceeded to bring his case for bibliographical rarities. 'This first edition is vital to understanding the translation of this wonderful text into European culture.'

'How so?'

'This, as with all future editions of the Burton translation, contains on the inside a frontispiece with the book's title in square Kufic, a geometric form of Arabic developed during the period of the Abbasid Caliphate. Although not a cryptic crossword, it resembles one. When first confronted with it, I bedevilled my neighbour who was a Sufi painter and although I don't think he had a clue what I was after he enjoyed the game and proposed that it might be a dance pattern, which in itself was valuable. I then went to the British Museum and produced a photocopy of it and was told it was a masterpiece of Arabic calligraphy and that within its complex pattern it repeats the Arabic title *'Alf Laylah wa-Laylah* four times. The ornate gilt cover provides the key to that puzzle. Burton must have said to this Arabic calligrapher that he wanted the covers done in black and gold, the colours of the Abbasid Caliphate.'

As to what those clues are, their complexity is beyond the reach of this book, but I advise the reader to go to the introduction of Caracciolo's pioneering work, wherein one may find the substance of a whole book poured into a few pages. As for Burton and his mighty rendering, Caracciolo described it as 'a magnificent piece of plagiarism, stolen from John Payne's translation.' We shifted onto the subject of *why books* and again he taught by example with an anecdote relating to his mentor and one-time colleague, Barbara Hardy, the brilliant scholar of nineteenth-century literature. After her death in 2016, her spacious Earls Court apartment was sold, but there remained the question of what was to be done with her library. One of her daughters managed to squeeze the whole of the library into two rooms at her own home.

'The books are redolent of my mother's presence,' she told Caracciolo, 'because they are impregnated by the perfumes she wore.'

I was here reminded of a late friend's copy of Shelley that he left me, which is imbued with his cigarette smoke.

'*That* is a lovely heritage,' Caracciolo concluded.

I wondered where in the Arabian Nights one might find a corresponding tale because, after all, as with all masterpieces, one gets the sense of the whole world and all the things in it. Well, almost. Dante's *Divina Commedia* is not one of them, for Arab scholars accuse him of stealing from their *The Book of Muhammad's Ladder*, the translation of which, *Libro della Scala Mochametis*, was published in 1264 about the time of Dante's birth. Influence, in my book, is not theft.

Pursuit is all. There is not a serious collector who has not felt the buzz that somewhere amid the chaos of a certain shop there is the ultimate book that awaits him. Maybe it is 'the Book' of which the Polish writer Bruno Schulz writes, the Book that contains all books, but which has yet to make itself known, or maybe it's a title he had all but given up hope of ever finding. This begs the question of what will happen when bookshops have disappeared for there is nothing else that can replicate the thrill of going into an unknown bookshop for the first time.

If I say female collectors are rare, I'm not being snide. Women tend on the whole to be more sensible, the words on the page being more important for them than the covers keeping the page in place. Occasionally, though, I do meet some, Wendy Rintoul, for example, also women who after the deaths of their husbands continue to add to their husbands' collections, which is a strange species of devotion. One such was Valerie Eliot who would buy books to add to the late poet's library. Female booksellers, on the other hand, are not so rare, maybe the queen of them all being the fierce and diminutive Margie Cohn of the House of Books in New York City who, when she gazed at the cabinet of rarities in Bertram Rota, cackled in her thick New Jersey accent, 'These are not in House of Books condition,'* and then in this country, one of the most mysterious booksellers of all, Veronica Watts.

As for the more extreme collectors who are no longer here and who most interest me, it is almost impossible to build a story around them because by and large what one saw of them is what one got. The business of collecting books is essentially a solitary one. A good collector will be hesitant to reveal his hand in any case. There is no need to explain himself or what drives him. Collectors are by default locked into themselves. They have to be, otherwise they might lose out to someone else. I tend to divide them into hawks and magpies, the first being those who collect books with a clear focus, say the works of a single author or titles on a specific theme, whereas the second collect whatever looks attractive to them at the time. I'm a magpie. Tony Fekete, whose acquaintance we will make, is a hawk. Whereas the magpie goes in search of the book which contains all the world, the hawk already knows what that book is. And the other distinction that has to be made is that between the bibliophile, the lover of books, and the bibliomane, who is perhaps a bit too crazed to love. Holbrook Jackson in his *The Anatomy of Bibliomania* (revised edition, 1932), the model for his work being Robert Burton's *The Anatomy of Melancholy* (1621), makes the distinction between bibliophilia and bibliomania. 'There is no greater cause of bibliomania,' he writes, 'than bibliophilia inordinately pursued.' The divisions between bibliophiles and bibliomanes are not, of course, as clear as all that, and it's the same for hawks and magpies. A magpie may

* Marguerite Arnold Cohn (1887–1984) was rightly described by American bookseller Chris Stephens as "Grande Dame of the Book business". She whose arrival at the shop we dreaded, her departure from life we mourned deeply. Carol Z. Rothkopf's excellent memoir of this remarkable lady can be seen in *Columbia Library Columns*, Volume XXXV, No. 1. November, 1985. http://www.columbia.edu/cu/lweb/digital/collections/cul/texts/ldpd_6309312_035/ldpd_6309312_035.pdf

have within his library a complete collection of books by a single author and the hawk may have books extraneous to his collecting activities. The hawk is the more puzzling creature.

Some clown with a medical degree recently described bibliomania as a mental disease. There are even a number of drugs that can be had on prescription for it although apparently none strong enough in themselves to effect a cure. There are cases, however, when the collecting of books really does become a serious problem. The most tragic case of bibliomania I have ever encountered was when I was called in to look at the library of a man whose obsession for buying books had become so extreme that unless he got rid of them his wife would leave him. Oddly enough, I had just recently read Elias Canetti's *Auto-da-Fé* (1946; *Die Blendung*, 1935) whose main character, Peter Kien, is so obsessed with books that he not only destroys his marriage but also the books themselves. When I got there I found an overweight, profusely sweating man who sat in a small clearing surrounded by tens of thousands of books, all of them stacked on the floor. All the rooms were similarly filled—a bedroom with a mattress in the middle of a sea of print, a toilet barely accessible, a kitchen about to go up in flames. The man sat in his cubbyhole, awaiting execution, a pleading look in his eyes.

'They've got to go,' he whispered, 'all of them.'

The books were so densely stacked one could see the spines of only a few of them. After a couple of hours of quarrying through them, I realised there was not a single book one could buy for resale. Maybe there was at the centre of one of those piles, if only one could get at it, but it seemed unlikely. One develops an instinct for such things. It was a graveyard not so much of the unreadable because, after all, surely there was something to be gleaned from any number of these volumes, but of the unsellable. There were enough books here to fill at least two shops although I wouldn't want to vouch for their success. When I told the man the books were not for me tears welled up in his eyes. I promised him I would call in a general secondhand dealer, Ike Ong of Skoob Books. A couple of weeks later, I saw Ike and asked him how he got on. He looked at me and replied, not without a hint of annoyance in his voice, 'Were you playing with me?' I never did learn of the sweaty man's fate.

I was once faced with the opposite extreme. I was called in to look at the library of John Horder, dubbed the 'hugging poet,' a follower of the Indian mystic Meher Baba. As soon as I got there, he began to tell me about all the wonderful books he had. I nodded enthusiastically. There was only one problem: I was standing in an empty room, the books he described nowhere except, so it would seem, in his own mind. Could it be he sold his books prior to my visit and was mourning their absence? I now discover he died a few years ago and of the several obituaries I found there is one by his sister in which she speaks of having to scramble over thousands of books to get to him. Another obituary has a photograph of him with rows of books behind him. I can only suppose he rebuilt his library after I saw him. 'In a time when I was nothing,' he writes in one of his poems, "There was an emptiness both inside and outside of me.'

Chapter Seven

THE LONELINESS OF THE COLLECTOR

ONE OF THE STRANGEST COLLECTORS OF ALL, WHO FORMS half the composite figure of J. Leper-Klamm, the 'unravelled pharaoh' in Iain Sinclair's *White Chapel Scarlett Tracings* (1987), was John Hale, who looked like he was carved from the wood of an ancient oak tree, whose eyes seemed as though they could pick out ghosts in broad daylight, and whose bony features, the skin tight upon them, were indeed suggestive of mummification. Whereas the 'unravelled pharaoh' is definitely John Hale, the 'biographical' details belong to the other half of Sinclair's composite who I'll come to. On the acknowledgements page of his book, Sinclair states the characters are fictional 'though invented more by themselves than by the supposed author.'*

* The most self-invented figure in Sinclair's gallery of characters is Driff or Driffield who also goes under several other variations of his name. My earliest memory of him is as a regular presence at the bookstall of the annual school jumble sale. With his head like a bullet, arms akimbo, hips swaying

John Hale collected stories of the supernatural and the macabre, or "weirds" as he preferred to call them, the more obscure the better. The modern was of scant interest for him, but Philip K. Dick and J. G. Ballard, dystopian writers both, stood high in his estimation. Although he was not easy to approach, the way to his mind a narrow path between saguaro cactuses, we would have, when he was in the mood for it, the odd chat, otherwise he would walk in and out of the shop with barely a hello or a goodbye. When he did talk it was mostly about books, the books he already owned because to speak of what he still needed might jeopardise his chances of obtaining them. There is fierce competition in the genre of fantasy literature, unavailability being one factor, inside knowledge another; also, when speaking to a bookseller, a dedicated collector of anything so rarefied will not show his hand because the other might take advantage of him. As a genre fantasy literature is as perilous for a collector to negotiate as the worlds it describes. Collectors of detective fiction are sissies by comparison.

---

in a circular fashion, elbows jutting into the ribs of anyone nearby, he would create for himself a space nobody else could enter, and with what seemed to be a third arm, for such was the perfection of his technique, he'd put his finds in a pile. Once he carried off an entire set of Anthony Powell's *A Dance to the Music of Time*. Maybe they were not first editions, but then maybe they were. This was some years before he became known in the trade as a collector of books on death and suicide and to complete the picture dressed up like an undertaker. *Driff's Guide to all the Second-hand and Antiquarian Bookshops in Britain* went through several editions, in one of which he describes bookseller and publisher Mike Goldmark as an 'oven-dodger.' He has been hailed for his wit for reasons not entirely clear to me. His comments are mostly ugly in the extreme, which in my book is not quite the same as wit. When face-to-face I took him to task for his anti-Semitism, his response was to smirk. This was at a point when by means of sneaky, though legal, methods he exposed Bertram Rota's finances, which were then in a parlous state. Apparently it gave him pleasure to feed upon other people's misfortunes. As "Xavier Driffield" he was cleared of charges of child abuse even though he had sent the girl's family a manuscript of a 'novel' describing his acts with her, using her real name. The abuse allegedly spanned three years when she was aged between eleven and thirteen. The jury accepted Driff's defence that the book was a fiction. Driff continues to be lionised in certain quarters of the book trade.

The collectors of weirds seem barely to live in the world at all and if proficiency lies in the intensity of one's separateness from it, which is to say one has sufficient ineptitude for life, then John Hale may be said to have been more proficient than most.

I was in the middle of cataloguing a collection of Edwardian literature, most of the authors unknown to me, when he spotted the first English edition of a Robert W. Chambers title, not his most famous collection of supernatural stories, *The King in Yellow* (1895), but one of the lesser ones. John Hale explained to me it was on the brink of weirdness and therefore qualified for inclusion in his collection. I knew nothing of the American author who had such an influence on H. P. Lovecraft and others. I never knew Barry Pain wrote weirds. Actually I knew next to nothing of the genre, which is always good news for collectors because it increases the possibility of error on the part of the bookseller. The seller who knows his stuff charges to the skies. I asked John Hale whether Kafka could be considered a writer of weirds or was he, rather, a realist ahead of his time. He lit up. At last I located in him a subject of mutual enthusiasm, although he took the former position and I the latter.

One day he came into Bertram Rota with a fine copy in dustwrapper of the first English translation of Kafka's *The Trial* (1937), a book that nowadays commands something in the region of £2,500. This copy, his second, was for sale. I said I would show it to one of the directors and he said, no, he had come to sell it to me. I laughed and said I couldn't possibly afford it.

'I haven't yet told you what my price is,' he said.

'It would still be beyond my reach,' I replied.

After he named his figure I said it was absurdly low and that I couldn't possibly take it from him at that figure. Something like anger shadowed his face.

'Twenty-five pounds was what I paid for it,' he said, 'twenty-five pounds is what you'll pay me, but only on condition that you will never resell it.'

Whenever I pause to study the stark black lettering against the yellow of the spine of the dustwrapper I remember John Hale's very strange smile. Only people who have suffered emotionally smile like that, a smile like a crack in a mighty edifice. It requires more effort to produce and is therefore all the more valuable. There was another book he gave me, gratis, the first English edition of Dino Buzzati's *The Tartar Steppe* (1952; *Il deserto dei Tartari*, 1940), which he rightly divined would be a work of some importance for me. *The Tartar Steppe*, written in 1938—the date alone is suggestive—relates the story of a young army officer, Giovanni Drogo, who goes to a remote desert outpost and there spends the best part of his adult life waiting for a barbarian horde, all the while solicitous of the glory a battle will bring him in its wake. As the years turn into decades, he barely notices the passing of time. When finally the enemy arrives, and then only as tiny figures in the distance, he sickens and dies. An allegory of life, it may also be seen as a rumination on work, the necessary illusion that what one does is, after all, of value. I read Tim Parks's essay on Buzzati* and discovered that when the author was asked about his book he said the idea for it came to him while he worked the monotonous night shift at the Italian newspaper *Corriere della Sera*, an endless routine he feared would swallow up his life. So, too, the days of sitting at my desk, cataloguing books, no end in sight because there'll be always more books to catalogue, and the sense of waiting for something, for anything, to happen, which may shock me awake, whether it be good conversation or a sudden insight into human folly because it is at bookshops that it is so often laid bare. Ordinariness is perhaps the most terrifying of all human challenges.

One day I got news John Hale had retired to Todmorden in Yorkshire. It was hard to fathom so sudden a move. Surely he was too young to retire. An 'unravelled pharaoh' maybe, but he couldn't have been much more than fifty at the time. I had no sense of him being moneyed although among collectors one can never be sure. Many collectors I know would sooner wear rags than pass up the opportunity to spend the money on a desired volume. Away from London's bookshops and book fairs, what would he be without them? This is not to suggest he was entering a wilderness, and

* *The Threepenny Review* (Winter 2001).

indeed ghosts do rather well for themselves in Yorkshire, but in terms of what it could give him would Todmorden suffice? And so it was John Hale took leave of my thoughts until a few years later I heard he'd died a sad and lonely death.

There is nothing like death to bring a man to life. I began to wonder about him. And now, for purposes of this book and because as I get older I think more about some of the people who've passed through my life, I wish I'd known him better. I have questions for him. One of the problems about interviewing the dead is that it is impossible to determine whether the answers they give are theirs or one's own. All too often they are canvases we fill with our own colours. There were, of course, mutterings in the trade with respect to the whereabouts of John Hale's marvellous book collection. I don't want to sound ghoulish, and there's nothing quite as contemptible as an ambulance chaser, but with the passing of a major collector there is always some excitation of feeling as to what will be released into the world. It is what John Hale himself would have thought with respect to his own collection had it been someone else's. Also where would we be without the wonderful journeys books make through the world? I found myself asking those few intimates of his for their memories of him, Tony Sillem who worked for Bell, Book and Radmall booksellers, bookseller John Eggeling and collector Charles Peltz. What they seemed to share was exasperated affection for him.

Peltz, a collector of erotica and the bizarre, says of him that he lived on pilchards eaten directly from the tin; John Eggeling, a book dealer in Todmorden, says tinned sardines. It is a very fine line, of course, between pilchards and sardines. Eggeling, who probably knew him better, widens the culinary range to include 'raw onions, which he ate like apples, and bananas' and stops there. Ascetics in remote desert places have lived on more.

"The Ayatollah," which is how Peltz dubs him, was born in 1942, in Uxbridge, which is at the end of the Piccadilly line. I think that to be at the end of any line has a bearing on one's life. A pilot with RAF Bomber Command, his father was shot down and was made a POW. After his mother became gravely ill with a burst appendix,

John's sister was taken in by a neighbour while the boy, suffering from developmental problems, was sent to a children's home. After the war ended, his parents divorced and he was sent to a boarding school. Peltz remembers him as hating his own father. Later, as a £10 Pommie (or "Ten Pound Pom"),* aged eighteen, John Hale went to Australia where he joined the army. Although he had the bare minimum with respect to educational certificates, there were just enough for him to qualify for the Army Surveying Section. When it looked as though Australia would enter the war in Vietnam, John Hale returned to England where he found a job in the surveying department of Westminster Council and from there moved to the Greater London Council, a job he described as easy because the houses were all alike and therefore afflicted with pretty much the same problems. Whether this was the surveyor one would wish to have on one's own case is a moot point. After the abolishment of the GLC in 1986 he secured a position in the London Residuary Body. It was a bureaucratic mess, but the thing about messes is that if one is equipped with sufficient shrewdness one can take advantage of them. Suffice to say that when he was supposed to be out surveying he grabbed the opportunity to visit as many bookshops as could be found inside his daily peregrinations.

'I first met John in a science fiction bookshop owned by Ted Ball and Dave Gibson,' Peltz told me, 'then situated in Chepstow Villas, West London, probably in the mid-seventies. By then I had a fair knowledge of writers and poets of the "Decadent" movement, most of it gleaned from *The Romantic Agony*,† and I had always

---

* A colloquial term used by Australians to describe British citizens who moved to their country after the war. The term, when broken down, refers to the ten pound sterling which was the adult fare to Australia, a scheme the Australian government ran between 1945 and 1972. My guess is that John Hale went there in the late 1950s or early '60s. Pommie, (or more commonly "Pom") is derived from 'pomegranate,' Australian rhyming slang for 'immigrant,' which gathers force when it was considered that English immigrants were more susceptible to sunburn, their skin taking on the reddish hue of the pomegranate.

† Mario Praz's *The Romantic Agony* (1951) is a study of the erotic, the morbid and the decadent in eighteenth- and nineteenth-century European literature.

read horror/ghost/weird fiction since the age of ten years old. So I started frequenting the Chepstow shop when I first read of its existence from an ad in one of the SF mags that used to be around at that time. There I met John, a dour, taciturn chap who took a shine to me when I made him laugh at some sort of cynical shit I was espousing. I then got to know him slowly over a number of years and he taught me quite a lot about authors I'd never heard of. Luckily, in my own small way, I introduced him to some authors he'd never heard of, so it was a good friendship. But he was always, quite rightly, cautious about revealing too much information because, as we always discover, such information leads to rivalry.'

Rivalry over books finally put paid to their friendship.

'He was a good friend unless you were offered by some unfortunate bookseller a book which he wanted. Then he went into a cold fury. I remember a bookseller friend of mine was offered a great collection of weirds, which he told me and a couple of others about, but did not tell John until we had taken our fill of what we wanted. John was outraged. My bookseller friend told me he kept getting phone calls in the middle of the night from someone who then hung up. He was certain they were from John. I didn't feel any sympathy since John had got in first when Blackwell's acquired the Dennis Wheatley library. John never mentioned it to me even *after* he'd taken what he wanted. Still, that is the nature of the game, isn't it? But John held that against me—he was a very sore loser—and never spoke to me again … I always made him laugh and he liked our meet-ups in London, usually in Becky's Dive Bar in Borough High Street or, when Karl Wagner was in town,* Peter's Bar in Southampton Row. John was his own man. I think he learnt from an early age not to trust anyone and was very lonely, hence his total immersion in books to the exclusion of all other activities. And we all know what bibliomania can lead to, don't we? Yes, John was a pretty unique character, but to me

---

The original Italian title, *La carne, la morte e il diavolo nella letteratura romantica* (1930), gives a better flavour of its contents.

* Karl Wagner (1945–1994) was an American writer of horror fiction.

a sad obsessive who may have turned out differently if he had a more loving childhood.'

There are few major collectors who have not had an apotheosis at some point in their lives. With John Hale it came in 1979 when he had first stab at the Dennis Wheatley library.* No sooner had the author died than John began making enquires after the whereabouts of his library. When he learned that it had been tendered and Basil Blackwell in Oxford won, he phoned them and was told that he would have to wait until their catalogue of the collection had been issued. John phoned them at least on a weekly basis, and when one day he was told the catalogue had been mailed out that morning he dropped everything, left the office, and rushed up to Oxford where he scooped up the very best of the weirds, many of which, because Blackwell's at that point were not up to scratch on modern first editions and their values, were absurdly underpriced. Among his purchases were copies of Frederick Cowles's *The Horror of Abbot's Grange* (1936) and *The Night Wind Howls* (1938), both of them inscribed by the author to Dennis Wheatley, both of them among the rarest books in the genre. They were sold by Blackwell's at £10 and £8 respectively; after John's death they appeared in 2009, in a catalogue, at £4,750 each. The copy of *The Night Wind Howls* still had the wraparound band with Wheatley's puff, 'Here is a fine collection of blood-curdling tales.' Cowles's last, posthumously published *Vagabond Pilgrimage*, was dedicated to Wheatley. Hale also bought a set of William Hope Hodgson, which Wheatley had rebound in white cloth and with his bookplate designed by Frank C. Papé on the front pastedowns, and M. R. James's *Ghost-Stories*

* Dennis Wheatley was the author of numerous novels of the occult, *The Devil Rides Out* (1934) having been cited by James Hilton as 'the best thing of its kind since *Dracula*.' In the third volume of his memoir *The Time Has Come* (1979), Wheatley writes, 'The fact that I had read extensively about ancient religions gave me some useful background, but I required up-to-date information about occult circles in this country. My friend, Tom Driberg, who then lived in a mews flat just behind us in Queen's Gate, proved most helpful. He introduced me to Aleister Crowley, the Reverend Montague Summers and Rollo Ahmed.' Wheatley died in 1977.

of an Antiquary (1904) with Wheatley's pencilled notes at the beginning of each story. So famous was the collection that even the catalogue has become something of a collector's item.

Tony Sillem tells me that during the 1970s and '80s John Hale had a basement flat just around the corner from where he lived, in Pimlico, but that during all those years he never once caught sight of him in the area, which led Sillem to believe that he was something of a recluse. Charles Peltz did visit him there, however, mostly in order to swap books. The place he describes as bleak and austere with a kitchen that clearly had never been used. The books were stored in metal cabinets of a vaguely medical appearance.

So then, the move to Todmorden in 1989: John Eggeling who had been friendly with John Hale in London, was taken aback when one day he received a phone call from him, saying he missed his 'best friend' and asking whether he could stay with him and his wife for a few days while he looked for a house. It is not always easy to be called upon as a friend when the one doing the calling is little more than an acquaintance. Of course it may have been in his mind true. Eggeling describes how John Hale came with nothing but a bag of books and a single pair of underpants, which he then asked his wife to wash. A surveyor he may have been, but not when it came to his choice of house. He ignored the tree growing in front of it, whose roots spread under and buckled the patio, and which, a year later, resulted in a massive split in the wall of his living room. His efforts to sell the house ended in failure.

As for the friendship between Hale and Eggeling, it was a rather strained one.

'He would pass the front of our house every day,' Eggeling wrote me. 'We have a high hedge but from our bay window, where we parcel up our orders, we can see through the gate to the road and the passers-by. When John walked past he would snap his head toward the window, see us, and snap his head away without any gesture of recognition. We soon stopped waving to him. John was only interested in seeing if we were at home. If a few days went by without him seeing us he would phone us and ask if we had been away book hunting and when I said yes he would invite himself round the next day. It was an easy way to have a quick turn over so I didn't object. I think the moment for me that totally epitomised John was when Judith, my wife, and I were heading off to a book fair. We arrived on the platform at Todmorden station and there was John. When he saw us his face dropped and he said, "Are you going where I am going?" to which Judith replied, "We might be. Where are you going?" John's response was, "Oh, I can't tell you that."'

And then Eggeling told me something that hit the mark.

'From my experience autistic males tend to lose themselves in fantasy fiction because mainstream fiction covers a world they don't properly understand. H. P. Lovecraft, who must have had an autistic streak in himself, is an author they naturally gravitate to. This is why John gravitated towards weird and supernatural fiction.'

Eggeling has a fond memory of what he calls John's "Haleisms," the nonsensical comments that would seep out during conversations. One night they met in a local bar for a drink.

'He asked me if I had seen a TV programme about the polar explorer Amundsen the night before and mentioned that whereas Scott and Shackleton had been kitted out in Savile Row, Amundsen had spoken to Eskimos and wore a coat made from polar bear pelts. He then followed up by saying, "Which makes sense, you don't see polar bears going round in Savile Row suits, do you?" He was also prone to mondegreens. He once said about a book I had mentioned, "Oh, it's as common as gardens." And when he noticed me looking slightly bewildered he said, "What, you haven't heard the phrase? Quite appropriate when you think about it." Mishearings like that happened from time to time.'

And then came his account of John Hale's final illness.

'John was rather paranoid about his health and would see his doctor for the slightest thing and be satisfied at being palmed off with a prescription for vitamin B12. We started to get worried about his health when he began to lose weight and look more gaunt, but when he visited the doctor he was told he was anaemic and given iron tablets. John had this strange diet, of course. Finally he saw another doctor and was immediately sent into hospital and diagnosed with cancer. He spent a fortnight in hospital, where he had two or three exploratory operations, before being sent to a hospice. We arrived soon after he had been admitted and spent three or four hours with him. He was heavily sedated and drifting in and out of consciousness, so around 6pm we decided to go home and return the next day. Before leaving we spoke to the nurse, then went for the bus. Soon after we arrived home we got a call to say he was dead. I should have stayed a bit longer.'

When I got the news of his death I had a peculiar mental image of John Hale in his brown leather blazer—I never saw him out of it—a vaguely contented look on his face, ascending through the air, his body tilted at an angle of forty-five degrees, one of his arms raised, a finger pointing not towards any Christian heaven but a heaven full of all the books he ever sought. What sort of heaven was this, though, where there would be nothing more to find? This is mildly ridiculous, I know, a bit like a picture out of some trashy 1920s occult magazine, but I see it still, the bodily translation of John Hale, such as Old Testament Enoch himself might appreciate were he a bibliophile.*

One time he told John Eggeling that the job he would really like to have had was Chief of the Secret Police. Eggeling says he would have been perfect in that role. A hawk in the extreme, John Hale, when he was dying, where did his thoughts reside? I picture the man slowly, but surely, becoming detached from the books on his shelves.

* * *

Who was Jimmy Kanga? There is considerably more of him in the figure of "J. Leper-Klamm" than there is John Hale. 'A long bandage of dirty cuff, unbuttoned, flapped at his wrist,' Iain Sinclair writes. Also there are references to his job in the tax office: 'Mr Klamm was a negligible presence; he filed letters, they were never seen again … He was a redundancy waiting to be found out.' Sinclair makes note

---

* 'The angels hasted and took Enoch and carried him into the highest heaven, where the Lord received him.'

of the brown paper bags in which J. Leper-Klamm keeps his books. I already knew about the bags because Ike Ong at Skoob Books told me. When Jimmy Kanga asked him the best way of preserving his books, Ike replied, 'Always keep them in the brown paper bags in which you buy them.' A trusting soul, Jimmy Kanga took him at his word and whenever he bought a book he would say, 'Please, sir, may I have it in a brown bag' or, if he bought more than one book, then as many paper bags as there were titles. There is a shade of the sadistic in Ike, but his advice was not wholly without substance. A book so kept will retain its freshness, the dustwrapper will not fade in sunlight.

When I first saw Jimmy Kanga I took him for some kind of vagrant with exquisite manners.

'Excuse me, sir, do you have any no yes?'

He had a strange high-pitched voice, not effeminate exactly, but sharp enough to cut through my drowsiness like a kukri.

'No yes?'

'Yes,' he replied, 'any of his poetry.'

I realised then he meant Alfred Noyes as in *noise*.

'No,' I replied.

'Yes,' he said.

'What I mean is that I'm afraid we don't have any Alfred Noyes.'

I can always feel affection for a man who collects Alfred Noyes, not that there have been any since Jimmy Kanga died and now, the more I think about it, I'm not sure I've ever sold Alfred Noyes to anyone other than him. "The Highwayman" was the poem of my boyhood and spurred me to write poetry in the first place.

One day I followed him into Bell, Book and Radmall which was down the street from Bertram Rota and, if anything, pricier than us. Chris Radmall said, 'I've got a book for you, Mr Kanga.' And when he said the price was £85—I remember the figure and not the book—without a moment's hesitation Jimmy Kanga replied, 'Thank you very much, sir, I will take it,' and then proceeded to pull the crumpled banknotes from his pockets. This was close to my weekly salary at the time.

Jimmy Kanga was a regular customer. A resolute collector of the uncollectable, the authors he most admired came out of a very narrow vein in this country's literature, between the end of the 1890s and the onset of Modernism, what for the sake of convenience has been described as Edwardian literature and, except for Hilaire Belloc, G. K. Chesterton and Edward Thomas who remain perennial favourites, the most unsaleable of any period in English literature. The authors he sought after included Mary E. Coleridge, Walter de la Mare, John Drinkwater, Michael Field, John Freeman, George Gissing, Edmund Gosse, Vernon Lee, Fiona Macleod, Viola Meynell, Alfred Noyes, Barry Pain, William Watson, Mary Webb and, for reasons I never quite understood, the Canadian poets Bliss Carman and Duncan Campbell Scott, the second of whom took me by surprise because very few citizens of that country know the name.*

The Modernists were anathema to him, James Joyce in particular. Tony Sillem relates how one time a customer came into Bell, Book and Radmall pursuing Joyce titles and Kanga, who happened to be there, spluttered, 'A charlatan, sir. An absolute charlatan!' I always suspected one reason he dwelled within that narrow vein of Edwardian literature was that for him it was literature's last chance to avoid modernity although he was slightly more adventurous when he turned his mind to foreign literature, one surprise being Julien Green, an American writer who wrote in French, otherwise he collected translations of Balzac, Zola, Gabriele D'Annunzio, Antonio Fogazzaro, Théophile Gautier, Maarten Maartens and François Mauriac. Also he collected books on Catholicism published by Sheed & Ward and Burns Oates.

As I said, his manners were always exquisite, albeit somewhat artificial, as if he had projected himself into the historical period

* As head of the Department of Indian Affairs, while Scott in his poetry was sympathetic towards the indigenous tribes as a bureaucrat aiming at total assimilation of the native peoples did them untold cultural damage. My guess is that Jimmy Kanga adopted the earlier, somewhat romanticised, image of the man as a force for good, which was how he was perceived when I first read him.

whose literature he loved best, but more often than not he was unkempt. His white shirts tended to be a size too big for him such that the sleeves reached the middle of his hands and the cuffs were usually dirty, almost black sometimes. I heard later that he worked for Inland Revenue and that he would arrive at work in such a state of disarray that on occasion he was asked to go home and change. The man I first took for a vagrant had a position of some importance. Peter Ellis tells me that when he phoned his office once to say he had a book for him a woman answered, 'Mr Kanga's secretary.' The wonderfulness of it all was that he was accepted for who he was.

One evening I was on the tube when suddenly, cutting through the din, from the other end of the car, I heard his high voice.

'Good evening, sir, I trust you are well?'

I shouted back my answer, which was always the same.

'Very well, Mr Kanga, and yourself?' (I never addressed him as Jimmy.)

'Thank you very much, sir, I'm well. I wish you a pleasant evening.'

Once he phoned the shop asking after books with prefaces by Walter de la Mare, another obsessive pursuit of his, and when I said, 'I'm sorry, Mr Kanga, nothing at present,' there was a moment's silence at the other end of the line.

'How did you know it was me?'

As to the question of *Who was Jimmy Kanga?* I spoke to a number of people in the trade, most of whom remembered him fondly but were at a complete loss as to actual details of his life. Only David Tobin at Walden Books seemed to know him a little, but even then it was the scatterings of other people's memories brought together in him. All anyone ever saw him eat were biscuits. One time he presented the staff of Any Amount of Books with a box of chocolates. When they opened it they found three chocolates missing and one half-eaten. There were rumours that his mother was a concert pianist. I sought her name in vain. It may be, of course, that she performed under her maiden name. After he died it was discovered he had quite a few books on classical music, most of them on Schubert, Schumann and Liszt. Nigel Burwood of Any Amount of Books says of him, 'Jimmy had a love for a fellow woman clerk and I think she moved away and it was heartbreaking. There was an element of tales of lost love in many of the books he collected.' Jimmy Kanga in love, the mind reels at the sadness of it all.

When Burwood went to clear his flat in Southall he found himself faced with thousands of books, all in brown paper bags. There were approximately twenty thousand books, although considerably fewer titles because Kanga kept buying the same books over and over again.

'I have heard of a Jewish idea that buying a book, especially a holy one,' Burwood told me, 'is a devotional act, an *hommage*, a tribute, and I feel that was what Jimmy was doing. He literally had twenty copies of many titles.'

By Burwood's reckoning the Alfred Noyes comprised somewhere between 5 and 10 per cent of the total, which, given the author only wrote thirty books, means a lot of duplicates. When the Any Amount of Books staff removed the piles of Noyes from his flat in Southall they did so to the refrain of the Slade hit, 'So come on, feel the noise.' One of them asked him once why he was buying books that he already had duplicates of, and he was said to have replied, 'Because I'm a very silly man.'

John Eggeling remembers him with affection: 'I knew very little about Jimmy, but I did see him regularly at book fairs. As well as selling to him there he would buy from my catalogues. Once he had ordered a couple of books from me and after five or six weeks without payment I sent him a statement. After another two weeks without payment I decided to phone him. He said, "It's nothing personal, Mr Eggeling. I owe money to lots of dealers. I can give you their phone numbers if you want to check up."'

Born Jamshed Manic Kanga in 1941, in Bombay, Jimmy Kanga died on September 9, 2012. He came to England in 1958, took the Civil Service exam and got a diploma in law, after which he joined H.M. Customs and Excise. A Parsee by birth, he became a devout Catholic. A funeral was held for him at St Anselm's Church in

Southall, with elements of Zoroastrianism and Hinduism thrown in, rose petals poured over his coffin from, not as he might have wished, a paper bag, but a plastic one. In his last years, when his home became too difficult to manage, with books taking up all the space, he was looked after by a local Sikh family and slept in their garden shed. When he got ill, true collector that he was, he ordered books from his hospital deathbed. There was so much endearing about him that when he died one could hear a paean of gratitude for his life, even from those who had previously thought him a nuisance. I rate him as one of the most genuine book lovers I have ever encountered in the trade.

* * *

A quiet man, the quietest of them all, so quiet one could easily imagine him wearing moccasins, sneaking past an owl in the branches, never the sound of a twig snapping, his books 'a pulped forest / rooting its printed weight indoors,' Alan Clodd was without doubt the greatest collector I have ever known. So extensive was his collection, so secretive the making of it, as if it were the erection of the Great Pyramid inside a sandbox, its parameters were not known until after he died. Only two people knew its full extent, the bookseller Ian McKelvie, maybe the only bookseller Clodd trusted enough to allow anywhere near his books, and the poet Jeremy Reed who is my invaluable source for much of what follows. Jeremy Reed's "Elegy for Alan Clodd," from which I quote above, serves as a template for his life. It's fitting that a poem should capture him more than any prose does, for poetry was his passion, which is not say his passions did not also feed upon vast tracts of prose. I first encountered him at a small press fair at the Poetry Society in the mid-1970s, many times again at Bertram Rota, and finally at Bernard Stone. He knew Bernard when he was selling books on a market stall. My brightest memory of Alan Clodd, which was maybe the closest I ever got to him, was when he brought me news of the poet Frances Horovitz's death, a journey he specially made, knowing such words would sit too heavily on the telephone wire.

Shy, deeply sensitive, a man who spoke only when it was necessary to do so, he invited me to visit him at his home at 22 Huntingdon Road, East Finchley, where he said he'd show me his Vernon Watkins collection. Why didn't I go? Was I not also shy and sensitive? We discussed from time to time the century's indisputable master of poetic form, both of us agreeing he surpassed Auden who often dabbled in verse forms merely to show he could do it, whereas for Watkins it was what the Muse demanded of him. Clodd brought me the beautiful quarto edition of Watkins's *Uncollected Poems* (1969) as well as *Selected Verse Translations* (1977) and *The Ballad of the Outer Dark and Other Poems* (1979), all published by his Enitharmon Press, which he set up in 1969 mainly in order to publish the works of the two poets then closest to his heart, David Gascoyne and Kathleen Raine, and, later, to rehabilitate authors such as Edgell Rickword, Ruth Pitter, Frances Bellerby and John Heath-Stubbs. Mainly, though, at the beginning it was Gascoyne and Raine.

Kathleen Raine's ego, though immense, was not monstrously so, for it was rooted in the assurance that she moved among angels and guides. She saw heaven much as did William Blake: as a stable place to be. When poets are thus blessed, their work tends to be variable. I still smile at the memory of a reading given by that very earthly rogue, Peter Russell,* who prefaced the evening with the announcement that 'the greatest poet since W. B. Yeats' was in the

* Peter Russell was not exactly shy. The evening before his reading we downed a couple of pints at the Museum Tavern (me paying, of course, for he was constantly broke and at that point, as at most, living on handouts). We discussed my going to Italy to examine, for purposes of sale, what survived of his archive, the greater part of it, including his correspondence with Ezra Pound, having perished some years before in a fire. It had been my aim to help him by offering the archive to an American university. If we were extremely lucky it might have realised four or five thousand pounds. I wanted first to sound him out on his own expectations because I didn't want the figure to disappoint him. I knew from his verbal description of the archive it couldn't be much more. 'Oh,' he replied, 'not much really.' I was relieved to hear this, and so I pressed him a little more, 'Well, Peter, what would *not much* be?' 'Well,' he said, 'shall we say a million?' 'A million *what*?' I said. I do not know of its eventual fate.

audience and just as he spoke her name I caught her response, a regal bowing of her head, an acknowledgement that yes, perhaps she was. She knew, however, she was only the second greatest. She wrote to me on September 27, 1985: 'I am so accustomed to being introduced (in France, or Italy, or India) as the "greatest English poet" at present writing—not true, David Gascoyne, and Jeremy Reed may be one day if he deepens his humanity, as he well may for he is a dear and loveable young man.' It is deeply troublesome, this matter of ascendancy, because what poet has not had the sneaking suspicion that he or she might be the best? The head of the pin is a crowded place. I suspect that with a magnifying glass one might see Geoffrey Hill, who never did get the call from Stockholm. Kathleen Raine was having none of it. She was harsh on Hill whose poems she describes as: 'though literate and literary, "contrived" and without one gleam or ray from the farthest star of Imagination. He writes English as the Schoolmen wrote Latin, as a dead language.' Vernon Watkins, on the other hand, was 'a great poet, of European stature.' She was not without opinion. Surprisingly few people collect her, or at least not as many as when she was still alive. The poets they do collect she would probably consider too terrestrial for her taste. According to Jeremy Reed, Alan Clodd was so intimidated by Kathleen Raine that before going to visit her at 47 Paultons Square, Chelsea, he would first duck into a pub on King's Road and down a whiskey.

'I never understood why,' said Jeremy, 'because I got on with her, had a fantastic friendship for twenty-five years, but he was terrified of her. He was daunted by her intellect. What he didn't realise is that once Kathleen got close to you she dropped her intellect completely and became a very compassionate friend. You could tell her anything, she was *unshockable*, and a big supporter of gay men who formed a large circle of her friendships. She found it difficult to relate to straight men because she had been badly treated by them. She looked after David Gascoyne for many years when he was in a terrible state.'

She was the immediate excuse for the founding of Enitharmon Press. Clodd went assiduously in pursuit of the ghost of a book,

Faces and Day and Night, which was meant to have appeared during the war. He finally located it at the printer to which it had been originally allocated and in 1972, twenty-six years after its initial publishing date, he published it for the first time. Also it was Enitharmon's first book.

'Shy man, reserve in you was integral / to a quiet humanity,' continues Jeremy in his "Elegy," 'your self-invention pivotal / to ways of living true and free.' It was perhaps a shyness born of necessity, the laws against homosexuality still very much in force, but then Alan was also a deeply private man. He lived in absolute secrecy with a Black Jamaican, George, who was a ticket inspector on the Northern line, who wore loud Hawaiian shirts and listened to reggae, and who Jeremy remembers as having a wide range of colognes in the bathroom. It doesn't quite fit in with the image of the quiet man I remember who, there being nothing of the peacock in him, nothing ostentatious, was almost a master of the art of not being noticed. So, too, his terraced house, nondescript, unnoticeable, the perfect place in which to hide. As Jeremy says, Alan would have made a good spy, anonymous in appearance, cryptic by nature.

'Alan and George were never seen in public together,' Jeremy continued, 'and when the latter died of AIDS in 1990, Alan, grief-stricken, had him buried in south London, as far away as possible from the neighbourhood in which they lived.'

While the secrecy was no doubt due to the criminalised sexuality of earlier decades, it was the same secrecy that enabled Alan to build one of the greatest collections in existence. He would refer to it as his 'work,' which he said would sustain him in George's absence. There was another reason for his having struck an anonymous note: he was terrified of being robbed of his books, which was why one of the conditions of friendship with him was that one must never disclose any knowledge of what was behind the plain façade. It was one of the reasons he lived in a nondescript terraced house. Apart from his friend the bookseller Ian McKelvie, the book trade was not allowed anywhere near his books although he did occasionally receive people in his small living room cum office, Martin Stone and Peter Jolliffe, for example, booksellers he admired, but all they ever saw was what he would bring downstairs in a small suitcase. Most of the books were kept in crates and cardboard boxes in three heavily curtained rooms upstairs.

Among the treasures Jeremy saw was a pristine copy of *Ulysses*, which Joyce had inscribed to Raymonde Linossier, an association copy that hums with significance. She is certainly worth a few lines here. The poet Léon-Paul Fargue dubbed Linossier "Violette noire" ("Black Violet") on account of her mysterious nature. The composer Francis Poulenc proposed to her. She rejected him on account of not wishing to be in a lavender marriage. Gay though he was, Poulenc was haunted by her for the whole of his life. She was, wrote Poulenc, 'the spiritual guide of my adolescence.' When she died suddenly in 1930, aged thirty-two, he placed the original orchestral manuscript of his ballet *Les Biches* between her hands in the coffin. 'All of my youth departed with you,' he later wrote in a song to her, and he carried her image with him in a cigarette case. There is also a deeply felt portrait of her in *The Very Rich Hours of Adrienne Monnier* (1976). A poet, a proto-Dadaist, an orientalist, a lawyer defending prostitutes, she remains nevertheless a silhouette. The seventh of nine typists, Raymonde Linossier got through forty-five pages of Joyce's manuscript of *Ulysses* before giving up on it, but at least she got to meet herself in the Circe episode: 'even their wax model Raymonde I visited daily to admire her cobweb hose and stick of rhubarb toe, as worn in Paris.' It is not known how she felt being put in the company of whores. When Alan Clodd showed the inscribed copy of *Ulysses* to a scholar from the University of Texas he was immediately offered $75,000, which he waved away as if it were an insult.

The same university later offered him a blank cheque for the entirety of his library, which he was free to keep until the end of his life, but this, too, he dismissed. Other treasures included the Hogarth Press edition of *The Waste Land* (1923), which Eliot inscribed to Virginia Woolf, thanking her for publishing the book when nobody else would, the rarest of Ezra Pound's books, *A Quinzaine for this Yule* (1908), the original autograph notebook of Christopher Isherwood's *All The Conspirators* (1928), the large-paper signed issue of Oscar Wilde's *The Picture of Dorian Gray* (1891), autograph letters from Djuna Barnes to T. S. Eliot complaining about the cuts made to *Nightwood* (1936), Sylvia Plath's first publication, *A Winter Ship* (1960), of which there were only sixty copies, the Black Sun Press edition of Hart Crane's *The Bridge* (1930), and John Keats's *Endymion* (1818). This barely scrapes the surface. There were complete collections of Samuel Beckett, T. S. Eliot, E. M. Forster, David Jones, James Joyce, Ezra Pound, Virginia Woolf, W. B. Yeats and one could go from there to the Hogarth Press editions published under the aegis of Virginia and Leonard Woolf, complete runs of the Cuala Press publications and Harry and Caresse Crosby's Black Sun Press books.

Clodd told Jeremy about how he once pursued T. S. Eliot into the toilet at the Institute of Contemporary Arts in order to get him to sign a copy of one of his early books. And then he would leave books at Faber and Faber for him to sign until finally Eliot had had enough of it and asked him to desist. Also he would go to Paris and leave books for Beckett to sign. Clodd accumulated upwards of a hundred copies of *Waiting for Godot* (1956) because it was never enough to have just one copy of a book he loved so there'd be ten, twenty copies. A hundred though? Where did he get them all? Not even with his intimates did he ever reveal any of his sources, not even the name of a mysterious runner in Paris who Jeremy remembers kept phoning him with offers of titles. On the back pastedown of each book he would pencil in his secret code, indicating what he paid, when and to whom. None of this, however, answers the questions of whether he was happy in his pursuits.

'It was the loneliness of the collector,' Jeremy continues, 'solipsistic, self-isolating, narcissistic, which is why he appreciated the very few friends he could share it with. If he missed a book from a catalogue it was a massive ordeal. He was a fetishist, he stroked the books, the binding, the boards … everything was fetishized, every detail.'

One of the great joys for Jeremy was when Clodd would invite him to go over the collection of a single author and that was how the afternoons were spent, looking at the rarest of books, autograph manuscripts, correspondence.

'Will it be H.D. today?'*

The spectre of death rarely diminishes a collector's appetite for rarities. Clodd, in the last week of his life, when he was dying from septicaemia, managed to purchase Harry Crosby's extremely rare second book of poems *Red Skeletons* (1927), illustrated by Alastair.† Crosby so disliked the book that later he bought the unsold copies, eighty-four of them, eighty of which he took to the Paris suburb of Ermenonville where he burned them, the remaining four he shot to pieces with his pistol, probably the Belgian automatic with which, in 1929, he took his own life and that of his lover Josephine.

Had Alan Clodd in his final days found contentment then? Well, not quite. What eluded him were the first editions of Count Stenbock's books, many of which his family destroyed after he died because of their homoerotic content. What about Stenbock's first book, *Love, Sleep, & Dreams* (1881)?

If only.

---

* The initials under which the American poet Hilda Doolittle published her books.

† "Alastair" was the *nom de plume* of Hans Henning Baron von Voigt.

Chapter Eight

THE TESTAMENT OF CHARLOTTE B.

'THERE IS NO SUCH THING AS CHANCE,' SCHILLER WRITES, 'and what seems to us merest accident springs from the deepest source of destiny.' A woman salvaged from another time, and the story she relates—one of rape, dark intrigue and abduction—may seem a touch familiar, it may even produce a doubtful smile, but as much as can be proved happens to be true. I do not think I exaggerate when I say that what follows had a decisive influence on my thinking with regard to how, on occasion and *for a while only*, we enter the inexplicable. While not given to spiritualism or parapsychology and, indeed, at the sound of those words will run a mile, I do think there is in this universe of ours something more powerful than chance. There is even, I suspect, an area where poet and physicist think and act as one. After all, what is the making of a fine simile but a brief habitation of some kind of interstice? I am reluctant, though, to allow my thoughts on the matter to congeal into theory, preferring, as Keats does, 'to move between uncertainties.'

Should one, in what purports to be the investigation of a historical document, resort continually, as I'm about to do, to the personal pronoun? My defence is this: the issues raised by certain events of a couple of hundred years ago are resolved in the present *and in the present only* and, necessarily, through me. A haunting is what they comprise and, as in all ghost stories, a ghost is not a ghost until it has a living audience. Also, there needs to be an outcome, a place where all the loose strands are neatly tied together and these, for better or worse, require my presence. Should events have proved otherwise, had these papers fallen into hands other than mine, what follows would have been the analysis of a social document, another sheaf for the department of eighteenth-century studies. I would suggest that circumstance has turned them into something else. On the other hand I do not wish to mystify because to do so would be to drain a good story of a potency that is found only in the real. I'm not out to produce atmospheres.

The history of the book trade is one of remarkable discoveries. A bookseller is not quite as surprised as he ought to be by the way objects move through the world. Perhaps it is because he is, by virtue of what he does, a net lowered into the water, the bigger the fishes he catches the better, the more profitable. On May 13, 1988, during preparations for a change of premises, Peter T. Scott called me over to look at some papers that had just been exhumed from a cupboard where they had been lying for some fifteen years. Should they be kept or jettisoned? Actually, like any experienced bookseller, he had caught from the papers before him a whiff of importance. These were originally in the stock of another bookseller, "Dusty" Miller, and when he retired Bertram Rota acquired them. This happened when I was still living in Canada with no thoughts of either staying there or of moving elsewhere. I had been working for Rota almost a decade when the present discovery was made. I relate all this as a demonstration of unlikelihood. The papers that are about to concern us here had been lying under my nose during all that time.

They included:

1. Several military commissions, in the name of Captain John Hitchcock and signed by George III.
2. An account of expenses, totalling £53.15.1, incurred by Hitchcock's funeral in 1823.
3. A blank Gretna Green marriage licence.
4. A letter, dated February 26, 1821, written by 'Charlotte B—' and accompanying this, in the same hand, a manuscript of several folded leaves, which had once been sewn together to make a booklet of twenty-eight pages.
5. Another letter, which, judging from the contents and style, probably dates from the turn of the eighteenth to nineteenth century and is from a man, possibly a notary (his surname is illegible, but he shall be remembered by his first and middle names, Edward Tyrell), to a Reverend J. B. Watkins of St James's Rectory, Dover; the letter, of which only the second page survives, describes the above items.

Subtract items one, two and three and begin with number five. Edward Tyrell makes mention of 'a curious feminine manuscript,' which he might have read through were it not, he claims, that his eyes gave out by the end of the second page. He feels assured enough in his doubts, however, to state that what he is now sending Reverend Watkins is 'an imitation of the stories which eighteenth century novelists used to incorporate in their stories—e.g. the *Memoirs of an Unfortunate Lady*.' It was to this feminine manuscript that my attentions were directed. It was, incidentally, only inches away from the open mouth of a refuse sack into which was being flung anything of unimportance.

The covering letter, headed 'Private,' begins:

> I fear, my dear General, your first impression on opening this packet will be that I am making you an extraordinary present & that I am taking a liberty with you which an acquaintance so long suspended does not authorise.—To this I have nothing to plead but the gratification I *myself* feel, & though I am

aware this could be no plea to your reason or your justice, I think it will be one to your friendship & kindness: for you have told me you still take an interest in my happiness & I am no longer of an age to be the object of *professions*—I *must* believe you—I should not, however, have chosen this time to offer you the resemblance of a form once dear to you, but for the very precarious state of my health & the desponding notions I entertain of the future.—Since I last wrote I have rapidly declined, I took cold after bathing (which it seems neither habit nor precaution will enable one to do in this Climate with impunity) & my Cough is daily becoming worse—I have not passed a spring in England since 1814 & both the opinion of my Physicians & my own feeling make me look forward with considerable dread [...] God knows then how this may end—the Doctors say my lungs are as yet untouched, but that they are in so very delicate a state as to give grounds from apprehending the result of the next three months if I am exposed to the usual vicissitudes of an English climate. When my letter reaches you all this will be decided, I shall either have escaped—or I shall be gone to that other that *better world* where it is soothing to me to imagine I shall again meet the person I have most loved in *this* [...] You have filled a large space in my humble existence—you were the first object of my affections—you have in some shape or other interested me during my whole life—if the afflictions or the dissipations of the world, my domestic duties, or my literary amusements have often banished you from my thoughts, they have never banished you from my heart. At my years & with the prospect of surviving a very few months I can have no reason for sacrificing truth to compliment—neither have I now a sentiment of female pride to combat—in my situation these considerations fade away & I tell you with the sincerity which becomes a last assurance, that I have never felt for another what I have felt for you. I will not say that the original romance of my nature might not have some share in this strange constancy—to love without *hope*—an *object*, a Being who was become

Private

I fear my dear General your first impression on opening this packet will be that I am making you an extraordinary present & that I am taking a liberty with you which an acquaintance so long suspended does not authorise. — to this I have nothing to plead but the gratification I myself feel, & though I am aware this could be no plea to your reason or your justice, I think it will be one to your friendship & kindness: for you have told me you still take an interest in my happiness & I am no longer of an age to be the object of professions — I must believe you — I should not however have chosen this time to offer you the resemblance of a form once dear to you, but for the very precarious state of my health & the desponding notions I entertain of the future. — Since I last wrote I have rapidly declined, I took cold after bathing (which it seems neither habit nor precaution will enable me to do in this Climate with impunity) & my Cough is daily becoming worse — I have not passed a Spring in England since 1814 & both the opinion of my Physicians & my own feeling make me look forward with considerable dread — I had hoped to go to the South of France or Italy, but am obliged to abandon the project, & the state of my health which renders this so necessary, happens to be one of the obstacles to its execution — Miss Harris the Daughter of Lord Harris is like myself never well in England

almost an imaginary one to me—one of whom I could hear only through the voice of fame; to cherish a secret passion for a man whose character & profession were well calculated to associate enthusiasm with mystery—was not only a very seducing state of mind to a girl of my disposition—but it was the most fortunate turn I could have taken—yes, my dear General, I owe to this affection that the most dangerous years of my life were protected from Vice & that I have through so many difficulties & disadvantages raised myself to a situation

> in society which if not splendid is honorable—& that with a very moderate fortune I enjoy more consideration than many who are great & affluent. My fear, my hopes, my wishes have followed you through a long & glorious career & there was a something of exaltation in this interest which would of itself have preserved me from debasement.

The style is pleasing enough, the sincerity of feeling unassailable, but it was not until my perusal of the following passage that something like a shudder moved through me.

> I should vainly attempt to describe the anxiety I suffered during the Mahratta War of 1803. I never could read a dispatch from India without trembling—never could I venture to read one in the presence of any third person—I believe I may reckon amongst my happiest moments that in which I once saw your name to a short report (I think of killed & wounded but I forget from whence) for it assured me of your safety—nor did I suffer less during the Wars of the Mysore.—I now sufficiently admire the Duke of Wellington—yet when he was in India I almost hated him—I had a thousand fancies about him too silly & too womanish to communicate, but it would indeed have been difficult to satisfy me because I was at once solicitous for your glory & your preservation—I dreaded your being placed in Posts of danger—& yet if I did not hear of your being employed I was indignant—I suppose my notion was for you to acquire distinction & honors without *fighting* or *risk*—I remember being very well pleased on reading in some account that you were left with the Emperor at Delhi instead of going to Agra. Yet these were only transient accesses of Cowardice—for no woman was ever more sensible to military glory than myself—your reputation has always been as dear to me as your Welfare.—During the greater part of the years 1814-15 I was in Holland—Germany—Italy—Switzerland—God knows where & did not hear of your Campaign, nor its

> results till the Spring of 1816 [...] The Hero of Nepaul little imagined that his early friend was on the 15th of May 1816 giving a Ball in celebration of the anniversary of his treaty after the reduction of Malown, to some of the prettiest women in Paris—But forgive me—I have wandered half over your Peninsula in recalling the tender & Constant concern I have ever felt for your safety & your fame.

It was as if the post had arrived over a century and a half late. I knew immediately from the historical details and dates, all of which were precise, *exactly* to whom she was writing. There is a single detail later in her manuscript, where proof would be absolute, where she had scratched through the recipient's name, which when held up to the light is clearly visible. 'The being she idolized' was my great-great-grandfather on my mother's side, Sir David Ochterlony. Some months earlier, I had stood beside Ochterlony's crumbling mausoleum in the haunting European cemetery at Meerut, north of Delhi, and for the past year or so I had been gathering materials on his life.

Ochterlony is one of the most fascinating historical figures to have never had a biography fully devoted to him. Although I had accumulated notes on his military career and in particular his victory over the Ghurkhas, the man himself remains one of those enigmatic figures of whom history leaves little more than a silhouette. The so-called twilight era of Anglo-Indian history of which he was such a fine example has only recently been touched upon by historians. The focus has been mainly either on the earlier period, of which Clive was the leading figure, for example, or the later, the Raj, but for me no period fascinates more than this one, when there was an extraordinary fluidity in relations between the English and the various peoples over whom they had economic rule. The history of colonialism is poorly understood in these days of self-righteousness, which is not to excuse the dominance of one country over another, nor is it to underestimate the villainy that often takes place, but the men who ventured there in the second half of the eighteenth century were not only commercial figures but Byronic adventurers and romantics, many of whom had a love and knowledge of the culture, spoke the languages, wrote learned books about what they saw and experienced. They included the likes of John Malcolm, Mountstuart Elphinstone and Sir Charles Metcalfe, any one of whom deserves a biography. Metcalfe, with whom Ochterlony shared a fine house at Shalimar Gardens in Delhi, and who later became Governor General of Canada, never travelled anywhere by horse, saying it was so much easier to read a book on the back of an elephant.

I will deal briefly with the historical references in Charlotte's letter. The Mysore War of 1780–83 against Hyder Ali (and, subsequently, the French) was Ochterlony's first military action, during which time he was twice wounded and imprisoned. Under the command of Colonel Thomas Deane Pearse he had made a gruelling thousand-mile march from Bengal to Mysore, through what Pearse describes in his journal as 'the shreds and fragments of a world, in Dame Nature's shop, producing nothing but sand and craggy rocks, brackish water, and pestiferous winds.' There is a gap of some twenty years before we hear from him again. In 1802, the English ousted the French adventurer General Perron from Delhi where he had held considerable sway over the Mughal emperor Shah Alam II. Shah Alam was a truly forlorn figure, a man whose position was, in Percival Spear's words, 'one of vacillation punctuated by alternate lamentation and resignation to the will of God.'* It is a clue to Ochterlony's character and statesmanship that when he was made Acting Resident at the emperor's court he showed every mark of observance to a man who was in fact his charge. Shah Alam died in 1806, still believing power was his. The defence of Delhi in October 1803 by three thousand men against a Mahratta force of fifteen thousand led by Jaswant Rao Holkar was without doubt a brilliant achievement. Some allowance must be made, however, for Holkar's penchant for brandy and women, for it was in pursuit of both that he paused in his march against Delhi, giving Ochterlony just enough time to strengthen the city

* *The Twilight of the Gods* (1951).

walls. Ochterlony took the unprecedented step of personally delivering sweetmeats to his Indian troops in order that their spirits might be rallied. The Indians remembered this. When during the Great Mutiny of 1857 (Ochterlony died in 1825), the insurgents swept through Jaipur burning the British residences, the house he had lived in, one of several houses he owned, was spared as a mark of respect. The greatest achievement of Ochterlony's career, one that made him a legend in his time (and little more than a footnote in the modern histories), was his conquest of Nepal. The running battle between him and the magnificent Ghurkha leader Amar Singh is worthy of an epic or would be were it not that such estimation is now despised. The Treaty of Malown, on May 15, 1815, was but an intermediary stage in a war that did not reach its conclusion until the following year.

I must confess that it is another side of Ochterlony that appeals to me more. The earliest biographical portrait I have found of him is in Captain Thomas Smith's *Narrative of a Five Years' Residence in Nepaul* (1852), in which he writes:

I am still less qualified to decide the moral and the theological question, which has been raised on the more delicate point of his domestic connexions. Some virtuous and well-meaning persons of both sexes, imperfectly informed on the subject, have blamed him for setting an example of what they deemed vice to the young men of the army.

When I first read this my thoughts ran to places they need not have gone. *Vice?* There is a famous Indian miniature of Ochterlony in the India Office, in London, which depicts him dressed in Indian robes, smoking a hookah and surrounded by dancing nautch girls. It is the image most commonly referred to when the discussion turns to those Englishmen who went 'native.' Captain Smith continues, 'He retained ever afterwards a relish for nautches, and the performances of the singing men of India, which could be accounted for, in one of his general taste, only on the supposition that they awakened associations of the spring-time of life.'

Edward Thompson writes: 'Tradition has preserved a picture of Ochterlony's thirteen wives on thirteen elephants, every evening taking the air in Delhi, heavily veiled—a story which almost seems to carry us across the borders of folklore.'* I have not been able to pursue the story to any earlier sources but I did go through the records of baptism, which are preserved in the India Office, and discovered rather more children than any one, two or three wives were capable of producing at any one time. (I was especially pleased to find a Roderick Peregrine.) It was not in the interests of officialdom to preserve the names of their Indian mothers. One name that does keep cropping up elsewhere, however, most specifically in Ochterlony's Will, is that of Beebee Mahruttun Moobarruck ul Nifsa Begume and it is on account of the name alone that I should like to think she was my great-great-grandmother. What it also means is that I have Indian blood in me.

It is a moot point whether it was she to whom Charlotte refers when she writes, 'If you married the lady who cost me so many bitter moments, whose name I could never hear without inexpressible anguish, she will scarcely be displeased at your possessing the Portrait of me at this age.' I would be greatly surprised if she actually knew of Beebee. It was not at all unusual for Englishmen to take on at least several wives and in fact they were encouraged to do so. After all, many members of the East India Company were domiciled there for life and European women were scarce. In the early 1800s, when the Englishwomen (*memsahibs*) went out to India in droves, social mores had begun to change. The idea of an Englishman with Indian wives became unmentionable and the likes of Ochterlony were being swept aside and the origins of their Anglo-Indian children heavily disguised.

I possess a painting of him in full military dress, probably painted at around the time Charlotte writes her letter. There is nothing much revealed in the face, maybe a certain vulnerability beneath the stiffness of the pose, also something a bit glazed across the eyes, but this could be a fanciful reading. In truth, it is probably little more than a likeness. There is a copy of the painting

* *The Making of the Indian Princes* (London, 1943).

at the National Army Museum. The note beneath it stated the subject never married. I protested. I was not listened to, but maybe now, with William Dalrymple's study *White Mughals* (2002), there is an unstiffening of attitude. Accompanying my painting are portraits of two young women, presumably his daughters. The written labels on the back of them describe them as having been born the Princesses Gorgii of Greece, a country that did not exist at the time. The "Greek" served to disguise the presence of Indian blood, which, ironically, is easily enough discernible in the paintings themselves.

A military gentleman, now deceased, who began to write a biography of Ochterlony, showed little interest in the information I had to offer him, which related to his subject's domestic affairs. It is an area of the life he was not prepared to countenance. When I first broached the subject with my great-aunt, in whose possession the paintings then were, informing her we had an Indian ancestor, she expressed her delight at the idea, adding, 'I wouldn't want to be of mixed blood, though.' 'Aunt Helen,' I said, 'you *are*.' 'Oh,' she replied, bringing the conversation to a quick close. All thirteen elephants were now released from the family closet. Although the temptation, if one is a male, is to mentally project oneself into the harem it ought to be remembered that in the real world of eighteenth-century India husbands were expected to take responsibility for their wives.

When Charlotte writes her letter to Ochterlony in 1821, and believes herself to be dying, he, nearing the end of his life, is already a sad figure, prone to terrible depressions. There are accounts of him quitting the dinner table in tears. The simple fact is that British rule in India had cast him to the side. Already he had begun to unhinge, both physically and mentally, and in the following year he suffered a major collapse. Also, he was crippled with severe gout. There is an unforgettable portrait of him in Bishop Heber's *Narrative of a Journey through the Upper Provinces of India* (1829), where the author records a chance meeting on a bleak plain in the middle of Rajputana. The date was July 27, 1824.

> We passed Sir David Ochterlony and his suite on his road to Bhurtpoor. There certainly was a very considerable number of led horses, elephants, palanquins, and covered carriages, belonging chiefly, I apprehend, (besides his own family), to the families of his native servants. There was an escort of two companies of infantry, a troop of regular cavalry, and I should guess forty or fifty regulars, on horse and foot, armed with spears and matchlocks of all possible forms; the string of camels was a long one, and the whole procession was what might pass in Europe for that of an eastern prince travelling. Still, neither in numbers nor splendour did it at all equal my expectation. Sir David himself was in a carriage and four, and civilly got out to speak to me. He is a tall and pleasing-looking old man, but was so wrapped up in shawls, kincob, fur, and a Mogul furred cap, that his face was all that was visible. I was not sorry to have seen even this glimpse of an old officer whose exploits in India have been so distinguished ... He is now considerably above seventy, infirm, and has been often advised to return to England. But he has been absent from thence fifty-four years; he has neither friend nor relation—he has been for many years habituated to eastern habits and parade, and who can wonder that he clings to the only country in the world where he can feel himself at home.

Ochterlony was in fact only sixty-six years old and had been in India for forty-six years. A year later he was dead. It is melancholy to observe in what contrasting lights Charlotte imagines him.

I began to read through the pages of the manuscript to see what I could glean of Ochterlony's life, and as my disappointment rose what emerged in the absence of any news of him was a narrative of considerable power. It was now Charlotte who claimed me, and I wondered at these two lives which were linked together as though by means of a most delicate clasp. The 'Unfortunate Lady' is, judging from internal evidence, approximately sixty years old at the time of writing. She believes she is dying, probably from consumption, and is now writing to the first love of her life, a boy she knew when she was barely sixteen and whom she has not seen since. The letter is studiously composed, whereas, as we shall see, the accompanying manuscript shows signs of having been hastily put together, as though the writing of it were a battle against the writer's reluctance to do so. What the manuscript loses in the epistolary grace of the former it gains in directness, almost modern in tone, which gives her story its particular emotional drive. And what a story it is. Although Charlotte may not, as she claims, have conquered vanity (she loves dropping names—Lord Harris, the Duke of Wellington, Mr Pitt, 'this vixen of a Queen [Caroline]', etc., etc. —) she is, as she approaches death, free of the strictures polite society places upon her. She is remarkably frank. She has improved her station in life, through a good marriage we may suppose, but it is to where innocence took a tumble, the years 1779 to 1784, that she now returns. She wishes to make her case clear. The audience she chooses is both near and far enough to make this possible, and the audience also happens to be famous. What we have here is not simply the case of a female suppliant seeking a hero, for although she may be in awe of him, in this remembrance of someone she once knew having risen to fame there is a vindication of her own worth. We know more than she does, however. She is spared the knowledge that she is writing to a broken man. Charlotte speaks of the miniature of herself that she sends him. 'You will find, dear General, that time which adds new verdure to the Laurel is fatal to the bloom of the Rose, & that while you have been gathering immortal wreaths for *your* brow, every charm has faded away from *mine*.' She pictures him again as passing his life between 'glory & pleasure,' 'between the cares of the Camp & the luxuries of the Palace.' Against this she contrasts her own fate.

With me it is very different—those days comprised the greatest felicity & the greatest misery I have ever known—when you *loved me* & when you *left me* are epochs to which I have never ceased to turn—they have been my points of comparison under every good & every evil which have befallen me—it will therefore (I repeat) be very pleasing to me to know you possess an object which may remind you of me when I am no more, & if as Gray says 'even in our Ashes lived their wonted fires' my spirit will be soothed should it be conscious that I am not entirely forgotten.

The rest of the covering letter is written in some confusion and the tone becomes a touch shrill at times, 'Good God, what you must think of me, to believe that I who could so young & inexperienced resist the object of my first my fondest affections, & when I was eighteen months older, with my understanding more cultivated & a perfect notion of the consequences, voluntarily throw myself into the arms of a Libertine half mad & half fool—& who has been my ridicule and aversion.' She refers a couple of times to a 'Mr H—,' but whether he is the above-mentioned Libertine is not immediately clear. The main thrust of her concluding remarks concerns her virtue.

I doubtless have had many [faults] of both omission & Commission, yet it is most true—that no woman ever had more strictly the virtue of the sex than myself. I thank God that I am naturally cold—my passions have been all in my heart—an ardent love of literature—constant occupation—early disappointment—early calamity—have tended to give me a sort of disgust—to the relations of love (as it is called) & Gallantry which I have seen possess in the world [...] You will see, my dear General, that I have through my life held in great dread the violent passions of men [...] & such has been the impression made on me by such scenes that I never heard a profession of love however respectful & decent without shuddering & repugnance.

I took the manuscript home and began making a typed transcript straight from the page, and it was in the slow fashion, word by word, that an incredible adventure took shape.

* * *

'It was about eighteen months after your departure,' Charlotte writes, 'that I concluded if you had been disposed to write I might expect to hear from you.' Ochterlony sailed out of Portsmouth Harbour on the *Lord North* on July 15, 1777. This much I had learned from my earlier researches. This is the date upon which we may construct a chronology of all that happens to Charlotte.

She assumes, correctly, that the average run to India and back was eighteen months and that the *Morning Post* to which she later refers would publish details of ships' arrivals and departures. She was not to know, in this month of January 1779, that the *Lord North* had sailed on to China and that it would be some weeks yet before news of its return to England. Charlotte describes how she applies for help from a Mrs Green, the wife of a small timber merchant. We know she lives south of the Thames because she speaks of their crossing the river to go to 5 New Palace Yard where, Mrs Green told her, she would find a file of *Morning Post*s. A boy meets them at the door and Mrs Green explains to him that the man at whose house they are is a family friend and that their purpose is to see the *Morning Post*s that are kept upstairs in the drawing room. She then leaves Charlotte to go through the papers, saying she has to go to Bridge Street to do some errands.

I had not the slightest suspicion. Lights & Coffee were brought by the Boy & the Coffee being already poured out I took some—almost immediately after I accidentally opened a Book (for at that time I was ignorant of all the etiquettes which forbid looking at Books) & to my great terror I saw Mr H—'s name—Still I did not suppose I was in his House (for I knew he lived in Parliament Street) yet I was alarmed & began to examine the room—on the chimney piece was a trinket which I had refused the day before—I no longer doubted where I was—my Head began to be heavy, & bewildered & terrified I flew to the door with the intention of getting away—at this instant this wretched man entered—I screamed dreadfully & I know not how it happened but in a violent effort to reach the door I struck my head: in an instant I was deluged with blood from my nose & the blow & the Laudanum together deprived me of my senses—oh General—what monstrous passions must a man feel who could abuse such a situation—I never think of this without an indescribable sensation of disgust & horror—.

Within the space of a few lines Charlotte describes not only her rape by the aforementioned Mr H—, but also her accidental opening of a book. I do not wish to muffle the terrible blow she receives but the aside is a fascinating one. The reading of novels, and especially 'fancy works' as Charlotte calls them elsewhere, was not recommended for women. Steele notes, 'insensibly they lead the Heart to Love. Let them therefore [...] be avoided with Care; for there are elegant Writers enough on Moral and Divine subjects.' The *Spectator* warned women against reading novels, which along with chocolates, and especially in the month of May, were believed to inflame the blood.

It was many hours before I became sensible of the outrage I had suffered—on first coming to myself—I was strongly convulsed—my Head was swollen—my white dress covered with blood & torn to pieces—my ankle sprained, one of my arms bruised—it is impossible to imagine a more pitiable object—my mind was a chaos of misery & I was in extreme bodily pain—I recollected too the alarm of my poor Mother—I was distracted by every sort of anguish—but I was helpless—I could not even turn on the soffa where I was placed—I sank again into a state of torpor & was put to Bed by a woman who I found afterwards had been in no way accessory to my sufferings—I saw no one else & Mr H—did not venture to approach me—but he began to be terrified at the state I was in—yet did not dare to call in medical aid.

She describes in some detail how over the next few days she sinks in and out of consciousness and is then removed, by carriage, to another place where she is tended to by medical people. She recovers just enough for her to be able to decide she will inform the physician of her plight but no sooner is she ready to do so than he is mysteriously discharged.

While I was planning some means of escape Mr H—came. It was a dreadful scene—he deplored his violence—offered every sort of reparation—acted one moment like a Madman the next like a person really penitent—he had brought a small Bible with him & Pistols—protesting if I would not take an oath to conceal what had passed that he would shoot himself—this I refused—but said if I should have some Books & work I would remain & consider of it. The Books & needles & threads were brought me & after cutting out capital letters to compose Mr Beaufoy's address I sewed them on a blank leaf—together with my own name—& a sentence descriptive of my situation cut from the Prayer book which I had desired to have. This paper I found means to give to the Apothecary who I learned after was a Mr Saunders of St James's Street—he had probably remarked something extraordinary & readily went to Mr Beaufoy—proper authority was immediately obtained—& Mr B—'s carriage & Housekeeper was sent to take me away—for the people of the house made no resistance.

What follows is a lengthy description, fascinating to any student of legal history, of the charges that are brought against Mr H— and how the prospect of seeing him hanged, together with the humiliation she would feel in becoming an object of public scrutiny results in the charge being changed from a criminal to a civil one. Mr H— is made to give his word of honour that he'd never attempt to see Charlotte again and now follows a 'peaceful' interlude during which time her mother dies. Charlotte is provided with a servant and she resumes her studies. What happens some months later is enough to make the sceptical reader scratch his head a little.

> One Evening about ten o'clock just as I was preparing to go up stairs—the servant made a pretext of some Household want for the morning to go out & returning hastily she said there was a great fire up the street which she believed was at Mary Belson's the woman who had nursed me & of whom I was very fond—instinctively almost I put on my cloak & ran out with the maid—there was in fact the light of a fire but at a great distance—but she drew me to the water side saying it was quite *visible* from thence—in an instant I was muffled in a Boat cloak—put under a tilt & rowed off into the Thames—the whole was so rapid—so sudden—that I am not sure I even screamed & I had Westminster Bridge before I could disengage my Head & mouth—so as to beg the men to put me on shore—they were very brutal fellows & only muttered something about 'Women running away

from their Husbands'—the only person in the Boat besides the rowers I could discern was a Mulatto who kept telling me I should not be hurt. I was excessively terrified, for my idea was that they were going to drown or to murder me in some way—it was in vain I cried & entreated—there were no Boats about at that Hour & when at last I was landed in a lone place I expected no other than that the Mulatto was going to assassinate me—so that when I was hurried into a carriage it was rather a relief to me otherwise. A few minutes brought me to the back entrance of a large Mansion situated in the midst of pleasure grounds—I saw no inhabitants but a grey headed man & his wife who took me up stairs in a state of passive terror—for I was really as much astonished as frightened—I had made an attempt to call for assistance in coming from the water side but if you recollect the *locale*—you will know it must have been useless [...] A paper was put in my hand which I saw was Mr H—'s writing, conjuring me to tranquilize myself for the night & protesting I should meet with no molestation—I found there was no remedy & hoping to get away in the morning & my cloaths being very wet & draggled by my struggling in landing I consented to go to Bed & have them dried. The room was covered with a sort of fresco paper representing the ruins of Ancient Rome & after fastening the Doors carefully I lay down, & worn out & harassed I sank into an uneasy slumber—but I had scarcely forgotten myself when I was awoke by the opening of a Door at the Head of the Bed—it formed the representation of an Archway in the Campo Vac[c]ino & unless closely inspected was not visible—so that it had escaped my search—you will imagine—what it would be so painful for me to trace. Suffice it to say that towards morning in some effort to escape I was thrown from the Bed on the corner of a chair & one of my ribs broken—I fainted from suffering & was for three months attended by a surgeon a Mr Churchill (the brother of the poet) in a nervous fever.

It is time to take a pause. Although I believed what Charlotte wrote—in the way one senses a story too outlandish to be true must be true—the many questions raised here demanded answers. I would accept nothing I believed. It was fortunate that Charlotte provides so many clues, for there is barely a page of her manuscript on which she does not mention a name or a place. These I realised would need to be verified. A hundred facts do not constitute a true story, however, and truth may be composed of many smaller fictions. It would be the rare author who did not, to some extent, reinvent his own life; verity becomes version, yet in Charlotte's account there is remarkably little speculation. The events she describes are dramatic enough to survive her own interpretation of them. Charlotte is at the mercy of 'a libertine half mad & half fool' whom she refers to throughout as 'Mr H—'. What she gives us with much 'Œconomy' of language is a character so exquisitely demonic as to make us wonder whether she did not invent him. Fortunately, she provides the two addresses where he lived—5 Palace Yard, Westminster, and Peterborough House near Parsons Green, which was then outside London. She mentions in passing that this last, her 'magnificent Prison,' was once 'the haunt of Pope & all the Wits of that day.' Whatever truth her story contained depended largely on my being able to identify the inhabitants of these two houses. The local history library in Fulham was the obvious place to go.

I asked the librarian in Fulham about Peterborough House. She looked through her records and found a small file. I asked her where the house was, for I was determined I should visit the place, but she informed me it had been demolished. She pulled out some descriptions of the place, first John Bowack's in his topographical guide *The Antiquities of Middlesex* (1705), which describes Peterborough House thus.

> This seat is a very large, square, regular pile of brick, and has a gallery all round it upon the roof. 'Twas built by a branch of the honourable family of the Monmouths and came to the present Earl in right of his mother, the Lady Elizabeth Carey,

> Viscountess De Aviland. It has abundance of extraordinary good rooms with fine paintings, etc., but is mostly remarkable for its spacious gardens, there being above twenty acres of ground enclos'd: the contrivance of the grounds is fine, tho' their beauty is in great measure decay'd. And the large cypress shades, and pleasant Wilderness, with fountains, statues, etc., have been very entertaining.

A watercolour of the house, done in 1794, which the librarian showed me, suggests that the house had not changed much by Charlotte's time. The walls were sparkling white and the roof a handsome blue. It was there that Charles Mordant, Earl of Peterborough, lived until his death in 1735 and, yes, entertained most of the literati and wits of the time including Addison, Swift, Pope, Locke and Bolingbroke. Swift makes reference in several of his letters to the hospitality he received there and even wrote a poem beginning,

> Mordanto fills the trump of fame,
> The Christian world his deeds proclaim,
> And prints are crowded with his name.

In 1727 Voltaire spent three weeks there, and, to make matters 'curiouser and curiouser,' it was only a stone's throw away from the villa where Samuel Richardson lived from 1758 until his death in 1761. The depiction of oppressed heroines was, of course, Richardson's forte. I asked the librarian who lived in the house.

'Why, the Earl of Peterborough, of course.'

The fourth earl, also named Charles, lived at Peterborough House until his death in 1779. It seemed just then that Charlotte's story was about to collapse.

'No, wait a minute,' the librarian said, pulling out some further bits of paper, which included an advertisement for the house, now owned by Robiniana, Countess Dowager of Peterborough, to be sold by private contract by Messrs Robson & Harris of Lincoln's Inn.

> A FREEHOLD CAPITAL MANSION HOUSE
> with the spacious and convenient outhouses, offices, stabling for 12 horses, dairy, dog kennel, very extensive pleasure grounds tastefully laid out, and large kitchen-garden, well cropped and planted with the choicest fruits, hot-houses, green-house, ice-house, and fruit-house, with exceeding rich meadow lands, close adjoining; the whole containing above 40 acres.

'Yes,' the librarian continued, 'it says here that Peterborough House was sold in April 1782, to Richard Heaviside, a timber merchant. He lived there until 1795 and he sold the house, in 1797, to a John Meyrick who demolished it and replaced it with a second Peterborough House.

Heaviside, *Heaviside.*

The name was almost too good to be true, the very stuff of Restoration comedy. *H* for *Heaviside.* I must allow for coincidence, I reasoned, and besides, the dates, according to my first calculations, fell a little late. I had reckoned the year of Charlotte's first misadventure to be 1780 and her second one a year or so later. My next step was to check the Fulham rate books and there, in the column for July 27, 1781, Heaviside makes his first appearance. So he had been living there, possibly as a lessee, prior to the sale. According to the rates he paid, £17.16.6 (a figure exceeding even that exacted from the bishop), he must have been one of the wealthiest men in the borough. The rate book for the previous year indicates 'empty or [sic] occupier,' so Heaviside could have moved in at any point after July 1780. It should be noted, too, that the names of ratepayers were entered in the books well in advance of monies being collected. I now had a Mr H— in the right place at the right time; all I had to do now was check the Palace Yard address. The Guildhall Library holds old business directories. A 1782 edition lists Richard Heaviside, timber merchant, Palace Yard, Westminster. Also, during these researches, I identified many of the people she mentions in her narrative, Mrs Green who led her to Palace Yard, for example. The *London Business Directory* for 1778 lists Thomas Green, timber merchant, of Cuper's Bridge, Lambeth, which would have been very close to where Charlotte lived. Mark Beaufoy, a Quaker from Bristol, was a vinegar merchant in Cuper's Garden. He began his career by distilling hard liquor but was so appalled by Hogarth's depictions of Gin Lane that he turned to the making of 'mimicked wines' and vinegar. John Dunning was one of the most outstanding lawyers of the day. The poet Charles Churchill gave his younger brother, John, financial assistance to train as a surgeon. These are just some of the names that I was able to identify over the following months.

I had identified Mr H— more easily than Charlotte may have wished anyone to. Perhaps justice has been done. Does she spill more clues than she means to, or is she mischievously spreading them? I suspect that she is, despite the years closing over her and despite her obvious intelligence, uncommonly naïve. It is this very combination of strength and vulnerability that makes her so attractive a figure. There is no secret that so breaks as the one most tightly reined in, but we must remember she is writing not for literary detectives but privately for a man she once and perhaps *still* loves. She struggles with the problem of what not to include in her narrative—that which most pains her, that which the world should not accidentally see and that which would mean little to someone as far removed as Ochterlony is. The joke on her is that she unstitches her own secrets while making them.

So where did we leave Charlotte?

> Surely General, sorrow does not kill or I must have sunk under these accumulated afflictions—I can hardly imagine a more desolate, a more forlorn creature than I felt myself at this time—I no longer complained—I no longer wept—my heart was half broken—the elasticity of my mind destroyed—& helpless & despairing I submitted to whatever was deemed necessary for my preservation. Mr H—'s mother was extremely kind to me, Mr Churchill really acted like a father, he brought his daughters to see me, & so interested one of the most respectable families in the Vicinage for me

> [...] all this while the evil genius of my life behaved very decently—never attempting to see me alone, & I lingered on in this strange situation till I was confined. On my recovery my position was changed & I now had a new embarrassment—I knew not where to go or what to do—I confess to you, though it is contrary to all experience, all one has read or heard of, that this offspring of fraud & violence did not inspire me with the maternal tenderness of which I *have* an idea—it was associated with degradation & misery & what I felt for it was rather pity than fondness & I deemed it a moral duty to preserve it if I could (for it was a female) from being as wretched as myself. I did not nurse it—& it was only brought to the House occasionally—I had bribed the woman who nursed me to send letters to my father & Mr B—but I could receive no answers for I found after, that the woman had betrayed me. Not knowing this I concluded I was given up—and at last I made a species of arrangement with Mr H— by which he agreed never to intrude on me, or to bring me any visitors—I had a wing of the House to myself—sombre groves & bright Parterres—music—Books—whatever I desired [...] I was become wild, savage as it were, & could not often be induced to receive anyone.

Clearly, she was living in a strange situation. With time, however, Heaviside returns to his old tricks.

> I was at times also subject to frantic intrusions from Mr H—. He was leading a very dissipated life—he endeavoured I believe to forget me & the atrocity of his conduct together, but it is certain he entertained a passion for me little short of insanity & which probably my coldness & aversion tended to encrease. He was once dangerously ill & made a Will by which he bequeathed me the whole of his property but nothing could conquer the dislike, the horror (I may say) with which I beheld him.

What are we to make of Heaviside? What is his problem? A man so absolute in what he does is not without interest and, possibly, charm. This is not to excuse him, his crimes are heinous, but the risks he takes to secure Charlotte are so immense that in the end even her father is silenced. Heaviside must be judged in his time, and although the noose might have spared Charlotte much sorrow there is little doubting his ardour. He lies, he cheats, he breaks bones, but otherwise he is prepared to give Charlotte what he thinks she desires, even the education she so highly values. Dissipated he may have been, but Heaviside manages to keep the books balanced. He was an immensely successful merchant, and as such was part of a social phenomenon then taking place. The merchants quickly rose to power, social barriers were broken, and upstart traders moved into grand houses. Heaviside, about whom I learned little, was born in 1754 in Bishopsgate. His father was a saddler of some repute. The son moved into timber. And into politics too. In the 1780 General Election he ran in two constituencies and lost in both. At some point he was made Justice of the Peace, a position that had more to do with local prestige than actual justice. In 1800, he married Elizabeth Ann Proctor. A son was baptized in 1804. Richard Heaviside died in 1815. He was, in terms of the social framework we have put him into, typical of the age. Whatever else he was, Charlotte has made him flesh and blood.

Now comes a critical turning point in her life.

> In this way I went on for more than two years till the Child died & I had no longer any reason for remaining [...] I then began to affect a desire to see plays & operas & to have valuable trinkets to appear at them—I pretended fancies for things which I had never worn or wished to wear, until in the course of a few months I procured enough for my purpose. Being now so far supplied as not to have the appearance of wanting to beg or borrow I related the whole of my story (which they had never heard from me) to Mr & Mrs S— & entreated their assistance in finding me some cheap place where the produce of my trinkets would support me

> for a year or a year & a half till the first search & the first rage of Mr H— should be over & I could claim the annuity. They entered into my project with the most benevolent Zeal & one of their friends a woman of fashion who was then on a tour of pleasure found & took for me a small cottage in Glamorganshire between Neath & Swansey & for which Mrs— insisted on paying the first year in advance.

She makes her escape and then begins a blissful interlude. I was to have one rather less so. I had already made considerable advances in my research, even though it had been barely two weeks since the discovery was made, but there were gaps in the typescript I prepared, certain words, which, no matter how hard I teased them, resisted decipherment. Whose property, I wanted to know, should have sunk in the Bay of Bengal? Which Roman campo was depicted on the fresco of a certain bedroom? Who was the Frenchman the guillotine took away from Charlotte? Whose house was supposedly in flames? I passed the manuscript to my colleague John Byrne, who is an expert in autograph materials and whose eye is much sharper than mine. Meanwhile, I had written to the three Heavisides in the London telephone directory, asking them if they could supply me with any biographical information on this figure who might have been an ancestor of theirs. Surely, I reasoned, Heaviside was not a common name. I may have gone too far, but my fascination was such that I was now willing to go trampling through the private gardens of complete strangers. Only one Heaviside answered: 'Thank you for your letter. I am seventy-one years old, born Londoner. My father was originally born in Durham City. His father was in a wealthy iron business in Darlington. He, like the prodigal son, left home & came to London about 1900. He married an actress. They had a son. She died, then he married my mother. Yours faithfully ———.'

Monday morning I was back at work and found myself wading through the silences of my colleagues. There was something they were not telling me. A few minutes later, John Byrne walked in and all was made clear. There were cuts and bruises all over his face.

The previous Thursday evening he had been brutally set upon in Pimlico Road and left bleeding in the middle of the street, and he had taken from him the black leather bag containing the original of Charlotte's manuscript. This was, in terms of what matters to me, a loss beyond loss. It seemed a mocking irony that from the violence of one century Charlotte should have disappeared violently into this. My wife drove around Pimlico in a futile attempt to find a discarded black leather bag. She even peered into the courtyard of one of the nearby housing estates. I sank into a kind of despondency and that week I dreamed about the manuscript, it must have been several times, and in those dreams I saw only the written pages, nothing surrounding them. I struggled with a memory of the shaped peculiarities of Charlotte's hand, and one night a *P* turned into a *V* and the word *Vaccino* came into focus. The next morning I consulted a plan of Ancient Rome, something I should have done in the first place, and there it was, the Campo Vaccino through the frescoed representation of which Heaviside made his dramatic entrance. Still, despite various other small mysteries I solved that week there was the underlying knowledge that gone forever was the proof that such a manuscript had existed in the first place.

I had resigned myself to the loss of Charlotte, and I had even persuaded myself that recent events were merely a continuation of the same evil that had befallen her. The mind constructs its own mysteries, it does so for the sake of coherence sometimes, and in a curious way I found myself not wishing to find the manuscript. I was to feel the same way when later I fretted over who Charlotte might be. Would I be puncturing the mystery? I think in both instances I was proved wrong, for no sooner is one mystery solved than another is made. The detective story with all its loose ends so neatly tucked in is for sophisticated simpletons. The truth is always odder.

Charlotte, now aged twenty, describes a period of peace.

> I lived in a sort of enchantment & there was nothing great or glorious which my fancy did not ascribe to you—& this is so true that your image is even now as much connected with the

> Bay of Briton Ferry as with the scenes in which I really saw you—in which I first loved you. It was here too my habits or order—of arrangement—& study were formed such as they still continue—my homely breakfast of herb tea—or milk and bread was always decorated by mountain flowers—& the repast which I called dinner & which was seldom anything more than Potatoes—an Egg or Oysters was served with all the ceremony of a dinner *en règle.* I dressed regularly with as much neatness as though I were to be seen—rose as early as though I had a thousand occupations & bathed in all weathers twice a week—in this inoffensive way I lived above a year—the poor people were much attached to me for though I had nothing to give I worked for them & when they were ill often cured them by simple remedies—I met with no sort of evil or embarrassment, the natural energy of my mind kept me from ennui & I had a good collection of books—Johnson's Poets—Hume—Gibbon, Robertson & many of our best authors both in History & ethics. But alas a Cloud was fast approaching which must soon change this serene sky to gloom.

Charlotte is down to her last ten pounds, her father and Mr Beaufoy, both perhaps under the influence of Heaviside, no longer support her, she speaks not a word of Welsh and although she could teach she cannot bear the idea of being 'surrounded by *dirty* children.' One suspects she has little by way of motherly instincts. She returns to Peterborough House where she is placed under the protection of Heaviside's mother who stipulates that her son remain in Kent. Arrangements are made for her to go abroad to a convent. Soon enough, however, her oppressor returns.

> Moreover the ungovernable passions of Mr H— rendered the House often a scene of nightly disorder—for in these frenzies he would break open the doors—get in at the windows & commit all sorts of outrages—so that I was often obliged to make one of the maids sleep in my room.

At last, and here I will spare the reader the complexities relating to her obtaining an annuity, she makes her escape. 'Thus, my dear General, I have brought you through the most melancholy part of my History … my residence in the Convent—my Marriage—& all the subsequent events you may (if I live) learn by degrees—.' The ending is not wholly satisfactory, all sorts of roots are left dangling in the air, but then this was never meant to be literature.

A week after the loss of the manuscript John Byrne received a phone call at work. It was Westminster police station. A policeman had discovered a black leather bag in an open space in the middle of a housing estate just down the road from where the mugging took place. It was the very place where my wife had had a brief look. It had been lying there for several days in the rain and not a single person was curious enough to investigate. I heard John Byrne ask after the contents of the bag. The bag itself was in a sorry state and all the papers inside had been either torn to pieces or else seriously damaged by water. Well, *almost* all of them. Charlotte's manuscript, which had been tucked in between the pages of a copy of *The Times*, because it was written in iron-based ink on handmade paper, was barely affected.

Quality is a passport to permanence.

* * *

While, during the first months of their separation, Charlotte was going through experiences that would forever alter the course of her life the young man who left her was going through various twists and turns that would forever alter his. In order to explain how will require a certain amount of backtracking and also, on the part of the reader, a submission to the curious workings of fate.

Ochterlony was born on February 12, 1758, in pre-Revolutionary America, in Boston, in the very house where, some years later, Paul Revere would pause on his famous ride. (There are, apparently, a number of such places.) His father was in the merchant service. At some point David Sr. fell in with one of London's underworld figures, Laughlin Macleane, 'distinguished in his day, it is said, for great abilities and lax morals.' There is even a school of thought that he might have been the author of the 'Junius' letters. An associate of his would later write, 'If he involved others he only did to them what he did without mercy to himself.' Macleane's biographer writes:

> He was a scoundrel with a host of faults, but a likeable scoundrel; and his courage was beyond doubt. The key to his character was his stutter. It drove him on, and, at the same time, held him back. Unlike Burke and Wilkes, who could dominate large gatherings with their golden-tongued eloquence, Macleane was almost inarticulate. With such a limiting affliction he had no hope of succeeding in the wider political arena, and so he exercised his talents in the shadows of the underworld.*

Macleane had gone to America, perhaps to escape his association with a highwayman, his very distant relative James, who was hanged at Tyburn. His biographer notes, 'People added two and two together and made five.' In America, in the company of his enormously fat and dumpy wife 'devoted to a lap-dog of swollen proportions which waddled along in front of her,' he took up the role of military surgeon and was not a bad one at that. After all, who, back then, needed experience? It was during Macleane's American period that he borrowed money from Ochterlony's father. David Sr. died suddenly in 1765 leaving his family almost destitute and Dr. Macleane was seen no more.

Soon after, the young Ochterlony went to England where some years later his mother remarried. He went to work for his stepfather, Sir Isaac Heard, at the Herald's Office in London although there he could 'never give his mind to the art and mystery of blazoning coats of arms.' Somehow he came into touch with Macleane who by now had become Under Secretary of State and First Commissioner for the affairs of the Nuwab of the Carnatic. Although he still did not have the money to discharge his old debt he offered to place the son of his creditor in the service of the

* James N. M. Maclean, *Reward Is Secondary* (Hodder and Stoughton, 1963).

above Prince at Madras. Ochterlony, eagerly accepting the offer, was taken for a short time into the Commissioner's Office in order that he might learn the forms of Indian business. It was during this time, one supposes, that he met Charlotte. On July 15, 1777, he sailed out of Portsmouth on the *Lord North*. Some eight or nine months previously, Macleane had gone ahead to Madras. It is here that I invite the reader to fix his eyes on the globe, imagining the *Lord North* on its journey from England, and HMS *Swallow*, the naval sloop Macleane was on, making its journey from India. The two ships met up at Cape Town in November. It was a fortuitous meeting because there Macleane furnished Ochterlony with recommendatory letters to the Nuwab and other people of influence. One might well ask why Ochterlony had not been given these before, for they were absolutely essential to his welfare. Anyway, Macleane would appear to have made good his promise. And it was there, in Cape Town, that Macleane had an uncanny premonition of his death. 'Considering the Perils of the Seas,' he immediately sat down and made out his last will and testament, a gloriously eccentric document in which he makes provisions not just for his wife but also for Margaret and Jane Satterthwaite, one or both of whom, sisters presumably, were mothers to his children. The HMS *Swallow* set sail on St. Andrew's Day and bobbed upon perilous waves while, in London, Charlotte swam against another tide. On June 10, 1778, Laurence Sulivan, MP, sent a letter to Lord Hastings: 'All hopes of Macleane are now at an end, as we have heard from the Brazils and all parts of America, but no account of the *Swallow*. At first I lamented his loss as a heavy misfortune, to myself particularly. I have now some reason to change that opinion, and perhaps his death has saved me an increase of misery ... I built too much on his remembering what he owed me.' Hastings wrote to Elijah Impey on August 10, 1778: 'Poor Macleane! It was believed in England that the *Swallow*, a crazy ship, foundered in a great storm in February.' As his biographer writes, 'In the end it was not a man but the wild elements that defeated the tough, brave, corrupt old roué.'

Ochterlony, meanwhile, quite unaware of his shady benefactor's fate, sailed on to Madras. And it is here that Captain Thomas

Smith, in his *Narrative of a Five Years' Residence at Nepaul*, picks up the story:

> A Chief Justice, who happened to be his fellow-passenger, accommodated the cadet on landing in the East; but falling in with another young officer (afterwards the Honourable Sir Thomas Maitland), they visited some place of public resort of that time, which was probably not as respectable as the modern clubs and hotels at the Indian presidencies, since it is certain that the destined conqueror of Nepaul there had his pocket picked of the letters which the commissioner [Macleane] had written to get him established, until he should make his fortune in peaceful employment.

Ochterlony, so quickly a novice in the ways of nautch girls, went to the various offices of the Nuwab, at which he was informed there was no need for his services. The letters of introduction were forever gone and so too, although Ochterlony was not to know this, was Macleane. The only thing left for him to do was to proceed to Bengal where he would await a fresh set of letters from England and in the meantime, so that he might survive, he joined the army of the East India Company. Little did he realise that he would wait forever. It is extraordinary to consider how Macleane, even in death, had been the determining factor in both Ochterlony's and Charlotte's lives.

* * *

The search to discover Charlotte's identity was not an easy one. At one point I had her eloping to Gretna Green with the notorious seventh Earl of Barrymore (a worthy successor to Heaviside). I never did get to the bottom of that blank Gretna Green marriage licence. I contacted the Bristol Record Office to find out who lived at 7 Pritchard Street and was informed that it was a Mrs Rachel Biggs. This, I assumed, must be the relative Charlotte mentions in her narrative. At least I had a B—, though. *B* for *Biggs*. A friend of mine, Wendy Saloman, confounded matters somewhat by turning up a Will in the name of Rachel *Charlotte* Williams Biggs. The path from one Charlotte to another is too labyrinthine to retrace, especially in an age abounding with Charlottes, and, quite frankly, I could not have strayed further in my researches.

A couple of months later, I checked the name Biggs in the British Library's manuscript index and found an entry for some letters from a Mrs R. C. Biggs to William Windham (1750–1810) who was a leading statesman and secretary at war under Pitt. When the letters arrived at my desk I saw immediately they were in Charlotte's hand. So the Rachel Biggs at Pritchard Street *was* the right one. I suspect that after Charlotte made her final escape from Heaviside she reverted to her original first name as a kind of subterfuge. She may have been the Charlotte Williams, daughter of John and Mary, who was baptized at St Sepulchre, Holborn, on December 10, 1761. There were Williamses everywhere, and nothing regarding them is absolutely certain, but a John Williams paid rates in Lambeth and a Mary died there in 1780.

The letters to Windham date from 1800 to 1806 and their contents are not immediately arresting. 'I have hitherto been so fortunate as to live in a domestic retired way,' she writes. 'And nothing would distress me more than to be thought a Person of literary pretensions by my neighbours.' The address she gives is Farrington House, 'at least eight miles from Wells, & out of every road except that to Bristol,' and the correspondence begins, unpromisingly, with a proposal that gamekeepers' licences be raised. I shuddered to think that between her and the days of Heaviside there had been only acre upon acre of rural stuffiness. This was not the way for my story to go. When I got to the third letter, however, something wholly unexpected began to emerge.

> The character of a female author, or female politician is not in my opinion calculated to create favourable impressions & it is certain that the situations I have been placed in, and the circumstances of the times only, could have tempted me to engage in pursuits of so unfeminine a nature.—It was impossible for any thinking person to witness (as I have done)

> the effects of the french Revolution, without feeling a deep & animated hatred against the principles which produced it, & in endeavouring to inspire others with the sentiments I had imbibed myself I have neglected no duty, & have only devoted those hours to my country, which I am at liberty to devote to amusement.

She then describes how, on her return from France in the summer of 1795, she made attempts to get a manuscript published.

> I apply'd in consequence to Mr Stockdale as a person I understood to be favor'd by Government, but I received only an impolite & repulsive answer and my work which I had exposed my life in writing, after having been discovered & detained at Dover, as probably seditious, & rejected with disdain by the bookseller as anonymous, was consigned to obscurity.—Alarm'd however at the supineness I observed in the rich, & indignant at the seductions practiced on the poor, & with a spirit perhaps imbittered by what I had recently seen & suffered in France, I devoted my leisure to conveying through the public prints such facts & reflections as I hoped might (tho' in ever so small a degree) tend to counteract the attempts then making to corrupt & ruin the Country.

During the course of her correspondence with the *True Briton*, she mentions having come to the notice of John Gifford.

John Gifford (1758–1818) has done rather poorly in the literary stakes: he has been described as 'a dull dog' and 'a feeble scarabæcide,' and his massive political life of Pitt gathers dust on library shelves. He was born John Richards Green, but after squandering a huge inheritance fled to France where he changed his name. When he returned to England he became a government pamphleteer and, later, founder and editor of the *Anti-Jacobin Review and Magazine.* As a reward for his political services he was made a political magistrate. It is a particularly cruel fate to be remembered as a bore, and redemption, however slight, must come to him who took up Charlotte's cause. I rushed to the British Library catalogue of books but found nothing under the name Biggs to fit the description of a book about France. I then checked under 'Gifford, John' and there I discovered *A Residence in France, during the Years 1792, 1793, 1794, and 1795; described in a Series of Letters from an English Lady: with general and incidental Remarks on the French Character and Manners, Prepared for the Press by John Gifford*, published by Longmans in 1797. Charlotte, it appeared, had escaped Heaviside only to be caught up in the French Revolution.

The reason she gives for not putting her name to the book is that she fears for the safety of those people she knows still living in France. While there is little doubting the integrity in this, I cannot but suppose that anonymity must have suited a woman so doubtful of her own abilities. When she writes to Windham of the mediocrity of her talents there is, I suspect, rather more here than just the usual apologia of the age. Although the book went into a third edition in the same year, its reputation did not survive beyond this final round of applause. Subsequently its authorship has been attributed to Helen Maria Williams, a lady of distinctly Jacobin sympathies, and in some instances to Gifford himself, although it is obvious that his blue pencil barely touched its pages.

'Most of these letters were written in the situation they describe,' she explains, 'and remain in their original state.' It was then fashionable to address a subject in the form of letters, and here the artifice, if that is what it is, works to great advantage. Charlotte writes in a style that is immediate, and as the Jacobins rise to power the French scene she describes gradually darkens. 'Our society consists mostly of females,' she writes. 'And we do not venture out, but rather hover together like the fowls of heaven, when warned by a vague yet instinctive dread of the approaching form.' As the printed text of *A Residence in France* runs to almost a thousand pages, concealment of the manuscript must have been a problem. In one extraordinary episode, during which armed men search Charlotte's room, she distracts them 'with the sight of a blue-bottle fly through a microscope' while a servant removes some letters which had been lying on the table. She manages to keep writing even through her imprisonment in Arras—yes, she comes close to losing her head—but this is a story which needs to be repeated in her own words elsewhere.

If the writing palls at times it is because Charlotte constantly analyses. She is motivated above all by a duty to explain to the English people the causes and effects of a revolution they might be otherwise tempted to imitate. As such her remarks are a testament to her mental vigilance, but the sense of *being there* is conveyed to us most vividly in those passages where she simply observes.

> The belief in religious miracles is exploded, and it is only in political ones that the faith of the people is allowed to exhibit itself.—We have lately seen exhibited at the fairs and markets a calf, produced into the world with the tri-coloured cockade on its head; and on the painted cloth that announces the phaenomenon is the portrait of this natural revolutionist, with a mayor and municipality in their official scarfs, addressing the four-footed patriot with great ceremony.

Her analysis of the French psyche borders on the tedious at times but she manages to make those who are her companions come alive. Madame de—, 'a French woman, who rouges, and wears lilac ribbons, at seventy-four,' tries hard not to look like an aristocrat. She dons revolutionary attire, but is unable to travel anywhere without her pet canaries, some exotic plants, a lap dog and a cat, and two servants to take care of them. I rather hope she survived. Despite my reservations, and these are probably of a meanness shaped by literature, the book is, in many respects, remarkable.*

I sought some kind of link between these experiences and her earlier ones, and found it in her mention of the convent she went to after her final escape from Heaviside. She is imprisoned in Arras with a friend whom she says she first met some years before at the

* The story of Charlotte in France has been taken considerably further in Joanne Major and Sarah Murden's *A Georgian Heroine: The Intriguing Life of Rachel Charlotte Williams Biggs* (2017).

Panthemont in Paris. This, according to one source, was one of the most aristocratic convents in France, '*"un immense hotel garni" ouvert aux femmes de la première distinction*.' It was inexpensive, had a huge library, and it was undoubtedly there that Charlotte furthered her education. Much mystery still surrounds Charlotte. Only once, in her correspondence with Windham, does she mention a husband: 'Mr Biggs has been lingering above eighteen months & is now in so deplorable a state that my only hope of his surviving the Winter is taking him to a milder climate [...] There was a time when Peace with the French Emperor would not have been remembered in my orisons, but I confess I am little of a Heroine & think more of my Husband than my Country.' The correspondence with Windham stops there, with this one and only mention of the husband who for now must remain a shadowy figure. Six years later, on May 15, 1816, presumably widowed, she is in Paris throwing a ball in honour of Ochterlony. What was she doing there so soon in the wake of Waterloo? Was she one of the fashionable ladies who followed the war almost to the brink of battle? In 1821 she is in Pritchard Street, Bristol, and the only other record I have found is that she died in a Versailles lodging house on February 24, 1827.

Not too long after he had been constrained to resign his high political office and was then planning a return to England, Ochterlony died in Meerut on July 15, 1825. One account has him turning against the wall, muttering, 'I have been betrayed.' Richard Heaviside died in 1815. A couple of years after the discovery of Charlotte's manuscript, while wandering through Bath Abbey, I noticed a tablet on the wall dedicated to the memory of Richard Heaviside.

HUJUS COLUMNAE SEPULTUS EFT AD PEDEM,
RICARDUS HEAVISIDE ARMIGER. IN
AGRO DUNELM NATUS, QUI BATHONIAE
OBIIT 12MO APRILLIS, A.S. MDCCCXV.
AMUM AGENS LXII R.I.P.

Bristol, Bath. Mr H— had remained geographically close.

Chapter Nine

THE DISEMBOWELLING OF PHANTOMS

'A MAN WITH HIS HAIR COMBED BACK LOOKS LIKE A MAN who is going somewhere.' This was not so much an observation from the Commander of TANKS as an injunction for me to do likewise. I do not have, nor have I ever possessed, a comb. The reader may infer from this whatever he wishes. Another ghost enters these pages, a ghost noisier than most, a ghost hungry for a fix, a ghost that rules by decree. William Hoffer was an antiquarian bookseller in Vancouver, a small publisher of poetry and prose, including some of my own, and the Commander-in-Chief of TANKS, a pseudo-military operation he devised in order to rid the world of arts bureaucracies and the collaborators who keep them in place. A fierce opponent of government subsidies, he sought to expose the system of favours that pervades every area of the arts in Canada and elsewhere. I became, during that short but heroic age, District Commissioner for Europe. We sent each other regular communiqués from our respective fronts, casualty figures and so forth, dwelling on our own dashing manoeuvres. Small silver tanks were awarded to heroes.* Hoffer wore a gold one. There were, apparently, four others to be given to the most distinguished fighters in the cause, but it seems that nobody could meet his stringent ideas of excellence. There were, of course, neither tanks nor casualties. We falsified figures. We pronounced as dead people who were still very much alive. And the front was wherever we decided it was. I think it's fair to say we were the merrily driven slaves of dubious enthusiasm. Should the reader conclude that Hoffer was wholly objectionable, the case can be made that to those whom he liked he could be wholly likeable. A man of Swiftian wit, he could make the glasses on the table dance. As to those whom he disliked, with them he could be cruel and unreasonable. What makes it particularly difficult to write about him is that no two people agree on his difficult nature.

My friend Norm Sibum makes a decent go of it in his essay "William Hoffer and the Theology of Snooker" (Des Antipodes, 2011) in which he employs the analogy of snooker, a single evening's game in particular, as the key to Hoffer's psyche. Actually it is by far the best thing I have read on him. Sibum is a poet and during the 1970s he was Hoffer's protégé, which had both its good and its bad side. Support is one thing, control another: it got so Hoffer would vet the women in Sibum's life. The two spent many hours together in the bookshop on Water Street in Gastown.† There was a single occasion when Sibum drank with him at the No5 Orange, a strip club where Bill, as I shall now address him, liked to do his business accounts, the writhing bodies on stage providing not so much an erotic as a sympathetic working atmosphere. A 'true democracy' was how he described the place. And then there was the Old Europa restaurant whose owner disliked Bill, possibly because he was Hungarian and Bill Jewish, possibly because of the latter's insulin rages. Bill suffered badly from diabetes, insulin

* Sadly I lost mine.

† The area got its name from 'Gassy Jack' Deighton who opened a pub there in 1867. 'Gassy' owes its origin to verbal flatulence and not, as some people might think, other causes.

shock a common feature of his life. When he was in a fix, and the service slow, he'd shoot up in the booth, which disconcerted the rest of the clientele. I remember occasions when he came to dinner at our place, almost frantic that we begin immediately on the first course. And finally there was the snooker hall where one evening he and Sibum had their high noon and, a familiar trope of western movies, one man measured the other. Bill, on occasion, wore a cowboy hat which sat oddly on his very Semitic features.

'Theology was entertainment,' Sibum writes. 'Snooker was, after all, theological. Snooker, within its rectangular confines, in the arrangement of the snooker balls at the outset of each game, had a vague cruciate aspect.' And then, most craftily, switching from the first to the second person singular, Sibum applies this to the art of bookselling although maybe not quite in the language of the stolid Antiquarian Booksellers' Association: 'If playing snooker was your religion, your default position, the collecting and selling of books was the secular expression of some creed or another, I'm not sure which. Or rather, it was the exercise of reason as opposed to faith. It was Aristotle as opposed to St Francis, Confucius as opposed to a squatting Buddhist wailing away on weird instruments. Perhaps, more precisely, it was politics. Civilization at stake, the arts of the book trade were imperilled too. The bookseller should hold himself apart from the consumerist hell we were all of us falling into head over heels; yet he should conduct himself as an honourable capitalist honouring proper market values. It was your romanticism.'

This is all quite excellent but, without wishing to better my colleague, I submit there may be a more accurate place in which to locate Bill's character and that is in the ancient Chinese game of Go. The most complicated game in existence, the number of legal board positions exceeds, so I read somewhere, *the number of atoms in the observable universe.* I should think that would just about accommodate Bill, give or take a few particles. The object of the game is to outdo one's opponent by surrounding as much territory as possible. It is for Go players rather more than a game; it is life itself. Sun Tzu, author of *The Art of War*, must have played;

Machiavelli, who also wrote a book called *The Art of War*, would surely have played had he known of it. When it becomes spiritual warfare then it is time for the player to pay close attention to the heart's occurrences. I broke mine at the chessboard. Bill broke his at the Go board. (There is no explaining this to one who does not participate in either game.) Wang Jixin, a notable Go player of the Tang dynasty, formulated the Ten Golden Rules of Go, the last of which enjoins the player to seek peace and to avoid fighting in an isolated or weak situation. If Bill had more closely observed the tenth rule, he might not have gone for broke. And indeed he might have inflicted more casualties. He must have been pretty good though or at the very least as good as his own description of himself as 'the best Caucasian Go player in town.' A former assistant of his, Cheryl Cooper, cannot remember him ever losing a game. She recalls the free-standing Go table with its two jars of black and white stones respectively, which followed him from his first bookshop to his last one, and the strange characters who would show up out of nowhere. The games, if the players were of equal stature, would go on for days at a time. A black stone sitting on its grid was the design Bill adopted for his business card and letterhead.

'He was always strategizing,' Cheryl tells me, 'always in war mode, always surrounding the territory of his opponents.'

She goes on to produce a most telling anecdote.

'He once told me he could follow the trajectory of rumours, who said what when and to whom and how much the story changed, because he himself had started the original rumour with the express purpose of seeing who betrayed him.'

I remember being disturbed by the way he could cut through, and frustrate, other people's moves. I'm speaking of life, not Go, although for players of it they are inseparable. I was largely spared the manipulative side of his nature. It might have been different had I been in Canada where he was at his most extreme. When he came to England he put on his best face. For one thing he was up against an older breed of bookseller. Also there were people here who appreciated his savage wit and intelligence. One of them, Susan Biltcliffe, who worked for the bookseller Peter Eaton, became his lover, or, rather, the woman with whom he sailed under a flag of convenience. She was the lady in his port of call and happy to be so. Another ghost, a pretty one. The first time I set eyes on her was at the 1984 Antiquarian Book Fair on Park Lane. She was going about in bare feet, which, in a situation I have always regarded as arid with impotence, greatly increased her allure. She was a deeply serious bookseller, however, and for her own pleasure collected Victorian ephemera and, in depth, the books of Herbert Read, among collectors not many of those. The last time I saw her was at a party where, absolutely skeletal, with only weeks to live, she danced herself into a frenzy, her arms spasmodic, her eyes closed, continuing alone long after the others stopped to watch this solitary dance of death, either embarrassed for her or for themselves.

The game of Go is applicable to bookselling or, more precisely, book buying, which is where the greater strategy lies. You don't sell a book, you let it go. Buying, on the other hand, is the art of the possible. As soon as one enters a room of books one enters uncharted territory and the thing is to be able to meet the other person's expectations without sacrificing too many of one's own pieces. The most awful thing is to make an offer that is refused, there being very little way forward and even less of one back. A wise offer is that which allows for a margin of compromise between buyer and seller and in this, of course, a certain amount of psychology comes into play. As a rule one has but a single chance at securing a decent collection and, more often than not, one can tell in advance whether the seller is going to quibble. One offers just a bit less in order to allow for a bit more. You can usually spot the difficult ones. Bill was, predictably, very good at it. And what he was even better at, surely the mark of a distinguished bookseller, was reading significance into books otherwise dull to the eye. 'I am a bookseller,' he writes in one of his pieces, 'a man who has literature in his profession. I am a successful bookseller at the midpoint of my professional life. The apprenticeship of an antiquarian bookseller is long. It is generally assumed that twenty years is too short a time to justify the unselfconscious use of the term bookseller. My profession is old, it has old rules. Honesty is a prerequisite, not an accomplishment. Because a bookseller has so many opportunities to be dishonest, it is simply the case that dishonest booksellers are not tolerated by the profession. One can always find exceptions, but even those are rare in the small community of professional booksellers through the world.'

The first time Bill came into Bertram Rota was in order to seek out first editions of Canadian authors, which, given his antipathy for the greater part of his country's literature, may be viewed as hypocrisy. I believe it was otherwise and that he would not allow prejudice to get in the way of selling a book. Almost immediately he fell upon a copy of *All That Is Mine Demand: War Poems of Nordhal Grieg* (1944). I tried to save him from error.

'Grieg is not Canadian,' I said. 'He's Norwegian.'

Bill looked at me with something like pity in his eyes. I was then given a brief lesson in Canadian literature. Grieg's novel *The Ship Sails On* (1927) had been a great influence on Malcolm Lowry's first book *Ultramarine* (1933) and Lowry, although English, by virtue of living in Canada, albeit briefly, has been co-opted as a Canadian author. *So there.* I stood corrected. We became friends, improbable friends maybe, but friends all the same.

Three books I most actively sought at the time, Joseph Conrad's *Nostromo* (1904), Bruno Schulz's *Cinnamon Shops and Other Stories* (1963) and the three-volume *Letters of Emily Dickinson* (1979), I bought from him. They were not unreasonably priced, but neither were they cheap because, a professional to the core, he was not about to make concessions to friendship. I was particularly happy with the Bruno Schulz, which had hitherto eluded me. Schulz seeded in me the notion that there are 'secret books' that act as keys to the universe. Bill gave me two books. They were expressions of who he was, which, I suppose, is one of the things that makes a gift a gift. The first was a modern edition of Moses Maimonides's *Guide for the Perplexed*, a stab at which left me more perplexed than before. It was, for Bill, a manual on how to behave. The other was Wesley W. Stout's *Tanks Are Mighty Fine Things*, published by the Chrysler

Corporation in 1946 as a commemoration of its contribution to the American war effort. Chrysler's Sherman M4 dominated its German equivalents, the Tiger and the Panther, which, although bigger and mightier, were quickly overrun by the smaller, faster American tank. A good historical parallel would be the defeat of the Spanish Armada by smaller, faster English ships. The book is inscribed on the title page: 'Office Copy—London Command—from William Hoffer cmdr of Tanks (retired). Nov 10, 1988.' The first title appealed to his sanity, the second his madness, which is not to suggest there is any great distance between the two mental states, only that one cost him more.

So why did he who abhorred so much of his country's literature specialise in Canadian literature? A sublimely rude answer can be found in his essay "Cheap Sons of Bitches: Memoirs of the Book Trade" (1988)*: 'I became a dealer in Canadian literature somewhat opportunistically, and because, when I first commenced bookselling, I was worried that I wouldn't want to sell books that I actually liked, Canadian literature recommended itself.' When he bought three thousand volumes of Canadiana in Iver, in Buckinghamshire, he had them shipped to Halifax, Nova Scotia, as far from Vancouver as he could manage. 'I flew across Canada to sort them out,' he wrote me. 'The thought of adding more volumes of Canadiana to the local ecosystem was sufficiently abhorrent to me that breaking them in the East seemed best.' In *A Statement* (1987), which he published under the imprint of the 'final judgement construction company,' he writes: 'I have encountered nothing good or interesting in what passes for Canadian culture. Not only are our authors not really authors, but neither are our booksellers really booksellers, our distributors really distributors, our reviewers really reviewers or our readers really readers. At the moment the most urgent "cultural" debate in British Columbia

* The title, as Hoffer properly acknowledges, comes from the American poet Kenneth Rexroth who declared, 'I've had it with these cheap sons of bitches who claim they love poetry but never buy a book.' It was John Metcalf who suggested it to him.

relates to dirt bike racing somewhere in the hinterland. The dance critic at the Vancouver *Province*, a cretin at the best of times, most recently devoted himself to a celebration of Dirty Dancing, thinking perhaps to make something Canadian of it by the laying on of his bloody Canadian hands. I am reminded I chose to become a bookseller in quest of shelter from the imbeciles I knew in my university days, thinking then, as I do now, that superior human beings tend to frequent bookshops.' And then he goes on to write: 'Contrary to what some of you may believe, my concern about the state of the arts in Canada is real; I have no argument with that real literature and art Canadians have made in the past. I am (and feel) Canadian. *I will not leave this country on any account.*' (The italics are mine for reasons that will soon become clear.) Certainly in our conversation, once he got beyond tirade or was sufficiently anaesthetised with wine, he did give the impression of one who cared deeply about literature. Sobriety put him in a less sympathetic mode.

Confrontational he most certainly was, but if you met him head-on he would back down not in fear but with the thought that here perhaps was someone he could talk to. Certainly he was "too much" for Anthony Rota, the Tory man of order as opposed to the Marxist bringer of chaos, and it was one of the few times I ever saw the former completely rattled. 'I watched his face turn white,' Bill told me. There was nothing in Anthony Rota's armoury with which to confront the likes of a verbal gunslinger from Saskatoon. A child of the Canadian prairies, it was there that Bill honed his own rhetorical style. Once more, Cheryl is my guide: Bill told her how as a child he'd watch for hours on end evangelical TV preachers. These were of a specific prairie vintage and, unlike their neighbours to the south, promulgated a socialist programme. Tommy Douglas, who founded the New Democratic Party, which is as far left as Canadian politics goes, began as a preacher. Bill was much further to the left than him, being rooted in Marxism and radical student politics, and as we all know, Marxists are most adept at capitalist ventures. Bill's politics was nothing new to me, and normally I bit my lip, but I was horrified by his defence of Felix Dzerzhinsky, leader of the Cheka and, under Stalin, architect of the "Red Terror." When I protested at the Soviet domination of Poland he said it was punishment for the country's treatment of the Jews. It was futile to argue back that the greater number of Poland's Jews were refugees escaping Russian pogroms. Bill was 'more Jewish' than he cared to admit. A rabbi in Saskatoon ached to denounce him as an anti-Semite. Others did. What he liked most about Israel, he told me, were the pretty women with dark eyes carrying machine guns. A favourite point of reference was the Yiddish proverb: *Der schelchter emes is besserer vi der bester lign.* ('The worst truth is better than the best lie.') Also he was fond of the Talmudic statement: 'He who pities the wicked oppresses the just.'

Bill's father, Abram, was probably the only man he ever truly feared. A physician and psychiatrist who, depending on which side of the fence you were, was either a charlatan or a scientific visionary cheated of the Nobel Prize. He was a pioneer of orthomolecular psychiatry, megavitamin therapy the be-all for mental illness, vitamin C his weapon of choice. The rebel psychiatrist and author of *The Myth of Mental Illness* (1961), Thomas Szasz, accused Dr Abram Hoffer of 'pure quackery.' The medical establishment trounced him. All I know is that I would choose orange juice over Prozac any time. Bill's mother, Rose, was co-author of *Everybody's Favourite (Orthomolecular) Muffin Book* (1980). Abram, together with his wife and colleagues, experimented in the medical use of LSD, which he advanced as a cure for alcoholism. I wonder how many experiments it took for him to arrive at that conclusion. Most troublingly, the father administered LSD to the son. Whether this was under strict laboratory control or within the confines of home is not known. Bill claimed he was given it when he was three, but then he also claimed it was in his early teens. Certainly he had it when he was eighteen because it resulted in a serious verbal haemorrhage, some lines of verse which begin, 'A million mindless echoes in my head / Nail me to my coffin-bed.' Whatever the damage, maybe even because of it, Bill revered his father all the more. A copy of *The Hallucinogens* (1967), inscribed by its co-author, 'To Pat & Bill /

Dec 15 '67 / Abram"* (an association copy if ever there was one), is the only book in Bill's personal archive. Shortly before he died, Bill wrote words to the effect there was a gulf between father and son, albeit a narrow one: 'My father's definition of recovery in the case of mentally ill patients is that moment at which they are paying taxes. Of course he is right; and yet, if my father were God and the ways in which he is right were universal, we would live utterly uninteresting lives. Our lives would undoubtedly be longer and healthier, and to that degree we would not invent devils or dream up purgatories in which to live with them.'

Poets, mostly bad ones, were the chief targets of Bill's ire. One could build an argument for poetry being, in his mind, the purest of art forms and therefore the most corruptible, but I suspect the main thrust of his campaign against poets had its roots in his inability to ever be one himself. This is not to say he didn't try; there is a typescript of an unpublished collection called *The Plague Year*. As publisher, he followed his fancies. As bookseller, he had a witch-finder's nose. As critic, he swung between the erratic and the precise. When he hit, he hit hard. Pity the poet whose intellect he described as being akin to a very thin layer of ice covering a very large lake. Pity the poet he described as walking about like some Greek god nobody has ever heard of. Pity the poet he described as 'a lump of lead that believes itself to be an intricate construction of glass threads that exchange light in ways never before known either to glass or lead.' And then there was the suppressed one-line obituary notice in which he wrote that although he had been saddened to hear of the manner by which a certain poet was silenced he was grateful for the silence nonetheless. Clearly he was not a man to be allowed airtime. The support he gave to several poets was, perhaps, a resolving of an inner conflict but in this, as in much else, he probably pushed too far. He sought control over what they wrote and in doing so traded critical acumen for a rather blunt and rusty knife.

---

* Pat was Bill's wife of the time.

Nor were booksellers spared his wrath. Pity the unsuspecting bookseller who had sent him a catalogue: 'I examined it with what charity I have surplus,' Bill responded, 'but it wasn't enough to prevent a prevalence of simply organic illness in its consequence. I withdraw my invitation of last year. I don't want to know you or to see you. Stay in your silly place and do whatever it is you use in place of honest brooding. I will prevent your entry into my honourable trade. You are no bookseller, you never will be one. You are what you seem, a fool with no future. I do not leap rashly to this conclusion. I have considered it all day. It is evening now. [...] I grant you your pacifism, indeed, I congratulate you for it. You made the right move; you qualify yourself to consort with cowards. Remove me from your mailing list. I have removed you from mine. I will be grateful not to hear your name again. I have more important things to do than to encourage cockroaches to play at being human.' Nor would he encourage humans to be booksellers. One hapless character in Vancouver, thinking he might enter the trade, walked into Bill's shop and offered to work for nothing to which the response was that those people who offer to work for nothing are worth *just that.*

Hair slicked back, Bill was a man *going somewhere*, his whole physical being concentrated in a purposeful stride, and yet, as Sibum writes, 'it was the body of clown ... as capable as it was of sudden and violent movement, it lacked athletic grace.' Lest the idea of neatly combed hair should bring to mind the image of an executive, Bill was nothing of the sort. He was unkempt, his beard untrimmed, and he wore jackets, often a size too small, that his mother bought him at rummage sales, the pockets of which he'd fill with cigarette ashes. Unkinder things have been said of him. I'm not out to challenge a man's hygiene. I am more interested in the good health of his mind. What's to be said of a man who could evoke such a wide range of feeling? He often told me that he had no overwhelming desire for respect or even love, but he did hope for people's *regard*.

Sentiment was an obstacle. A customer had asked him to find the missing two volumes to an incomplete set of books—I can't remember what they were, but they touched on some aspect of Canadiana and were very rare. There is nothing in the world more painful for a collector than an incomplete set. My set of Turgenev lacks a volume, which in some obscure way makes me feel incomplete. I only have to look at it for my soul to wince. I know, too, that if I ever do find the missing volume it will be an impostor with identical features. Other people won't notice, but I will know. Bill had already supplied his customer one of two missing volumes and quite by chance, in the most improbable of places, in England, he located the other. This was when the terrible news came; the collector had died in the meantime. I thought I saw, just then, a flicker of sentiment in Bill's face, and even, if one had the instrument sensitive enough to measure it, a slight quaver in his voice. Bill stared fixedly into the distance. I was about to wax lyrical on the workings of fate when, muttering a curse, he wondered aloud how he'd be able to persuade the widow to let him have the other volumes. An incomplete set was for him infinitely more terrible than the very complete end of a man's life.

If there was poetry in Bill it was not in his poems, where every word hobbled across the page, but in his letters. I took pleasure in stealing from them: 'It's a universe all rusty fish-hooks and spiritual collapse'; this, ironically enough, appears in the poem of mine that he hated most. John Hudson's printing of it, *Doctor Honoris Causa* (1991), saw him expelled from Bill's court. After he died, I wrote a poem for Bill, which, again, contains the spoils of my looting sprees: 'Wicked men gnaw at their own ankles', '… lovers who seem to stand for lovers, / Children who seem to stand for children,' … 'What gastric condition leads to such grimaces,' etc. There are, reportedly, collectors of Bill's correspondence and there's a mighty heap of it at the Lilly Library in Bloomington, Indiana, including the letters he wrote to his close friend and mentor, Peter Howard of Serendipity Books. Some of the best letters to me are those in which he describes everyday events in the bookshop. 'It has started to rain; the crazed inhabitants of the street are being flushed out, and stagger past the shop with their huge heads grimly positioned a foot or so off centre. Indians, postgraduate drunks. The dark menace of the shop's black iron bars and recessed entrance keep them out; occasionally one will crawl up the stairs and gape, like a sea creature accidentally hauled to the surface. I walked up to the corner store, wandering through the antique shop across the street. The talk is about a pimp murdered in a club a few hundred feet from here, at midnight. Anything is preferable to Salman Rushdie.'*

What distinguished Bill from many of his tribe was that he could be just as ruthless in the business of *not* selling a book. Cheryl provides an example. One day a man brought a book to the desk for purchase and after looking it over Bill asked him why he wanted to buy it. Unsatisfied with the response, he told him, 'I can't sell this to you. You are not worthy of it.' Bill put into practice what most booksellers think but rarely activate. Yes, it is painful to sell a book one likes to someone one dislikes. I am happy to say that on occasion I've refused to sell a book to a customer. Another story concerns a man who wandered into Bill's shop, asking for books on astrology. According to his assistant of the time, Bill strong-armed the man out of the place.

'Out of here,' he told him, 'and don't ever come back.'

Bill turned to see the shocked expression on his assistant's face.

'What's *your* problem?'

'The man you threw out ...' she stuttered.

'Yes,' he barked, 'what of it?'

'That was Leonard Cohen.'

Interestingly enough, Sibum touches on the very same, only there is no poet/singer in the picture: 'You regarded with a cobra's eyes any client unsound enough in body and mind to enter your shop looking for books of astrology. "You can't spiritually afford it." And so you pronounced the dark oracle's dark admonition to some goose of a mongoose. You scared such a customer within an inch of his life. "A public service" you contended. As, indeed, it was.'

---

* This was written at the time of the furore surrounding the publication of *The Satanic Verses* (1988).

Argument, Hoffer claimed, was a poor substitute for action. 'I don't want your ideas about literature,' he cried. 'I want body counts!' The day would come when "war criminals," as he dubbed his foes, would crawl towards, climb onto and willingly immolate themselves upon heaps of smouldering bodies. There was no area so delicate he did not risk being puerile. Once, at a party in London, catching sight of a buxom woman who choked the room with her perfume, he pointed to her, crying, 'There, *there* is the dolphin to which we'll attach our missiles!' At his best, though, he could be brilliant: 'We live in an age in which intellectuals have imagined that miracles could be made with the mind alone. A writer isn't someone who writes, he is someone who is read. An architect without a carpenter is nothing but a dreamer. Regarding it, I decided that I must be a carpenter more importantly than I could ever be an architect. There is more honour in architecture, or at least there was once.'

What was TANKS exactly? An answer may be found in the title of the second book Hoffer gave me. 'The book was about clear purpose,' he writes, 'the defeat of an enemy of human freedom and dignity, however crudely represented and understood. There was an understanding of obligation in it, a recognition that there was a job to do … I realised that these were all qualities lacking in what we call culture these days.' And what was all this talk about 'war criminals' and 'war heroes'? We who supported him were the war heroes or, rather, his 'armadillos,' which I suppose is a nice enough instance of nature imitating military hardware. 'There is no way to abolish badness in the world,' he continues, 'least of all by wishing it away, but the system made badness unimportant to the work it found itself supporting.' Was TANKS the making or the unmaking of him? I'd say both, simultaneously. Certainly it was madness of a kind, which cost him dearly, both in peace of mind and pocket, $100,000 finally. Why the martial language? Sibum hits the mark when he addresses Bill's shade: 'You were fond of military metaphors, as are many men who carry about a slight whiff of the effeminate in their natures.' The letters Bill wrote to me at that time resemble military communiqués. 'I am taking a bit of a rest in a small overlooked cave in the middle of the battlefield. My Commander of Tanks self doesn't approve of human frailty, being vastly inhuman himself. He keeps reminding me that one kills inhuman enemies with inhuman instruments, and I shut up again.' In the same letter he returns to the reality of the bookshop: 'It is 2:30 pm and I have been writing letters all day. Nothing much has been sold; I bought a book for two dollars.'

The greatest offence to the greatest number of people was his use of the phrase "war criminal" to describe those benefiting from state subsidy or who sought and won favours or who profited in the vapid poeticising of their own measly existences. 'I understand your distress at the manifesto,' he writes me, 'because I am similarly distressed. It is evidence of our own war criminality that makes dignity more important than we can afford to let it be.' The objections flew at him from all directions, academic and otherwise. While some were mere yelps, others were reasonable. Bill fought back all the more, adding, wherever possible, injury to insult. Puerile? Yes, of course it was. It was puerile in the way almost all fledgling literary movements and manifestos are. Sadly, though, the bird never got to fly or at least not far enough. It was not that objections couldn't be made; it was that they were too *easily* made. We have since been beaten over the head with other people's moral rectitude. What would Bill have to say to our current climate of self-righteousness? Woke and cancel culture? And he thought he saw the worst of it! I wonder if he can hear from where he is my nervous tapping of fingers on the keyboard. The language he used was in order to achieve an effect, which is one of the more doubtful aspects of any cultural revolution. Did I laugh? Yes, I did. Was my laughter allowable? That depends on who I speak to. Was it wrong? Yes, probably. A lapse of taste? Certainly. 'As we ask many to become intelligent,' he continues, 'let us try to be a little more stupid. Remember Gorky and his heroes. This is a limited operation. In May, it will be history.' Was it though? Was it ever history? For something to be so it must first, if only for a moment, reach a pinnacle.

If TANKS was a state of mind it was also the imprint for a series of six titles, its opening salvo, alas, mine. *The Machine Minders*

(1986) is no longer a piece by which I stand, not because I necessarily disagree with the opinions of my younger self but because my younger self mistook gut reaction for critical acumen. My arguments, such as they were, were poorly put; I was priggish too. It was an attack on the poetry scene then current in this country and as such it would be quickly out of date. I took aim at certain figures whereas the sensible course would have been to take aim at what produced them in the first place. I claimed religious justification when it was never mine to use. Shooting wildly (to resort to militaristic language) resulted in collateral damage. I named people who did not deserve to be named. They have my apologies. Somewhere, though, at the back of it all, in some dimly lit room, there was, I think, rightness of judgement, but everything in front of it was obfuscated. I don't think Bill agreed with much of what I wrote either. He had another purpose in mind: those who were sent the essay and wrote back to complain about it were automatically served a single-page notice: *Indictment: War Criminal.* The statement reads:

> *The Machine Minders* makes a simple statement, essentially a religious statement; it is an inquiry regarding Faith. Not myself a Christian, I find it relevant, but not helpful to my own inquiries about the nature and purposes of literature. I did not publish it in order to convince you; I published it in order to identify those of you who are too far gone to be included in the literary and ethical discussion we so urgently require. It is a litmus test. If you have received this xerox instead of a letter, you may understand yourself to have been found unsuitable to engage in that discussion. Your name has been removed from our mailing list; your presence is not desired.

I think he got it wrong in the first two sentences. It was never a religious statement, although I did employ language that might have made it seem so. What Bill knew was that the piece would cause offence, his indictment even more offence. 'You will be entertained to learn that absolutely no one in Vancouver finds the war criminal indictment entertaining. The most usual response is dumb incomprehension, followed by a plaintive "What does it mean?" This war I am conducting with rare grace and beauty is invisible to the sheep and swine herders who walk the local streets and fill the bookshops and art galleries with their fingerprints and dabs of shit on board.' Again: did I laugh? Yes. Mine was the laughter of banshees.

Sadly the essay contained terrible illustrations serving absolutely no purpose. Robert Bringhurst designed the pamphlet while, presumably, holding his nose. Certainly its content was anathema to him—an 'adolescent squawk' he called it. Holding his nose, however, might be said to be his default position: I say this while acknowledging the excellence of many of his poems, the pity of it being they were not enough to save him from being served the indictment. I salute him in his calaboose.

What Bill lacked was an aesthetic. We had an almighty spat a few years later. I objected to the typographic design on the cover of my pamphlet *The Wolf Month* (1992). This resulted in a three-page explosion.

> I am not prepared to discuss this with you. I am unprepared to be told what to do. Sternness, a euphemism for war, must be reserved for last, not trotted out at the first sign of disagreement. We are in this, like it or not, for good and forever. We are allies more importantly than we are friends. Our friendship is our own business. The initial type forms are not twee. George Sims' cottage in Reading was twee.* You

* George Sims was a bookseller and writer, a friend of Anthony Rota although this did not prevent him from taking business liberties with him, and he took against me for being half Polish, the Poles having been his collective *bête noire* during the war. He had been worsted by them in a pub squabble. He complained bitterly of a Polish pilot who flew his plane *under* the Hammersmith Bridge and he disliked me all the more when I suggested that he ought perhaps to be more grateful to the derring-do of Poles during the Battle of Britain. There are certain people who have an aspect of a kitten-drowner in their features.

> are not so universally more British than the commander of Tanks in any of his manifestations. And, even if you were, you cannot claim authority in every form of life ... I expect a broader mind from you, a better ability to separate yourself from a poem when it is finished ... Please don't shrink the universe to those few enthusiasts you think of when you think *audience*. We want more people, not fewer. We want fire instead of wax to make all surfaces even ... Besides, the design I sent you is neither twee nor archaic; the fact that you have to use such tired words to describe it is simply further proof of how new it is ... A finished book is like a statue hidden in the stone; different eyes may see it differently. By definition a bookseller is supposed to protect his customers from bad books, and a publisher is supposed to protect his author from anything that may make his work unfortunate.

Amazingly I won the battle. Bill's assistant John Hudson devised a new cover although, as with those unlucky enough to be in Henry VIII's court, he would later lose his head. As for *The Machine Minders* I am not being hard on myself nor am I being hard on its publisher. There is a certain amount of health to be accrued from one's mistakes. My own pleasure was in inducing hysteria in other people. We had succeeded in our aim to be a little more stupid. 'There are strange howlings in the street,' Bill writes me. 'The desk is littered with bits and pieces. Incredibly there is still no organized resistance to the terrible gathering of the Tanks.' Among the more outrageous things he did was to seek an arrest warrant for Margaret Atwood for misuse of Arts Council funds. It was all so exhilarating.

Where I disagreed with Bill was in his own dismissal of the worth of literature. 'Literature is genuinely unimportant and always was,' he wrote to me on August 7, 1988, when perhaps he realised the blows he'd struck were blows struck at himself. 'It is an affectation of the rich and self-important. Aristocratic democrats and democratic aristocrats are equally difficult to accept.' With this came the announcement, with something vaguely Keynesian in the wording, that he had been working on a new general system of bookselling and to this end had produced three definitions:

1. Booksellers are individuals who solve problems caused by books.
2. A good book is a book one has a use for.
3. The term 'book collector' was invented by people who don't buy books to describe people who do.

The first is acceptable, the third funny, the second an instance of the utilitarianism that blighted much of his thinking. Something, meanwhile, had begun to go badly wrong with him; it could not be put down to depression alone. If his campaign began with tanks, towards the end of it, when failure began to bite, he spoke of mysterious airships that would rise slowly from the ground, firing in all directions at once. TANKS had been a financial disaster but, far worse than that, it had not achieved anything of lasting value. Canadian literature went on as before, unruffled, the same people winning the same prizes. What Bill had not bargained for is an innate Canadian ability to simply *ignore*. It broke him. Their regard, which he sought above all else, was the very thing denied him. 'The war was not good for me,' he wrote on April 22nd, 1991. 'Time, perhaps, to leave.' He once said to me that the only cure for Canada would be to remove the entire population and replace them with other people. I didn't ask what plans he had for the deportees. It was time for a move, although nobody could have anticipated what that move would be.

Then began a second campaign, perhaps the silliest of his life, when he took against other members of the book trade. Toronto was, for some reason, his main target and in this he may have adopted old literary prejudices between west and east in the way that in many countries the conflict is between north and south. His machinations became increasingly absurd, and with respect to them he lost not only my sympathy, but also those of booksellers he admired, Peter Howard for one. Bill had arranged for a booksellers' conference to be held four hundred miles north of

Vancouver. Was this some kind of Siberian exile, where with luck his colleagues in the trade would be fed one by one to the local wildlife? Scornful of book fairs, in his booth he played Tetris, deliberately ignoring the customers. What he had done in effect was to sign his own death warrant. Could it be, though, he was seeking an exit strategy?

Something happened during this period, but what it was exactly remains a mystery. Was it madness or inordinate sanity? The answer may lie in the vast archive of the American bookseller Peter Howard, which is housed at the Lilly Library. It was probably the closest relationship of Bill's life and perhaps Howard's as well. An aside is called for. Peter Howard was a bigger than life character, a man at once generous and terrible, with maybe a pinch of the psychopath in him, certainly something unreachable. A poetic equivalent might be the American poet Robert Lowell or rather Lowell's superego, Caligula. I remember Howard well. He came to Bertram Rota several times. There was really nothing much there for him, but then this would have been equally true of any bookseller dealing in modern literature. Whatever you had on offer, he had it twice over. Bill wrote of him, 'He is like the hunter who kills the whole buffalo to use three ounces of its tongue and leaves the rest to rot. In the ecology of relationships he has always been a menace.' And again: 'He is only vaguely conscious of it, but his understandings are too much like God's understandings of prayer. He doesn't quite see what it has to do with him.' Peter Howard was the greatest American bookseller of his generation and what he most admired in other booksellers—Bill and in this country Martin Stone and Peter Jolliffe—was what one most admired in him, a sense of the absolute. Howard began Hoffer's obituary: 'Bill was snuffed out Sept 28, 1997. He had burned very brightly. No filter. There was a vapour trail. He was my friend. I tried to be his.'

After the collapse of TANKS, and in the midst of his second campaign against the book trade, Bill became an agent for the KGB, *or so he said*, although I have no reason to doubt he believed *what he believed to be the case*. The quality most expected of spies is that they do not go about saying they are spies. Also he ran his own private detective agency, *or so he said*. What is certain is that he had begun to study Russian, getting up at five in the morning and studying for three or four hours, and became proficient enough to be able to read *War and Peace* in the original. Bill was nothing if not bright. His teacher was a man called Moorad Agagieyiev, who was from Makhachkala, the capital of Dagestan. (I insert the last sentence mainly for its exotic perfumes.)

When Bill came to London he sat at our table, speaking in the brightly lucid sentences that are so often the attribute of people who have had a mental collapse. There is a clear logic to be found in them but only through the agency of one's own sympathies. One must defer to madness. This was the failing of Rosencrantz and Guildenstern. They simply didn't *get it*. The talk that night was of the KGB, the detective agency and a Russian sailor. You could say there was a running theme. Sibum writes: 'Your breakdown was a thing of the past as was that Russian sailor in Vancouver. He, I suspect, dripped some poison in your soul that very nearly destroyed you altogether, but this is only conjecture. You went mad in the classical sense. Your eyes shone with madness when your eyes didn't use to really shine, at all, but perhaps memory serves me badly.' There have been suggestions that Bill's infatuation with the Russian sailor was not strictly platonic. I doubt this. I may be wrong, but often the attraction between men verges on the erotic and what is made love to is not the body but a wild abstraction. That ramshackle visit to London was the last time I saw Bill in the flesh. The flesh was not wholly recognisable.

On February 29, 1992, after he settled or was *settled down* by antidepressants, he wrote to me:

> Next month Peter Howard will take another load of books away. This has led to the rumour that I am going out of business, which is not true. I continue to buy books. It's just that I have finally accepted that no one in Western Canada is interested in an antiquarian book shop, and that holding a quarter of a million dollars in inventory is crazy. One

> doesn't need books to be a bookseller. Though I will say that the international book trade bears more and more heavily on me. I despise the conversion of the book to artefact, and the preciousness of our generally held assumptions ... I have resigned my position as National Secretary of the ABAC*, my enemies having inadvertently provided me with an opportunity to do it with no danger to myself but with the likelihood of doing great damage to them. And my detective agency, elaborated into a more formal system of espionage which I entirely believed myself from time to time, has crashed. I can put it down to reading too many spy novels. Suffice it to say, I am still curious about opening a bookshop in Moscow, but will be doing it on my own. I actually don't know any other spies than myself, and it seems unlikely that any such agencies would be very interested in an ageing bookseller who is far too obvious in a crowd. So I am sorry to have implicated you in a rare fantasy. Since I have worked so hard at always telling the truth, it is easy for me to lie.

I'd somehow missed that line about opening a bookshop in Moscow or perhaps I'd lumped it in with other dreams of his. And so, in the spring of 1992, carrying with him a single volume of Emily Dickinson, which is not at all what I would have expected of him, all the better for doing so, he set off on the final great adventure of his life. He flew to Moscow where he billeted himself with the woman who later became his wife. She had two children. I have described her elsewhere as the warrior queen of a forgotten tribe. I will repeat here what I wrote there: 'I can easily picture her in a chariot not dissimilar to the huge Pazyryk one made entirely of birch, fourth-century BC, which I saw at the Hermitage in St. Petersburg. She is not merely tall—she is, in every respect, a giantess. When I first met her, the sun's rays picked up the gold in her teeth, which in ancient times would have been the gold hanging from every part of her. She dresses wholly in black and her hair

* Antiquarian Booksellers' Association of Canada.

is black too.' Masha Valterievna Averyanova brought him, so it seemed, the happiness that had so often eluded him in the past.

My communication with him was at first sporadic. One night very late, in his cups, he phoned me from Moscow to inform me that he was going to abandon the English language and that henceforth I would have to communicate with him by means of an interpreter. Already he was growling Russian phrases at me. Acquiring the language was one of his chief concerns:

> I am constantly in a state of weirdly unimportant terror that someone will try to speak to me. And, as if to reward paranoia with paranoia, I am often quite incapable of saying anything for several seconds, even for several minutes, as the huge wheels of Russian syntax and grammar resolve themselves into something usable, some more useful than a group of obscurely related paradoxes. But I have started telling old jokes again, in Russian rather than in English, aware that the trick of keeping them funny lies in something other than translation. Every once in a while, I suddenly realize that I have no idea whatever is coming out of my mouth. To say that it is automatic now is to understate the matter. This is deep and distressing stuff. But the jokes are still funny, if tilted seriously from their previous orbits around a dimmer historical and cultural sun. Russian permits the speaker much more freedom to create everything, including new verbs and other parts of speech. It is one of the reasons that writers are so honoured in Russia; among the many great users of language they are the greatest. Yesterday I fell into conversation with an old man quite by accident. At some point I wanted to say something I didn't know how to say and apologized to him, referring to my bad Russian. 'Where are you from?' he asked. 'From Canada,' I said. 'What! I thought you were a Georgian!'

An old communist, Bill got there just in time to witness communism's demise. The pulling down of Soviet statues appalled him. Still, I believe he found happiness of a kind, not least with Masha who herself was an old communist although not a starched one. Sadly I say of her *was*. Another ghost. I do not remember Bill as being musically inclined although I knew he played guitar 'as if with a belt buckle' according to one of his bookshop audience. Masha told me he dismissed Chopin as 'music for rabbits.' She was wounded by this. She loved Chopin. Who would have thought it possible, but in the last year of his life, *before* he knew he was ill, Bill became obsessed with Mozart's *Requiem*, playing it over and over. Would he have continued to be a bookseller if he had found the right ropes in Russia? I think probably yes. He wrote to Sibum: 'I am one of the few interesting and talented booksellers of my time. I am sitting in Moscow without a bookshop. It doesn't make me less a bookseller. When I have resolved the contradictions that made it impossible for me to continue selling books I will sell books again.' There were several mentions in his letters to me of opening a bookshop devoted to publications from the West, in particular books about Russia.

As for his observations about the country they make interesting reading.

> 'Russia cannot be encompassed by the mind,' Tyutchev's poem says, 'She can only be loved.' Perhaps that is one of the reasons that I feel so comfortable here in my uncomfortable but improving condition … I am reluctant to generalise about Russia or Russians. There are a lot of cheap observations one can easily make. Russians are very difficult to trust or *not* to love. They are childlike, particularly the men. There is no disfiguring women's liberation to trouble one's classical mindset. Women use their bodies as they use their hands, to do work, and because of it they seem more attractive, more normal. I am, I think, out of the great game, but I remember it together with all its puzzles. The distance between women on the street and strippers in Vancouver is much greater than the same distance in Moscow. There is a vast sense of something, freedom, hell, I don't know what … I am as happy

> here as I have ever been anywhere. I feel much more at home, in spite of my handicap, than I did in Canada or England, anywhere I stayed for more than a few days. Knowing very few people has been good too. I don't know why. Perhaps it was the dreadful sense of death and futility that rose like swamp gas from the histories of the deteriorating lives of my old acquaintances in Canada that was the source of my growing depression. I have traded all my old depressions in on one larger and more tractable depression here, *Russian*. One must always convert political and emotional problems into financial problems, I used to say, on the grounds that financial problems are the only ones that can be solved. You just have to learn to live with the other kinds ... What to say? Russian love affairs tend to lead to much suffering and a considerable number of actual children, unlike love affairs among the poets of the west, which lead only to unnecessary poems. Katya, the 24-year-old lover of my best friend here (who is 59 and married, with two grown sons) is in danger of bearing their child exactly tonight and is worried about being in the '*rod-dome*' (literally, 'birth house') when all the doctors and nurses will assuredly be drunk. Anything is an adequate excuse for a drink in Russia. If all else fails, the Russian joke is, one can drink to the 700th birthday of the balalaika.

Although he never fully abandoned the book trade, particularly when it came to seeking scarce Russian publications, mostly unfindable, another passion took over and this, which, in terms of *his* life, I found inexplicable, was the amassing of a collection of wooden and clay toys. Together he and Masha accumulated over five thousand pieces. Scarcity and beauty were not prerequisites—they had to be whatever was still being made.

> We bought a Xloodnovsky toy by some young new artist, for 45,000 roubles and a tiny clay horse whistle for 20,000 roubles. The price of bus and metro tickets just increased from 1500 roubles to 2000 roubles. The Xloodnovsky toy

> was not essential. I don't like them very much. They were made by certifiably insane and bad-tempered *babushki* in the 1960s and 70s for sale to Soviet museums for what were really very high prices at that time. But they satisfied the world of socially correct art theory and were the basis of an art industry of teachers and scholars many thousands of times greater than the few old women who were clever enough to make them. Aleksander Naumovich Frumkin,* a dwarf alcoholic Jewish art historian with a speech impediment and a rolling limp, has described his arguments with said *babushki* thirty years ago. I will say that anyone who can understand Sasha Naumovich's Russian is no piker in the world of Russian as a theory of life in our time, and I can understand him well enough.

Bill, with an eye to publishing, asked Frumkin to write a book on Filimonovski clay toys. (Might this be a fugitive item in the bibliography of Hoffer's publications?) One day, should anyone wish to know the state of Russian wooden toy production at the end of the second millennium, it will be to the apartment on Universitetsky Prospekt that he'll need to go. I visited the place after Bill died. The shelves were banked three or four rows deep with wooden toys of every description, among them goat ladies, sawyers and blacksmiths, gentlefolk, nesting dolls, Pinocchios, mechanical, pull and pendulum bob toys, merry-go-rounds, bird whistles, dream vehicles, red-painted roosters and horses, pecking hens, bears chopping wood, bears ice fishing, bears playing chess, fantastical *balyasy* being those gay and comical figures that spring from the minds of wits and jokers, and, moving away from there, towards the ceiling, wooden birds dangling for a breeze. Their effect, *en masse*, is Hitchcockian.

I was trying to get a grasp on the man he had become. *Bilochka!* Masha and her two children, Vasya and Anya, called him "Bilochka." I can't imagine him in the role of father and I knew

* Not to be confused with the famous Soviet electrochemist of the same name.

that he was hard on the one child, gentle on the other. After he died, Anya conferred sainthood on him; Vasya remained sullen. When I knew Bill he seemed to have neither the domestic nor the frivolous in him although I think he may have made heavy with both, such that his pursuit of toys became feverish in its intensity and sheer drive. What could have been his plan? I find it hard to believe he did not have one. And what of the photo of him Masha showed me, which she took late one night when he returned home, weary but ecstatic, his arms a cradle to still more wooden trophies? Who was this man for whom sentiment had been a bourgeois disease? The decision to move to Russia had been an extraordinary one, dictated to him in childhood, when, in the company of his father who was visiting Vienna in the early 1950s, he saw a couple of Russian soldiers marching with their peculiar grace, a memory that was to haunt him all his life. A Jew, he actively sought Russian citizenship while thousands of Russian Jews were quite happy to lose theirs. I asked him once whether the Russians were not anti-Semitic, to which he answered, yes, but with them it was all in the mind. So was it something of the mind when Masha's mother arrived with equipment to fumigate her daughter's apartment of the Jewishness that had seeped into it? Masha related the story after he was gone. If he never mentioned it to me, doubtless it was because he did not want his Russian dream crushed. I will have to assume the unthinkable: he was content. There was something like equilibrium in his life when fleetingly he spoke to me of being 'vaguely ill and dogged by old demons.'

Bill flew from Moscow to Victoria, BC, to put himself in his father's care. Dr Abram Hoffer, ever the believer in megavitamin theory, bombed his son with such massive quantities of vitamin C that his skin glimmered a shade of orange. Masha, abandoned in Moscow, was ordered not to come. Bill felt her presence would have annoyed the father he was always at such pains to please. He wrote to her, saying, 'I have no experience in dying so I don't know how to behave.' In his final letter to me, dated September 12, 1997, he writes, 'I have been remiss. A large part of the problem is that the leaky gourd of my secrecy, battered already at birth by Peter

Howard, clumsy for that and in consequence of my amateur standing in matters of life and death, the whole infinitely complicated by people telling one another and people wanting to demonstrate their status as holders of information, has resulted in a siege … I have no principal objection to dying and no evolved understanding of what dying is, but I am anxious not to be dreadfully uncomfortable and suspect that I can manage that more easily here than in Moscow.' And in the very last lines the old literary warrior writes, 'I don't recommend Canada. There is a new effort to debunk Margaret Laurence.* She committed suicide. She was a drunk and smoked too much. She was a bad mother and wife and had affairs. When literature becomes a subtext of Diana's underwear there is nothing left to say.'† And so indeed there would be nothing left to say, no more words from the wordsmith groomed beneath Saskatoon skies. When he was taken into hospital the nurse, trying to find his pulse, sought to distract him, asking, 'And what was it like living in Moscow?' And he replied, 'It wasn't *Gabereau*. It wasn't *Saturday Night*.‡ It wasn't the hideous assassination of Margaret Laurence. I knew they'd turn on her in the end because she drank.' The nurse, confused, thought he was suffering from dementia. William Hoffer, bookseller, publisher, Commander of TANKS (retired) died of lung cancer at the Jubilee Hospital in Victoria, BC, on September 28, 1997, aged fifty-three. One of the last people to

* Margaret Laurence was a Canadian author best-known for her novel *The Stone Angel* (1964). One reason she may have been on Bill's mind was that, like him, she had been diagnosed with lung cancer for which there was no treatment beyond palliative care.

† Diana, Princess of Wales, had recently died. 'I have been wondering about Princess Diana,' Bill writes. 'The most terrible thing is that nothing else seems as important, without regard to how utterly unimportant she was and is. Even the fate of Russia and suicide bombers in Jerusalem are shouted out and trivialized by this banal nonsense. She has, for the moment, become the moral ballast that we have lost as we wander without promise of redemption by art or civilization, an afterimage, a burst of energy that marks a place we all know must exist but which doesn't exist any longer.'

‡ *Gabereau* was a CBC Radio interview show; *Saturday Night* was a Canadian general interest magazine.

see him was the Canadian poet Susan Musgrave, who had been a friend of his since 1970 when, at the Falstaff Bookshop, the first of his bookselling ventures, she spooned bookbinder's glue into her tea by mistake, thinking it was honey. 'I've always said such stupid things to you,' were his last words to her. 'And in that final room,' she wrote in her obituary of him, 'I held his magnificent hands and said something equally stupid back.' Bill was buried in the yard of his parents' house, which begs the question, with them now both gone, who has taken over custody of his remains? I wish, in a way, he had died in the arms of Mother Russia.

Some months after he died, Masha sent me something she found in one of his files, a five-page obituary he wrote for himself, the greater part of which was written in late July, a couple of weeks before, on August 6, 1997, he was presented with a prognosis. Afterwards, on the final page, he writes, 'There is nothing for it except to continue. My current occupations are so few and so uninteresting that dying will be almost a distraction.' This extraordinary document touches on a number of perennial concerns—literary warfare, old loves, youthful poems, the nature of love, and a stunning childhood memory of the sun over the prairies. Most revelatory, perhaps, is the opening paragraph.

> When I was 14 or 15 my favourite poet was Walter Savage Landor. I didn't read much of his poetry, more committed to Shelley above all, and to Keats, if very much only in theory. I was particularly taken by Landor's careful preparation for death. He wrote his own elegy every five years from the age of 75 until he did finally die at 96. I, 53 this year, have decided to write my own elegy, reminded by almost everything that much of my life has already happened and the possibilities of finding new meanings in what is done and forgotten by almost everyone but me are fewer every year. In a long series of letters to an old friend I tried to construct a new and improved model of my life, a summing up of much that was always too private to describe when I still needed myself as a weapon in real or imagined wars. As a reward for

> faithful service, or, possibly, as a result of too many well-intentioned mistakes, I find myself not at war, not required to be a weapon, and with no such horizons to consider. I could, I suppose, start a war; but I have never started one before. A soldier out of necessity, a man unwilling to accept what didn't have to be accepted or what was morally unacceptable no matter how inevitable, I was in that sense hopelessly romantic. I have rejected that description, even knowing that it was always partly true. My methodology has never been romantic, and descriptions of people are in the end descriptions of what they have done or are doing or might do in future. What we call psychology is that fund of suspicion we use to justify our opinions in that regard. Whether psychology, philosophy, sociology or anthropology rise to being sciences, I don't know; I suspect they don't. But we can measure what men and women do and remember what they say. In order to remain aware of what I have done and seen and heard I have used my own life as a puppet theatre, illustrating my moral tales with appropriate vignettes. At the same time I have kept most of the secrets I was entrusted with, revealing them only as they degenerated through time. There are no old secrets. Secrecy is by its nature youthful, a process rather than collections of facts that no one knows. A secret is something that someone in particular doesn't know. How they are prevented from knowing what by whom and for how long are what matter most.

So what does any of this have to do with my life as a factotum in the book trade? Everything in fact: my friendship with Bill was woven into the very fabric of what it is to be bookseller or at least what it was once upon a time, before computers crashed the scene. Maybe the ghost of some eighteenth-century bookseller has crept into my bones, which ache for a time when for booksellers pamphleteering came as naturally as drinking gin. I've never much liked William Hogarth. I can't put my finger on why this is so. I feel inclined to respect his grave, which is at the end of the walk my wife and I take most evenings. Aesthetically I am full of lacunae. I've never read Evelyn Waugh. There's something in his profile I don't like. Hogarth and Waugh were both abrasive figures. Bill was abrasive. As I have always been attracted to a certain jaggedness in human nature, maybe it's time for me to rethink them, maybe even read and look more closely at their achievement. I will repeat myself just in case I wasn't heard the first time round: the book trade has been for me about books and people. Abrasive as hell, a wire brush taken to one's teeth, William Hoffer was a mighty presence.

A scourge of the slight and the mediocre, such was the task which he took upon himself, but often it amounted to not much more than the disembowelling of phantoms. 'When I attack,' he once wrote me, 'I imagine the fire bird guides me to the exact centre of battle; of the thousands of arrows that I fire, not one fails to find its mark.' And so it was that he could be devastatingly accurate. When he was wrong he was wrong in the extreme or, in that delicious Russian turn of phrase, *not even wrong*. 'I don't know the truth,' he said. 'I know only what seems true to me. I will not surrender the right to insist on my responsibility to my understanding of what it is to be a human being. A man who can't keep promises to himself is unlikely to be able to keep promises to anyone.'

I may never fully understand the nature of my friendship with him. I wonder if Sibum does his. We were so far apart on so very much, mostly in matters of the spirit, but he told a friend of mine that I was the canary that a miner might reasonably take down a mineshaft with him and that I have an uncanny ability to smell danger, to smell it on other people's skins, to smell it before it becomes conscious of itself. Maybe, for him, these were soldierly attributes. As such, I'd be of use. And maybe, for me, it was his sense of absolutes. What I got of him was always true. I could see beyond other people's dislike of him. Maybe the oddest thing about him, odd because it doesn't quite fit the picture, was that he went 'hookless' fishing. I think he was something of a pioneer in the practice, which involves getting a fish to rise and take the fly and then let it go again unharmed. There was uncustomary gentleness in his voice as he described this to me. I more than liked him for it. Maybe he was giving the world a second chance. Why does a man cast flies? Why do some men fish with dynamite? Why does this man write poems? A ransacker of people's vanities, was there not also something vainglorious in Hoffer's crazy scheme? Maybe. If sometimes he played the clown, so be it; anyone who thinks a man putting on a clown's face doesn't mean serious business ought to go to the opera more.

Chapter Ten

BLACK MISCHIEF AND SUBTERFUGE

AN ELF, WHEN FED ON THE RIGHT SUBSTANCES, VODKA and suspicion, will become a demon in no time at all, the world he creates one of black mischief and subterfuge. Such was the bubble in which I found myself after I left Bertram Rota in 1992 to become, ostensibly, manager of Bernard Stone's Turret Book Shop. It was to be the wildest and, ultimately, the most humiliating year of my working life. So promising were its spring notes that I almost immediately, indeed willingly, let my guard down. After years of wearing a tie, I was ready to cut loose. It was Bernard Stone who first described me as 'a factotum in the book trade' and so I owe him at the very least this book's title. Also he got me out of a rut. My brain had been in a sling. If I was finding it increasingly difficult to see outside the frame it was because I had forgotten about the frame. Security shoos away adventure. Some people need a solid base for their imagination to prosper, others thrive on uncertainty and movement otherwise their imagination finds no release. There are no guidelines, nothing one can trace, and with respect to the direction one takes the first has no superiority to, or advantage over, the second and vice versa. Some people operate best from inside a thimble. The open field has been for me perhaps the most serious of my limitations in that I find it difficult to write on things closer to home. I have always sought the *elsewhere*, whether it be Damascus or Naples or even my own shadowy alcove but now, as I move into my seventies and I've begun to wear green shoelaces, the past becomes another kind of elsewhere.

I'd been at Bertram Rota for fourteen years and although I learned a great deal there I had begun to stagnate. If I may be ruthless with myself I wanted for courage. I had a young family to support, true, but all too easily that can be an excuse for somnolence. What should have been my years of adventure were yet to come and indeed I may have gained from being a late developer. With respect to bookselling, I'd been given the opportunity to go elsewhere on three occasions, one of them, with Bill Hoffer acting as midwife, a job with the legendary Martin Stone. Martin has been granted more column space than any other bookseller of our times, deservedly so, and even before his death in 2016 he burned brightly in bookselling discourse. A true maverick, he could churn up out of the most barren field buried treasure. Many were the stories of him going into street markets in Paris and spotting what nobody else had seen, his knowledge of the lesser French Symbolist poets, for example, being second to none. One of my earliest memories of Martin was when I bumped into him at Skoob Books and from his briefcase he gleefully produced a copy of Hemingway's *Across the River and into the Trees* (1950) which, not long before his death, the author had inscribed with words to the effect that one day soon he would take a gun to his own head.

Martin Stone who had the best nose in the business could smell out a rare volume blindfolded. A brilliant guitarist, it was good news for the book trade that he failed in his bid to replace Brian Jones of the Rolling Stones. The story is that he was deemed too unsightly, which was rather odd given his ethereal presence. There is nothing that will ever replicate his smile when he located a treasure, when his whole face came alive. There was always laughter in the wings of his wonderful private theatre.

We had dinner at a Greek restaurant in Notting Hill, Bill's enthusiasm ever growing as mine continued to wane, Martin smiling his big toothless smile—this was before Peter Howard of Serendipity Books awarded him a set of teeth for his services to the book trade. Martin had recently opened a small bookshop, the Forgotten Shelf, in the Kings Cross area, so brief its existence it has slipped out of most people's memories. Where else could one hope to locate a copy of J. Fogerty's *Mr. Jocko* (1891), which Martin, in one of his very few catalogues, described as 'an anti-clerical novel of Darwinian ideas, dedicated to Professor T.H. Huxley; set in the circus world, its discussion of Mr. Jocko, an intelligent monkey, as the "missing link" just tilts it into the science-fiction category.' *Just tilts*, thus spake the Great Persuader for his truly was the power of suggestion. There was never such a thing as a hard sale, only a subtle appeal to other people's intelligence. Martin would not have been interested in a first edition of *The Collector* or *Midnight's Children*. The books had to be outré.

So why didn't I go with him? Why didn't I take a gamble? The answer, quite simply, is that a shop was not in keeping with Martin's style. He was too restless a figure to be tied for long to any such venture. And because I knew this, and because I could see that Martin, already merrily in his cups, was allowing Bill's words to wash over him, we both, without ever saying so, knew it wouldn't work. Also his lady friend of the time was perfectly capable of the day-to-day running of a bookshop although, as I knew would be the case, it didn't have much longer to go. Still it might have been more interesting to fail with him than to succeed with someone else.

Another thing about Martin, while his ghost hovers over the page, is that he had an innate grasp of the literary connections between people and so—I could batter the reader with a thousand examples—it was obvious that Austryn Wainhouse, translator of the Marquis de Sade and Georges Bataille, and author of yet another candidate for the Twentieth-Century Pantheon of Unreadable Masterpieces, *Hedyphagetica* (1954)* would be in possession of some remarkable books. Who other than Martin would have acted upon this arcane knowledge? The things he found there still circulate through the trade. A while back, I sold Austryn Wainhouse's copy of Samuel Beckett's *Watt* (1953) which Martin sold to Peter Ellis. And one last thing about Martin, which eclipses all else; only he could have got away with wearing a French beret and winkle-pickers at the same time.

It was tempting to accept Rick Gekoski's invitation to work with him when he was still located in Chalcot Square. One of the shrewdest people in the trade, with 'a gift of the gab,' there was no book he could not talk out of another person's hands. What he knew was that there is always a point when a seller can be persuaded to

---

* If your goal is esoteric literature, why not go instead for Francesco Colonna's *Hypnerotomachia Poliphili* (1499), the first half of its title a compound of three Greek words, *hypnos* (sleep), *eros* (love) and *mache* (strife). The first complete translation of it into English appeared in 1999, exactly five hundred years after the first edition was printed in Venice by Aldus Manutius and which is said to be the most beautiful of all incunabula. At the time of writing there is a copy available for £200,000. I first learned of it from an introduction the violinist Peter Sheppard Skærved gave to the deeply challenging music of my composer/friend Michael Hersch: 'I suddenly heard behind me the falling of some tesserae, and finding myself solitary, in a deserted place, I was quite frightened. I quickly turned around and saw a gecko or wall-lizard which had caused this accident.' The strangeness of Colonna's lines anticipates the strangeness of certain passages in Michael's music. I read the book on a return journey to Llangollen, finishing it just as the bus pulled into Victoria Coach Station. I have just pulled the book from my shelf and, lo and behold, tucked inside is a National Express ticket which informs me I took the bus to Wrexham, where I was met by my friend Peter Meilleur who ferried me from there to his home in Llangollen, on Tuesday, November 25, 2014, and that the return journey was on Thursday, November 27, 2014, which seems to me of monumental significance although I'm at a loss to say why. Maybe it is because the reading of that book brackets the time I spent with a dear friend who is no longer with us. This is just one example of the many associations a book can have. As to the timing there is a mysterious pleasure when one is able to complete a book within the precise time frame of a long journey. This happens on a more modest scale when on a tube one completes the chapter just as the train arrives at its destination.

overcome his reluctance; money was the extractor of the seemingly immovable and he was prepared to go the distance. His cunning was in putting his cunning on full display, there being no hidden clauses. A different kind of smart from Martin Stone's smart, a measure of his smartness can be best located in his two books, *Tolkien's Gown & Other Stories of Great Authors and Rare Books* (2004) and *Outside of a Dog: A Bibliomemoir* (2009), both of them witty and urbane. I can't remember why I didn't take him up on the offer although it might have been failure of nerve, while, from his side, Gekoski was all nerve. Maybe, though, I was reluctant to go more deeply into the trade, which would certainly have been the case had I gone with him. Gekoski moved in another stratosphere. I would have struggled for oxygen there. I have never wanted to be in a position where I dealt only with 'high spots' when for me a £5 book could be just as valuable. Also I feared any such commitment would throw my inner balance and I wouldn't be able to write. It didn't stop Gekoski, of course, but then he was unstoppable.

Another invitation, welcome though it was, I had to refuse. Paul Rassam dealt in the kinds of books I liked, and had a flair for continental literature, which was squarely in my own zone of interest. I liked him too. There was a problem however. Paul had a showroom on the second floor of a building directly opposite to, and absolutely level with, Anthony Rota's office. A pair of binoculars would have been sufficient to monitor his activities and from his side mine. I would have been too embarrassed working at such a close range. Ridiculous? Yes, maybe, but then I suffer inordinately from embarrassment. As it turned out, Rassam folded his tent and worked from the more stationary position of home.

I was going nowhere when one day there was a phone call for me. At first there was silence or, rather, something akin to the gasping of a fish pulled out of water and then came a nervous jumble of words, a man telling me he was getting old and that he was looking for someone to take over the management of his bookshop. Also whoever that would be would eventually inherit the business. *So he told me.* I was forced to be circumspect as my colleagues were within hearing range. A bit of cheek, phoning me at work, but it was the only way he could reach me. This was an opportunity that would surely alter the course of my life. The Turret Book Shop was this country's answer to Shakespeare and Company in Paris; the only other comparable shops, Compendium Books in Camden Town and, before my time, Better Books in Charing Cross Road, were long gone. Turret Book Shop was a poetry bookshop with literary associations already firmly in place. It was everything I could have hoped for, certainly for someone who was a bit of a square with bohemian tendencies. I had frequented the bookshop in its heyday when it was in Kensington Church Walk, and again when it moved to Floral Street, but the shop, now in Lamb's Conduit Street in Bloomsbury, had begun to slide. The stock never changed, which is fatal in a bookshop, and Bernard had become almost wholly reliant upon the same people he had known for decades, among them Christopher Logue and Ralph Steadman, whose presence had to a great degree defined that scene.

Steadman, one of the most savage illustrators of our time, had knocked about with Hunter S. Thompson and illustrated his *Fear and Loathing in Las Vegas* (1971) as well as his book on Nixon's 1972 reelection campaign. He had also illustrated a couple of Bernard's books for children, *Emergency Mouse* (1978) and *Quasimodo Mouse* (1984). Word has it that Bernard was so afraid of Hunter S. Thompson that when Steadman brought him into the shop once Bernard hid under his desk quaking. *Fear and Quaking in Kensington Church Walk.*

Quite simply, and credit where credit is due, Bernard Stone was a legendary figure in the poetry world, the generosity of the public man being such that a good many poets owed him not just their gratitude for the free wine but also for the beginnings of their careers. Among the earliest of Carol Ann Duffy's pamphlets was the Turret Books edition of *Thrown Voices* (1986) and other people he published included Alan Brownjohn, Sylvia Plath, Ted Hughes, Anthony Thwaite, Edward Lucie-Smith, Jeremy Robson, Harry and Ruth Fainlight, Alan Sillitoe, Lawrence Durrell, Brian Patten and Christopher Logue. Any history of the 1960s and '70s poetry scene would be incomplete without reference to him. Also, and this could not but have sweetened my disposition, he had just recently published a broadsheet of one of my poems.

I met up with Barry Miles, sometime bookseller, biographer of Allen Ginsberg and William Burroughs among others, and, most vitally, able chronicler of London's sixties counterculture. Miles had been in charge of books at the Indica Gallery where Yoko Ono met John Lennon. Miles fed Paul McCartney hash brownies. Miles, for all that he lived at the centre of pop culture, was never superior with it, which for graduates of the Age of Aquarius was quite a rare quality. It had been his idea to get Bernard to poach me. We agreed that with the times no longer being what they were, the lily having gone rancid beneath a Thatcherite sun, a certain amount of rigour would be required in order to prop up a bohemian façade. I would bring my own expertise, which would involve the building up of a first edition section. This would be in addition to the new books. The aim was nothing less than to have the best poetry bookshop in existence. I could not have had a better champion than Miles.

This was how I came to be with the man whose reputation, ramshackle though it was, would help to reboot the poetry scene. Or so I imagined. I was at an age when I could still muster faith in the support of a wider populace. There were, I thought, still enough sparks to light up a darkening world. If I have become considerably less optimistic with age it is not only due to a hardening of the arteries. It is what the poetry scene itself has become. What had been a sacred vocation has become a profession, so now you have poets with their damnable CVs milking the system for all it's worth when, really, the system ought to be anathema. Most vitally, the spirit of generosity necessary to any thriving of the arts has all but disappeared. What is left is a mere shell and it is hard to speak of the arts without distaste. They have become a forum for smug certainties. Three decades ago, I still *believed*. Three decades ago, my first full collection of poetry was about to appear. Three decades ago, the time was ripe for a change. One thing was clear: such ideas as I had for the bookshop could not have been put into practice without Bernard's support. I was not his usurper. I was meant to be his factotum and, if necessary, his dacoit.

The private man was another tale. Certainly he was circumspect and waved away any questions about his past and even the present was a dense fog through which he sent different signals to different people at different times. The poet Brian Patten has noted that 'trying to prise any information out of him was like trying to open a safe with a bookmark.' One could begin by saying Bernard was born in Nottingham in 1924 of an immigrant Jewish family from the Ukraine. And then what? It's a patchy picture. Not even those closest to him knew for sure the details of his early life. Christopher Logue writes that when Bernard was conscripted in 1940 he was sent to work at the Quartermaster's Stores in Lagos, which served the army in East Africa, and it was there that he decided to become a bookseller dealing in poetry and that he would use his army gratuity towards such a purpose. This sounds a shade apocryphal or maybe even a deliberate obfuscation on Bernard's side. Logue speaks of a stint as a book dealer's runner. What came in between the war and running books was his involvement with a Jewish defence organisation which had been set up in London's East End in the late 1940s when there was a resurgence of Mosley's British Union of Fascists. A woman with a curvaceous figure volunteered her services. Bernard was all agog. She resisted his advances with a brisk humour of a kind the world could now use more of. It was, in a sense, 'the decade of Ooo!' and Ealing comedies. England was, in so many respects, a sweeter though sillier place. She was Diana Mary Fluck, better-known as Diana Dors, England's answer to Marilyn Monroe. Smut is porn's sweet alternative; it acknowledges that we are, at heart, ridiculous creatures. At least this puts the younger Bernard in a recognisable frame. After working in street markets, he set up bookstalls at poetry readings, which is where some of his earliest literary associations were formed.

There were hints of a tragedy in his life, an engagement to a woman who close to their wedding day committed suicide. One day, while I was clearing bookshelves, there slipped out of a book a black-and-white photograph with perforated edges of a naked woman on a chair, striking an amateurish pose. It shouted 1950s at me, all of it, her hair and even, if such a thing is possible, her bodily curves. There was something infinitely silly about that image and yet it deeply touched me. It could only have been her and the clumsy pose she struck was the precious contract a woman grants the man she loves. I slipped it back inside the book. Was it *really* her though? Was I merely trying to put together a picture of Bernard's life? There again, it was impossible to know with him what was or was not true. I have been asked on occasion if he had literary enthusiasms and, if so, where they lay. It is easy enough to say he liked Irish poetry, Seamus Heaney and Derek Mahon in particular; one could also say he relished the literary life; what fascinates me more, and is perhaps revelatory of 'the inner life,' is that he collected every edition he could find of *Don Quixote*. One could never send such a man to Siberia, whatever his flaws.

I am here presented with a problem and whichever way I look at it I see no escape, only the imperative that I describe things *as I saw them*. A friend advises me that I'll be skinned alive. I'll never forget what my assistant Germaine Hampton said to me, that nobody would ever know what it was actually like *working there*. This is true of most working situations, but this was truer than most for it was becoming increasingly difficult to reconcile the man at his desk, shakily reaching for his bottle, and the public persona of a generous and genial figure. The consumption of a bottle of vodka a day did not make Bernard the most logical of people to deal with although, according to boozers' wisdom, vodka is the poison of choice, the one on which one might continue to function for the longest time. After all, one of the most powerful countries in the world has been fuelled by it. This said, I never saw Bernard drunk to the point of being uncontrollable. Certainly he was not lacking in charm and because he was old enough to be relatively harmless and also because he was bountiful with his purse, attractive women would flock to him. This was the prince who had become a toad, toadiness being the secret of his attraction. There was also something of the dapper yachtsman about him, the only thing missing, a skipper's hat. The women came and went and he would take them, sometimes one on each arm, to the Chelsea Arts

Club. One of them, sadly when I was out on a break, did a strip-tease in the shop; another was a Dutch actress who would later become my sugar-coated assassin.

One of my main tasks was to move Bernard from the cramped quarters in Lamb's Conduit Street in Bloomsbury to a bigger, brighter place. Although I rather liked the shop as it was, and after working for Rota where not a hair was out of place I welcomed a certain amount of chaos, there was barely room for a poetry audience. And the stock suffered from fatigue. Visitors never looked at the shelves. Such places one can take in with a single glance. So that a move might be facilitated it was essential that I apply some sense of order in advance of it. The first two months of working with Bernard were akin to a whirlwind romance. There was nothing I could do that was not in his eyes precisely what he himself would have done had he still had the energy to do so. We went at least twice a week for 'a bit of nosh'—Bernard's favourite phrase—to a nearby Italian restaurant where one night a member of his retinue bared her breasts to all at the table before inviting me to apply lipstick to her mouth while her lesbian partner looked on in agonised horror. Then there were frequent lunches with the likes of Martin Bax, editor of *Ambit* magazine, and the Irish novelist Benedict Kiely, whose store of literary anecdotes, going all the way back to Yeats, was inexhaustible. Kiely was probably a much better raconteur than writer; it was all in the delivery and could not be bottled for the page. The illustrator Ralph Steadman was a constant, as were the authors Ken Smith, Judi Benson, Ivor Cutler, Alan Sillitoe, Ruth Fainlight and Laurie Lee. (Bernard Stone tried once to present Ivor Cutler with a copy of my poems, which he strenuously refused, crying, 'Please, no, I might have to read them and *say something nice*.' I can well sympathise with such a position.) The Laurie Lee we knew was Laurie Lee, collector of dirty French postcards, a rather valuable collection they were too, and he was the owner of a *pied-à-terre* in London where Bernard went once and found a stark naked girl in her teens lying on the sofa, her sole purpose, so it seemed, to be decorative. This was not so much cider with Rosie as absinthe with Monique. She never bothered to cover herself or flee. She never once spoke. It was one of the few times I saw Bernard nonplussed.

There was the poet Fiona Pitt-Kethley whose main preoccupation was sex and talking about it endlessly. At the time she was doing research, as punter and prostitute, for a travelogue called *Red Light Districts of the World* (2000). She claimed to have recently smuggled herself into a Turkish brothel for research purposes. It was hard to know whether she was being serious or just playing with us. Who subsidised this Grand Tour of the world's fleshpots? She inscribed my copy of *Gesta* (1986): 'don't forget to give me info on the brothels of Warsaw etc,' which strikes me as perhaps revelatory of her code of practice. Did she get most of her information from other people? She spoke in a flat, colourless voice. So persistent was her conversation with respect to sex that Bernard and I began to suspect she was a virgin, which, had we leaked it, would almost certainly have torpedoed her literary career. And we reckoned, too, that she'd been nowhere near a red lightbulb other than the one she screwed into her vivid imagination. There was something indelibly prim about her, but then primness is very often the precondition for scarletude. Smuttiness cohabits with primness. More subtle, although with a bawdy sense of humour, was the cartoonist Posy Simmonds, author of *Gemma Bovary* (2000) and *Tamara Drewe* (2005), who is one of the funniest women I've ever met, funny because she knew precisely what *not* to say. With Pitt-Kethley one had the sense of watching footage of the day before yesterday's horse race. We knew the results well in advance. Pitt-Kethley did what bad girls do and married a British chess grandmaster with whom she moved to Spain and she has dyed her hair blonde.

One of the poets most closely associated with the bookshop was Christopher Logue. I admired him for his versions of Homer's *Iliad*. Homer made Logue. There is nothing in his own verse that touches the heights of his theft of Greek fire. The mistake is to call it Homer; it's Logue at his best. At his worst he provided me with one of the most delightful illustrations of a poet's vanity. Surely there's an anthology to be done of poetical vainglories. Prior to a reading he gave he arrived at the shop and handed my assistant Germaine Hampton a bouquet of flowers, saying to her, 'Now, when I have finished my reading you are to present me with these.' One can almost feel affection for such a figure. I got along with him after a fashion, keenly aware that he was a man not to get too close to. I turned a blind eye when he helped himself to books from the shop, some of which he later presented to the London Library as gifts from himself. A rogue he may have been, but was he a lovable one? What I have to say about him is no worse than what he says of himself in his surely ironically titled memoir *Prince Charming* (1999). Bernard surrounded himself with people about whom he complained bitterly in private, but what I had yet to learn was the psychology behind this: he *wanted* to be taken advantage of—he *wanted* to be the victim. The day I finally understood this was the day I put my head beneath the guillotine's blade.

A single event, although small in itself, rattled me. One day Bernard called me into his office and handed me £200 in cash, asking me to hide it in a safe place. It was not for me to reason why, although it might have been a secret stash to ensure his daily bottle. I took the money to the downstairs storeroom, which was kept locked and to which nobody but he and I had access. I pulled some books from a shelf on my immediate left, beside the light switch, and deposited the envelope of money there. It was not the most ingenious of hiding places, but what did it matter if the room was barred to other people.

A month later, Bernard summoned me.

'You remember the money I gave you to hide, could you get it for me.'

I went downstairs, reached behind the books and … nothing. I was sure it was there. A sense of panic building in me, I began to pull more and more books from the shelves above and below. Nothing. I went back upstairs, a sick feeling in the pit of my stomach.

'Bernard, I don't know what to say. It's not there, the money's gone.'

With a faint smile, his head bobbing up and down, he said, 'Don't worry, you'll find it sooner or later.'

It was the first time I felt something like a cloud move over me. I reckoned that he had gone looking for money, which, after all, wouldn't have been that hard to find, and that he had merely forgotten about it and yet ... and yet he was not a man to forget anything.

Something else troubled me. The shop income was mostly generated by a single figure, Raymond Danowski, the darkest of dark horses. It would be a while before I got to meet him and when finally I did he stared right through me. A stout, bearded figure with a long ponytail, who moved like a steamer through a narrow canal, Danowski was a New Yorker who grew up in poverty on a Bronx housing estate. After working his way through the art gallery world he married Mary Moore, daughter of the sculptor, and became a wealthy man. A master of psychology, he played Bernard with greater skill than Bernard played other people. Danowski was the puppeteer, Bernard his puppet. I'd already suffered a dose of Bernard's psychological warfare, so I was not ready for more. It was Danowski who had kept pushing Bernard for a move to new premises. I began to wonder whether this might not have been a condition he set for his continued custom. There is nothing more dangerous in the book trade than relying on a single source and even Bernard warned me against killing the goose that lays the golden eggs and yet it was not advice he himself heeded.

One evening, Danowski took Bernard to the most expensive Indian restaurant in Mayfair and for the two of them ordered enough dishes to cover the whole of a very large table. As was always the case, Bernard ate a sparrow-like portion. Meanwhile Danowski sat and dreamily gazed at the colourful array before him. When asked why he wasn't eating he replied that he had grown up in poverty and that now he was wealthy enough to treat this as a feast for the eyes. This, for me, was a unique take on poverty, allowing a mountain of food to go to waste. After hearing this, and registering Bernard's own disquietude, I could not help but question Danowski's altruism. I kept asking Bernard whether he could guarantee Danowski's continued support because if we were to lose it we would be finished.

'Stop worrying,' he said, 'it'll all come out in the wash.' This was another of his favourite phrases. This was one cliché too many for me. I wanted reassurance.

Raymond Danowski died in 2018. If one looks for him on the internet and elsewhere what we are presented with is a hero to learning and culture. An avid reader, although I had no evidence of this, he aimed to create what he called *une bibliothèque imaginaire*, a collection of first editions of every book of twentieth-century poetry in the English language. This would be extended to include small magazines, ephemera and recordings. Danowski describes his aim on the Emory University website: 'I intended to set a contextual collection, envisioning a snowflake, a symmetrical structure relating to issues in the 20th century which impacted upon or influenced poets such as the Spanish civil war, Vietnam, Provo, Black Panther ... Strong author collections would be crucial and be as complete as luck would have.' I never spoke to him about book collecting, and of course the 'snowflake' had yet to materialise. What if he were to lose interest? Big-time collectors can be fickle. They can also be passionless, but I will accept what he also wrote on the Emory website: 'I want to say book collecting is fun; serious fun possibly but always an antidote to the idiocies of life and the pretensions of academia. Book collecting is an outlet for fanaticism, passion, love, and rationality without their drawbacks.' Also he mentions the bitter discouragements of early home life, a father who kept his books out of reach of the child yearning for them. Danowski was clearly a complicated figure.

Bernard had already been supplying him for some years and there was always an open box into which he would drop books of verse, both old and new, and these would then be sent to Geneva where they went into "the Hole," Danowski's gigantic warehouse. Needless to say, these were not books Danowski read or even bothered to handle. One time I watched Bernard drop yet another book into the box and I asked him whether he kept a record of the titles he'd already supplied. Bernard said his memory was up to the task. Whether or not this was true, I'll never know, but I can't help but think that among the reported seventy-five thousand volumes there were not multiple copies of many of the titles. In 2004, Danowski donated the bulk of the collection to the Rose Library at Emory University in Atlanta, Georgia. The collection bears his name as is only right and proper.

The greater amount of our income, however, came from the schoolbooks and academic texts that Danowski donated to schools and libraries in the South African townships. The story is that when he lived in Stellenbosch he once went into a shop and bought up all the food vouchers, which he then distributed to people living on the streets. Generosity can wear several faces, of course, ranging between the generosity that is private and the generosity that calls for witnesses. I will never know what was on his mind—also I am fully alive to the fact that many a human being is a composite of his own contrarieties—but what happened later would forever force me to question his motives. One evening he took me out to dinner and I had the sense of being measured, but for what I couldn't tell. It was an unsettling experience.

After checking out several potential places for the shop's new location, Bernard and I settled on a magnificent space in Great Queen Street. There was a massive basement which would house the hundreds of boxes that Bernard had kept stored for several years in a couple of warehouses. Those boxes contained the rare books of which Bernard continually spoke. *Stop worrying*, he kept saying to me. The very idea of all those books pacified me. A month was spent painting, putting up shelves, sanding the wooden floors and hanging pictures. Also, to my joy, we had the donation of an upright piano. We brought in the enormous curved Henry Moore–designed desk, a thing of beauty akin to his sculptures, with hidden drawers and extensions, which both commanded and defined the new space. Although I might have wished otherwise, Lyn Bamber's extraordinarily lifelike waxwork of Sigmund Freud took its position by the door as it had done in the previous shops. I have always felt an antipathy to Freud, but it was a pill I was prepared to swallow. Admittedly there was much pleasure to be had in watching people say 'Excuse me' or 'Good morning' as they brushed past him.

One day a vivacious woman walked in and told me she was a chanteuse and that she would love to perform there. She must have spotted the piano from the street. I invited her to audition right there and then. No sooner did the first deep notes come out than I knew hers was the voice I wanted for the new space. She went under the stage name of Cécile Sauvage, which presumably the very real Celia Stothard took from a French poet of that name although at the time I was thinking more along the lines of François Truffaut's *L'Enfant sauvage*. She performed at several events, accompanied on accordion and piano by David Harrod, singing from the great French repertoire Charles Trènet's "Reste que t'il," Edith Piaf and Louiguy's "La vie en rose" and Dino Olivieri and Louis Poterat's "J'attendrai." She did so once to the great annoyance of a group of poets who felt I'd allowed her to invade their poetical space. They protested. A most horrible yelp it was too. I told them that a poet who fears the presence of a singer is a poet who had better attend to his own craft. I have just checked to discover her whereabouts only to discover she died ten years ago. I also learned that together with her husband, Alan Kitching, she became a printer/designer at the Typography Workshop. *Celia, Cécile, I thank you for who you were. Merci.*

We had yet to have a proper opening for the new shop and so we planned one that would coincide with the presentation of a festschrift *The Shelf Life of Bernard Stone*, compiled by Camille Whitaker. Brian Patten is in there, so too Dannie Abse, Martin Bax, Judi Benson, Ken Smith, Gavin Ewart, Adrian Henri, Hugo Williams (for whom, by the way, Fiona Pitt-Kethley, also present, had an unrequited love), Adrian Henri, Roger McGough, Jeremy Reed, Alan Sillitoe and Ruth Fainlight. I see from its title page it was May 8, 1993. While the musicians played trad jazz in the street outside and people celebrated inside, a black cab stopped in front of the shop. The driver came in with a small envelope. It contained a folded slip of paper bearing a one-line note: 'Today marks the end of Bernard Stone.' It was from Raymond Danowski. I'll never know whether the puppet master cut the strings and the puppet crashed to the floor or if previously the puppet had said something to the master that was beyond the pale. Whichever it was, it was a savage doom. Whatever issues Danowski might have had with the new premises he never addressed them to me. Years later, I was told he didn't like the space. Surely, though, it was something more. I was out of the loop and no longer party to the whims of two highly inflammable figures. With Bernard now released from Danowski's psychological clutches I realised we had to rescue the shop. A certain amount of money would come in from the last of the orders for South Africa. After that, everything depended on the contents of the two warehouses. They would be our rescue package.

Bernard had continually spoken of the 'treasures' he had in store. At last with the enormous basement there was room for them. The day came. A couple of vanloads arrived with close to two hundred boxes. So many of the titles, I reckoned, would have ripened over time. I opened the first box. It contained multiple copies of a remainder as unsaleable then as it was ten years before and as it would be now. I opened another box that contained multiple copies of a single title published by the Fortune Press. It was not, as one might have wished, the suppressed (unauthorised) edition of Wallace Stevens's *Selected Poems* (1952), but one of the publisher's many vanity titles. Panic took hold of me and I began to tear into more and more boxes. There was the odd Steam Press Ralph Steadman title or copy of Sylvia Plath's *Uncollected Poems* (1965), but for the most part the books were of no value whatsoever. I remembered the scene from *The Treasure of the Sierra Madre* where Howard and Curtin go to reclaim their sacks of gold dust only to find their contents had been dispersed to the winds. The final scene has them roaring with laughter. There was no laughter, however, no philosophy, in me. The best books from all those boxes filled no more than a single glass-covered cabinet in my office.

Meanwhile the book launches and readings were a success. I brought in fresh faces such as John Ashbery, Christopher Middleton, Les Murray, Ivan V. Lalić, Gabriel Levin and Mimi Khalvati. Ashbery hadn't forgotten my *Kismet* moment. He inscribed my copy of *Shadow Train* (1981): 'for Marius and auld lang Long Acre, John Ashbery – 13 October 1993.' Jeremy Reed read there. I remember it well. A hooded figure was sitting at my desk, away from the rest of the audience. Why did he feel he had to hide? The audience had come to hear Jeremy Reed, not him. I was greatly tempted to ask Elton John to move. Also I was determined to break free of my own prejudices and invite poets who were not to my personal taste. It was my aim to create the most inclusive poetry venue in the country. Moreover, given the opportunity to grab a slice of literary history, the poets read for free. Publishers were only too pleased to launch their new titles with us. It was rumoured that the nearby Poetry Society in Covent Garden, realising it could not compete, put a stop to its reading programme.

There was one strange interlude. Bernard announced he had to go away for a few days. He was a bit shakier than usual. The news from Israel was that his sister had been the sole casualty of a scud missile fired at the country by Iraqi forces. After behaving outrageously at the funeral, so I heard from my Israeli sources, he was asked to leave. Bernard, always secretive in matters of family, had made no mention of a sister although later I heard he had a niece.

One day Allen Ginsberg came in, fresh from a trip to Poland, and was on the hunt for translations of Polish poetry. I pushed Zbigniew Herbert at him. I stayed quiet about Czesław Miłosz who had begun to irk me and who very soon, in one of poetry's most cringeworthy moments, would kiss Ginsberg's arse.* My recently published collection *Doctor Honoris Causa* was on display. Ginsberg added it to his pile. I found myself in a moral quandary. I told him that the author of the title, although he had a Polish name might not qualify because he wrote in English. Ginsberg asked who he was and I said it was me. There followed a moment of confusion: Ginsberg removed the book from his pile and then gingerly put it back. After thinking a few seconds more, he returned it to the display.

It was the second time he disappointed me. Some years before, in 1979, I met him at the Cambridge Poetry Festival. He was together with Peter Orlovsky who was scraping dead skin from the

---

* "To Allen Ginsberg" in *Facing the River* (1995).

bottoms of his feet. Orlovsky had no time for the world's niceties although it is quite possible he never knew what they were. He was a kind of Caliban minus the good lines. Joseph Brodsky had just finished reading, his voice like a cantor's, a poem that surely was a masterpiece but which in its translation amounted to an exercise in the utterly mundane.* C. H. Sisson took to the stage and courageously endured the catcalls of the ill-informed who howled disapproval of his youthful, which is to say *pre-war*, enthusiasm for the Action Française poet and philosopher Charles Maurras. I could not say at the time whether I was for or against him, but I was keenly aware of how quick people were to condemn some writers as fascists and others not at all. Why was Maurras in their ledger of evil and not Ezra Pound, who at that time had still escaped censure? When I met Sisson a few years later, I found him to be a paragon of bonhomie and tolerance. As for Pound, I will always

---

* One of the most celebrated poets of the second half of the twentieth century, for me Brodsky was no more than a pompous windbag. I went to see him together with Czesław Miłosz, Derek Walcott and the Arab poet Adonis at the National Geographic Society where they took part in a symposium on the future of poetry in the new millennium. Brodsky held forth on the absolute necessity for rhyme and illustrated it with a poem of his own, which was so bad I could only assume his intention was to insult his audience. When someone in the audience spoke of the poetry of the King James Bible he retorted it would have been better in rhyme. Then Adonis spoke of the need for a return to spiritual values. The argument would have been cloying were it not for his eloquence. Brodsky sneeringly bobbed his head up and down while Adonis spoke and when Adonis finished, said to him, 'Your culture is steeped in garbage.' The audience froze. Walcott and Miłosz stared straight ahead, saying nothing. Adonis does not speak English and so missed Brodsky's quip. I am to this day ashamed that I did not stand up and challenge Brodsky. This was the man who said once that he would go back to Russia only on the back of an American tank. Would Akhmatova, Tsvetaeva, Mandelstam or Pasternak, all of whom suffered under the Soviet regime, have said such a thing? I doubt it. Years later, I had my own private revenge. I visited the Anna Akhmatova Museum at Fountain House in St Petersburg where I was conducted by a charming woman who was the director of the museum. After we finished she said that a Brodsky exhibition was due to open the following week but she would take me in for a preview. I declined the invitation.

defend the poet, the great mover, the literary brawler, but never his anti-Semitism which he himself at the end of his life called 'a stupid suburban prejudice.' Such was the scene: the Anglican Sisson was reading and the Jew Ginsberg seemed not to notice the boos and hisses. There was a bar at the back of the auditorium for those who'd had their fill of poetry. There seemed to be more people at the bar than in front of the stage. We spoke for a few minutes and then Ginsberg asked me what I was drinking. I said half a pint of ale would be lovely. He went off in the direction of the bar and that was the last time I saw him.

The cracks began to …

… but hold fire: there had been an earlier occasion on which Ginsberg abseiled through my existence. In 1973 I was in a greasy spoon on Bank Street in Ottawa, drinking coffee or something vaguely resembling it, when he walked in and sat at the table adjacent to mine. A bored waitress slapped the menu in front of him. What could he possibly want to eat here? There was no brown rice; tofu was the food of lovers with strange appetites; the mung bean belonged to a future state. I already knew the place to be dedicated to the desecration, rather than the preparation, of food. Ginsberg ordered. I strained to listen but couldn't quite make out what it was. I ordered another coffee. I simply *had* to see the outcome. Meanwhile I contemplated the man whose books I had on my shelves. Allen Ginsberg was by then already in the business of writing Allen Ginsberg poems, with William Blake duly summoned to their defence. I knew of his kindness to many people and so he was not to be dismissed, but the poems of late had been execrable. They had nothing of the mighty surge of *Howl* and *Kaddish*. Ginsberg no longer wrote, he ejaculated. And here he was, sequestered, or so he thought, from the world's scrutiny, a man with a growling stomach. I felt a strange intimacy growing between us, between observer and observed, which would have been shattered were I to acknowledge his presence. I took great care not to. At the same time I couldn't help sneak glances. The food arrived. Ginsberg beamed. It was the delicacy perhaps known to Canadians alone, the infamous hot chicken sandwich, which comprises two slices of white bread, its texture as close to cotton wool as possible, and tucked in between them slivers of cold chicken sometimes a week old or more, a side order of French fries, the potato reconstituted, the whole of it drowned in a thick sea of tinned gravy composed of some unspeakable residue. Ginsberg, stripped bare of his poeticals, tucked in with gusto. So this was what he was like in private. I can't remember whether he chose the jelly or the rice pudding that came gratis with all meals.

So yes, the cracks began to cover the whole blasted jug and spread from it to my fingernails and from them to anything one might care to call peace of mind. There is nothing new in the battle between the older and the younger man. It's the stuff of a thousand small tragedies and comedies. Such successes as I managed to achieve irked Bernard. At the readings and book launches that I'd arranged he would disappear into the office, and the bigger the audience the more irritable he became. This is where I am forced to take stock of myself. Maybe I should have been a shade more subtle in dealing with him. The fact he didn't want to let go was perfectly understandable. This was his creation, after all, and I had burst onto the stage in the final chapter of his life. Say I should have been just a bit more careful, say I should have pretended my successes were his, how was I to deal with the fact that he tried to sabotage my every effort to keep the bookshop afloat? I had struck deals with the main poetry publishers—Carcanet, Anvil and Bloodaxe—they would stock the entirety of their catalogues on a sale or return basis. There would be launches for newly published books. So what did Bernard do? I was struggling to build up the poetry stock and out of the blue there would arrive twenty copies of a remaindered book on goldfish, which he put on the display table.

'Bernard, what this?'

He put on that quizzical face with which I had become familiar, only this time there was something in it I hadn't seen before.

'Bernard, we desperately need more poetry titles. Why twenty copies of a book on goldfish?'

'Shut up,' he replied, 'it's my shop!'

The jug was no longer covered with hairline cracks, it was now in a thousand pieces. I was powerless. Yes, it was his shop. So why was he out to scuttle it? As time went on I began to realise that he had not paid the publishers who let us have their stock on sale or return. I had secured their trust. One obituary said that the reason the shop collapsed was due to our being unable to meet the exorbitant rent for the place. This was untrue. We had been given a year's free rent, when in the property rental market such things were still possible. Bernard never paid a penny's rent for the place. The worst, though, was yet to come.

Christopher Logue delivered a box containing the annual instalment of his archive, which was to be automatically sent to an American university library. As I already had considerable experience in cataloguing literary archives it was only natural that I should see what was inside. The box was already on the packing bench, ready to be shipped. Nobody had opened it. I did. When I looked inside, I was horrified. The greater portion of it was junk mail—travel brochures and the like—much of it still inside their plastic envelopes. I would find the odd page of autograph notes, but nothing one could properly describe as a working manuscript. I knew that sometimes it was years before boxes were opened by librarians at the other end. We would be sued if anyone checked this one. I showed the box to Bernard, asking him whether in his mind the material within constituted an archive. He buried his face in his hands, saying he had no idea what to do. I said I would take on the responsibility. I phoned Christopher, saying that the material he delivered did not match my idea of what an archive should be.

'You little shit,' he screamed, 'who in the hell are you to speak to me?'

I said I was the manager and therefore responsible for the running of the place.

'You've *got* autograph material!'

'I've got a few pages of notes and a lot of junk post.'

'You bastard, do you seriously think I am going to let you have *my good stuff*?'

It was a while before I learned 'the good stuff' had gone to another institution.

'Actually, yes, I do.'

Christopher slammed the phone down on me. About half an hour later, a cab arrived. Logue stormed into the shop, shouting to Bernard, 'Sack him! Sack him now!' I said nothing. My fate was in the balance. The very image of innocence, Bernard offered Christopher a drink and Christopher cast a mocking eye at me. I knew then I was finished.

The situation continued to deteriorate. A priest who I already knew to be an avid collector of poetry came into the shop. As we dealt in both old and new books, and with a bigger range than he'd seen elsewhere, he gave me his card, saying he would like to open an account with us. Over the next hour or so, he made a tall stack of books. Bernard rolled in from his lunch. Quietly I showed him the card, saying we had just got ourselves a valuable customer. Bernard grabbed the card out of my hand, staggered up to the priest and waving it under his nose said to him, 'I bet you pick up little boys with this.'

The priest walked out.

The party was over.

The paycheques I was given began to bounce. I told Bernard, but my desperation only seemed to amuse him. Something happened that still haunts me. A painfully shy Japanese girl, a student, newly settled in the country, without friends and acquaintances, attached herself to the place. When she first came in, Bernard behaved charmingly towards her, invited her to events and the odd 'bit of nosh' and, as one might expect, she became a regular. Bernard nicknamed her "Yum Yum," which she accepted with giggles. One day I caught out of the corner of my eye something I was not supposed to have seen. "Yum Yum" had gone into Bernard's office, they were chatting and suddenly he slid his hand up her skirt. She froze in horror and then quickly sped out of the shop, never to be seen again. I waited a couple of weeks although really I should have taken immediate action.

'Bernard,' I said, 'what's happened to Yum Yum?'

'Well, you know,' he replied with an impish smile.

'I think I do, but maybe you should tell me.'

'She said she can't come back here.'

'Oh, and why's that, Bernard?'

'She has fallen in love with you.'

Contempt was all I could feel for him then.

I won't say who informed me, but there was a Will, its executor Bernard's niece. It contained a key sentence. It stipulated that upon his death the business would be dissolved. The Will had been made some time before I worked for him. Clearly he had never intended for anyone to take over the business. I might have worked for him in any case, but I had been brought in on a lie. Thinking back, maybe I'd been spared the headache of running a business. I knew then it was time for my departure. The only positive thing I managed to achieve was to get stock returned to the publishers who had let me take books on a sale or return basis. I did this without informing Bernard because he would most certainly have prevented it. I'll never know why I clung on for another couple of weeks. Maybe I was hoping I'd be paid the salary owing me. A couple of friends, the author Alan Wall and former publisher and bookseller David Elliott, took me out for lunch and got me drunk or rather they didn't prevent me from emptying one too many glasses. When I got back to the shop I collapsed on the floor, opening my eyes just in time to see Bernard stepping over me. He was grinning. I almost liked him for that.

Maybe I held out because I had not been definitively sacked. That honour was granted to the young Dutch actress who I note once played the role of Magda Goebbels. She sat on the floor, flashing her eyes at me. She purred. She pouted. She shook her blonde mane. It was some of the worst acting I'd ever seen. She began by asking me about my future plans. I wasn't about to tell her anything. I was, in effect, being dismissed by someone who was a mere hanger-on, Bernard her meal ticket. Meanwhile, Bernard, who always shied away from confrontation, sat reading a newspaper in his office.

That evening there was a celebration of Bob Dylan. It was not a particularly good note on which to end. There is always something vaguely embarrassing when adult males, poets in particular, abase themselves before Dylan, which is not to deny my own esteem for the man, but that kind of worship is all so desperate somehow, a negation of people's own lives. Small wonder Dylan himself shuns them. Songs were sung, bad poems read. I felt ghostlike. Some people who had been my familiars were giving me the cold shoulder. I said goodbye to Bernard and he said goodbye to me as if it were a day like any other.

A couple of months later, the bailiffs came. Bernard, meanwhile, had gone into hospital with various complications. The last I heard of him was that he'd gone off the bottle and, most incredibly, that there was no marked change in his behaviour. Bernard was Bernard, either on or off the wagon. Presently 36 Great Queen Street is the site of Stephen Jones Millinery. It has been there ever since Turret Book Shop closed.

Twelve years later, in February 2005, I was waiting for the number 9 bus in front of Charing Cross station. I was going home after a day's work at Ulysses Bookshop. It was a windy day. A sheet of newspaper was blowing about in the air—something so very captivating in that, the wind as choreographer, every dip and rise of the paper a hypnotic dance—as if all the news in the world amounts to nothing in the face of nature and the only thing that matters is the dance. It landed, and then, somehow dodging the traffic, it rolled across the street and spread out in front of me, right way up, and because I have a primitive urge to go looking for signs and wonders, for messages that might be destined for me, I looked down at my feet only to see Bernard Stone's face staring up at me from the obituary page. I chuckled. *So even here you find me.* I did not actually pick it up but stood there, my body at an angle, trying to make out the words when another gust of wind took it elsewhere.

Chapter Eleven

THE SQUARE ROOT OF OBSESSION

SADNESS IS THE SQUARE ROOT OF OBSESSION: I ASK MYSELF whether the equation does not apply to Peter Jolliffe more than to anyone else I've known in the book trade. I worked with him at Ulysses Bookshop. It was not easy. Once he so exasperated me it was only good fortune that the tall ladder I was holding at the time did not bear down on his shiny dome. I did make ready to, I did *think* it. Strange the quizzical look on the face of a murderee. When I first wrote about Peter Jolliffe a few years ago, a piece designed to be, while taking note of his manifest eccentricities, affectionate in tone, I was astounded by the efforts of a couple of friends of his, not booksellers but civilians, to have me drummed out of the book trade. I was accused of libelling the dead by people who saw nothing of what I saw, who were nowhere in the vicinity of the belfry where proverbially the bats career through the workings of people's minds. (Only now have I investigated the origin of the phrase *bats in the belfry* and am startled to discover this seemingly Anglican construction, which John Betjeman regurgitated as the title of one of his books of verse, *New Bats in Old Belfries* [1945], comes not from here, Merrie Olde England, but has its origins in an 1897 issue of *The Paducah Daily Sun* in Paducah, Kentucky, where the phrase was employed to describe an unfortunate woman who would not relinquish the decomposing body of her daughter. It was picked up again in 1907 by Ambrose Bierce in an article he wrote for *Cosmopolitan Magazine* as meaning '"possessed of a devil," the Scriptural diagnosis of insanity.' I am pleased that it has since been distilled to a milder use, so that I may apply it without injury to my ex-colleague.) As for my accusers, one of whom concluded that I must be the packer, which I should say is a most revealing charge, what they did not know is what I know about them. Also, as I'm sure most booksellers will agree, there is something oddly pleasurable about packing a book—it's an unwinding of sorts, an expression of contentment.

After the debacle with Bernard Stone I sought a cure, not, as perhaps ought to have been the case, with opium in a Turkish *hammam*, but with a residency at the Mount Pleasant writers' retreat in Reigate. It was there, so local lore has it, that Deputy Führer Rudolf Hess was taken to be interrogated after his mysterious flight to Scotland in 1941. I found no Nazi ambience, but there was a very proper, very precise, young Austrian woman, dressed in black, with a frilly white apron, who excited in me memories of Jeanne Moreau in the film *Diary of a Chambermaid* (1964). She was responsible for the day-to-day running of the place. If there were other people, cooks and cleaners, then things were so arranged that they would never reveal themselves, very much like the mad king in Palermo who had a system of underground tunnels built beneath his ersatz Chinese pagoda so that he would never have to trouble his eyes with servitude. Maybe, though, Shiva-like, my Austrian lady covered all bases. There were no telltale stains on her apron, but then she may have been such a miracle of exactitude that even the fat in the pan spat elsewhere. Mount Pleasant was rather like a gentlemen's club, only stranger. Among the people staying there at the time were the novelists William Cooper (H. S. Hoff) and Peter Vansittart, both of whom are now largely forgotten, undeservedly so, and the exquisite Robert Ponsonby, music historian and arts administrator, with whom I went on walks, the two of us behaving as if we were school truants fleeing our strict Austrian mistress. We made silly purchases at a village fête. Otherwise we stayed in our rooms, creative industry being our reason for being there, although nobody ever confessed to the vulgarity of setting pen to paper or note to stave. (The retreat was also open to composers.) One day I climbed nearby Box Hill where I had a most disturbing experience. Some boys were playing on the crest of the hill and in their collective, tightly wound, childlike imagination they took me for an evil figure. I listened to them discuss me, their voices shrill with panic. Suddenly they began to pelt me with stones. I was the adult who accidentally strayed into the pages of William Golding's *Lord of the Flies* (1954).*

A struck gong heralded mealtimes. Here, too, the Austrian lady was a paragon of mathematical precision, her summoning to table never a minute too early or too late. I began my stay on a bad note. Unthinkingly I sat down at the head of the table. There was a deadly silence followed by theatrical coughing and then, more devastating still, a polite lesson on how to behave. There was great sensitivity on the matter of seniority and who should be entrusted with control of the buzzer, which was hidden beneath the carpet at the head of the table. A pressing of it with one's foot would be a signal for the next course to be served.† One had to be observant and mark the last spoonful or forkful of food going into the last mouth before doing so. On my final day there, I was made Master of Ceremonies. Conversation steered well clear of anything of importance. The faint whiff of absurdity, the stuff of a Terence Rattigan play, was what I most required at the time. Also I wrote a little, which after a year of drought was abundance.

---

* A copy of which can be had for anywhere between £2,000 and £20,000, the higher figure being an expression of misplaced optimism.

† I am put in mind here of a favourite cat of mine who would bring frogs into the house and hide them in odd places. How was I to know that was not an air pocket beneath the carpet in the hallway?

When I returned home, my future very much in the balance, I was offered a brief sojourn in the august quarters of Maggs Brothers in Berkeley Square, where my job was to produce the catalogue of a Rudyard Kipling collection, quite possibly the most complete in existence. I was summoned just the once to the office of John Maggs, inheritor of a mighty lineage. Apropos of nothing I'd said to anyone there, he cautioned me never to speak of Sir Winston Churchill in derogatory terms. Clearly he had met Poles who'd never got over the carve-up in Yalta. (There was a real as opposed to imaginary Pole—not always distinguishable—with a Lech Wałęsa moustache, who worked in the packing department and disappeared on occasional binges, which, presumably because of his untreatable Slavic origins, were met with resigned tolerance.) This was the substance of my one and only conversation with John Maggs, although there may have been small matters of state, but I came out of the meeting with the answer to what had been a mystery to me. An odd sound came at regular intervals from the direction of his office, somewhat akin to the reverberation of the struck chord in Chekhov's *The Cherry Orchard*. I was with him when it sounded. High in the corner of his office was a TV monitor, which he watched with fascination while on its screen shadowy figures entered and left the building, the eerie sound being that which was produced each time the front door opened. Why hadn't I made the connection before? It seemed to me that his fascination was with something other than the possibility of actual theft and actual thieves; it was almost as if he were a hermit observing life on the outside.

Maggs Brothers, founded in 1853, is one of the most prestigious booksellers in the world, among its many triumphs having been, although not in the same transaction, the purchase and sale of the fourth-century *Codex Sinaiticus*, one of the two earliest Christian Bibles, and Napoleon's desiccated penis, sensitively described in their 1924 catalogue as 'a mummified tendon.' The latter ended up, as many things do, in New Jersey. The *Codex* was purchased by the British Museum in 1933 for £100,000 while the intimate Napoleonic relic went for £400 which, allowing for inflation, was a not insignificant figure. Ed Maggs, with whom I shared the office, and who was then heir to the throne he now occupies, spoke wistfully of his time as a bass player in a reggae band, which in a recent interview he describes as 'a rather doomed attempt to modify my genes.' Something in the way he spoke, some curious inflection, seemed to preserve those musical sonorities.

The strangest thing of all was the staff tearoom where nobody ever spoke. One day I found myself sitting opposite a man wearing a silk tie with horizontal stripes. I blundered into his territorial space, asking him where he got the tie. Mortification spread into all the corners of the room. We had never spoken before and it was as if I had broken some golden rule. I explained that my wife, a weaver, had made it. Its style was uniquely hers. This was too much for him, that he should have upon his own body some part of my own existence, and he hastened back to his upstairs quarters.

Maggs Brothers was said to have a resident ghost, but it felt I was among more ghosts than one. It was quite the most fascinating place. There was always the sense that it could produce surprises from any one of its many cubbyholes. My brief spell there, enjoyable though it was, exposed a major handicap in me: I was not computer literate. I simply couldn't get the hang of it when it came to doing catalogue entries of the Kipling books. Ed Maggs, a magnanimous figure, allowed me to bring in my own portable typewriter on which I would produce the catalogue entries, which he then had a secretary re-type into a computer programme. The doubling of the workload may have halved any possibility of my remaining there.

Soon I'd have to make the switch only because in order to survive one has to be computer literate. This raises in my mind fundamental questions with respect to how our brains operate. The computer, the most powerful memory tool we have, has shrunken our own memory storage. Mnemonics, once upon a time a subject in school curriculums, when it was dropped resulted in a mighty slab of the brain falling into disuse. I am quite convinced that before the computer, when I had to produce index cards for every book, which involved the physical business of putting a card into the typewriter and removing it and then putting it into a file drawer, I could remember where every volume in the shop was, what every book looked like, its colour, its weight in the hand, maybe even its smell and the sound of its pages as one turned them, which in old books can differ from volume to volume; I could remember issue points, variations in binding and whether a top edge was stained red or blue; I could remember the smallest blemishes; also, when seeking out a particular passage, I could remember whether it sat on the left or the right-hand page, whereas now, rather than resorting to my own mental faculties, I find myself going more and more to the database and if the information I'm seeking is not there then I go to the spurious safety zone of Google, which is fine until, when one least expects it, the whole damned thing crashes. It may be, of course, that I'm losing my faculties with age. As it is, I find myself having more and more recourse to the words W. S. Graham spoke when during his poetry readings, befuddled with booze, he would say to his audience, 'Am I not deteriorating, my dears?' And when I say it *crashes*, I don't mean just the machine; I mean our own mental capabilities. We have been party to the most powerful technological revolution in history, the printing press notwithstanding, and so fast are its workings that if we have to wait twenty seconds for a result, a mere fraction of the time it would take to cross the room and pull a volume from the shelf, we find ourselves taken to the very limit of our patience. The world is getting faster and faster and our evolutionary development cannot keep pace, and with the imperative that we move faster still, what has happened is that there has been a shift from active knowledge, which demands of us that we aggressively *pursue* answers, to passive knowledge, whereby we are *fed* information.

At home I discover to my dismay that rather than turn my body the thirty-five degrees it requires to reach for my *Concise Oxford Dictionary*, a slightly chewed volume bound in red leather and with gilt edges, snugly held between the "Pushing Men" bookends designed by Chris Collicott, which are a gift of my dear friend Irena Murray, unthinkingly, idly, I search for the same information online. Very rarely do I rise to my feet and pull from the shelf behind me a tome of the immense twenty-volume OED, the gift of my dear friend Eric Ormsby, whose wife happens to be Irena Murray. I am so deeply privileged in being able to move from the concise to the expansive, the whole of the English language at my disposal, not to mention the thin-paper eleventh edition of the *Encyclopaedia Britannica* (complete with the three supplementary volumes, the last great work of scholarship in the field of reference) which, at some point in the 1970s, I proudly lugged home from Arthur Page on Museum Street, not to mention the other dictionaries and books of quotations I have, which include a facsimile of Captain Francis Grose's *A Classical Dictionary of the Vulgar Tongue* (1785) wherein I discover a 'fart catcher' is 'a valet or footman, from his walking behind his master or mistress' that really I have no excuse not to use them. It's all there, but I find I have moved willy-nilly into the Machine Age that previously I had spent so much of my life resisting. My only plea to monkishness is that I do not possess a mobile phone. I do wonder what the consequences will be for the young, the greater part of whose common knowledge is derived from the internet. Almost every day I speak to customers and book runners for whom the ultimate authority resides in Google. Okay, it might be argued that the internet is only as good as what we feed into it, and as such it is a forum of the mentally ungovernable, its benefits often immense, but I wonder if by taking on more than we can handle we do not diminish ourselves. The computer has likewise turned the antiquarian book trade on its head. As for the books that surround me as I write, bugger it all, I'll chuck the lot in the skip and watch the scavengers coo. And so yes, with respect to our culture, the whole damned thing crashes.

After my stint at Maggs in the autumn of 1994 I found myself in the ghastly position of seeking Jobseeker's Allowance. *'Well then,' he said, 'you can sell shoes.'* A few days later, I received a phone call from Joanna Herald, one of the four partners who ran Ulysses Bookshop at 40 and 32 Museum Street, the other three being Peter Ellis, Gabriel Beaumont and Peter Jolliffe. She interviewed me and although I seem to remember being a shade facetious in my responses apparently I was no more so than usual. She dazzled me. I accepted and was of course relieved to be back in the saddle. Ulysses was quite the most elegant place, maybe the most distinctive since Bertram Rota on Long Acre, although within a very few years it would fall into decrepitude. The idea for the partnership was arrived at almost by happenstance, a single phone call from Peter Jolliffe enquiring after a space in the basement of 40 Museum Street, which then, within minutes, metamorphosed into the idea of a partnership, as simple as that, although Joanna had her worries. Why so? What did she see that the others failed to see? Was it female divination, a reading of ashes?

At first it was difficult for me to get a grip on the mix, four people strikingly different from each other and all with strong personalities—Joanna with her flashing Egyptian eyes, a stickler for order, her husband, Peter Ellis, who beneath his calm liberal exterior might have been a northern mill owner in another age, Gabriel who was bottled chaos, or, rather, the chaos born of the bottle, a Stalinist who never ceased to believe, and finally Peter Jolliffe, who will be the focus of what I write here.

Chubby, sweating profusely, wearing a winter coat in June, soft-spoken, polite, a somewhat intergalactic look in his eyes: this, from some point in the early 1980s, is my earliest memory of Peter Jolliffe. The sweetness of character with which he is remembered by those who did not have to work closely with him is the sweetness I remember or, rather, it's the picture I choose to preserve. There was also his rather beatific smile. When I think back on him, my guess is that it was the happiest period of his life. A lone trader, the proverbial tortoise who always wins the race, he was most often seen lugging several bags of books and very rarely was he not going somewhere for more. As is commonly the case with bulky people—Sumo wrestlers, for example—he was quick to move when needs be. I didn't yet know his rotundity was due to a medical condition that necessitated the heavy use of steroids, which in turn was responsible for mood swings and weight increase. A gentle, rather shy figure, Peter was at that point in his life no hostage to avarice.

When Bertram Rota acquired the Leonard Clark library he became a daily visitor, ready to pounce on some of the many hundreds of volumes of poetry as they appeared, stage by stage, on my cataloguing trolley. While I am usually annoyed by hoverers, weary of the greed in their eyes, I made allowance for him. I could see that poetry was at the centre of his existence. A few years later he would publish some pamphlets of his own verse, a couple of which I have before me as I write. He did not buy books for their resale value alone. They were something he *had* to have even if only for a while. I was happy for him to plunder my shelves. The conversation was welcome. Leonard Clark, a poet himself, seemed to have known everyone: he was an intimate of Walter de la Mare to whom during the war he sent fresh eggs when eggs were scarce; the World War One poets F. W. Harvey and Ivor Gurney, and Andrew Young who of late has slipped the world's notice; he met countless other poets, Seamus Heaney, Ted Hughes and so forth, and so it stood to reason that his library would contain many presentation copies. I bought his copy of Vernon Watkins's *The Lady with the Unicorn* (1948), inscribed by the poet to him. Also I have his copy of Skeat's *Etymological Dictionary of the English Language*. Even now, forty years later, there are very few booksellers who will not have in their stock a title or two from Clark's vast library and of those a good many will have passed through Peter's hands. I wonder, though, what it was about Leonard Clark that when we went to collect the books his widow should have taken such umbrage. She instructed us to remove everything we could see. I pointed to a small glass-fronted bookcase filled with Clark's own titles. 'Except, surely, these,' I said. 'No,' she snapped, 'I want *everything* out of here.' It was not the first time I'd see women behave so. After the novelist William Gerhardie died, and we emptied the room where he spent his final years in mental and physical isolation, the woman whose apartment it was, was insistent that we take absolutely everything. 'Yes, the records, too.' She could barely contain her distaste. 'I want it *all* out of here,' she said as if asking us to remove a curse. When later I took a peek at Gerhardie's final manuscripts I caught an inkling of something terrible. There was a single notebook in which the same sentence was written over and over, a kind of hellish mental loop the author had fallen into.

I had in my own collection something Peter wanted, Seamus Heaney's first pamphlet, *Eleven Poems* (1965) and he had something I wanted, Geoffrey Hill's untitled Fantasy Press pamphlet of 1952. We did a swap; I bettered him; he bettered me. The current value of the Heaney is far greater than that of the Hill, but with respect to what eternity holds dear mine is the more valuable as I'm sure that for Peter the Heaney would still be. And besides, Hill was my lodestar whereas Heaney I could never more than like and admire. I believe Peter and I were of like mind with respect to our hearts' desires. We both came away from the deal happier. This was the Peter Jolliffe I still revere.

Wherever books appeared, so would he, but little did I realise that the man with beads of sweat on his forehead, clutching his plastic bags, would probably do more than anyone to alter the profile of bookselling in this country. The slow man stole a march on just about everyone, even the firm of Bertram Rota. What I read somewhere about him being the first to put value on modern first editions is nonsense, but he was the first to stretch those values to the very limit, such that all that was required now were people prepared to pay his prices. Whether he realised he was a pioneer of sorts is a moot point because he was driven first and foremost by a love of books. I don't think he had an economic plan in mind. The stiff prices he put on his books were not set in such a way as to squeeze the most money possible out of people but rather to discourage them from buying anything at all. This is where the bats began to swoop through the darker areas of Peter's psyche. It is not a principle exactly, that one should be prepared to pay dearly for what one loves, but that he should have paid dearly for books that only hours before had been his made him the object of humorous anecdote. Paul Rassam recounts the story of when he went to the office on Fulham Road, which Peter shared with Julian Nangle. Paul made a purchase of five books and took the tube back to Long Acre where he still had his office, directly opposite Anthony Rota's, and there, waiting for him, was Peter who had jumped into a cab, desperate to buy back at least three of the books he'd sold an hour before.

And then there were the books he'd missed. Charles Peltz told me he'd gone to the Russell Hotel book fair and purchased from the stand next to Peter's, for £60, a copy of Arthur Symons's first book of poetry, *Days and Nights* (1889), inscribed by him to John Addington Symonds. What lover of decadence could resist a book containing the poem "The Opium-Smoker"? Symons later wrote an essay titled "The Gateway to an Artificial Paradise: The Effects of Hashish and Opium Compared" (1918). And what smokier association copy than one inscribed to the man with whom he smoked hashish? Peter had had every opportunity to buy it, but it was the fact that someone else bought it that drove him into a Baudelairean nightmare. That evening he phoned Peltz in tears, begging him to sell him the book. Peltz was, in his own words, *sternness personified.* Some decades later, the book remains in his collection.

So, of what was Peter Jolliffe made? Or what made him who he was? The fact I later worked with him for almost five years does not mean I had special access to his character and indeed I might have got to know him less than when I hardly knew him at all. A man with no close relatives, no amours other than those he nursed within, the only kinship he could claim was with the books with which he surrounded himself. There were friends such as Veronica Watts, who flits swallow-like through the pages of one of Javier Marías's novels, and then there was Stephen Francis Clarke who, although maybe from one side only, was Peter's closest ally in the trade and who, when I last saw him, had painted his fingernails blue. Peter's deepest friendships, however, lay elsewhere. Was there ever anyone for whom books were so totally the life? Well, yes, there are and there *were*, but never have I been at such close range to such a one. This separateness from ordinary human discourse was all the more pronounced when he was thrust into a social occasion, when one could observe the fidgety look of one who did not quite 'get' the human race, and yet, on a one-to-one basis, especially when one touched on some enthusiasm of his, some poet whose work he admired, R. S. Thomas, for example, he could be all sweetness.

A babyish rage, a horrid whine, was the flip side. It was what countless others had to endure. At Ulysses we used to dread the Any Amount of Books catalogues, not for what Peter was able to buy from them but for what he failed to secure. The tantrums would last a day or more at a time. The joyfulness I first encountered in him had begun to degenerate. *Bibliomania?* Yes, I suppose. Where mania is, death hangs close. Death has many guises. It can be registered in the turning down at the corners of one's mouth. As to the actual life, as opposed to imagined life, there are the cold biographical facts that point to an early existence of unremitting sadness.

Peter Benedict Jolliffe was born in 1947 in Trowbridge, Wiltshire, to Michael Jolliffe, a librarian at the Wiltshire County Library, and Jeanne née Pitt. In 1947, his father was appointed librarian at Gordon Memorial College in Khartoum. Maybe one should remark a bookish connection between father and son, although in my experience librarians tend to torture rather than caress books. There's no saying what the move from Wiltshire to Sudan may have engendered in the boy's mind. Maybe it is measurable in the properties of light, so often the case with people who grow up in intensely sunny places. Two years after the move, his mother died while giving birth to twin daughters neither of whom survived. Peter's father, either in the folly of sorrow or else foolishly thinking himself wise, decided it would be best for the son if all trace of his mother were erased. Small wonder Peter had a strange beam in his eyes. At first he was farmed out to the family of the college dean who sent him to a convent school in Khartoum, and then, five years later, he was shipped back to England to live with his grandparents in Trowbridge where he attended St Mary's Convent. A memory of Sudan survives in Peter's poem "Leave." I've always been irritated by the use of the lower case in poems, which strikes me as a stab at a modernity unachieved, although here, and this I owe to the perspicuity of Peter Ellis, it may signal the reluctance of one who did not wish to emphasise anything in his life. I was grateful to him for gifting the poem to me. I am not unmoved by it as it affords a very rare glimpse of his inner life.

as the train straggled
into one of the mid-way stations
— was it Atbara or Shendi? —
the desert moon silver, the night
deep with stars like orange blossom,
my father shooed me out of sleep
and we buffeted our way
to the carriage door to catch
the commotion

    the manhandling
of baggage by desperate porters,
the peanut sellers, the urgent crowd

fringed with infantry relaxes
with rifles in the evening of empire

the sergeant strolled to me
on the carriage steps,
so where are you off to, then?,
and when I had replied
winked 'you lucky blighter'

my father invisible
behind me laughed
beneath that storm of stars

how his laugh still sweeps
through me like radar, reclaiming
memories, isolating loss

how little we knew
how soon we would all
be going home, in a train curving
northwards into the night

I think, given the 'desperate porters, / the peanut sellers, the urgent crowd' it must have been not Shendi but the town of Atbara, commonly known as "Railway City," in northeastern Sudan and that Peter was on the way to Port Sudan from where he would sail home, and, because I have a tendency to follow things through, it might have been aboard the SS *Hendrik* whose final destination was Hull in Yorkshire. The National Archives in Kew has a passenger list, but that is one journey too far for me. What I take away from the poem is a boy's solitude, a father invisible, the 'we' surely the poetical *we*. I noticed that towards the end of his life Peter started buying books on Sudan, presumably seeking memory traces. It is highly probable the seven-year-old travelled alone; it is what children so often had to do in those days. I chanced upon a record proving his father was still in Khartoum in 1957, the sole European librarian in the whole of Sudan. A man alone, a child alone. There is, although I have yet to see it, a photograph of Peter, aged about five, sitting on some steps, an appreciable distance away from his adoptive family in Khartoum. Peter said once he had no recollection of ever having been hugged.

A bright boy, he went from St Mary's Convent to St Mary's Hall, Stonyhurst, and from there to Stonyhurst College. In 1966 he won a place at Merton College, Oxford, where first he read classics and then English literature. It might have been philosophy had he not overheard through the open window of his college room a tutorial, which I fancy might have been the tutorial I heard in another country, in another time, the old chestnut about whether the chair we sit on exists anywhere other than in the mind. I may often find myself in a fool's paradise, but solipsism has never been my mode. I doubt it was his either. A year later, when he moved into a shared house, one morning he awoke to find a cat sleeping on his chest. Soon after, he suffered a catastrophic lung collapse. I don't know whether a cat can provoke such a crisis, but a cat was held to blame. Peter was diagnosed with pulmonary fibrosis and diabetes insipidus and told he was unlikely to reach the age of thirty. I was with him when he celebrated his sixtieth birthday.

A third-class degree in hand, his first job was in the paperback section of Blackwell's in Broad Street, Oxford. What really interested him, however, were the modern first editions around the corner at Blackwell's antiquarian department on Ship Street. Meanwhile Peter's father returned to England where he became librarian at Royal Holloway College. A bicycle accident forced him to retire early and in 1977 he died. This was a major turning point in the son's fortunes. Michael Jolliffe had left a large interest in a horse-racing course, which Peter cashed in, thereby allowing himself to become a bookseller from his Oxford home and then in Eynsham where he bought a sizeable house. I was there once although I can't recollect the circumstances. It is difficult not to believe the geographical choice owes much to Oscar Mellor's Fantasy Press, which was in Swinford, near Eynsham, and which published the Geoffrey Hill pamphlet I was so keen to obtain a few years later.

Occasionally dealers would go to his house in Eynsham, one of them a major league bookseller from New York, who made a selection of books and agreed a global price. The dealer then said no, that actually he wanted one title only, and paid Peter the global price divided by the original number of books, a mean trick that would haunt him for years to come. One might say, of course, that Peter agreed to it and so had only himself to blame, and, besides, in such instances theft is not so much an actual problem as an abstract one well beyond the reach of justice. Peter was not a difficult man to swindle. A few years later, the same dealer cheated him of the Dedication Copy* of one of Seamus Heaney's books, when he claimed never to have received it in the post. What Bill Hoffer said of the trade comes back to me: 'Honesty is a prerequisite, not an accomplishment.'

As well as producing catalogues, Peter exhibited at provincial book fairs including the one where he narrowly missed the Arthur

* For those unfamiliar with the term, the Dedication Copy (usually capitalised) differs from a presentation copy in that it is the copy presented by the author to the person to whom the book is dedicated.

Symons. He then shared an office with Julian Nangle in Fulham Road, where I attended the opening party with Bill Hoffer who there spied the heavily perfumed woman to whom he said he'd strap his missiles. Sooner or later, everything links up in the universe. And then Peter shared a space in a small shop in Soho with Charlotte Robinson and Stephen Francis Clarke. The next step was Ulysses. A lone trader such as he was, nothing was quite as alien to him as a partnership. This he ought to have recognised in himself before the other partners, perforce, recognised it in him. Joanna Herald was right. His blunders became, perforce, *their* blunders. So great was his desire to obtain a scarce title that he would be prepared to take a financial loss on it and, there again, his loss became, perforce, *their* loss. A man alone might be able to handle it, or dilute failure in one area with success in another, only that with Peter success could make him as unhappy as failure. Very often he would be full of remorse about having made a successful purchase and then would feel even more remorse when he made a sale of it. What defined his business attitude was not loss or gain but the quest and in this respect actual business became secondary in importance.

What made him a bookman, a great one at that, was not deep knowledge, which, after all, is the province of many booksellers, but the fact that for him there was no separation between books, the transit they made through the world, and the workings of his soul. It was a state as terrifying as it was sublime. As such it bode ill when it came to working with other people. When I arrived there, in 1994, Ulysses was arguably the most powerful bookseller in London and not least because of the efforts of three of the four people. It seemed invincible. Gradually, though, I began to observe cracks in the edifice. The partnership would die with the century.

A free agent inside a partnership, the implications do not need spelling out. There was no unity of vision, which may be a baggy word when applied to the trade. If there was anything approaching a 'house style' in the Ulysses catalogues it was not adhered to by Peter who often used the opportunity of the printed page to produce wildly exaggerated descriptions of the books and with autobiographical elements, mostly sad, seeping into them. It is said many people relish the memory of his catalogues, but then I think there was a fine line between admiring his descriptions and laughing at them. The factor common to almost all the books he described was the refrain of 'top edge dusty' even if the dust was only a single mote. It was the unhappiness of one for whom there could be no possibility of perfection. It got so he saw flaws where there were none. It became for him a kind of hell. Peter would describe a book to death, the details so heavily layered that the object itself was rendered invisible to the mind's eye. The catalogues, in particular the ones he later produced on his own, were the blue devils on a rampage.

An unguided missile, Peter went on spending sprees without reference to his colleagues, one of whom, Gabriel, was driven to a breakdown during the course of which he either imagined or had really discovered he was related to a Nazi war criminal. Alcohol was the lubricant for these wild fancies, reality the spur. It would be too much to say Peter was the direct cause of Gabriel's problems, but the money Gabriel needed to keep his side of the business going, travel and topography, was swallowed up by Peter's uncontrollable spending. At one point Peter took all the profit from the sale of books at a New York book fair and blew it on a collection of E. McKnight Kauffer posters, which he accidentally left behind in a hotel room. Was he not becoming the willing victim of his own contrivances? And then there was his purchase of John Lehmann manuscripts from Peter Howard, which by and large proved unsaleable. Also he bought books and, fearing the censure of his colleagues, squirreled them away in cupboards, always pleading innocence when it came time to settle the monthly accounts. The question is whether Peter was venal or addictive or if he simply didn't know how to function with other people. I would say the latter, although perhaps I'm alone in thinking this.

I witnessed the rows. Such were the extremes to which Peter drove people. One day Joanna said to him, 'Peter, are these books your family?' I sat there silently saying, *yes, they are. Yes, they are all he has*. I watched his face crumble. The jibe may have been cruel, but it was born of desperation. It was already the end, although the actual end had yet to come. I watched helplessly as the partnership collapsed. The branch across the street closed and Peter Ellis, taken to the very limit and too exhausted to be able to battle for the control of Ulysses, went his own way and worked from home. Joanna had already made her way, setting up a gardening business, which was much closer to her heart. Gabriel took his side of the business, travel and topography, home. Gone was the most powerful partnership of the nineties. The shop had by default fallen into Peter Jolliffe's hands. Was he any the happier for it? I don't know, but, there again, what species of happiness would allow for the place to deteriorate the way it did?

After the partnership broke up, I stayed with him for another couple of years. Any partnership requires checks and balance, and without them, as he increasingly lost command of himself, his uncontrollability would prove to be the biggest factor in its breakdown. These are matters almost too delicate to go into. Although he still owned the house in Eynsham he spent hardly any time there. The once-beautiful shop became his home. Squalor set in and from all over there would be a smell of rotting food. The inevitable happened. The place became infested with mice, such that at one point I thought it might be the first bookshop in history to be closed down by the Public Health Department. One night Peter caught a mouse, and, holding it in his clenched fist, slowly, very slowly, squeezed it to death. Should I say he was a sadist? Or was it a story he concocted? Who would speak thus of himself? I think it was true and although this may come as a surprise I don't think he was sadistic. I believe he fell prey to the vespertine.* Those empty nights must have been strange. Night terrors, the spawn of solitude. As he did not own a bed, not even in Eynsham, he slept in a chair, his slumped figure often drawing the attention of the police, or, more worrying, young hoodlums who would peer through the window, taunt and terrify him. At

* The Latin for 'bat' is *vespertilio. Vespertine* is also the name of an album by Björk.

first he tried to make friends with them, but they tormented him all the more. When I came into work in the morning it was to the sense of a man having awoken from a nightmare. All day long, he saw night creatures.

Something else inexplicable: at night he would undo the work I had done earlier in the day. Whatever tensions might have existed between us, they had previously been subsumed in our daily routine, and as such they were kept in check by my sympathies for him, but now, with the other partners gone, they were fully exposed. There was absolutely no reason for this other than the fact that *this* was all he had in life. I could go home. This, for him, *was* home. *This* was his family. This was *this* alone. As for my role, as factotum, it was becoming less and less sustainable. Any initiative of mine was immediately crushed. I'll provide two instances. One day, when he was out of the shop, I purchased the first English edition of Jack Schaefer's *The Canyon* (1955). Admittedly it was a whimsical purchase, but the book was written by the author of *Shane* (1949), a milestone in the history of the western, and so was not wholly negligible, and besides I paid only a fiver for it. Peter returned. I showed him my purchase. An hour later, after continually turning the book over in his thoughts he took it and without a word flung it across the room.

The second instance was of a rather different magnitude. Some explanation is required. Again I was on my own when a woman came into the shop with a framed galley proof of six poems by Rupert Brooke, which were published in the fourth and final issue of *New Numbers* (1914). This short-lived journal was the literary organ of the Dymock Poets, a literary group which comprised Lascelles Abercrombie, Edward Thomas, W. W. Gibson, John Drinkwater, the American poet Robert Frost who was then living in England, and Rupert Brooke. The printing of the final issue was delayed so that Brooke who at that point was with the Hood Regiment preparing to take part in the Dardanelles campaign, could finish his war sonnet sequence, the last of which is "The Soldier" with its famous opening line, 'If I should die, think only this of me.' Brooke posted the poems to Lascelles Abercrombie in January. The proofs reached Brooke at a military camp near Blandford in Dorset, at which point, on January 24, he wrote to Eddie Marsh, 'These proofs have come. God they're in the rough, these five camp-children—[Sonnets] 4 and 5 are good enough, and there are phrases in the rest.' Later that month, he wrote to John Drinkwater, 'Come and die. It'll be great fun. And there's great health in the preparation.' And so, *come and die*, in February 1915 Brooke sailed to the Dardanelles. The poems, meanwhile, were praised for their 'selfless patriotism' and Dean William Ralph Inge read "The Soldier" from the pulpit of St Paul's. It was reported in *The Times*. When Brooke was told of it he was already on his deathbed, felled not by a Turkish bullet but by a mosquito bite. All he could do was mumble, which is not to say his wit was impaired, for he got across words to the effect that he was sorry Dean Inge did not think him quite as good as Isaiah. Two days later, on April 23, 1915, he died.

Whatever one may think of Brooke's patriotic sentiments, which, when compared to Wilfred Owen and Isaac Rosenberg, are now a little too easy to deride—actually had the poem been kept to its original title "The Recruit" it might have been read as ironic, the romantic vaporings of a young man who had not yet seen action—the poem is important if only as a heartfelt expression of its time. One could go further and say it was the last time in our human history that such a poem could be written. What I have yet to say about the framed galley proof is that at the bottom, right beneath "The Soldier," is Brooke's autograph inscription to his last love, the actress Cathleen Nesbitt. There have been many words wasted on the true nature of Brooke's sexuality, which could profitably be whittled down to a Bloomsbury via Oxbridge muddle, the sting in the tail being respectable marriage. Cathleen was his promised one and nothing sexual had passed between them. There is good reason to suppose this was the last thing he inscribed. This literary artefact stands as one of the most potent items I have handled in my forty-five years in the book trade. Admittedly it took no more than a glance for me to register its importance even though what I write here has been gleaned from various sources.

Confronted with this treasure, it was incumbent on me to not let it 'get away.' After all, all the lady selling it needed to do was to walk over to Pied Bull Yard and show it to Rick Gekoski who would certainly have made a purchase of it. I had to act quickly and so I devised an offer, which she accepted. As I could not write a cheque she said she would return for it in a couple of days, which struck me as a pleasant enough expression of trust.

Peter returned. I showed it to him. He sulked. He whined.

I went out for lunch, absolutely furious with him. What he could not bear was that something that should have been his discovery had been contaminated with my involvement and experience. When I came back I found the shop completely empty. The front door was wide open. At the entrance he had placed a chair on the seat of which was the framed Brooke, facing outward onto the street, there for anyone to take. Suppose it had been stolen, and it's a miracle it wasn't, would I have been held to blame? Would the woman who left it be paid for something which perhaps Peter would claim he'd never seen? What was his game? The first dealer to come into the shop was Paul Rassam who wrote out a cheque for an amount not much greater than that which I had arranged to pay for it and sped away before Peter could change his mind. To say this was an extreme case of bibliomania would be to understate the matter, for this was bibliomania turned inside out, from a negative into an even deeper negative.

As time went on and his health worsened he became increasingly erratic, often deliberately alienating his best customers, that is, those who could afford his prices. I cultivated a Canadian who had become an excellent buyer.* One day he put on reserve a copy of Samuel Beckett's *Whoroscope* (1930) and as a show of goodwill he gave Peter a holding figure of £100. A couple of days later, he returned, saying he'd decided against the purchase. Peter replied, 'Well, you can't have your money back.' This put the end to any

* Later, when I joined up with Peter Ellis, he sold us some valuable Russian books, which included an inscribed collection of Akhmatova's poems and, for me the prize, a first edition of Osip Mandelstam's first book, *Kamen* (*Stone*, 1913).

further business with the Canadian. It was only the first of several such occasions.

One of the most valued customers was lost on account of a single strawberry.

There was no period when Peter was more dangerous, more unpredictable, than during the Soft Fruit Season (SFS). He would buy vast quantities of the most expensive strawberries, cherries, blueberries, more than he could possibly eat, which he would then distribute in bowls throughout the shop. Woe to the customer who thought the fruit was there for the taking. A collector of note extended a hand towards a strawberry when from the other end of the shop Jolliffe bellowed, 'Don't touch them! They're mine!' Needless to say, we never saw him again. I watched thousands of pounds walk out the door. Once SFS was over it would be a standard fare of green grapes, again the most expensive he could find, and pink lady apples. When the partnership was still in existence, I was among those who made a sport of stealing the odd grape. One day, when he walked over to inspect them, he found several missing, not *all of them* taken by me, and in what later became known as 'the grapes of wrath' incident he took the bowl and hurled it down the stairs. The scattered grapes and broken shards remained there for the next week or so. Another incident involved the pink ladies, when he discovered one of them had been replaced with a banana. This took him into a zone beyond rage. He kept returning to the offending banana, staring at it, walking away and then coming back. He spoke not a word for words could not possibly give voice to incomprehension on the order of a psychic disturbance. The culprit I discovered later was my young daughter, who having heard from me about the pink ladies, dropped into the shop on the pretence of coming to see me, and made the switch. My aforementioned accusers find in this evidence of my cruelty towards him. A better acquaintance of the workplace might enable them to see this for what it was, a mere lark; it's what people who work together do. My daughter is certainly not cruel, but if it pleases them I will say several *mea culpas* but only for the several grapes I pinched. A pink lady, on the other hand, would be serious theft.

Why couldn't we talk when there was so much to talk about? There was, if nothing else, poetry. Peter was the rare, perhaps fatal, instance of a bookseller who was also a collector. He was the "Collector" in Byron Rogers's *The Man Who Went into the West: The Life of R.S. Thomas* (2006).

> Call him the Collector, he does not want his name mentioned. It took months to set up a meeting, in the course of which there were many excuses.
>
> 'My house is in a terrible mess."
>
> Oh, I won't mind."
>
> You don't understand, I might want to sell it one day.'
>
> A low room in a small cottage in the main street of a Home Counties village, with books everywhere, books on tables, on chairs, on the floor. And where no books were there were magazines, and manuscripts, and the only thing missing was furniture. That must have been around somewhere. Forced beneath this weight of print, perhaps fossilised. Through this there moved a man attached by tubing to an oxygen machine, for the Collector was in poor health. It left the impression of an astronaut in an archive among the stars, which in its way was appropriate. Images of space will recur in this book.

How curious that Rogers should also have reached for an image from outer space. He, too, must have noted the intergalactic stare. What he does alter is the house, reducing it to a cottage. I have done the same when hiding the identities of people I've written about. Speaking of his subject, R. S. Thomas, Rogers describes his search for the poet as 'a bit like a space probe in science fiction, with there being very little evidence of a personal life.'

> And then, on a hot summer afternoon, I came on it, or rather, I came on its remains assembled on shelves. It was all here. The first editions were here, the rarest of all, the books printed by small provincial presses, one of them above a chip

> shop in Carmarthen. And not just one or two, but four, five, six copies, each of which would fetch upwards of what? God alone knows, for these books were those the poet had given his wife, his son, his parents.

Rogers goes on for another few pages describing the many treasures he saw in Eynsham. A few years later, when I worked for Peter Ellis, I would catalogue every one of them. Clearly at this point in the visit the Collector became more loquacious.

> 'I got interested in him when his book *H'm* swam into my ken,' said the Collector. 'What a bloody stupid title, I thought, what sort of man could have chosen that? So I began to read him, and there were these incredibly deep poems constructed out of such ordinary language and so few lines. They seemed to me quite magical. So I became a collector. I had one great advantage. I am a bookseller by profession, and my interest in him coincided with what I suppose was a lull in the market for his books in the 1970s. So many of his books came into my hands, with nobody to sell them to, and that was when I thought to myself, I will keep these for myself. And I kept adding to them. At this stage my collection consisted of just basic copies, but then something extraordinary happened. I met his son Gwydion.'

Although Peter would get himself into financial difficulties he did eventually buy the world's best R. S. Thomas collection. Rogers couldn't believe Gwydion Thomas would part with all this, so he rang him.

> [Gwydion] was in no way abashed. 'When we first met I asked the Collector what he would like. "Everything," he said. And that's what he got ...*everything*.'

If Rogers couldn't believe Gwydion would part with the books inscribed to him by his father, including one which contained a poem dedicated to him, I couldn't believe it either. And then I met him. All became clear. Gwydion came into Ulysses with his very young Vietnamese or Cambodian wife. I saw them later on Great Russell Street, he striding ahead pulling his wife by the arm, almost dragging her. They didn't notice me. What I saw, just then, was fear in her eyes. Gwydion, a sometime actor, played the role of Lechery in the 1967 screen adaptation of Christopher Marlowe's *Doctor Faustus*. I would meet him again when I was at Peter Ellis, actually in the process of cataloguing the R. S. Thomas collection. Gwydion expressed outrage that the books were being sold separately, crying that this destroyed the integrity of the collection.

'So why did you sell them then?'

Gwydion produced a reptilian smile.

When Peter made purchases of books he knew would interest me, he hid them. I read on someone's blog that W. S. Graham was Peter's favourite poet. I disagree, Seamus Heaney or R. S. Thomas maybe, followed closely by Elizabeth Bishop, Derek Mahon and Paul Muldoon, but yes, Graham was on the fifth or sixth rung of Peter's literary ladder. I know: I put him there. Peter had a way of absorbing other people's enthusiasms into his, which, in a way honours those from whom he took them. What was not quite as easy to accept is that he would become possessive of them to the point of excluding me. This may sound peevish of me, but then I, too, am smitten with bibliomania although only to the degree that the books were affordable. There were two such instances, one involving Graham and the other, the Polish poet Zbigniew Herbert.

Herbert is another of my literary heroes. I was desperate to get my hands on a book Peter purchased from Peter Howard, Herbert's first poetry collection, *Struna światła* (*Chord of Light*, 1956), inscribed by the author to the man who would produce the first translations into English of many of those poems, Peter Dale Scott. One of the highlights of my collection is the hardback issue of the Penguin Modern European Poets edition of *Selected Poems* (1968) which Herbert inscribed to me when he gave a poetry reading in Oxford on May 5, 1980. A moment ago, checking on the date, I held the book in my hands and I see that already the poor quality paper has become brittle and I can't help but wonder what this little volume will be like a hundred years hence. Will it still *be*? So many of our productions will become dust whereas one will be able to turn without fear the pages of Shakespeare's first folio. I saw Herbert a couple of days later, when, in the company of a rogue friend of mine, we spent a beer-soaked evening in London during which time he inscribed the later Oxford University Press edition of *Selected Poems* (1977). He incorporated in his inscription a drawing of a cityscape and beneath it, as if in opposition, a solitary tree on a hill. I now see that tree with different eyes. Was it not the poet himself, alone? Maybe I read too much into this. I have written elsewhere on my intermittent relationship with Herbert.*

Another of my treasures is the German edition of *Pan Cogito* (*Herr Cogito*, 1974), which on May 28, 1975, he inscribed with 'love and admiration' to the poet Christopher Middleton. They were in Freiburg im Breisgau, on a boat on the Dreisam River. On the verso of the title page is another inscription: 'and passed on with love, admiration, gratitude for Marius from Christopher – October 9, 2013.' My eyes begin to smart. A close friend, Christopher was nearing the end of his life and he wanted to be sure the volume came to me. What an addition to my collection that copy of *Struny światła* would have made. It is difficult to imagine a more desirable copy although presumably a second one was given to Dale's co-translator Czesław Miłosz. When I asked after it, Peter claimed he couldn't quite remember where he'd put it. It would be mine when it appeared, he said. It failed to emerge after his death. Where did it go? Did the mice in the cupboard speak and consume Polish?

When I learned that Peter had made a purchase of a rare W. S. Graham item, *The Journeys of Alfred Wallis* (1948), I asked him if I could see it as I'd had never seen a copy before. I should have known better. Peter gazed into the distance and said he couldn't remember where he had put it. He had bought it at auction the day

* "A Meeting with Pan Cogito", in *The Pebble Chance* (Biblioasis, 2014).

before. I knew he also had the rare issue of Graham's first book, *Cage without Grievance* (Parton Press, 1942) with the illustrations by Benjamin Creme and Robert Frame hand-coloured by them. After he died, Peter Ellis bought both the stock of Ulysses and Jolliffe's private author collections including the W. S. Graham, which contained manuscript material as well. I bought the collection from Ellis. I wonder if that would not have infuriated Jolliffe, the idea of my having it. *Cage without Grievance* wasn't there. It didn't make sense, I knew he had it. Otherwise, as a collection, the Graham is almost complete. I have yet to find the two broadsides printed by Guido Morris of the Latin Press in St Ives, so rare I wonder if I am not imagining them although surely I set eyes on them once.

One of the highlights (terrible word) of the collection is the first edition of *The Nightfishing* (1955), which Graham inscribed to fellow poet G. S. Fraser. It is by any standard an extraordinary copy. On the front free endpaper is a solitary inscription: "From where we are it is not us we see. / Disguise is mortal. 25-1-55." The lines show up fifteen years later in Graham's poem "The Constructed Space," collected in *Malcolm Mooney's Land* (1970) where they become amplified: 'From where we are it is not us we see / And times are hastening yet, disguise is mortal.' Turn the page of my copy of *The Nightfishing* and on the first blank Graham has written out, sans title, the first stanza of that same poem now considered to be the epitome of his later style. What is significant is that his new mode was already there, fully seeded, on October 25, 1955. But where was *Cage without Grievance*? Where could it have gone?

What can I say to those who have no idea who W. S. Graham and Zbigniew Herbert are? They were drunkards both. They were wonderful poets too. I hope that such words as I've quoted will be enough to drive the curious to look for themselves.* It is a strange thing, but when an author dies his 'stock' falls for as long as a decade. This puts paid to the nonsensical remarks of people who on the death of an author say that booksellers immediately double

* *The Pebble Chance* also contains an essay on W. S. Graham.

the prices. Their stock plunges. I've seen this too many times to be mistaken. When Samuel Beckett died it was more than a decade before people started buying him again and at the moment it is true of Seamus Heaney and Geoffrey Hill. There are those very rare instances when the opposite happens; of all the poets of the 1960s and 1970s it is Graham's star that continues to rise. I am speaking of the first edition rather than the new book trade, although I think what happens in the first is a kind of measure. Graham's contemporaries, who were much better known in their time, have almost totally ceased to sell. I can't remember when someone last purchased a title by George Barker, David Wright, John Heath-Stubbs and other poets of Graham's generation. Another unjustly forgotten poet, Nicholas Moore, the only book of his that sells is *The Glass Tower* (1944) and that is only because it is illustrated by Lucian Freud. There is no accounting for the vicissitudes of fame. Some of the most expensive modern first editions in the 1930s were John Galsworthy's novels. A younger generation may very well say *who*? End of lecture.

During that final period my father died and I went to Canada for the funeral. When I returned a week later, Peter said, 'I'm not paying you.' I look at him quizzically. 'I'm not paying you for the time you were away.' I hadn't thought about being paid and I hadn't thought about *not* being paid; I would not have asked for it nor would I have refused it; it was simply nowhere in my thoughts. Why did he say this when I had had not so much as his condolences? And then I think back to when he failed to give Joanna the telephone message that her mother was gravely ill, I understand her taunt all the more. And yet what a reflection this was on his own life, where sympathy and family feeling were like weeds to be pulled out at first growth. The idea of family was completely alien to him and so I don't think he was deliberately cruel to me. It was simply that within such a context he didn't know how to behave. A few weeks later, after one of his many peeves, when I found myself about to crown him with a ladder, I gave my notice. A big library had come up via a friend of mine and I approached Peter Ellis, saying it was a perfect occasion for him to consider taking on a shop in

Cecil Court that had just become vacant. When I told Peter I was going to leave, there were tears in his eyes. He pleaded with me to stay with him. And then the next day he pleaded again.

I found it difficult, I really did. I did not dislike him, but I disliked the situation in which he put me. I could see he was deteriorating. Already, for want of adequate hygiene, he had to contend with a horrendous rash that covered his legs and then when his lungs began to deteriorate further he had to put himself on an oxygen machine. There were days his lips were blue. He hated to be put on display like this and I did everything I could to persuade him it didn't matter, that anybody with a sympathetic bone in his body wouldn't mind. But it *did* matter. People would walk into the shop, see him, and quickly leave. What I can say is that never once did I hear him complain about any of his medical conditions. And indeed he was proud to have outlived his doctor's terrible prognosis of over thirty years before. I knew there was nothing more I could do to support him, and besides, I was carrying too much of the burden, and yet I wish some part of me could have seen him out. The other, more pragmatic, side of me couldn't have got out of there fast enough.

Afterwards, he grew again in my affections. One could appreciate him maybe only at the distance which he put between himself and the world, but it was enough. Any attempt to move up close would only result in exasperation. He died on December 27, 2007, the multiple causes of his death bronchopneumonia, pulmonary fibrosis and histiocytosis X. Gabriel Beaumont was at his side and held his hand and now Gabriel, he, too, has joined the ranks of the departed. Shortly before Peter died, I saw him sitting at his desk, surrounded by boxes of books, too weak to get at them, breathless, his face deathly pale. We chatted and the smile was his old smile. Maybe he'd slipped back into the man I first knew, only now he could barely move. I wish he could have made his departure, in his chair, in the bookshop, surrounded by his treasures. I went to the funeral which struck me as a drab affair for one who deserved more. I heard later that his ashes were scattered on the Westbury White Horse, not far from Trowbridge. Could it be, I wonder in my best Thomas Lovell Beddoes mode, that his ashes whitened the white horse still more? Peter Jolliffe was one of the worst booksellers who ever lived. One might be tempted to say he always shot himself in the foot but for the fact he always missed. But then Peter Jolliffe was the greatest bookman of our time.

Chapter Twelve

IS GOLDILOCKS JEWISH?

SOME YEARS AGO, I CAN'T REMEMBER WHERE, I READ AN eighteenth-century account, clearly written by someone who'd been chiselled once or twice, in which the author speaks of the lowest dregs of society as comprising thieves, prostitutes and booksellers. Cecil Court, the pedestrian alley in central London where I have worked for close to two decades, has been party to all three. In the early part of the twentieth century "Flicker Alley," as it was nicknamed, was home to the film industry in its fledgling stages. Cecil Hepworth who made the first film adaptation of *Alice's Adventures in Wonderland* (1903) and James Williamson who made a film called *An Interesting Story* (1904) about a man so engrossed in his book that he is oblivious to the dangers surrounding him, had their offices there. Where there's celluloid there are bound to be whores. This I learned from an old-timer who had worked there in the 1930s. Their beckoning ghosts occupy the upper storeys. An earlier manifestation of Cecil Court boasted a house of ill repute called The Ham.

At another address the young Mozart, aged eight, stayed a few weeks and, what a brat, wrote his first symphony. The original buildings are no longer there, though, and I have never been overwhelmed with feeling when I read that 'on this site once stood the building *where* ...' I want to know that whatever it is that asks of me that I bow my head in reverence is tangible. I want to be able to walk about the room with a metaphorical tape measure and a spirit catcher too. The Cecil Court we see now was constructed between 1895 and 1902. It's rather handsome. A recent refurbishment has made it even more so. Thieves are a constant: I gave chase to one not long ago; I was fired up with adrenalin, with no thought as to what might happen had I actually caught him.

Cecil Court is as good a place as any to see me out. Although I'd never worked there I frequented it in the 1970s and so it feels like I've gone full circle. I work three days a week and then skedaddle. After the collapse of Ulysses, Peter Ellis continued from his Martello tower, issuing catalogues. When in 2003 I got word on a house full of books I contacted him and suggested that perhaps this was the moment to take over a shop that had become available in Cecil Court. Also it was the springboard I needed in order to be able to leave Peter Jolliffe. Our shop used to be the premises of Lady Edith Finer's Frognal Rare Books, which specialised in economics.* She designed rolling shelves in the basement so that if one were sufficiently on the ball one could squeeze someone to death between them and then say it was all a most unfortunate accident. And then it was a father-and-son team, Reg and Philip Remington, who specialised in travel and topography. Cecil Court had been going through a period of rejuvenation as it must do every ten years or so, and with Peter Ellis's arrival it was given a boost and with his departure it will probably require another one.

* An immensely likeable woman, such that I wish I had got to know her more. I have no interest in economics but I'd often go in there just to shoot the breeze. In an interview with Sheila Markham for the December 1992 issue of *The Bookdealer* she said, 'There's a difference between books as a way to make money, and books as books. It makes me sad when I hear of people going into the business as a business. I love my books and I want to sell them as books.'

Only will it be there, the desire for continuance? I strike a glum note.

Peter Ellis offered me a partnership but at the same time, and wisely, advised me against such a move. I wouldn't be able to write, he warned me, as I'd be wholly absorbed in the running of a business, paperwork, taxes and so forth. He has my gratitude. I have never made provision for the future, which for me has always been an abstract notion (or perhaps an inability to grow up), but at least I have been largely free to do as I like. It's hard enough to manage myself, much less a business. Almost certainly I would not have seen the publication of a number of my books had I chosen a mercantile course. Most vitally, Peter was accepting of the fact I would disappear for a month or so at a time to Damascus, and later, Naples. They had become the stomping grounds for my deeper enquiries into human nature.

What did change for me was that now I had a greater illusion of autonomy than ever before. I had a limited hand in buying books together with him, which is a tremendous way to keep one's interest from flagging, a sense of involvement a firm such as Bertram Rota would never countenance. I will not pretend this did not put additional administrative weight on Peter, but as for myself it resulted in the best years of my working life. Also my relationship with customers was more direct than ever before, on Saturdays in particular when I worked alone and the bookshop became for me a sort of theatrical space. It was not that I sought to make it so. The Saturday people are different to the weekday lot, most of them having been set loose from the madhouse, the schoolhouse, the workhouse, the doghouse, and sometimes, one suspects, the jailhouse. There tend to be more thieves on the loose. Almost always, the day begins with young, starry-eyed American women, a sympathetic lot by and large, who fresh off the plane come in looking for Jane Austen. Some of them ask if I have any first editions, and I say to them that if we did we'd probably close the shop because they are so rare and valuable. Some of them settle for a late-nineteenth- or early-twentieth-century edition, almost always, if we have one, *Sense and Sensibility*. Or else it's

Emily Brontë, *Wuthering Heights*, or Currer Bell, better known as Charlotte Brontë, *Jane Eyre.*

* * *

Is Goldilocks Jewish? In the autumn of 2019, a rabbi walked into the shop with a copy of the Koran in his hand for sale. Although by no means a scarce edition, it was a handsome enough copy, bound in black leather. The rabbi was ultra-Orthodox and dressed in full Orthodox mode—the long black *chalat* coat, wide-brimmed hat, sidelocks and a *tallit* with knotted *tzitzis* at the corners. It seems I had entered the realm of unlikelihood. I was prepared to offer him thirty pounds for it, but thought it would be advisable, courteous even, to ask him whether he had a figure in mind.

'It cost me a hundred pounds,' he replied, 'but I'd be happy to get my money back on it.' Good thing I asked.

I said I wouldn't be able to come anywhere near that figure.

'What would you be prepared to offer for it?' he asked.

'I would rather not say because I don't wish to offend you.'

'Believe me, you won't offend me. Say what your offer would be.'

The rabbi had me in a corner. I stated my figure and then told him that he ought to visit some other booksellers to see if he could get more and, if not, then he'd be welcome to return and I'd honour my original offer. And he went away, only to return a couple of hours later, somewhat crestfallen. I gave him the thirty pounds.

'I hope you don't mind my saying this,' I told him, 'but not even in the wilder recesses of my imagination could I have expected to see a rabbi wandering down Cecil Court with a copy of the Koran in his hands.'

'One of the loveliest sounds in Jerusalem,' he replied, 'is hearing from the minarets the call to prayer.'

Clearly I was speaking to a rather special man, someone able to rise above the Middle East divide. Then he expressed the hope that America would not attack Iran. I can't fully recapitulate all that was said, but I discovered Rabbi Benjamin spoke old Hebrew, Yiddish, Arabic, Aramaic (the language with which Christ would have been familiar), French, Russian and even, if I remember correctly, a smattering of Persian. One of his relatives, he told me, the brother of his great-grandfather on his mother's side, was the great cantor Moshe Koussevitzky.* For those unacquainted with cantorial music this would be the equivalent of saying one's uncle was Caruso. When I extolled the beauty of the cantor's voice, Rabbi Benjamin asked me whether I would like to hear a couple of examples.

'What, really?'

He began with "Ashamnu Mikol Am" ("We have become the guiltiest of all people") which is sung before the *vidduyim* (confession) at Yom Kippur. A work of great beauty, melancholy yet sensuous, it was composed by the Russian cantor David Roitman who is often referred to as 'the poet of the pulpit.' Rabbi Benjamin then sang to me in different cantorial styles, including a mystical prayer in Aramaic from the Zohar, "Brich Shmei" ("Blessed be the name"), which was made famous by the other great cantor of the twentieth century, Yoselle Rosenblatt; it is sung when the Torah is taken out of the ark to be read. I remember being aghast when a late friend said to me that had the Nazis listened to klezmer and cantorial music, the Jews might have been spared their terrible fate. I wished I could agree and yet Rabbi Benjamin told me of another distant relative of his, also a cantor, who, together with scores of other Jews, was taken out to be executed in front of the pit that would be their common grave. Stripped naked, he sang one last time. The Nazi commandant was so astonished he set him free. The others were shot, of course, but it says something for a music that tames, if only for a second or two, the most bestial in human nature. The visit brightened what had been a grim day, not least

---

* I had been exploring his music along with that of Yoselle Rosenblatt. I would be hard-pressed to choose between them although not being able to speak Hebrew who am I to judge? Incredibly Moshe Koussevitzky's three brothers were also outstanding cantors. Koussevitzky, with the help of Soviet agents, managed to escape Nazi-occupied Poland to Russia where under the name of Mikhail Koussevitzky he sang opera, sometimes with Stalin in the audience.

because for several months the whole of Cecil Court was lined on both sides, from top to bottom, with scaffolding, making it dark and miserable and bad for trade. Also there was an incessant sound of drilling immediately outside. As soon as Rabbi Benjamin began to sing, the scaffolders outside fell silent.

A rabbi had stopped time.

A few weeks later, he returned, this time with a copy of *Goldilocks and the Three Bears*, one of those insipid productions of the 1950s with illustrations in pastel colours, which adults seemed to think would please children although I think they must have been pleasing only themselves. Most children's books are, in a sense, adults' books. And this one came from the decade of cotton wool bread and processed cheese. Children enjoy menace. They don't want their world delivered in pinks and baby blues. The main protagonist in Robert Southey's original published version, published anonymously in 1837, although it already existed in the oral tradition, was an old hag who might be better placed in a House of Correction than in children's tale.

'What makes you think I'd be interested in this?' I asked him.

'I think it's a very nice copy,' he replied.

'Yes, but it's not even remotely what we deal in.'

It wasn't even a nice copy of a bad book, but I didn't immediately dismiss it because I wanted to keep Rabbi Benjamin talking. It was near closing time. I suggested we go for a coffee, but he had to decline because the cow from which the milk came would not have been milked under strict rabbinical supervision and the cup in which it was served would first have to be immersed in a *mikvah* or ritual bath although a disposable cup would be alright. While I was tempted to say why don't we get a takeaway black tea or coffee I didn't, thinking there would be even more religious obstacles. When I told him how much I enjoyed his singing last time he was positively gleeful.

'Do you want to hear another?'

'Well, why not?'

He sang another melancholy piece.

'I can also do the Muslim call to prayer.'

'Really?'

'Allahu akbar, Allahu akbar, Ashhadu alla ilaha illallah.'

I found something ineffably moving in this. Some months later, I visited the Rabbi Benjamin at his family home. A delightful woman, his mother asked me whether I had been sent by witches. And I was able to say that I had been in correspondence with one, Kala Trobe, at which the rabbi interjected, telling me that his mother is psychic. The discussion turned to the witches that were employed by the British Army during the war in order to protect with their spells the coastline.

Again, is Goldilocks Jewish? What at first seemed a spurious notion, my weak brain conflating the 'gold' that so often features in Jewish surnames and, dare I say it, Rabbi Benjamin's sidelocks, has now acquired a solemn dimension. A silly question demands a serious answer and so I did a bit of research. All too predictably *Goldilocks and the Three Bears* has been given the psychoanalytic treatment although by no means is there a consensus on what its interpretation should be, Bruno Bettelheim seeing in it the child's struggle to get past oedipal issues while Alan C. Elms sees it as Freudian pre-oedipal anality. I should think there are conferences all over the world devoted to this thorny issue. I then discovered the story has been analysed from a Hassidic perspective. ("Goldilocks" in Hebrew is "Zahavah," which means "Golden One.") According to Hassidic thought one should strive for the middle way, a prime instance of this being the Giving of the Torah which involves the synthesis of the spiritual and the physical. I don't want to pretend to have knowledge of matters well beyond my ken, and Judaism is akin to the unlocking of a new universe, but in its rudiments I find the Hassidic take infinitely more attractive than any psychoanalytic hogwash.

Goldilocks seeks a middle way in which the porridge and the bed are *just right.* The temptation might be to strangle her or to say that if the porridge is too hot now it won't be in five minutes or that if the bed is too hard try putting on it one of those memory foam toppers which have been developed by NASA to keep astronauts comfortable. There is also, derived from the search for a happy medium, the Goldilocks principle which may be applied to cognitive science, biology, engineering and even economy, and from there we come to what is called the Goldilocks zone, which is the habitable area surrounding a star or what is called the circumstellar habitable zone (CHZ). Our planet is just the right distance away from its sun—not too hot, not too cold, not too cushy, not too hard—and as such it can support the existence of booksellers, prostitutes and thieves.

* * *

One Saturday a man in a blue fedora very much like mine, only with a narrower brim than I would find acceptable, aged somewhere in his mid-fifties, came into the shop with some poetry pamphlets he found outside. I hope he will not take it amiss if I were to say there was a goofy aspect to him, the goofiness that is so often an attribute of searching minds. (Goofy, the Walt Disney cartoon character, an anthropomorphic dog, wears a crumpled fedora, only his is green not blue.) My friend James Sutherland Smith, poet, was in the shop at the time, over from Slovakia where he lives, to launch his new book *The River and the Black Cat* (2018). You might say the stage was set for an agreeable farce. As I said earlier the shop is often a theatre and I had the sense of someone with whom I could make sport and who would not take offence. When I misfire, I misfire badly. There was the time a woman came into the shop looking for mountaineering titles, who was not amused when I said I bet she could climb to the top of any mountain. I am such a fool sometimes. Anyway I studied the poetry titles, all of them small press publications of a fugitive nature, all of them well away from the literary mainstream, all of them imbued with the desperate aura of the poetically disabled. These were not books a civilian would purchase.

'You a poet then?'

'Well, yes, I suppose I do write verses,' he replied, obviously pleased to be recognised as one.

'In that case I think you'd better leave,' I said in my best Harold Pinter voice.

As perverse in his nature as I am in mine, he stood his ground, undeterred. We got into conversation. Although it was true, he did commit the cardinal sin of weighing down the planet with yet more verses, he was, in the main, a classical composer. This piqued my curiosity as I have always been in awe of classical musicians and composers. Poets are a dime a dozen and even at that, more often than not, overpriced. What emerged was an extraordinary story. A composer for the whole of his adult life, actually more if you include his early to late teens, David Hackbridge Johnson has composed fifteen symphonies and close to four hundred other works including opera, chamber music, works for piano, ballet music and so forth. The incredible thing is that he had heard hardly any of it in performance. There were no recordings either. The compositions had gone into his bottom desk drawer, so to speak.

A few years ago, he had a serious illness that left him hovering between life and death for a whole month, a malady which even now leaves him somewhere between sunniness and torpitude. At the end of this struggle, the thought occurred to him: supposing he had died, what would have become of all the music he wrote. At the urging of a friend, record producer Martin Anderson who, by the way, had no idea his old friend was a composer, he sent his Ninth Symphony to the conductor Paul Mann who read the score and realised it was a work of genius and subsequently recorded it with the Royal Liverpool Philharmonic. When Johnson listened to the orchestra recording his Ninth and was asked whether it was what he imagined he replied it was exactly what he heard while composing it. *Good, good.* The thing imagined is not always the thing realised. Another two recordings have appeared since, but they only scratch the surface of a sizeable body of work and I'm irritable for want of more. We have become friends although he is on constant probation for he keeps producing verses. Any deeper consideration of David Hackbridge Johnson's music must be dealt with elsewhere, but for now let's just say there is a most singular David Hackbridge Johnson soundscape.

Among book collectors he is definitely a magpie, seizing upon whatever sparkles. Although he'll buy books just because he likes the look of them, a terrible flaw in a man of intelligence, I have rarely encountered anyone who as a reader is more democratic in allowing authors, particularly unknown, unfashionable or forgotten ones, a first, second or third chance. And whatever author takes his fancy, he'll drain to the dregs the whole of his or her oeuvre. It was in this spirit that he bought the two-volume edition of John Drinkwater's *Collected Poems* (1923), a poet whose very name tends to raise a smirk and yet who in his day was much admired as one of the Dymock Poets, whose number included Edward Thomas, Robert Frost and Rupert Brooke. And who reads John Masefield anymore? Well, David Hackbridge Johnson does. And so he will move from the perceived stodginess of the Georgian poets to that old scoundrel, Peter Russell, and from there to the radically innovative Bill Griffiths.

Another ghost, Bill Griffiths: I knew him when I worked at the Poetry Society and under my imprint Earthgrip Press* published a couple of pamphlets by him, *The Song of the Hunnish Victory of Pippin the King* (1976) and *Six Walks around Tenby* (1976). We together, on my Adana letterpress, printed and pulled pages, collated and stitched them together. I fed him and he ate as one who eats but rarely and with no time to meditate on what he

* 'Earthgrip' was not taken from the science fiction stories of Harry Turtledove, but is Anglo-Saxon for 'the grave,' as in Michael Alexander's translation of "The Ruin": 'Earthgrip holds them—gone, long gone ...' I also published work by Jean-Pierre Dupray *Temporal Flight* (1976) in the translation made by Pierre Joris; and Nathan Whiting *The London A-Z Poems* (1976). A selection of Marvin Cohen's stories, *How the Snake Emerged from the Bamboo Pole but Man Emerged from Both* (1978) was published in conjunction with Oasis Press. Four of the titles were printed on the Adana letterpress, which was my sole foray into the world of fine printing although the results were anything but. Printing requires patience and patience has never been my strong point. What can be said in its favour, though, is that there were several bookshops in London that accepted small press publication, the most important of them being Compendium in Camden Town. Also I'd produce ten numbered and signed copies, the sale of these usually covering the costs of printing. Bear in mind that regular copies rarely sold for more than a pound. Still I found myself with insufficient funds to publish more.

ate. A onetime biker with the Harrow Road Rats, which regularly clashed with the Hells Angels, and briefly a Brixton prison inmate, Griffiths galvanised those experiences, making them the substance of one of his best works, *Cycles* (1974), with its electrically charged fanfare:

> Ictus!
> As I ain't like ever to be still but
> kaleidoscope,
> lock and knock my sleeping.

LOVE and HATE were tattooed on his knuckles and covering almost the whole of his back was a tattoo of the Crucifixion. Christ squirmed upon his cross as Griffiths bent to the Adana printing press. Was he irreligious? I think not. There was a savage biker's probity in him. And there was a softness in his voice that could easily become menace. William Rowe was surely right when he spoke of him as 'possessing an intense gaze that was embedded in some inner place of delicate shyness.'* In another age, Griffiths would have been a North Sea raider, declaiming verses as he hacked his way through the mediocre, but he would also have been the monk that same raider put to the sword. There truly was a gentle side to him; he was courteous to women, the very young and the elderly, kindly to stray dogs, and with some proficiency played Scarlatti on the piano. My mother adored him. One morning, in September 2007, I was sitting on the top deck of the number 9 bus and opened the pages of *The Independent* and there, on the obituary page, was my auld acquaintance. Fifty-nine years of age, only. *Jesu*, my eyes pricked. I found him the most interesting, the most unpredictable, of the so-called British Poetry Revival of the 1970s, Eric Mottram its cicerone. Bill Griffiths's poetical sun, though visible, has yet to fully rise. What I can say for sure is that he would have been mightily chuffed at the thought of a composer's appreciation of him.

---

* Rowe's obituary of Griffiths appears in the *Guardian* (September 22, 2007).

I asked David Hackbridge Johnson for his written thoughts on books and collecting, confident in the knowledge that he would produce something unusual for he is, in both chapter and verse, quite the most peculiar of writers, such that I wonder sometimes from what planet he comes. I asked for a gavotte; I got a symphony. And it even had a title "Sniff the Red Gauntlet." It affords a rare glimpse into the unpredictable mind of a magpie. What was I to do with it? Was I to extract only what I wanted from it? I could see that to do so would ruin its sure rhythm. So what I've done is to present it here whole in order that I might slip out for a tumbler of absinthe.

> If I am to think about books, can I start with what is *not* in them? Nothing then of stories, poems, history, mathematical formulas, maps of Norfolk, what-have-you. Just the book as an object, a rectangle open on three sides, a hinge for rifled pages, a pinched sheaf of paper that only age will release from the author's grip.
>
> My parents had a modest collection of hardbacks which sat in a couple of shelves in the living room. They were not easy of access; no one read them so they needn't have been. The books were those that my parents had read and kept; an ossified group to which nothing was added or taken away—I never saw them pull out any of these books; they must have read them many years previously, perhaps before I was born. Their everyday reading requirements were met by a steady feed of cheap paperbacks which were usually dispatched when read, never staying in the house long enough for me to know. But the immobile frieze of spines in the bespoke collection was captivating to me as a very young boy. Book spines—that uneven wave they make when a finger is run parallel to the shelf, one whose amplitude could be altered by pushing books of smaller width to the back of the shelf, for, yes, my father was fastidious enough to have the spines as flush as he could make them—my interference must have been ruinous to his nerves. Then, pulling a book from its

rank to discover a colourful dust jacket, or a woven cloth in purple, or, and this the best of all, the marbled boards of Walter Scott's *Redgauntlet*, a volume of which, the third, my parents possessed. First, the pattern of the boards—of paisley 1970s shirt design (we wore them), the spine in tooled leather, the gold gilt lettering of the author and title—then, open the book to hear again and again the crumpling of the pages, for damp had intruded into the volume making another wave, this time of the warped leaves. How many times did I stay by that corner shelf, cramped between various pieces of free-standing furniture, with *Redgauntlet* as my sole companion, in awe of its feel, its shifting planes, its musty smell? And not having a clue about its contents, since my trance state precluded an actual reading of the story. This was an object of desire.

Having established a love of books based on the sensual, I should add a brief aside on the Wallington High School for Boys Book Sniffing Club. This august organisation I am proud to say, was founded by me in 1977. It ran informally until 1982 when I left the school. One of my piano students, who later attended WHSB, resurrected the club in the late 80s. I cannot say if it reached the venerable third school generation of existence. Suffice it to say that a lot can be gained about the activities of this club by its title. Imagine a row of boys, no doubt bored with sines and cosines or with the kinships of the Boro tribe, hunched over books in silence; pages of assembled volumes are rifled and a gentle sniffing is heard—each boy with his own unique nasal cavity with which to impart his 'tone.' Slow and thoughtful were the inhalations, as if vintages of the Côte d'Or were being held to the nose. Woody, with a hint of lychees. It was safer than glue.

But at around this time, 1977, I had graduated beyond the sensual, to actually reading books. As a residual of my past fascination with the feel of a book, I accompanied my reading with rapid fannings of the pages as a comfort to dry spells in the plot or to tedious descriptions of the faces of characters, faces which I had already pictured for myself—how often authors got the look of their characters wrong! After a few years of saved pocket money and with money from my first jobs as a pit violinist for local operetta companies, I was able to start my own collection. New books held little interest, unless they were the *Playfair Cricket Annual*, or something on the planets by Patrick Moore. I needed books that matched the spell of Walter Scott's dank tome. Replication—that obsessive trait. Soon I had entire runs of Scott in the cheaper, smaller editions. Sets of Trollope, Thackeray, Dickens (with Phiz), Galsworthy, G. B. Shaw, Blackwood, Machen, followed. All unread as I ploughed through paperbacks of many of the same authors—my page flicking watched by the rows of blinking gilt. I thought of them as the real books that could not be penetrated by my scanning eyes—the paperbacks were sullied by my doing so.

That I bought so many books, to the despair of my parents as the unread volumes spilled out of shelves and into carpet-based towers, is partly due to the rather wonderful pair of peculiar shops in the locality. There was the Cheam Bookshop and there was the Croydon Bookshop. First peculiarity: the Cheam bookshop was in Belmont and the Croydon Bookshop was in Carshalton. At a stretch one might include Belmont in the edgelands of Cheam, but Carshalton couldn't by any geographical sleight-of-hand come within the orbit of that skyscrapered metropolis, Croydon. Had these shops been uprooted and replanted? Had they caused literary offence in their original localities and been expelled to the illiterate hinterlands? And where had the Sutton Bookshop gone to? Penge. Second peculiarity: the rabbit warren layout of both shops—as if a Sheridan Le Fanu plot had been made visible as a labyrinth of shadowy internal spaces, each with its dim, bare bulb flickering over thousands of arcane volumes, wherein the dismal secrets of benighted families lay. The Belmont had outbuildings, garden sheds really, where an avalanche of unsorted books, all having a faint odour of fertiliser, would tumble forth upon opening the rickety doors. The Croydon was manned by a couple—he, a terrifyingly silent pipe smoker—requests for Walter Besant met with a disdainful sucking—she, only by her smiles less silent. The Belmont seemed to be run by a jovial family of red-faced OAPs who greeted one with gusto, fought over broadsheet newspapers and said, 'Have a look in the Fourth Shed.' Third peculiarity: I was peculiar, so I fitted right in.

Forty years later and I am in a position to offer useless advice. The best way to build a collection is not to have a plan. I discovered this when I had grown tired of not reading the regiments of Victorian fiction on parade in my room at home. The type of collection I have in mind is that eclectic one led by the nose for the curious—I needed more topics. No more Lyttonian 'dark and stormy nights' or Hardyesque wife-auctions; I needed the neglected book by a major author, the panned author, the once all-the-rage forgotten author, the *poète maudit* of impossible sonnets, the poet who punched other poets. The strange, the odd and the overlooked. Regional Scottish Check (not to be confused with Tartan). Insect Noises. Sewage Hydraulics. And that Holy Grail—the yet to be unearthed *Encyclopaedia of Manhole Covers*.* The eclectic bent of my collection (remarked upon by friends) might have a further source beyond curiosity, in that motley book assortment of my parents; in addition to the marbled *Redgauntlet*, I might mention my father's weighty volumes of English history, particularly the Crimean War period, his absorbing but utterly impenetrable (to me at any

* What is one to say of a man who lists as his top treasures: J. B. White, *The Design of Sewers and Sewage Treatment Works* (1970), P. T. Haskell, *Insect Sounds* (1961), W. S. Chevalier, *London's Water Supply 1903-1953* (1953), the last with a signed presentation letter to members of the staff of the Metropolitan Water Board, and Eric Bligh, *Tooting Corner* (1946), memoirs of life in Victorian Tooting. Bligh was a bookseller and owner of the Vintage Book Shop in Dorking. One could, I suppose, put a Dantesque spin on the first title. (*ed.*)

rate) *Canadian Rubber Company Standard Mathematical Tables and Formulae*—how I still thrill to the Witch of Agnesi and the Ovals of Cassini*—the beautiful books on the flora of Madeira and Tenerife, with photographs from the 1960s in what seem now somewhat hallucinogenic colours, and two of my mother's favourites: the poems of Rupert Brooke, and George Eliot's *The Mill on the Floss*; the former with an inscription to my mother from 'Daddy.' My parents revealed their own eclectic taste by what they read—and this trait passed to me.

More advice: don't alphabetise books. This tissue of order is a disaster for the collector. You can spend a week obsessing about the alphabet, shuffling the letters backward and forward, deploying book ends every twelve inches and desperate, pronated thumbs to stabilise the teetering books—and finally you have the perfect A to Z order! Only you find that the just purchased slimmest of slim volumes will not fit under the letter K, however hard you squeeze his verse, and that no subsequent letter with its tranche of books can be eased the fraction of an inch required—and the whole of the letters subsequent to K (perhaps several thousand volumes) have to be shifted to space that doesn't exist.† All systems fail for lack of space. The non-system goes where it will. One well-known record collector (I have a collection of these too but will leave this other-madness for other times) swears by the order-by-purchase format—in other words the Haydn quartets, the opera by Puccini, the symphony by Magnard will ever remain together in a slot that preserves their union by having been bought at the Gramex on 23rd November

* In mathematics the Witch of Agnesi is a cubic plane curve defined from two diametrically opposite points of a circle and a Cassini oval is a quartic plane curve defined as the set (or locus) of points in the plane such that the product of the distances to two fixed points is constant. I hope this is not to state the obvious (*ed.*).

† "K." Dare I live in hope? (*ed.*)

1994. This method has much to commend it; I prefer sort-by-subject, but within subject alphabetising is forbidden.

Apart from moments of low ebb, my collecting has continued to this day, nose to the heights and depths of towering shelves. Need I cover in detail the nineties, the thousands? The mill race of Charing Cross? The Harrods-like scramble at Book Fairs? The mystery of the sealed case at Watkins? The seismic shift of sheet music in the basement of The Archive? The man who enters the shop with his fanfare, 'Any bus tickets, got any bus tickets?' Every collector will have his stories of elation and despair: the book that by its absence is a wound in the shelf on which it surely belongs—its sudden appearance at a fraction of the price expected; the book of Henry Moore drawings so yearned for, found at last, yet the discovery that its plates have been removed by means of a razor. Everyone knows that feeling of grovelling at the lower shelves in Any Amount of Books for the one missing volume of the Byron letters, only to find the smiling face of Jeremy Reed level with your own. Or knows of that man foaming—I never saw a lady foam—at a clutch of Rudolf Steiners, only to find the etheric plane quite beyond him.

Can collecting from the wonderful old shops continue? Might the dream end, as bookshops are squeezed by Rachmanite landlords and falling literacy?* For it is in dreams that I journey through dark streets, into gloomy shops, to discover perfect arrays of unknown books suddenly met by their glowing titles, inviting in their red morocco, their enigmatic inscriptions, their paperback simulacrums fluttering around in well-thumbed homage. A Quest in the mind as much as in materiality. The Quest is all. And the reading, a bonus.

* The dream ends for reasons that would have been inconceivable at the time of writing (*ed.*).

I'm back. Has he finished? Will David Hackbridge Johnson demand his share of royalties? Splitting the atom would be comparably simple to my splitting the even more infinitesimal with him, for my sales more often than not enter the minus zone. As it turns out, he is honoured to be sandwiched between a rabbi and an erotomane.

* * *

I can't present a magpie without its opposite, a hawk, and so I turn to one of the most fascinating collectors I've met in recent times, Tony Fekete. Although born, bred and educated in England, Fekete has the air of an aristocratic foreigner. There is something in his clipped voice that bespeaks the drawing-rooms of Venetian palaces. There is even in his curly hair tinged with white some hint of rococo intrigue. I can say this because I don't really know him. One may allude to simple facts, of course. His parents, Hungarian Jews, came to England after the Second World War and then had a brief spell in South Africa before returning and settling in Millom in Cumberland where there was already a small population of Hungarian émigrés. The Hungarians are difficult to understand at the best of times, but that they should converge on a small town of ironworks makes them even more inscrutable. Millom is home to the Cumbrian Heavy Horse Centre and it is said of Hungarians they are inseparable from their horses, but theirs would be light horses reared for swooping over the Great Hungarian Plain as if they are acting out the fast movement in a Bartók string quartet. Some years later, the Feketes moved to London. As a child Tony Fekete frequented the bookshops in Flask Walk in Hampstead where presumably he caught collectors' disease. The English boy goes in search of culture. His parents wanted him to be English and to *not* speak Hungarian. This he puts down to the double stigma of being refugees from a communist country and being of a tyrannized race.

'When you are persecuted,' he said, 'you either feel proud of the fact that you've survived or you feel that maybe there was a reason for it and that your children will be persecuted as well. So *let's hide it*. They brought me up to be English, they gave me an English name. So I had nothing Jewish and nothing Hungarian. I had to rediscover those things. My father told me not to go to Hungary because I'd be locked up. When you are student what is the first thing you do? You do what's forbidden, yes? So I went to Hungary, developed a fascination for the place and built a mystique around it. When I went in the eighties to work there with an American bank I still couldn't really speak Hungarian, but because I understood what my parents said to each other it was basically a process of *activating* my passive knowledge. I learned to speak relatively fluently within a year.'

This penchant for language, whether consciously or not, would have consequences for him as book collector, but first he collected Baedekers and then erotica. The latter was one of the most important collections ever assembled, the bulk of it sold in auction by Christie's in 2014, one of those landmark sales of which even the catalogue is of collectible value. It included the first edition of one of the rarest books in existence, Marquis de Sade's *La Nouvelle Justine, ou les malheurs de la vertu, suivie de l'histoire de Juliette, sa soeur* (1797 [1799, 1801]), in ten volumes, complete with 101 engraved plates. It was the work that saw its author arrested and incarcerated in the Charenton Asylum, without trial, for life. It titillates still. The copy belonged to the notorious French author, diplomat and pederast, Roger Peyrefitte. Obtained for 7,000 euros, from someone who did not realise it was a first edition, it sold at Christie's for £86,500. Tony Fekete has one of the most effective weapons in a collector's arsenal: knowledge.

I suggested that, as with Don Giovanni, for him the object of desire, once obtained, loses its lustre. The analogy is not an idle one. One can observe rapacious hunger in Fekete's eyes. I'd cast him in Mozart's opera any time.

'But you *must* know that!' he replied as if somehow I'd overlooked the obvious. 'That is what book collecting is all about. It is about dreaming for three decades of obtaining a book and then as soon as you have it you think about what to get next.'

After the erotica collection was dispersed, although he has held back some rarities, Fekete developed a whole new area of collecting, one so unique that it invited itself to be included in this book. The Private Polyglot Library, as he calls it, comprises grammars, glossaries, dictionaries and works of translation, but not just any translations or any books of etymology. They must first have upon them the patina of unlikelihood and, better still, a story attached to them. A first French translation of *War and Peace* would hold little or no interest for him whereas the first edition of *Robinson Crusoe* in Maltese does. As well as being one of the first printings of a book in the modern Maltese orthography, which up to that point had employed Arabic script, *Il Haÿa u il Vinturi ta' Robinson Krusoe* (1846) is the first non-religious book to be printed in Malta. A solitary man on a solitary island in a solitary language, what better fit for Tony Fekete?*

These are the sorts of things I look for,' he continued. 'Shakespeare in strange languages. I have him in Armenian, Ottoman Turkish and West Frisian, and now Defoe in Maltese. These books were important because they enabled people to read the classics in their own language and therefore strengthen the status of endangered or minority languages. If you could read *Robinson Crusoe* in Maltese as a Maltese it would enrich your literary knowledge—you wouldn't have to read it in English—and similarly with Frisian, you've got a literature printed in the Frisian language. That is important for the language, otherwise it would just get lost as a colloquial way of communication.'

Applicable to Tony Fekete's grand scheme is the Hungarian proverb *'A nyelvében él a nemzet'* ('The nation lives in its language'). I found the idea of collecting obscure translations quite extraordinary, but I divined in this a bigger scheme. I was not disappointed by his response especially when it brought into play a wedding of sacred and profane.

* An in-depth study of this edition by Jay Mifsud, *Translation and adaptation in extracts from Il Haÿa u il Vinturi ta' Robinson Krusoe* by Daniel Defoe translated by Richard Taylor (2016) demonstrates the extraordinary degree to which Taylor's translation was tailored for a Maltese audience.

'The translation is just one part of the whole,' he explained. 'The collection is about language in culture—the development of language, the development of cultural and national identity, and the use of language in special situations as well, whether it be the language of erotica or the language of the church. It was important that as part of their work missionaries translated things into vernacular languages. It is all about the development of language through books. So we go from the fifteenth and sixteenth centuries when they were simply recording languages, producing grammars and dictionaries, into the seventeenth century where, with the beginning of the Enlightenment, language was seen as a way of expressing the ways people think. Also it was about transmitting ideas from one culture to another. Here it becomes very interesting. You have, for example, the rare 1660 *Port-Royal Grammar* by Antoine Arnault who was a Jansenist and therefore among the first free thinkers. It is a very important grammar which separated or, rather, freed language thinking from the fairly rigid classical way of looking at things. Bibles are also interesting because you see in them an early attempt to structure language and to establish some sort of consistency in the orthography and grammar, the Luther Bible, for example. I don't have that, but I do have the first edition of the Ostrog Bible of 1581, complete.'

Speaking to Fekete is an education in itself, which makes good his vaunted ambition to create, as it were, a collective intelligence. The Ostrog Bible is not only one of the earliest translations of the Bible, it is the first complete edition in Church Slavonic, the liturgical language used by the Orthodox Church in Russia and neighbouring countries.

'It is one of my big treasures,' Fekete continued, 'a book of 1,256 pages, and the most important statement of the Slavonic language to date, and going on from there I am interested in the development of grammar. Take Russian, for example. In the seventeenth century you have the Smotrytsky *Slavonic Grammar* (1619) which I have,* which is the Moscow dialect, if you like, or a variant of

* It was already scarce in 1726 when Fedor Polikarpov in his foreword to a new edition of the Smotrytsky wrote it was like looking for 'a spark amid the ashes.'

Church Slavonic, and then the eighteenth century when Russian has a structure of its own, and forward into the nineteenth century where you see the Russian language used as a way of controlling the empire. I am also very much interested in minority languages, in particular the grammars for languages that are not particularly well-known. You look at the development of Hungarian and the Romanian languages, and how from the end of the eighteenth to the beginning of the nineteenth century they went through a period of self-discovery and structuring because in both countries there was the desire to establish a language that was worthy of placement in the languages of Europe. With Hungarian there was a problem in that there was no consistency in the orthography, there were doubts about grammar, debates on how you put words together and whether you should be conservative in your vocabulary or accept new words. All this was settled by about 1830. In Romania it was even more exciting because there was an attempt to get rid of the Slavic background, when the language was written in Cyrillic, and so there was a movement to exchange Slavic words for words that are Latin- or French-based. This interests me very much. Translations come into this because not only were they important in transmitting ideas, but also, particularly in the eighteenth century with philosophical works, you find that translations were sometimes an inspiration for creating a new vocabulary. I have some examples of this. I have a book which was translated by Antioch Kantemir who was a prince and son of the great Moldavian soldier and statesman Dimitri Kantemir, Fontenelle's *Conversations on the Plurality of Worlds*, which was hated by the Church because it suggested there was life on other planets. This book has importance as a work of the Russian Enlightenment and also because it introduced new words into the Russian language at a point when it was still in formation.'

It ought to have been obvious to me, but then my thoughts had never ventured there, that religious works often preserved languages that have since disappeared.

'I have a second edition of the New Testament published in a creole language called Negerhollands [Negro-hollandic], which was spoken by the slaves on the plantations of the Danish West

Indies. It was published in Copenhagen in 1818. The Danish West Indies are now, after being sold to the USA in 1917, the American Virgin Islands. It is perhaps the only literature in this language. I also have the *Gospel According to St Matthew* in another Caribbean language, Black Carib, a language spoken on St Vincent. Similarly it is one of the very few books, perhaps the only one, in that language.'

Very few are the collectors who own a book bearing a saint's ownership signature. Fekete has a Church Slavonic-Greek-Latin Lexicon published in Moscow in 1704, the first trilingual dictionary published in Russia, which was owned by the Georgian-born monk and theologian Saint Antim Ivireanul otherwise known as Saint Anthimos the Iberian.* Clearly this was the object he used for the many translations he made. As for the book itself, it was an important milestone in the origins of the Russian Enlightenment, its inclusion of Latin very much in line with Peter the Great's policy of opening up Russia to the West.

Where else under a single roof can one hope to find, in addition to countless glossaries, grammars and dictionaries, Hans Christian Andersen's fairy tales in Yakut; *Tiomnadh Nuadh* (1767)

* Captured by the Ottomans as a child, Antim was sold in the slave market in Constantinople to the Patriarch of that city. There he took orders and trained as an artisan in sculpting wood, painting, embroidery and calligraphy. Patriarch Dositheos took him to Iași in Romania where he would become a guiding light in the development of its language. An interesting figure in the history of typography, in 1691 he was put in charge of the newly founded printing press in Bucharest where two years later he published the Gospels in Romanian. Also he was instrumental in bringing Romanian into the church as an official language. In 1709 he founded the first Georgian printing press in Tbilisi. He was martyred in what is now modern-day Bulgaria, quite possibly on the orders of Prince Nicholas Mavrocordatos, Grand Dragoman to the Divan, which is ironic given that the prince was a polyglot and surrounded himself with learned people from all over Europe. 'What shall I say of the great callousness of the people of this world?' Antim wrote in his book of sermons called the *Didache*. He was canonised by the Romanian Orthodox Church in 1992. One might say that with his grasp of language, printing and translation, Saint Antim was a born candidate for Fekete's collection.

which is the first translation of the New Testament into Scots Gaelic*; the first German edition, published in Vienna in 1774, of György Kalmár's *Grammaticalische Regeln zur Philosophischen oder Allgemeinen Sprache,* which aimed at the establishment of an artificial universal language†; the 1942 Calendar of the American Ukrainian Workingmen's Association; Johann Pollak's 1899 translation into Viennese dialect of Paul Verlaine's erotic poems *Femmes*; *Bubatul de vaca*, the 1804 translation into Romanian of Edward Jenner's book on cow-pox and the vaccination against it; Christian Moller's 1770 translation of the New Testament into Yiddish; the first Hungarian edition of Dickens Károly's *Nehéz Idök* (*Hard Times*, 1855); the 1880 edition of Shakespeare's *Othello* in Armenian; an erotic collection of poems, *Sektretaj Sonetoj* (1930), by Peter Peneter, pseudonym of the Hungarian Esperantist Kalman Kalocsy, which created an erotic vocabulary for Esperanto, just imagine, the whispering of Esperanto endearments; a 1936 book, in Russian, on the Shanghai Chinese Dialect written especially for the Russian émigré population living there; a "restricted" 1943 Romanian Phrase Book issued by the US War Department in the event of American military action in Romania; a 1664 edition of Thomas à Kempis *De Imitatio Christi* in Arabic; the 1782 second edition of the Hungarian translation of Bunyan's *The Pilgrim's Progress*; a parallel text, in Latin and Russian, of Ovid's *Tristia* published in 1795 and which was to be such a powerful influence on Osip Mandelstam's poems of banishment and exile; and, while not exactly a translation unless the translation is one that occurs in the soul, a guide for those coming to London in search of vice, *Sinks of London Laid Open: A Pocket Companion for the Uninitiated, to which is added A Modern Flash Dictionary containing all the Cant Words, Slang Terms, and Flash Phrases now in vogue, with a list of*

---

* One aches to think that this appeared during the period of the Highland Clearances which were a near death blow to Gaelic culture.

† A truly fascinating figure, on his Oriental travels Kalmár consumed only vinegar and grains. I refer the reader to Béla Hegedüs's essay on him, "The Ideas of György Kalmár: Theory behind his Universal Language Plan." https://core.ac.uk/download/pdf/78471086.pdf.

the Sixty Orders of Prime Coves, the whole forming a True Picture of London Life, Cadging Made Easy, the He-She Man, Doings of the Modern Greeks, Snooking Dens Depicted, the Common Lodging-house Gallants, Lessons to Lovers of Dice, the Gaming Tables, etc, embellished with humorous illustration by George Cruikshank (1848).*

The day I spoke to Tony Fekete he bought from Peter Ellis a copy of John Bowring's two-volume *Specimens of Russian Poetry* (1821, 1823). It was interesting to observe the hawk circling for a kill, the intensity of the gaze, the tug-of-war going on inside him, not as to whether or not he should catch the prey but as to how vital it was in terms of feeding his ravenous appetite, and, finally, I watched the tough bargainer trying to bring down the price a little when, really, he might have found it less painful to pay triple the price. I saw the suffering of the dedicated collector come alive on the surface of his face. The buyer's psychology was pitched against the seller's and it is safe to say both sides won. When we spoke later he was still holding that inner debate with himself. I could almost hear the ellipses in his voice.

'This Russian book on its own ... *nobody* knows Bowring. Firstly, nobody would bother ... you look at it and you say, "Russian poetry in English translation" ... *not interesting* ... but you then have to look at it one step further, which people won't do because they look at it once and move on. "Bowring, who's Bowring?" So you get the story of Bowring, which is really interesting. This book has a great story. Bowring was governor of Hong Kong and he claimed he spoke a hundred languages and understood another hundred, but he was a liar ... although there is no reason why he should have lied because he really did have a command of many languages ... and he was a gifted person ... but he was so full of himself. So this book has a place in my library because it has a story. If you create a story, you increase its value. A £400 book becomes a £700 book. And then you ask, "How many translations of Russian poetry had there been before this one? Had there been any at all? Was this

* One learns that an 'academy' is a brothel, 'aunt' or 'baggage' a prostitute and 'barking irons' a pistol.

the first translation of Russian poetry into English?" It may very well have been. So then it becomes interesting to collectors of such material because it has a place in the Russian section of libraries. And so in my library it has a place, it being one of the first, if not actually *the* first, translations of Russian verse. If it is not the first then it was one translated by a nutter.'

'It seems to me,' I proffered, 'that you are building for yourself a citadel of culture. There is a sense of protecting culture against disintegrating forces on the outside.'

'Maybe, but not consciously. I don't think that I'm protecting or building anything. I think I'm *creating* something. This is an original area. Nobody has ever collected like this before. That is what is so exciting for me. It is the collector in a creative role. You say there are very few interesting collectors. They come in, they are interested in an author and so they collect him, but they haven't got anything to contribute. They are simply consumers of the culture they are looking for. It's great that there are people who do that, but I have been collecting for a long time and I have a good feeling for these things and so I think, okay, now I am going to branch out and create something myself. I will create an area that has not been collected before. It is not a defined collecting area, like birds or erotica or anything which has a bibliography that can be used as a reference point. You have to create the limits yourself. My limits are that it has to have something exciting about it, it has to be relevant and it has to have something to do with the development of language. It has to have something *exceptional* about it.'

'And yet you create and then sell your collections. Although I've been a bookseller for some decades I've never been able to get my mind around that. How can you let them go?

'The psychology is very simple. When you are collecting you are always thirsting for something new, but then you get to a point when there isn't anything more to collect.'

'Alexander the Great wept because there were no more worlds for him to conquer.'

'There are two points to make. The first is, well, if you get to the point where there is nothing to collect then you can't buy anything else and so the hunger disappears. Secondly, you reach a point when you are taking rational rather than irrational decisions. A book collector will think irrationally. I will think very carefully about spending £200, but to buy a really important book for £3,000 is not such a problem. I have been offered this Welsh-English dictionary published in 1547. The first complete Welsh bible was not published until 1588. We discussed the price, which could be £6,000 or £7,000, but it's worth it because it is unique. You can see I am still hungry, I'm excited, whereas with my erotica and travel guides I was no longer excited by anything. I began to think there are so many other things one could buy for £5,000 or even £1,000. I could go away somewhere for the weekend. As soon as you begin to have profane thoughts about what else you could be doing with the money then the hunger is not there anymore. This explains why I can sell a collection and build another.'

Another book Tony Fekete is considering is *Finnegans Wake* (1939). I mentioned the fact that I'd sold a copy of the second edition to Johnny Depp the day before. Depp was trying incredibly hard not to be recognised and with predictably comic results. I found him polite. Depp can act other people, but he seems unable to deactivate himself. Will he read it? Would Fekete? It is, of course, a language all its own, ripe for inclusion in the Private Polyglot Library. I had always maintained that nobody has ever actually read it, but then another favourite customer of mine, Andrew Malone, has read it twice. I can't vouch for his sanity. And of course with a name like Malone he collects Samuel Beckett too. Poor man. As we reached the end of our conversation Tony Fekete had a sudden coughing fit and went red in the face. I thought to myself no, these are still early days. Should one jump at every cough? Very soon, I would.

Chapter Thirteen

THE MAN COLLECTING NAMES

CUSTOMERS OFTEN ASK ME IF I AM A COLLECTOR TOO. I'M never quite sure what to say. I own several thousand books, but still I balk at the idea of being called a collector. It feels just a little alien, as if to describe myself so would be to put a distance between myself and the books I love. I can understand calling someone a philatelist, and at one point early in my life I collected stamps, but books are another matter. They are vehicles of the word and as such their significance lies not only in the objects themselves but also in what they seed in the mind. There is something essentially wrong with the phrase *book collector* although there is such a creature. It would be the end of the antiquarian book trade otherwise. Surely, though, *bibliophile* is the better word in the same way *antiquary* feels truer, more solemn, than *antique collector.* I can say without hesitation that I'm a bibliophile. The fact that I buy, when affordable, first editions in as good a condition as possible is secondary in importance.

I am more accumulator than collector, more magpie than hawk. From time to time, I weed out what's not central to my interests, otherwise the story of my books is, though not wholly, the story of my life. Was this not the trap Don Quixote fell into? I don't want books in lieu of life—all too often I've seen that happen—but the books I have are, en masse, the deepest expression of my contemplative life. That's why I could never be anything more than I am, a factotum in the book trade, because for a bookseller it is a deadly mistake to get too attached to his books, just as a farmer should never name his cattle. We have already seen what happened to Peter Jolliffe. One needs to be able to let them go. Ultimately, of course, one does.

I've had this dream, more than once, of stepping inside a bookshop, one I'd never been to before, and there finding all my books for sale. *Who could have done this?* I ask myself in the dream. *Who could have sold them from under me?* Panic seizes me. Somehow, between my leaving home earlier that day and arriving here, the owner of this bookshop had gone to my home, and, whether by theft or trickery, got hold of my books, priced them, and then shelved them, just in time for my arrival. Suddenly I twig: I'm a ghost. Somehow I missed the dying bit, although does one ever really die in one's dreams? And so, ghosts being ghosts and not terribly good at the mechanicals, I am unable in the dream to pull any of those books from the shelves and look inside them to see whether certain titles are inscribed to me. Yet I know they are mine and not some magical replication of my library at home. The books are beyond my command, irretrievable, soon to be wed to other existences. At this point I wake up. I see before me, in the darkness, the silhouetted rows of my Robert Louis Stevenson books, their covers as dark as the dark they inhabit. Wouldn't it be strange if one day some of them end up with a fiddler from Milwaukee. As I keep saying, it's remarkable the journeys books make. I shuffle about a little, then go back to bed where I hope the dream will not resume. I have been granted, my books too, a temporary stay of execution.

When I think of all the house calls I've made, my own library is the one that I would most like to have. It is not that it includes so many rarities, although there are some, but because I am of the view that one's library should be an accurate reflection of one's own personal tastes. The books are not there for show, but to be read and loved for what they are. It seems superfluous to even say this, but when I am confronted, as is often the case, with people asking what they should collect I am brought back to first principles.

'Collect only what you love,' I say to them, 'the most valuable books are those on which *you* place value.'

Sometimes I entertain the notion my books will continue, together, without me. They will be, as it were, my *mind* and so to scatter them would be for me to die twice. This is absurd, I know. I should like in my next life to reread the books I have most enjoyed in this. A man who has as many books as I do is already fighting to preserve his balance. The collector, as opposed to the accumulator, has an even bigger struggle with his inner demons because he is more likely to fetishize his books and become so caught up in their particulars that what they contain diminishes in importance. At least I can take pleasure in, and be enriched by, the sheer worthlessness of my books.

I almost became a collector. I didn't have the money to be one, but I did manage to get most of my better books for relatively little. One consequence of being an accumulator is that now I have more books than I would have had if I become a collector. It is easier for me to justify my craving and say, 'What's the harm of having just one more?' There is no more room for them. I've double-banked them, shoved some under the bed, and there are piles of them all over the place. I forget where many of my books are. And then I have to ask myself: what would my library be, were it not for the fact my books were in other people's libraries? People die, their books scatter, I benefit. The eventual dispersal of my library is something I should take comfort in, the thought that my books will bring joy to other people. But do I really? I do and I don't and I do. All I can hope for is that people know their significance.

I stare at my books with something like bewilderment. Patricia Rieff Anawalt's *Shamanic Regalia in the Far North* (2014), I saw it at a reduced price and I had to have it. It quietly petitions me, but whether I'll ever read it is another matter, and the same goes for the three-volume translation of Ibn Khaldûn's *The Muqaddimah: An Introduction to History* (1958), so austere, so demanding of my attention.* What both titles ask of me is more than I may have. I might not read them, but I *need* them to be there. A personal library must also be a pantheon of good intentions, which is not quite the same as a pantheon of unreadable masterpieces.† There are still a few too many of those and I have to ask myself whether they are there because one day I might crack them open or whether it's because I haven't yet fully extinguished the desire to *appear* knowledgeable. And there, too, reprimanding me, is the magnificent Yale edition of *The Letters of Robert Louis Stevenson* (1994–95) in eight volumes. Why, though, does it exclude that masterpiece of invective, *Father Damien: An Open Letter to the Reverend Doctor Hyde of Honolulu* (1890)? 'I rejoice to feel the button off the foil,' Stevenson writes, 'and to plunge home.' Skewer him, he does. A man of no great religious persuasion, a Presbyterian according to his birth certificate, Stevenson rises to the defence of a Catholic priest unjustly charged by one—can one believe it?—Reverend *Hyde*! So what was *his* Jekyll like? Answering Hyde's charge that Damien was dirty, Stevenson replies: 'He was. Think of the poor lepers annoyed with this dirty comrade! But the clean Dr. Hyde was at his food in a fine house.' The pamphlet, which could easily serve as a template for all who wish to bring a charge against injustice, is one of my treasures.

* Robert Irwin relates that when Ibn Khaldûn moved to Egypt he arranged for his family and his library to be sent to him there. The boat sank with the loss of all. Why do I lament the library more?

† There, too, I wobble a little. I did, however, sell my three-volume set of Robert Musil's *A Man Without Qualities* (*Der Mann ohne Eigenschaften*, 1953–60) and my two-volume set of Heimito von Doderer's *The Demons* (Die Dämonen, 1961). I can take only so much Teutonic worthiness.

Not long before he died, the poet Geoffrey Hill extracted from his own library a selection of books that held special significance for him. I was called upon, in my professional capacity, to put a value on them. They were at his son's house close to where I live, approximately two hundred books filling a single case. The usual thing is to evaluate for purposes of probate or insurance a person's whole library and not just a selection from it. There were many books of greater value at Geoffrey Hill's home in Fulbourn, Cambridgeshire; this I know because Peter Ellis and I sold them to him. Among the chosen were titles I expected to find, Yeats and Pound, and then a few surprises, a first edition of Beatrix Potter's *The Tale of Peter Rabbit* (1902), Edith Sitwell's *Popular Song* (1928) in the Faber and Faber Ariel Poem series, which sat oddly with the Modernists. Several titles sparked happy memories. Many years ago, well before one could get on a computer and quickly obtain titles, Hill asked me if I could find him copies of David Gascoyne's *Hölderlin's Madness* (1938), which is my own favourite Gascoyne,* and Dylan Thomas's *The Map of Love* (1939). It took me, in both cases, a couple of months, but I did find them and here they were. And then, alone of his own works, I found something I'd given him when he came to visit me, an issue of the periodical *Poetry and Audience* (1955), containing two of his early uncollected poems. When he saw it on my shelf he lamented the fact he didn't possess a copy. Who was I to deny a man his own offspring? As for his buying habits, he once wrote to me, 'I like having books which are to me iconic, but I'm not a bibliophile or bibliomane, and many that I have are far from mint condition. My copy of Dylan Thomas's *18 Poems* (Parton Press 1934) has a knitting-needle sized hole in the spine, deftly concealed (by the Welsh Wizard himself?) with shoe-blacking.' It was almost as if he had managed to turn a fault into a virtue.

---

* My copy is inscribed: 'For Peter Joliffe—Encore une fois!—David Gascoyne. Cambridge, 8.VI.79.' I never knew why Peter let this go; it was not like him to sell books personally inscribed to himself although I'll hazard a guess and say he might have been displeased that Gascoyne misspelled his surname.

I was then shown the manuscript notebook of his final long poem, *The Book of Baruch by the Gnostic Justin* (2019). This, together with other notebooks and correspondence, was destined to join the main bulk of the archive at Leeds University. Geoffrey had told me on a couple of occasions that he was working on an 'angry poem' that could not be published until after he died. Well, published it was and there was mass critical applause, some of which I found hypocritical in the extreme, coming, as it did, from people who denied the author that pleasure while he was alive. Many poets disliked him almost as much as he disliked them. I was shocked by how few attended his funeral. Stephen Romer was there, so too Kevin Perryman who translated some of Hill's poems into German, Elizabeth Cook and Andrew McNeillie. Where were the others? There were more clergymen than pen pushers. The pallbearers, following the poet's instructions, wore pink socks. Sometimes there was more Benny than Geoffrey in him.*

As for the 'angry poem' I had expected something on the order of a Villonesque testament. What I got instead were the concerns of the moment, his anger at Brexit, for instance, some peculiar fanfare for Jeremy Corbyn that will not sound very deeply into the future, and many other matters, but nothing of a grand recapitulation such as one might find at the end of a Sibelius symphony, not even a settling of old scores. I think he began to believe a little too much in his own voice. Old men do. This said, what he had set out to do, he did, and if he confounded our expectations, so be it; I salute him. Absolutely himself, he was a poet of absolutes. What I saw that day, at his son's house, was something which to my amazement the book's editor, Kenneth Haynes, neglects to mention in his editorial notes, the single most incredible thing about that manuscript. On the day Hill died it would appear he had begun work on a new section, a couple of lines at most, which

* For the sake of any transatlantic readers I might have, Benny Hill (1924–1993) was an English comedian known for his slapstick, burlesque and double-entendre and quite lacking in the subtleties for which English humour is more widely esteemed.

he then covered with white correcting fluid and over which he penned a row of asterisks. Was the clock in his body alerting him to the fact his poetic journey was soon to be done? '* * * * *': those asterisks, for me, say more than the poem does, there being a terrible finality in them while at the same time signifying a noble departure. I've heard he died in his garden and had just received author's copies of his Penguin translation of Ibsen's *Peer Gynt* and *Brand* (2017), the first of which contains the line, 'I really admire the way her bum twerks.' Was this a stab at relevance?

Geoffrey Hill was a frequent buyer from our catalogues. I can still hear his agonised, Job-like lament at the other end of the telephone.

'I suppose I am too late. Yes, *of course* I'm too late. The books are already gone, I'm sure.'

'Oh Geoffrey, I replied, 'nobody would be interested in any of the books *you* want.'

There was a grumpy acknowledgement. 'Yes, I suppose so.'

As it turned out, they were all available. The people I have most enjoyed selling books to have always been the least predictable in their tastes. There could be no gauging his. Why did he want the *BBC Handbook* for 1943? What was he going to do with the enormous photograph of R. S. Thomas which I catalogued, thinking to myself, 'Who'd want to hang this grim mug on his wall?' The only time I met R. S. Thomas was over dinner when he bitterly accused the English of introducing electricity into Wales as a means of controlling his country. Small wonder Geoffrey appreciated his better in the doom stakes.

Looking back on our conversations they were never livelier or more packed with knockabout humour than when he was on the telephone. The medium seemed to free him up whereas in person, within seconds, he could disappear into some dark place inside himself where he became quite unreachable. Oddly enough, we very rarely discussed poetry unless we did so wielding machetes. We discussed composers. Music was important to him, and he spoke of his almost torturous decision as to whether Bruckner should be allowed to displace Mahler in his affections. 'Why not both, Geoffrey?' Likewise he agonised over David Gascoyne: 'I've been reading his *Journals* and *Selected Prose*,' he wrote me. 'I like the *idea* of him, as I like the *idea* of the purity of Anton Webern; but I can't endure much of A.W.'s music and Gascoyne's poetry, like that of his mentor Jouve, seems flat on the page: lumpy obvious sentiments and no sense of rhythm. That's unfair, of course, several things in *Poems 1937–1942* are fine, and there's a most beautiful translation of Supervielle, "Rain and the Tyrants". I also admire him for coming through all that he did; and for going out writing. He *certainly* survived his desolate years; & holds out hope for us.' Was Geoffrey Hill contemplating his own desolation?

I never missed an opportunity to send him up and he rarely failed to provide me with one.

'Can you imagine,' he said proudly, 'there is to be a reprint of my *Collected Critical Writings*!'

'Oh Geoffrey,' I cried, '*another* fifty copies.'

'I can always count on you,' he replied in mock anger, 'I can *always count* on you.'

I have all his books including the Fantasy Press pamphlet I got from Peter Jolliffe, but chief among them is the Dedication Copy of *Odi Barbare* (2012), which he dedicated to Christopher Middleton and myself. When he came to my place, on October 8, 2009, he thrust into my hands, almost as if wanting to be shot of it, a copy of the typescript to which, incidentally, he would later make numerous changes. The poem was written in response to *Palavers* (2004), the book of conversations which I recorded with Christopher Middleton. What struck Hill in particular was Christopher on the subject of Sir Philip Sidney's poem "Cleophila." On the recording I made, Christopher reads the poem, with music for oud, accordion and piano by Anouar Brahem playing in the background. Nothing was planned. Christopher was drinking cognac, me grappa. It was coming on evening. Quietly he picked up my volume of Sidney and read from it. The recorder was on, the music was on. What came of that conjunction of circumstances was an unlikely though perfect synthesis spread over, and bringing together, the ages. A beautiful accident may be a plainer way to describe it. Also Christopher had a lovely reading voice. 'It's one of the best Sapphic metre poems that I have ever come across,' he said. 'And it's strange, I was reading it after the *Astrophel and Stella* sonnets, by which I got more and more bored, because they seemed just to run through endless amorous routines and then, quite suddenly, this much more profoundly and complicatedly formal metre *enshrines* a voice that speaks with a direct and extraordinary vehemence of a *real* passion than with a sort of décor of Elizabethan wooing.' *Odi Barbare*, which employs the same form and metre Sir Philip Sidney uses, was written as a response to that conversation. And now they are both gone, Christopher and Geoffrey, two ghosts too many for me to be able to write about them with equanimity.

Would I be able to do as much for myself and make a selection of key titles, the books most significant for me? I think not. I want them all. What I will do is make an intermittent journey through my own shelves, skipping over most of my books, but pausing here and there for whatever stories they may have to tell.

* * *

I will begin with Pirandello, his short stories in particular. There's a good title, *The Naked Truth and eleven other stories* (1934).* Next

* It has the ownership signature of W. George S. Whiting. Who was he, I wonder. Over the years I have seen dozens of books with his neat signature and always with the date of purchase written beneath his name so that the tails of the two *G*s of "George" serve to bracket the month in Roman numerals, and the day and last two numbers of the year, both in Arabic numerals, are on either side of them. He seems to have been possessed of an orderly mind. The closest I have come to identifying him is that he might have had something to do with music because he wrote a letter to *The Gramophone* in 1930 on the subject of Augusta Holmès's symphonic poem *Irlande* although in the main he was quoting an article by the English composer Ethel Smyth. I'm intrigued. Augusta Holmès who first published under the pseudonym "Hermann Zenta" was Irish and when she became a French citizen in 1874 she added the accent to her surname. After she declined an offer of marriage from the French composer Camille Saint-Saëns she lived with the poet Catulle Mendès. There would be no end of it if I were to begin to discuss Mendès and his mysterious

to it is his almost forgotten novel about Sicily at the time of the Risorgimento, *The Old and the Young* (1928; *I vecchi e i giovani*, 1913), which anticipates Giuseppe Di Lampedusa's *The Leopard* (1960; *Il Gattopardo*, 1958). What both authors do is to mark beginnings and endings, with perhaps just a bit more nostalgia in the latter and the smell of the sulphur mines in the former. I recommend the Pirandello although sometimes it is hard to keep track of the many characters. It has colourful paper-covered boards; I suspect the abstract design comes from, or is inspired by, a Sicilian folk textile. When my wife and I were in Agrigento we stayed in a villa where it is claimed Pirandello stayed for a while, and indeed we had, at no extra cost, "the Pirandello room." I wonder if it was true. I doubt it. We visited the Casa Luigi Pirandello, which I am happy to report is in a suburb called Il Caos: 'I am the son of Chaos,' wrote Pirandello in his *Frammento d'autobiografia* (1933). What I remember best about the museum were the photographs of his muse, the hauntingly beautiful Marta Abba. Pirandello's great plan was to write a story for each day of the year. I recommend "The Madonna's Gift" in *Better Think Twice About It* (1933), one of the most terrifying short stories I've read.

I move from there to the Swiss writer Robert Walser. He may be the closest modernist literature has come to producing a holy fool and I disagree with those critics who say he was a chronicler of the inconsequential because what he did surely was to make everything of equal importance, which maybe explains the strange light that envelops his prose. Very little happens in a Walser story and the less there is, the more exciting it becomes. The fact I became hooked on him I owe to Christopher Middleton who with *The Walk and other stories* (1957) brought Walser's work into English for the first time, and it was Christopher who sent me his translation

death in a railway tunnel in Saint-Germain-en-Laye by which time he had left Augusta Holmès and married a poet called Jeanne Nette. None of this, of course, brings us any closer to the identity of W. George S. Whiting who clearly was a man of rarefied musical tastes. He is not to be confused with the American George Whiting who composed the song "Give Me Just a Little Bit of What You've Got a Whole Lot of."

of *Jakob von Gunten* (1909; trans. 1969). Walking was Walser's release from the turmoil that saw him spend the last twenty-seven years of his life in mental asylums. Whether he was actually mad is a matter of conjecture. When finally he was moved into the sanatorium in Herizau and was asked by his friend and legal guardian Carl Seelig whether he was doing any writing, he replied, 'I am not here to write, but to be mad.' Awareness of this kind suggests inordinate sanity. As if plotted well in advance, on Christmas Day 1956, during one of his long walks, he collapsed and died in a snowy field. A photograph shows him lying where he fell, his own footprints leading up to the body.

The most expensive book I ever bought was the first edition of Joseph Conrad's first book, *Almayer's Folly* (T. Fisher Unwin, 1895). It has a missing *e* in the word *generosity* at the bottom of page 110; there's also another missing bit of type somewhere. The errors were spotted during the printing of the book and immediately corrected. This doesn't mean the corrected version is not a first edition, but that it is the second issue. My copy is the first issue. I paid £400 for it, which in the 1980s was a staggeringly high figure for someone of my low salary and with a young family to support. The only justification I can make is that I paid for it through the sale of books I bought elsewhere. I paid not nearly as much for the other Conrad titles. I have already mentioned *Nostromo* (1904), which I bought from Bill Hoffer, often spoken of by people whose intelligence I respect as Conrad's best book, which makes me wonder if they are not congratulating themselves for making it to the end of this story about a cardboard figure in a cardboard country, committing cardboard acts of heroism, surely one of the most tedious books ever written by a great writer. It's there only because it has to be there, its lovely blue spine set against the green and red and charcoal grey of the other Conrad volumes, and maybe, too, waiting for the day I realise I've judged it too harshly. I have more sympathy than most Conradians for *Victory* (1915) in which one can draw pleasure from its two lines: 'Dreams are madness, my dear. It's things that happen in the waking world, while one is asleep, that one would be glad to know the meaning of.' Conrad was hopeless, for the most part, when it came to writing about women, but I'll allow him Winnie in *The Secret Agent* (1907).

This year it is Wolfgang Koeppen who claims me, in particular his novel *Death in Rome* (1992; *Der Tod in Rom*, 1954) which mercilessly dissects the German psyche. The books are not a laugh a minute. I'm not sure how much misery I can take, but I do better at it than most people. I was reading it the day I was treated for benign paroxysmal positional vertigo (BPPV) or "crystals in the ear" by a German doctor, a very intense, very beautiful, woman with piercing eyes, who cured me in a single session. She held my head at an angle, staring deeply into my eyes. I told her the room was spinning in circles. She said she could read it all in my eyes. And then she turned my head at another angle. And that was that, I was cured. She deeply unsettled me and wanting to say something, *anything*, I showed her the book. 'Have you read this?' I asked. She stared at it, and, pausing for a moment, as if translating it back into her mother tongue, she gave an involuntary shudder as if I'd dealt her an electrical shock. 'No,' she said, 'no!' What is the German for *faux pas*? A writer not exactly revered in his time, at least during the years covering the publication of his three post-war novels, *Pigeons on the Grass* (1988; *Tauben im Gras*, 1951), *The Hothouse* (2002; *Das Treibhaus* (1953) and *Death in Rome*, he never wrote another novel although his late childhood memoir *Youth* (2014; *Jugend*, 1976) is impressionistic enough to count as one.

Other author collections include: Isaac Babel, Baudelaire, Borges, Lord Byron, Camus, Bruce Chatwin (fibber though he was), Chekhov, Emily Dickinson (who my friend Norm Sibum outrageously accuses of knocking out epiphanies like someone sitting at a cash register), Dostoevsky, T. S. Eliot, Patrick Leigh Fermor, Witold Gombrowicz (the most horrible man in literature), W. S. Graham, Henry Green, Zbigniew Herbert, R. C. Hutchinson, Kafka, Danilo Kiš, Milan Kundera, Leopardi, Lorca, Osip Mandelstam, Javier Marías, Gabriel García Márquez, Christopher Middleton, Czesław Miłosz (who aggravates me more and more), Eugenio Montale, Orhan Pamuk (who is in danger of expulsion from my shelves), Ezra Pound, Rimbaud, Joseph Roth, C. H. Sisson,

Stendhal, Stevenson, R. S. Thomas, Miguel de Unamuno, Verlaine, Vernon Watkins and then people who became friends through the book trade: Adam Thorpe, Paul Rossiter and Henry Glassie.

Henry Glassie, American folklorist: I had just turned down a copy of *Brick Lane* (2003) and it was not because the author had recently come into the shop and was rude but because the seller trying to convince me it was scarce was also rude. He stomped angrily out of the shop. A browser, overhearing this, made a quip. Somehow, exactly how I can't remember, but within minutes he and I were discussing Sufi orders in the Middle East and then it turned out he was the author of the magnum opus *Turkish Traditional Art Today* (1993) as well as works on African art, Ireland, Bangladesh, vernacular architecture, American bluegrass music, pottery and folk culture. He spoke not only Turkish but also had a decent amount of Ottoman Turkish, which is more than most Turks have. My friendship with Henry Glassie is one of many I have made through the bookshop.

The year I bought *Almayer's Folly* I also bought, for the same price, a wood engraving by David Jones, the first of fifteen signed copies of "The Oblation of Noe" from his *The Chester Book of the Deluge* (1926). It is vulgar saying how much I paid for these objects, but their purchase was the high point of my bibliomania. Thereafter I came to my senses and stuck to more modest purchases. This is not to say I don't have some wonderful books in my collection, but that I obtained them through other means, judicious swapping or occasional sacrifices from my own shelves. I still find it difficult to come out of a bookshop with nothing in my hand. I am very much a magpie, acting not just on what I already know but to perhaps a greater degree on what I do not know. Very rarely do I keep a book about which I have ambivalent feelings. I buy what I need, what I want, and for reading at some point deep into the future. It may take me a full decade or more before I finally get around to reading a book and it's then that my instincts are put to the test. I am not a little proud in declaring my instincts have served me well.

* * *

Yesterday, at Any Amount of Books on Charing Cross Road, I found, for a mere fiver—it's probably worth no more—the *Journal of Maurice de Guérin* (1891), with a biographical memoir by Sainte-Beuve. A God-intoxicated poet who breathed pagan fumes, 'the André Chénier of pantheism,' Guérin was already dead by the age of twenty-nine. Why hadn't I heard of him? Was I missing something? Was he the missing link between all that I've read and all that awaits me? I was holding the book when somebody behind me said *sotto voce*, 'You won't live long enough to read all the books you have.' I spun around and his face was only dimly familiar to me. A stranger had crept into my thoughts. Yes, I have made rough calculations as to how many years I may have left, erring, perhaps, a little on the generous side, and assuming reasonable mental health. Considering I am a slow reader and that even if I did nothing but read twenty-four hours a day, there is virtually no chance of my getting through them. And then I have considered reading again the books that have meant the most to me, which puts any possibility of reading them all at an even further remove, and then, of course, I make these calculations on the assumption I will stop buying books. This, too, is impossible. If I am honest with myself I have been buying books at a rate considerably higher than ever before. I have been squirrelling them away, claiming imminent retirement as an excuse.

'And you,' I replied, 'will you read all yours?'

'I doubt it even though I've retired,' he replied. 'Also I've no one to leave them to.'

Maybe he was the man collecting names.

'Do I know you from somewhere?'

He produced a vague smile and left. *Who was he?*

My library is a kind of bridge, a bridge more firmly constructed than myself, its bolts in the right places, and over which knowledge will be ferried. All I'll say for now about my recent purchase is that its red and black cloth, the gilt lettering on the spine, greatly pleases the eye. Jeremy Reed was in the shop and he had never heard of Guérin either and he's hugely knowledgeable on French poets of the fin de siècle. Martin Stone would know, but Martin Stone is no more.

Now here's an association copy with which to reckon: George Seferis, *The King of Asine and other poems.* (John Lehmann, 1948). This is the first collection of the Greek poet's work in English, the translators being Bernard Spencer, a fine poet in his own right, Nanos Valaoritis and Lawrence Durrell, and with an introduction by Rex Warner who later translated a selection of Seferis, *Poems* (Bodley Head, 1960). The book is inscribed by the author: 'To Professor Thomas Whittemore, with kindest regards George Seferis—Ankara, Oct. 19, 1949.' Loosely inserted is an autograph letter from him at the Greek Embassy in Ankara to Whittemore care of the American Embassy in Istanbul. At the time Seferis had a diplomatic post in Ankara. In the letter Seferis speaks of his gratitude for Whittemore's 'wonderful work—I should say your most courageous salvage.' Thomas Whittemore (1871–1950) was an American archaeologist and scholar who founded the Byzantine Institute of America and it was he who with the blessing of his friend the first President of the Turkish Republic, Mustafa Kemal Ataturk, removed the plaster covering the magnificent Byzantine mosaics at Hagia Sophia. Built in AD 537, Hagia Sophia had been converted from a Greek Orthodox patriarchal cathedral to a mosque on May 29, 1453, and remained so until 1931 when, after holding discussions with Whittemore, Ataturk put a sign on the door of the cathedral, written in his own hand, saying: 'The museum is closed for repairs.' Whittemore's next great task was the restoration of the Byzantine Church of the Chora, the Kariye Camii,* and it was there that he personally conducted a tour for the Greek poet who would describe him as 'the unforgettable venerator of the monuments of Orthodoxy.' Its restoration may be the 'most courageous salvage' to which Seferis alludes although there is as much reason to suppose he meant both. At the end of the letter Seferis expresses his hope that the two would meet the following summer, but it was not to be. On June 8, 1950, Whittemore

* As with the Hagia Sophia, perhaps even more shockingly, the Turkish President Recep Tayyip Erdoğan has issued an order for it to be transformed into a mosque.

suffered a fatal heart attack while visiting the US Department of State in Washington, DC. There is an asteroid that bears his name.

Some books radiate mystery. They are like a code waiting to be cracked. One such is my beautifully bound copy, in James Thomson's translation, of the first English edition of Giacomo Leopardi's *Essays, Dialogues and Thoughts* (*Operette Morali* and *Pensieri* [1905]). The morocco binding by Morrell has gilt floral decorations, green silk pastedowns and endpapers. It is clearly a gift binding, the upper cover stamped in gilt 'L.M.B. DEC.1905.' On the first blank is an inscription in Persian, which translates as 'a distant dream' beneath which is written 'Christmas 1905.' On the following blank, in the same hand, is a quotation from Edgar Saltus *The Philosophy of Disenchantment* (1888) and on the rear blank a further quotation from Saltus: 'In brief then, life to the Christian is a probation, to the Brahmin a burden, to the Buddhist a dream, and to the pessimist a nightmare.' What is it about this book that exudes significance? Am I being too fanciful in thinking its secrecy owes to it being the gift of a thwarted lover, which would be in keeping with Leopardi, or perhaps it was meant to be a disguise.

One of my literary touchstones is Cecil Collins's introductory essay to *The Vision of the Fool* (The Grey Walls Press, 1947). A book that has been central to my own writing, in particular *The Street Philosopher and the Holy Fool* (2004), I have had numerous occasions to refer to this book. It contains reproductions of the artist's paintings and drawings, which form a cycle. On the front free endpaper is an inscription: "To Elisabeth from Parc – The Studio. Cambridge, October 12th 1947." This is the Dedication Copy. On the dedication page is printed 'for Elisabeth'; Parc was his wife's nickname for him. Elisabeth Ward Collins née Ramsden was also an artist and appears in her husband's work as an angel or anima representing the inner self. One of Collins's most unusual paintings depicts her sitting in a tree and clutching a trophy symbolising eternity and on her lap a bird representing freedom. On the back of the painting is a Christmas card from the artist to his wife whom he nicknamed "Bell." Incredibly I found the book at Marcus Campbell's art bookshop close by the Tate Modern. The book had been discarded by the Tate Gallery to whom the bequest of the artist's archive was made.

The only book I took with me to Iran was Robert Byron's *The Road of Oxiana* (Macmillan, 1937). Loosely inserted in my copy is a menu, dated 'Le 17 Septembre 1935,' on the back of which Byron drew a bearded satyr clambering onto the bed of a woman pointing her finger at him, clearly admonishing him. During this time Byron spent a fortnight in Leningrad, assisting at the Third International Congress and Exhibition of Persian Art and Archaeology held at the State Hermitage Museum, which opened on September 10 and then moved to Moscow on September 16, where presumably the banquet took place on the following day. Byron presented a paper on Timurid buildings in Afghanistan. His wealth of knowledge on Islamic architecture in Central Asia was derived from his journey there in 1933, which in turn is the basis for his classic work. The British art historian David Talbot Rice was also present at the conference. The cartoon was given to me by the author's niece, Setitia Simmonds née Butler, as a token to celebrate twenty-five years of friendship.

Paolo Dall'Oglio: I devoted a chapter to him in *The Street Philosopher and the Holy Fool* and then again, in rather darker hues, in "The Saddest Book I'll Never Write."* On July 29, 2013, in Raqqa, Father Paolo was seized by members of Islamic State. He has not been seen since. There are rumours that he is in fact in the custody of the Syrian regime, but this strikes me as improbable. Nine years earlier, Ivo Saglietti produced a book of black-and-white photographs of the religious community at Deir Mar Musa in Syria, with an introductory letter by Paolo Dall'Oglio. The last time I saw Father Paolo he presented me with a copy of *Sotto la tenda di Abramo—Deir Mar Musa el-Habasci* (*Under the Tent of Abraham*, Peliti Associati, 2004) with the inscription, "a Mr. Marius Kociejowski con un cordiale grazie! per il suo libro sulla Siria ... amicizia - Paolo 13-4-06.' What I wrote elsewhere, I will repeat here: 'Whether he be alive or dead, I imagine the

* Collected in *Zoroaster's Children and other travels* (Biblioasis, 2015).

stunning desert and mountain landscape around Deir Mar Musa humming—yes, *ensouled*—with his presence.'

Wilfred Thesiger was the last great travel writer, an explorer in the way the word would have been understood a century earlier. A great photographer as well, his *Visions of a Nomad* (1987) is the first of several publications drawing on the thirty-eight thousand negatives which he donated to the Pitt Rivers Museum in Oxford. I met him briefly at the signing he did for the book at Stanfords on Long Acre, the magnificent travel and specialist map bookshop established in 1853, which now, sadly, is only a shadow of its former self. Among its customers were David Livingstone, H. M. Stanley, Florence Nightingale, Ernest Shackleton, Captain Scott of the Antarctic, Francis Younghusband, Amy Johnson and "Doctor Watson," who in *The Hound of the Baskervilles* (1902) is commandeered by Sherlock Holmes to go to Stanfords and get a map of Dartmoor. So nervous I was in the presence of this greatest of twentieth-century travellers with his head like an eagle's that all I could think to ask him was the identity of some birds that years before I'd seen flying in extraordinary formation above the Sahara. They flew in a constantly shifting pattern too intricate for language to describe. I can see them still, but I can't tell you *what* I see. I made a stab at it with Thesiger. He thought for a minute and said, gruffly, and with great authority, 'Sand birds.' When I mentioned this to someone who knew him the response was, 'Oh, Wilfrid knows bugger all about birds.' My copy of *Visions of a Nomad* is inscribed simply "Wilfred Thesiger—To Marius." Well, he did lead a spare existence.

The finest Gaelic poet of the twentieth century was Sorley MacLean. Such was the beauty of his voice I can just about forgive him the absurd politics, which he expresses without so much as a blush in "The Bolshevik" and which just occasionally blights the sheer magnificence of his *Poems to Eimhir* (1971; *Dàin do Eimhir*, 1943) and yet what Gaelic poet has not had his moral compass bedevilled by the Highland Clearances? Those ghosts are yet very much alive. (What Jewish poet two centuries hence will not still feel the pinch of a distant history?) During World War Two Sorley MacLean fought in the Royal Horse Artillery and was wounded three times. The experience of warfare in the North African theatre was enough to shake his lyric voice. In February 1942, he wrote to Hugh MacDiarmid: 'If I am ever to write any more verse, it will be very different from what I have written, that it must be less subjective, more thoughtful, less content with its own music.' The most serious injury he sustained was at the Battle of El Alamein when on November 2, 1942, a shell exploded near him, resulting in his hospitalisation for the next nine months and eventual release from further military action. One particular battle, at Ruweisat Ridge, ten miles south of Alamein, would produce one of his finest war poems "*Glac a' Bhàis*" ("Death Valley") and it was this which he read on the publication of the revised edition of *From Wood to Ridge—Collected Poems in Gaelic and English* (1990). He prefaced his reading of the poem with a description of something he saw during that battle, the body of a young German soldier, and while talking he was clearly transported to that scene, his voice almost breaking when he spoke of that boy who in the poem lies dead 'with his forelock down about his cheek and his face slate-grey.' A poet of deep humanity in inhuman times, MacLean allows his young enemy the benefit of the doubt. The poem concludes:

> Ge b'e a dheòin-san no a chàs,
> a neoichiontas no mhìorun,
> cha do nochd e toileachadh 'na bhàs
> fo Dhruim Ruidhìseit.
>
> Whatever his desire or mishap,
> his innocence or malignity,
> he showed no pleasure in his death
> below the Ruweisat Ridge.

After the reading I asked Sorley MacLean to inscribe my copy of his book, which he did in Gaelic: 'do Mharius—Somhairle

MacGill-Eain' and which, still inside the moment of that poem, he dated '29.10.42.'

This seems as good a place as any to stop this very brief journey through my books.

Chapter Fourteen

THE POLISH FOR GOODBYE

THE GREATER PART OF THIS BOOK WAS WRITTEN DURING the first COVID-19 lockdown. On Sunday, March 15, 2020, I got a message from Peter Ellis that I was not to come in to work the following morning and so it would be until further notice. The shadow moving across my plate had not yet reached full eclipse. The first thought that occurred to me was that I'd left on the desk at work a brand-new glasses case of midnight blue. There's nothing like the major to flush the minor out of one's life. Peter was right, of course, and acted with the decisiveness that is one of his strongest attributes. A floating world was not to become on his watch a floating hospital. It would be another week and a single day before a smug and muddled government followed suit by which time what damage there was to be done was done. Already it had been a year of false starts and lousy finales. As it turned out, as month followed month, the period of the lockdown overtook my scheduled date of departure. After all that I had been dreading with respect to my final day at the shop, the sound of my key turning in the lock one last time, a pangolin, while others say a dead Chinese bat, stole a march on me.

I had started this book earlier and then let it lie dormant for several months. Suddenly the writing of it became urgent and not merely a means of marking time. I was watching my world slide. The opening chapter of this book, an elegy for what I was about to lose, belongs to an earlier existence. The seam between it and what follows is, I hope, invisible. As I write, there are fears of yet another pandemic wave. A few months were enough to demonstrate just how fragile our society is. It ought to be made of sterner stuff. Some of the worst societal collapses come not of conflict but of being too comfortable, too prissy, too sure. The politicos, in an attempt to make themselves look credible, resorted to militaristic analogies. In this, as in so much else, they got it wrong. Pandemics have little regard for front lines. They make sport with the flesh, then go for the soul, which also is subject to damage. Rimbaud writes: '*La combat spirituel est aussi brutal que la bataille d'hommes.*'* It is a motion I'd like to see tabled at the next meeting of the Antiquarian Booksellers' Association.

The economy behind the running of a bookshop is markedly different to that of most other businesses. It depends to a great degree on whatever's in the air. It had been Brexit and the uncertainty it induced in people's minds. Whenever anything big happens, which rattles the nerves, there is a reluctance to indulge in luxuries. The week Princess Diana died we sold nothing. The day it was announced Donald Trump won the election we sold nothing. The day after England narrowly missed winning the World Cup we sold nothing. There is also a curious phenomenon, which every bookseller recognises, which resembles the middle passages of "The Rime of the Ancient Mariner" where there is no friendly breeze. There is no explaining it, no albatross in the works, just stagnation. Check with other booksellers on the street and you find it is the same story. And then suddenly it breaks, the sails

* 'Spiritual combat is as brutal as the battle of men'—from "Adieu" in *A Season in Hell, trans.* Louise Varèse. (New Directions, 1961)

billow (from the Old Norse *bylgja*) and business goes back to normal.

Such reports as I get from the "Inner Zone" put me in a dark place. Several bookshops are on the brink of collapse. Quinto is gone. Apparently even Foyles is like the *Marie Celeste*. There'll be stragglers of course, survivors in odd places, but the trade as we knew it is imperilled as never before. No amount of guesswork would have arrived at what is happening now, a dystopian nightmare. It puts mind in a strange place. This morning, in the small hours, I began in my reveries to journey through the London of forty years ago—Richmond (three bookshops), Kensington (eight), Chelsea (two), and so on. They've all gone. Go into the provinces and it's the same. Rare books will continue to be sold, at auction or over the tops of walnut tables, but we are about to be robbed of the mystery and serendipity of the old bookshop. The mistake is to think it's the pandemic alone that is to blame. It is merely the coup de grâce.

After so many gripes about writing this book, a reluctance to say anything at all about the book trade, I find I have only just managed to scrape the surface of a life that has not been wholly objectionable. I have handled extraordinary books and manuscripts and, more important, I have met and worked with remarkable people. I wish, though, I'd taken notes. Who was that man with whom I discussed Emily Dickinson? Why didn't I act on Edmund Kurtz's invitation to visit him? Why didn't the fellow who showed me J[ohn]. D[onne]'s *Poems. With Elegies on the Authors Death* (1633) come back when I told him we'd definitely like to make an offer for it? These are, of course, pointless regrets. As it is, the greater part of existence slips through our fingers; the aim of the writer is to preserve at least a fraction of it. I had suggested the trade might be taking leave of me. And so it has, only not in ways I could have imagined.

A couple of reports come as stabs to the heart.

The happiest collectors tend to be those who deal in the lowest stakes, who delight in finding a book for a pound or two, and so it follows they are the ones most fun to sell to. Adrenalin belongs to the higher stakes and that, too, affords another kind of pleasure, but I'm more in sympathy with those who in penury find riches. Every Saturday, at 12:30 p.m.—one could almost set one's clock by him—Patrick Bollard would appear, spend half an hour or so looking at the books on the outside shelves and when he finished come in for a chat before going to place a bet of ten pence on the horses. First, though, he would go to the National Portrait Gallery for a pee and as payment, which for him was a moral issue, buy a postcard, often randomly so as to surprise himself with some new historical or literary personage. Such are the small rituals of solitude, which make the clawing world bearable. A tall and lanky figure, in his seventies, thinning white hair combed back, Patrick wore bell-bottoms, maybe the last person on the planet to do so, which he had specially made, and a full-length Australian bush ranger coat which made him look taller and lankier than he actually was. His eyes were deep-set in a way that often indicates ocular trouble.

What he looked for in particular were signed or inscribed books, which he would buy regardless of their content and no matter how obscure their authors were. If they were in any way related to World War Two or what life was like on the home front then so much the better. I think, from various things he said, that he was trying to recreate his mother's world. I know of no collector who delighted as much as he did in making a find. The signed or inscribed books he bought would be his research material for the following week, when he'd go to his local public library and find out as much as he could about the authors and, if possible, the dedicatees as well, entering the information in his childlike cursive in a fat little notebook he carried everywhere and about which he put thick rubber bands as if to stop it from bursting with fresh knowledge. I very much doubt he read more than a handful of his books, but he did read and that's what matters. The following Saturday, he would tell me of the discoveries he'd made over the previous week.

A man of very little formal education, he could get things in a frightful scramble sometimes, muddling names and often whole sentences. It would have taxed any grammar hound to keep track of the mistakes he made; he'd actually say *was you* or *they was*. If a writer were to put such dialogue on the page he'd be accused of striving for effect. Patrick had put himself on a course to learn as much as possible. At the same time he was highly considerate of other people's interests, buying books for them. Although no aficionado of opera, he would tell me of any forthcoming radio broadcasts, almost always getting the composer's and opera's names wrong so it became for me a kind of game working out what it was. And because his eyesight was so poor he would read word by word, sentence by sentence. This made him valiant in my eyes. The presence of such people in the world is enough to make me think that the bookseller's life and all the drudgery it entails is worth it.

Patrick could say "hello," "goodbye" and "how are you" in several languages. It became for him a point of honour to be able to address people in their own languages. Without fail he'd walk in, and even when the skies were clear, wipe his shoes on the doormat, and say '*Dzień dobry, jak się masz.*' (Good day, how are you?) When he picked up his prescriptions he'd say the same in Bengalese. *Hyālō.* Āpani *kēmani* āchēna. *Bidāya. Bidāya*, goodbye. I think his dentist was Chinese. *Nĭ hăo. Nĭ hăo ma. Zàijiàn.* And each time he spoke those words it was slowly and clumsily as if he were giving them utterance for the first time.

I had been wondering who among the people I knew would be the first to fall to the pandemic. A childhood neighbour on Jig Street, a gravel road in rural Ontario, died of it. I very much doubt Glen Hutchins, a farmer's boy, whose parents Orval and Violet Hutchins worked themselves to the bone, ever read a book and so I imagine he'd be baffled to find himself in the pages of one. I offer my condolences to the breeze. This is not to say his death did not affect me, but it was all such a long time ago and I struggle to keep his face in a single frame. Another face, however, will not quit my thoughts, there being barely a day it does not visit me at least once. I got news of Patrick's death a month after the fact. I knew he'd had throat cancer although the impression he gave was of not attaching too much importance to it, but then he was, for all his apparent openness, a very private man and may have kept his fears hidden. He went into hospital for treatment at a point when hospitals were deemed to be relatively safe and there contracted COVID-19. Sometime in June, at Charing Cross Hospital, a ten-minute walk from where I live, he died. When I gave Peter Ellis the news, he told me that he had only just spoken to a friend of his, telling him who he'd miss the most when he left Cecil Court. Patrick was at the top of his list. I should think the same holds true for the people who work at Any Amount of Books, Quinto and James Tindley.

An innocent in so many ways, a man of simplicity, whose love of books opened up a new world for himself, Patrick was also one of my most loyal readers, always coming to me with questions about what I'd written, which sometimes would exasperate but, more often than not, surprise me. I always did my best to answer them. Somehow, according to something I'd written in one of my books, he got the idea I was born in November and so, despite my protestations to the contrary, every year, towards the middle of November, he would bring me a fine bottle of Rioja.

'But Patrick, it is not my birthday.'

And he would smile the smile of one who wasn't going to be fooled for a minute.

After I got news of his death, I wrote to his brother Mick and discovered more details of his life. I learned that in the 1960s he was a lathe operator. He began to frequent Eel Pie Island in the Thames. The old hotel there had a dance floor, which saw the beginnings of many a band, among them the Rolling Stones (when Mick Jagger still wore a tie), Long John Baldry, John Mayall's Bluebreakers, David Bowie, The Who and Pink Floyd. Patrick was at those performances before any of the bands were famous and then he got a job on the island with a boat builder. Also he had a girlfriend called Berenice, who was probably the one and only love of his life. They were still in occasional contact. And then he got a job as an engineer at Isleworth Sewage Works where he became ill with some mystery disease and never worked again.

After his parents separated, he moved back home to take care of his elderly mother who had arthritis. Almost every day he would take her out in her wheelchair for a new adventure. On those outings he would take photographs of everyone they met during the course of the day, whether it be a railway worker, a ticket collector, a postman, a café owner or a waitress, and filled whole albums with them. One could say he was a conceptual artist without knowing it. Certainly it would have been the last thing to occur to him. I suspect a simpler motive: a lonely man sought to engage with, and preserve, the world.

Patrick also knew the Polish for goodbye.

Do widzenia, my friend, may your heaven be more of the same.

* * *

On May 17, 2020, a date I had already noted with melancholy, it being the anniversary of my mother's death, I learned that my octogenarian/bookseller friend Helen Hardy died, not from COVID-19 but from complications following a stroke. Again the news was late in coming to me. She worked for Travis & Emery Music Bookshop diagonally opposite Peter Ellis. Much to the bafflement of medics, she survived a brain tumour that ought to have taken her life a couple of years earlier. Rather than grow, it shrank. She proudly showed me the medical report and we agreed she had a record to achieve. She seemed indestructible. Sadly, though, she would not become the oldest bookseller ever, but at the time of her death she was, I believe, the oldest in London.

I first met Helen in the early 1980s when I sold her a copy of Constant Lambert's *Music Ho! A Study of Music in Decline* (1934), which was then a sought-after title but not so much anymore. (Surely there is room still for a book of such vivid prose.) She bought the book in a bit of a huff as if she were doing me an immense favour. I avoided her for another three decades. After I moved with Peter Ellis into Cecil Court, she and I would exchange morning greetings that gradually evolved into conversations and it got so she would always come into the shop for a chat before commencing work. Sometimes she reverted to the fierce manner of earlier times. She upbraided me once, angrily, for mispronouncing "Gesualdo." I had asked her if she had any books on the composer. I don't have a clear recollection of our last conversation, but then probably there was nothing of note, merely the pleasantries we exchanged from one week to the next. We dwelled mainly on trivial matters, the smaller the better, because I think they were the glue that held her world together. Triviality can be, on occasion, a good indicator of depth of feeling between two people. I pretended to be an informer so if she were a few minutes late I'd make a note on a scrap of paper, which I would then pretend to put into a secret file. She always enjoyed the joke. Very often we could have a perfectly viable discussion without ever once touching on the same subject. A colleague of hers once described our banter as utterly surreal although it seemed to me perfectly normal.

She asked very little of life and such as she was given made her girlishly happy so that weeks later she would still make mention of it. She described a small celebration for her many years of service as the greatest event of her life. I believed her absolutely. I gave her flowers on her birthday. They bloomed in her talk for weeks to come. She gave me a wonderful present once, a programme for a performance at the Wigmore Hall by my favourite pianist, Dinu Lipatti. The concert was on Sunday, April 4, 1948, Lipatti already seriously ill with the cancer that a couple of years later would claim his life. Helen, aged thirteen, was there. I gave her in return a copy of my book containing the poem "Dinu Lipatti plays Chopin's Sonata in B minor." She was horrified.

'Oh,' she said, 'I see.'

She then said poetry was not her thing, especially modern; it was too late to undo the giving of the book, which was already inscribed to her, and she could not undo the receiving of it. It was never mentioned again. One had to tread delicately with her and observe the peculiar limitations of her existence. Opera was not to her liking either nor did she indulge in exotic foods such as pasta, which she'd never tasted—*what, really?*—preferring, rather, the simplicity of chicken and potatoes. One consequence of her brain tumour was that she'd lost all sense of taste. This said, I don't think food for her was anything other than what one takes in order to stay alive. When I told her about an octopus I ate at a market stall in Palermo she stared as if into the black hole that will one day swallow our universe. She was, however, highly discriminate on the matter of chocolate. She told me she was brought to music when, aged ten, she was taken to a screening of the 1945 movie *A Song to Remember* which starred Cornel Wilde as Frédéric Chopin. It was no great task to imagine her at that age because she continued to carry the little girl she was into senescence. Whether she ever fell in love with anyone was not for me to know nor would ever I dream of asking, but I can't imagine there was anyone.

Violet was the colour of her lipstick and clothes.

The framed Lipatti programme hangs above the entrance to the small room where I work and is one of several things I have about me that serve as apotropaic devices. There is a Pulcinella which rather cleverly turns into a red horn, which a friend in Naples gave me, and to the left of me, again from Naples, there's a porcelain bell, an abstract figure of San Gennaro, which another friend gave me. You would think that with such a squad I'd be inoculated against trouble, and still it comes, but then I have to consider how much worse things might have been without them. That Sunday afternoon in 1948, Dinu Lipatti played the Chopin sonata, Ravel's "Alborada del gracioso," Bach's Chorale, Debussy's "La soirée dans Grenade," de Falla's "Ritual Danse du feu" and Liszt's "Sonetto 104 del Petrarca," which he never recorded because, perfectionist that he was, he recorded very little; he also played Brahms and Bach, the chorales in both G minor and major. It was a demanding programme for a man in his poor physical state.

What had been Lipatti's memorial will now serve as Helen's too.

* * *

I have already mentioned the obscure eighteenth-century reference to prostitutes, booksellers and thieves. I met a man whose distant ancestor might have fleeced the author of the piece, an antiquarian bookseller from America who described to me, without so much as a tremor of shame in his voice, his method for buying private libraries. If, say, there are a thousand books, among which are a number of rarities, he will choose several titles that are attractive to look at but of little value in themselves and leave them jutting out maybe half an inch on the shelves. After presenting the seller with a global figure for the collection he will then retire, leaving him or her—this works, so he told me, particularly well with widows—to consider his offer. If the answer is positive, which usually it is because, after all, he is a dealer of some repute, with some letters after his name to prove it, he'll discover that a few titles have been quietly removed or else the seller asks whether they can be excluded from the deal because they are of sentimental value. And, naturally enough, being of good heart although I wouldn't have put it past him to huff and puff a little and reduce the offer by a token amount equal to the pain of his loss, he will say okay, then, fine. These, of course, are invariably the ones he had left sticking out.

Surely this is a somewhat lamentable way for me to take my leave in a book that ultimately is meant to be a defence of the trade, but I think it is important to reveal, by means of an extreme example, the human frailty that underlies the transaction between buyer and seller, seller and buyer, and the psychology this often involves. I think the dealer I've just described deserves to be pilloried and just in case I am thought to be prejudiced, underhandedness is not an exclusively American trait; there are instances on these isles every bit as bad if not worse. Widows, beware. This said, the trade is just as much about life as it is about books and a certain amount of cunning goes into it as it does all other transactions where objects are of indeterminate value. I am experienced enough to know when a seller is going to haggle, and there, too, psychology is of prime importance, so I will make an offer a little less than the amount I am prepared to pay in full expectation that I will have to increase it by a percentage. There resides a bit of the Phoenician in all who negotiate. I would like to think I've been fair in my transactions, but fairness itself exists on a sliding scale. There is always a possibility of error and I am put in mind of John Byrne, who on several occasions, realising his offer was too low, would later send another cheque to the seller of the book to make up the difference.

And then there are those instances when a seller is presented with an offer higher than he expected and will decline it, saying he hadn't realised it was worth that much and then go to another bookseller with *that* figure in mind in the hope that he will do better. Sheepishly he will return, realising that the initial offer was the best, only to discover it has been withdrawn. I am of the view that Peter Ellis is fair and indeed often rather fairer than I am. He will make an offer in the belief that the books he buys will sell whereas I take the pessimistic route and assume a large number of them will never sell or at least take many years to. When we went buying together we would each work out an offer without letting the other know what it was and then compare notes. I am impressed by how often we arrived at roughly the same figure. If not, then we split the difference.

What about the seventeen years I worked with Peter, surely I have more to say about him? I'd rather not write about people still active in the trade. I reckon it was in him from the beginning to be a bookseller. It was not something he entered as a chancer. Growing up in Birmingham, where there are hardly any books to be found, might have been a factor. He is a reader and it is never less than interesting to hear his judgement of a title. We had many a laugh together. I would say he has more of a Protestant work ethic than I have, which is not to say I was idle. I pretended to be, and this was the stand-up routine Peter and I devised for the visiting world: I was there only because he couldn't get rid of me or he had sacked me and I kept coming in and he was too embarrassed to sack me twice. I enjoyed the role. I trust he did as well.

I think it is reasonable to say that the better organised a bookshop is, the less there is to say about it. There were fallow times, of course, when I had to convince Peter things would improve and that when things were difficult for us, they were difficult for everyone. I always felt honoured when he sought my advice.

* * *

I will make good my earlier promise that I'd be back in a frenzy of extreme prejudice. And so here he is again, the dealer who has just asked me whether I have any 'high spots' and to whom I reply *yes, all of them*. Awful though he may be, he is not quite as annoying as those who ask in an even more weaselly voice, 'Have you got anything I should know about?' Such dealers rarely lift their heads the few degrees it requires to see what is on the shelves. Should he ever read this, which I doubt, and recognise himself, which almost certainly he would, and should he take umbrage, so much the merrier, at least he will know from which direction the bullet comes. It is not his name alone on the bullet, however; he stands in for a good many other dealers. More than the pandemic, more than the economy, more than the general decline of intelligence, more than the internet and its spurious paradise, the species of bookseller I'm about to describe has all but destroyed the book trade.

The book upon which the following illustration of bad behaviour centres means not all that much to me, but it does to people who care for the genre. It is a first English edition of Erle Stanley Gardner's *Murder Up My Sleeve* (1938) in a pictorial dustwrapper depicting a Chinese villain whose physical characteristics may cause delicate souls offence. Ours is a deeply sensitive age, maybe the most sensitive in history, such that we are at pains to apologise for the behaviour of even people who have been long in their graves. Once upon a time, the image on the dustwrapper would have passed unremarked, especially when people living in the 1930s were already inured to the "yellow peril" as depicted on the covers of Sax Rohmer's Fu Manchu series. Actually the Gardner cover is rather lurid and if this Chinese man is representative of maybe hundreds of thousands of Chinese men then one might justifiably cry prejudice in which case one should tear off the dustwrapper, scrunch it up and throw it in the bin, thereby turning a £2,500 book into a £250 one. Ah, but do I not detect a weakening of resolve? The blurb on the dustwrapper of *Murder Up My Sleeve* tells us 'Jacob Mandra has been murdered by a queer device, a Chinese sleeve-gun.' The author was onto something because the sleeve gun was soon to be developed during the Second World

War by "Station IX" of the Special Operations Executive. The dustwrapper is in excellent state with just a few tiny nicks at the top edge, the white of the spine a brilliant white, and the book beneath the skin, while not perfect, there being just a little spotting to the edges, is in excellent state. Naturally enough, as a member of the Antiquarian Book Association the dealer who looked at it would have been entitled to a 20 per cent trade discount. At the time of writing there are no other copies on the market.

The dealer, who specialises in crime, first dismissed our very bright copy of Arthur Conan Doyle's *The Hound of the Baskervilles* (1902) because it was not inscribed by the author, and besides, he already had several copies in stock. Well, bully for him, but that was no reason to sniff at our all too humble copy. When it came to the Gardner, however, he found good reason to pause because in all his years of dealing he had never set eyes on the dustwrapper. Nor had we. He turned the book this way and that and then put it back in its place, saying, 'When you get a good copy, let me know. I'll take it at any price.' *At any price* is, of course, big dealer's big talk.

Why am I so het up about this? Why not go for a sprint along the Thames instead? I don't mind if he thought the book was too expensive for him to realise a profit. What I do mind is that he thought our copy unworthy of consideration and all because of a few nicks on a dustwrapper he himself professed never to have seen. What I also mind is his attitude towards a fellow bookseller. Why *should* we supply him with a perfect copy? Not only am I weary of these people, but they have also done the reputation of the trade incalculable damage. For one thing, they have been responsible for imposing upon the minds of collectors an utterly false set of values. The collector has been bamboozled into thinking that a copy with a dustwrapper that has been price-clipped, for example, cannot be considered a collector's copy. Clearly something has happened since I first entered the trade, when once I saw a collector so overcome with being offered, after twenty years of searching for it, a rare book that he was close to tears. I wish I could remember what the title was, but what I do remember is that it lacked the dustwrapper and the covers were none too bright. Nowadays he will have been deceived into thinking that without the dustwrapper it is not a book. I am not suggesting that there ought not to be premium put on a perfect copy nor am I saying one should be content with an imperfect one, but clearly something catastrophic has happened in the trade; it has been the fetishization of the book as object to the degree that we forget it is, first and foremost, the vehicle of the word. And human nature being what it is, where fetishization occurs pleasure is diminished or, rather, it is only a poor facsimile of pleasure.

As this book is aimed at people who suspect, not always wrongly, that there is some kind of mystique in the antiquarian book trade, maybe they would like to know why a book should be considered of value when its literary worth is not nearly as great as a book a fraction of the price. A guide to the perplexed, as this is supposed to be, I'm still at a loss to understand why a copy of *Casino Royale* (1953) is pricier than a copy of Joseph Conrad's *Youth* (1902), which contains three stories, one of them arguably the greatest novella of modern times, *Heart of Darkness*. One may safely ignore the idiotic health warning from politically correct quarters that, although it pretends not to be, it is a story shot through with the author's innate racism. It won't be long before we will have to speak in whispers of Ian Fleming's cavalier attitude towards women. This is not to say *Casino Royale* is not splendid entertainment, but it is difficult to argue that it is more than that or that it approaches the condition of great literature. I think that somewhere along the way, when I was slightly more than a fledgling bookseller, I might have been able to argue the case for it being the more valuable of the two books although I'd still have to put a harness on my voice.

'Mistah Kurtz—he dead,' writes Conrad at the end of his masterpiece. 'Mistah Kurtz—he dead,' writes Eliot at the beginning of his masterpiece, "The Hollow Men," lines from which Francis Ford Coppola had the wit to put into Colonel Kurtz's mouth in his film masterpiece, *Apocalypse Now* (1979) in which, of course, he deploys Conrad's story to extraordinary effect. As we are talking about values, however, I will focus on Eliot's greater work, *The Waste Land* (1923). At the time of writing one can purchase a bright copy of the Hogarth Press edition for £7,500, a mere snip when compared to, from the very same bookseller, £50,000 for *Casino Royale*. (Actually the first edition of Eliot's poem was published in America by Boni & Liveright in 1922, but for various reasons the one hand-printed by Leonard and Virginia Woolf is preferable.) *Casino Royale* had a print run of 4,760 copies, of which 4,728 were bound, leaving 32 sets of sheets unaccounted for; the Hogarth Press issue of *The Waste Land* had a printing of about 460 copies although if one is in the mood for splitting hairs one could say it comes in three variant states, the copy to which I refer being the most desirable one with a pattern of asterisks surrounding the title on the paper label mounted on the upper cover. *Casino Royale* is a sturdier book, which means there is a greater likelihood of finding a very nice copy in dustwrapper than an equally nice copy of *The Waste Land* which is in paper-covered boards, therefore more fragile, and quite often lacking the spine. The copy currently on offer is in very nice condition.

So what is going on here? I could go on with numerous examples. Quite recently a customer asked why the price of a first edition of Mark Twain's *Huckleberry Finn* (1884)* was considerably less than the figure we had on another book beside it in the display case, *One Flew Over the Cuckoo's Nest* (1962). Where does a book's value lie? It is, first and foremost, in what it is, a skilled assemblage of words. It begins there, and in the convoluted world of rare books, ends there. What goes on in between is why I have written this book. The intrinsic value of a battered paperback reprint of T. S. Eliot's *The Waste Land* is the same as the copy of the Hogarth Press edition, the first issue, which Eliot placed in the hands of *il miglior fabbro*, Ezra Pound. The first copy may bring about a transformation in the mind of the reader and indeed may encourage him to take up the pen himself, but I would dearly love to possess

* The first edition, published in this country by Chatto and Windus, precedes the American edition published a year later. The American first tends to be the more expensive of the two. In collecting terminology this is called 'following the flag.'

the latter copy, if only for the thrill of having in my hands such a piece of literary history. Desire determines value.

The worst damage to the trade has been done by the trade itself. We saw the seeds of this in the late 1970s and continuing through into the early '90s when books published only months before were fetching ridiculous prices. Michael Ondaatje's *The English Patient* (1992) is a perfect instance. The price peaked for several months, mainly because of the fuss that was made of it, and the film, and then it fell sharply. The same is true for Louis de Bernières's *Captain Corelli's Mandolin* (1994) a book I greatly enjoyed at the same time as everyone else, when one couldn't step onto a bus or train without seeing *somebody* reading it. It, too, was turned into a rather feeble film. Absurd prices were charged for a fine copy in dustwrapper, the first issue in white as opposed to black cloth. This is bookselling of a kind that has been dealt a lethal blow by the internet when it became apparent just how many copies were out there. The reason this is not happening so much anymore is that the internet, while being a forum for idiots selling to other idiots, has also forced the serious bookseller's hand so that it is now incumbent on him to become a bit more realistic on the matter of what constitutes scarcity. There is no bookseller as foolish as he who describes a book as rare while on the same website there are perhaps a hundred copies available. There are still some out there who seem not to have got the message, who will stand in a queue at readings and signings and slide a mountain of books over the author's table for him to sign and thereby raise their value a little. What has happened is that there are countless signed copies available on the web. The sad fact is that anybody can become a bookseller. You can find them in their thousands on ABE (Advanced Book Exchange). There needs to be a culling of sorts.

* * *

Some days the bookshop is dead. Other days it comes alive. One Saturday, I decided to take notes. As it happened they are all related to people I saw but once. There are customers who come, make a splash, sometimes a *very* big splash, and then vanish, never to be seen again. A Greek living part of the time in England came in and announced that he was disinclined to add any further volumes to his library of forty-five thousand books in Athens. All he wanted was to browse. We fell into conversation. We spoke of Brexit, which would be the subject of three conversations that day, all of my customers in agreement that this country was operating on a suiciding principle. I argued with the Greek nevertheless, saying that while economics is an issue, and yes, there really is a worldwide shift towards the right, resulting in the worst kind of populism, there is something else, the closing of the English mind to outside influences. We agreed that English literature is never as alive as when it allows for the admittance of other cultures.

'I suspect you are a writer,' I told him.

Apostolos Doxiadis is the author of *Uncle Petros and Goldbach's Conjecture* (2001) and a graphic novel *Logicomix, An Epic Search for Truth* (2009). We spoke for almost two hours, covering a wide range of subjects and he left and came back with a copy of the latter title, which he presented to me. It will be my first venture inside a genre that has thus far passed me by. It is based on the early life of Bertrand Russell. Doxiadis, a mathematician by training, brings those skills into what he writes. It is claimed that *Uncle Petros* is the first mathematical novel although I wonder if we can know this for sure. What has not been done at least once?* We closed our discussion with an attack on Edward Said's *Orientalism* (1978) and its thick web of falsehoods to which countless students blindly subscribe.

As it turned out, he did buy a book, Ezra Pound's *Drafts and Fragments of Cantos CX–CXVII* (1970). He might not have done so were it not for our conversation. This is just one of the reasons the bookshop is a magical place.

---

* I have read it now and as a mathematical nincompoop, a position from which it is probably too late to be rescued, I declare the book a success and, even more important, a pleasure to read.

A bit later, an Irishman living in New York, a collector of James Joyce, and on his way to a Joyce conference in Dublin, came in. With Brexit still in the ether, he told me how his Irish father volunteered as a pilot in World War Two but that with things going as they were he might as well have joined the Luftwaffe instead. Maybe that was pushing it a little, but I did catch the exasperation in his voice. If only, he said, those politicians in favour of Brexit could hear the conversations in his New York office, one client after another pulling their money out of the United Kingdom.

I had been trying to articulate something else that might account for the sinking fortunes of the book trade when a young, strikingly handsome Italian man walked into the bookshop, looking for a copy of Elliott O'Donnell's *Strange Cults & Secret Societies of Modern London* (1934). Giorgio Vingiani is a marine biologist working for Stazione Zoologica Anton Dohrn in Naples. I was greatly cheered by the arrival, even though it was almost closing time, of this emissary from what has become a favourite city of mine. When I told him of my love for his city, he seemed surprised although he may have been playing with me a little. Many Neapolitans have a habit of knocking their city only in order to elicit other people's defence of the place. As for the title he wanted I had to disappoint him, adding that surely there was plenty in Naples to feed a craving for the esoteric.

'Yes, sure,' he replied, 'but there is one big difference. We have these cults in Naples and they're real, but the ones O'Donnell wrote about never existed. He made them up and then his readers went looking for them.'

Giorgio then went on to explain how during the interwar years there was a real appetite for the supernatural and spiritualism.

'The Great War was to a degree responsible for this. In 1914 there were 145 societies affiliated to the Spiritualists National Union. By 1918 it had more than doubled. There was the so-called Crewe Circle who claimed they could photograph the spirits of lost loved ones. Arthur Conan Doyle endorsed spiritualism.'

I marvelled not only at Giorgio's command of English but also at his ability to summon facts and figures. What he was saying was true. There are any number of books from that period which prove the case. Sir Oliver Lodge published a book called *Raymond, or, Life and Death* (1916), which details his communications with his son who died at the Battle of Ypres in 1915. And then there was the publication of Arthur Machen's *The Bowmen and Other Legends of the War* (1915) which introduced "The Angel of Mons" legend about ghostly archers from Agincourt coming to the rescue of British soldiers at the Battle of Mons. Machen's story was accepted as fact and soldiers returned from the Western Front with reports of dead enemy combatants with arrows stuck in them. The very first casualty of the war was inflicted by a Captain Hornby who on horseback killed a lancer. Could Machen's story have been inspired by this mediaeval-like encounter? That appetite of which Giorgio spoke was not so much pre-war as post-war and is most commonly located in people who had suffered terrible losses. Could it be that in the wake of a reality too terrible to absorb people had become all the more gullible? Maybe. The current crisis, although not nearly as terrible, has resulted in bizarre behaviour, the 'COVID parties,' for example, a distant echo of those mediaeval people who tried to dance away the plague. Musically the sense of loss following the Great War was caught in "Marietta's Song," the aria everybody remembers from Erich Wolfgang Korngold's opera *Die Tote Stadt* (*The Dead City*, 1920). A lament for a lost one who has been 'seen,' how it must have resonated with the audience of the time.

The scene was set for Elliott O'Donnell.

I've never set eyes on a copy of *Strange Cults & Secret Societies of Modern London* although I've handled other titles by him, almost all of them on the subject of ghosts. There is now little call for him, not even among aficionados of the supernatural of whom there are quite a few. They are fussy about their ghosts and will not be fobbed off with cheap facsimiles. Although O'Donnell was transparently a fake, he managed to publish over fifty titles and was called upon as an authority on the subject and invited to write newspaper articles and deliver lectures. A professional 'ghost hunter,' O'Donnell cornered the market. He lived to be ninety-three at which point he became what he had hitherto pursued. In his Will he left £2,579, which I find interesting because not long ago his archive sold for £25,000. Given that he died in 1965 and the archive sold in 2016, his 'value,' taking into account inflation, stayed roughly the same. What interests Giorgio is the phenomenon of a writer who manages to cash in on a willingly deceived readership. As long as this remains a part of our human condition, magicians and charlatans will continue to thrive.

Giorgio told me that every time he goes into the old centre of Naples another bookshop has gone. I told him that here it is likewise.

'So what's *your* excuse?' he asked.

I came up with the usual stuff about increasing rents and rates, and people buying books more cheaply online. It was then that he sprang a surprise. He asked after my age, apologising for doing so in advance.

'Yes,' he replied, 'I figured it would be close to that.'

Clearly no flatterer he.

'The real problem,' he continued, 'is that your generation failed to pass on to the next what it knows. There has been a break in the chain of knowledge. Our generation has been left stranded, not knowing which way to go, and now with computers and other distractions it is unable to focus on anything. It certainly doesn't read books. The problem is not just with the things you mention. It has more to do with the culture itself.'

So there in a nub was what I'd been earlier trying to articulate.

When Giorgio left I was startled to see it was already close to half an hour past closing time. I got up to lock the door when two Armenians from America, father and son, came in, asking after books by William Saroyan. All day nothing happened and now, as I struggled to make my escape, people kept coming. I showed them a copy of *One Day in the Afternoon of the World*, the second English edition of 1966, inscribed by the author to the film director Karel Riesz and his wife, Betsy Blair. It was a good association copy, which, for those readers unfamiliar with book trade jargon, is a book inscribed by the author to another person (in this case two people) of significance. This makes a book all the more valuable, the better the back story the higher the price.

Saroyan had been friends with Betsy Blair since 1941 when she played the role of Agnes Webster ("Saint Agnes of the Mice") in his play *The Beautiful People.* She was seventeen at the time and had just married Gene Kelly, who the year before played Harry the Hoofer in the 1940 production of Saroyan's play *The Time of Your Life.* All in all, it is a nice chain of associations. 'He's a big bruiser,' Gene Kelly said of Saroyan, 'as regular as they come, and looks like a contented ice man.'

My Armenian customer then told me about how one day he was offered a lift somewhere, but that first the driver had to stop off to see a friend of his. They got to the place and the friend came to the door dressed in nothing but his underwear. It was William Saroyan.

'That's how I began collecting him,' my customer told me. 'Saroyan is of Armenian ancestry.'

I mentioned how much I liked Armenian sacred music, telling him I first heard it many years ago while leaning against the wall of a church in Aleppo. I heard the choir inside and thought I'd gone to heaven. He told me about the Armenian church of St Sarkis in London which was built by Calouste Gulbenkian in the 1920s and modelled on the ancient bell tower at Haghpat Monastery in Armenia. And then I told him about the beautiful seventeenth-century Vank Cathedral I saw when I was in Isfahan and how in front of it I spoke to a young Iranian couple who expressed their desire to become Christian, the first and only time in my life I'd heard such sentiments from Muslims. 'What's stopping you?' I asked them, and the man with his finger drew a line across his throat.

A purchase made, the Armenians left. I was actually in the act of closing the shop when an American woman put her foot in the door.

'Sorrrreeeee, I can see you're closing,' she said. 'Do you have a copy of *How to Be Sexy with Bugs in Your Teeth*?'

This was rather late in the day for practical jokes. I was getting hungry too.

'I think I'd remember the title,' I replied.

'That's what all you bookseller guys say,' she answered.

'You mean there really is a book of that title?'

I should have known better. It turned out to be a comic history of women and motorcycles. After she left, I checked ABE, on which most booksellers list their books online. A single paperback copy is available from a bookseller in Portsmouth, New Hampshire, for $795. It is not even a first edition. After all these years in the trade, I know nothing.

I closed up shop and went home.

* * *

Quite unbidden, a couple of lines of poetry come to me: 'Pull down thy vanity, / Paquin pull down!' It is from Canto LXXXI of Ezra Pound's mighty, though often abstruse, opus. My copy of *The Pisan Cantos* (1949) in which those lines first appear once had a short autograph letter from the author tucked inside. The content was of scant importance, its only value residing in the signature. Still it was a nice thing to have. Should the man I entrusted with the keys to our place ever read these words, I ask him to return it to me. Silly of him to think I wouldn't notice.

Who is Paquin? When I first read the lines, in my mid-twenties, I associated the name with troubadour poetry, a moniker one might happily attach to a rebec or a lute. I now discover it was a well-known Paris couturière, Jeanne Paquin, who briefly had a fashion house in London in 1912 when Pound still lived there. She made the costumes Picasso designed for the Ballets Russes production of Erik Satie's *Parade* (1917). The deployment of her name makes good sense, fashion being close to the top of any list of the world's vanities, but it is also an example of how sound alone can be enough to make one believe in a poem's inner truth. Paquin, the gravitational pull of it; actual meaning seems to me of little consequence. The lines have always haunted me, and when we look at what immediately precedes them we find the calm and measured voice of a monstrous ego brought to heel by nature.

> The ant's a centaur in his dragon world.
> Pull down thy vanity, it is not man
> Made courage, or made order, or made grace,
> Pull down thy vanity I say pull down.
> Learn of the green world what can be thy place
> In scaled invention or true artistry,
> Pull down thy vanity,
> Paquin pull down!
> The green casque has outdone your elegance.

Why did it take Pound so long to be contrite? The world no longer accepts his apologies. It did once. Now we are invited to see only the objectionable side of the man, which was indeed objectionable. The mistake was to have made excuses for him in the first place. What matters is that he was finally brought to the truth of his folly, which is more than can be said for many people. Were it not for *The Pisan Cantos* and the final *Drafts & Fragments of Cantos* CX–CXVII in which his remorse could not have been clearer—'To be men not destroyers'—the whole of his enormous poetic venture would have been a cranky failure.

The only time I have ever vandalised one of my books, and the shame of it sits heavily on me, was when I removed from Alvin Langdon Coburn's *More Men of Mark* (1922) his photographic portrait of Ezra Pound which now hangs on my wall. Even as the image of an unknown man one could mistake it for a Renaissance prince. A friend chastises me, not for what I did to the book, but for giving place of honour to a traitor and anti-Semite, and all I can offer him as a defence, which I offer to all who in condemning Pound also condemn his achievements, are the lines I have just quoted, arguably the greatest in twentieth-century poetry. It is not a bad time in which to revisit them now the world's vanity has been pulled down into the mire. We've made a pretty poor show at demonstrating our might in the face of nature. I'm only sorry that a pangolin paid for it with its life.

One sunny day, early in the lockdown, I took a walk along the Thames to where there is the reservoir on the other side. Such traffic as there was, was barely audible. The breeze rattled the leaves and the birds seemed to sing louder than ever before, although I fancied they sang expletives at me, as if to say, *Look at the fine mess you've made of things, you and your feckless species. Paquin pull down.* Once again I look again at my books, my trophies if you like. They are a kind of shoring up against one's own mortality, a composite of one's own vanities, and words I wrote some years ago come back to haunt me. *All will be gone, all we ever were will cease to be.*

CODA

MELANCHOLY IS AN OLD HUNGRY HORSE. IT NEEDS TO BE constantly replenished. After the second wave of the pandemic, although it was never quite over, I ventured into central London where my barber is, who understands that my haircuts end where other people's begin. It's why I brave the malevolent particles; there's nobody else I can trust with my skull. A collector of sorts, he subscribes to not a book club exactly but something close to, which 'curates' signed first edition copies of new titles. He doesn't choose them. They are automatically supplied, monthly. I know from where and it is not a collection I'd ever want to own. As he really believes those books are an investment, with an estimated 300 per cent increase in value, I bite my tongue. (Some bookseller, I'm glad he knows the future course of our literature.) Anyway the loss will not be all that great and, who knows, my barber might read one of them. Also he collects original movie posters and with the one for *La Dolce Vita* among them what he'll lose in one place he'll recover in the other. After clinging on for dear life, two lockdowns later, he has just had his rent raised. Where's the dog's muzzle for human greed? How many shorn locks will it require for him to be able to survive? Will this become yet another empty space?

The city was drained of life, so many shops and cafés familiar to me gone. Our politicos haven't got a clue. A bounder by nature, a bounder politically, our leader knows not of what people are made. So he knows not what they value. And after a while they fail to notice what is being lost. It's how the cornbread crumbles. They are losing their culture. I went to see what had become of the old shop. Maybe I shouldn't have. All that remained of it was Peter Ellis's name in gilt letters above the window; its interior was gutted, and inside the window display was a weighing scale. Was Peter being ironic? Certainly he is pleased to have the burden of running a bookshop taken off him. Stripped bare, the place looked so small, so insignificant, and indeed customers, who bought from our catalogues, when they visited the premises for the first time were often surprised by its size, that it could have issued so many treasures. What they didn't see was that the basement has three times as much space and was always close to bursting with stock, catalogued and uncatalogued.

Size matters not, quality does.

Small, large, I have always been sensitive to spaces. There are those which work and those which don't. Also I have a feeling for dead zones. There's no remedy for them. Whatever moves into them flops. There is no logical reason for this other than there are presiding spirits just as there are weather gods, mythical tricksters and trolls. There may have been shops smarter in appearance than ours, bigger, brighter, but very few with the buzz that allows a bookshop to thrive. Ours was a pleasure to walk into, or so I've been able to gauge from the people who strolled in. 'What a wonderful shop,' they'd say or some such. Maybe it was not quite as chaotic as I would have liked, but it was, and Peter may laugh at this, a charmed space.

Where is everyone? Where is young Master Jack Kendall? One of the most ethereal people I've ever known, he dressed in a long brown cape and wore multiple bracelets and bead necklaces.

Swinburne was his first love, a dangerous love to have, a corrupter not so much of souls as of people's epistolary and conversational style. I miss Jack's purple. And where's the Saturday morning visitor who was obsessed by Thomas Lovell Beddoes? Actually I think he had all there is to have, but it didn't stop him from wanting more. Those are the customers one likes. The last time I saw him he told me he'd just fallen in love. So happy he was, I feared for him. Something in his voice told me he'd jumped the gun and whoever jumps the gun does not want to revisit the jumping scene. That was seven years ago. Where did he get to, hell or paradise? What happens if either of them ever strays into Cecil Court again, chasing after Swinburne or Beddoes? One more bookshop gone, what dies with each one is a book's worth of stories.

ACKNOWLEDGEMENTS

I AM GRATEFUL TO THOSE MANY PEOPLE WHO HELPED ME, some of whom may take issue with what I wrote, and to them I say that any errors I have made are mine alone. Thank you, David Berridge, Jonathan Brodie, Mick Bollard, Nigel Burwood, John Byrne, Peter Caracciolo, Jaqi Clayton, Cheryl Cooper, John Eggeling, Peter Ellis, Tony Fekete, David Hackbridge Johnson, Nathalie Kay-Thatcher, George Lawson, Patrick McGahern, Gillian McMullan, Julian Nangle, Charles Peltz, Paul Rassam, Jeremy Reed, Anthony Rudolf, Peter T. Scott, Norm Sibum, Anthony Sillem, Anthony J. Simmonds, James Sutherland-Smith, Vanessa Stauffer, David Tobin, Kala Trobe, Charles Unsworth, Camille Whitaker, and a special word of thanks to my wife, Bobbie, who went through the manuscript and spared me countless embarrassments, and to Chandra Wohleber and her wondrously sharp editorial eye. I'd better say thanks as well to the book's dedicatee.

PHOTO BY BOBBIE KOCIEJOWSKI

MARIUS KOCIEJOWSKI, born 1949, is a poet, essayist, and travel writer. Among the books he has written are *The Street Philosopher and the Holy Fool: A Syrian Journey*, now reissued by Eland, and a sequel, *The Pigeon Wars of Damascus*, published by Biblioasis in 2010. His first collection of poetry, *Coast* (Greville Press, 1990), was awarded the Cheltenham Prize. His most recent books are *God's Zoo: Artists, Exiles, Londoners* (Carcanet, 2014), *The Pebble Chance: prose & feuilletons* (Biblioasis, 2014), *Zoroaster's Children and other travels* (Biblioasis, 2015), and *Collected Poems* (Carcanet, 2019). He has recently completed another travel book, *The Serpent Coiled in Naples* (Haus, May 2022). He lives in London, England, where, until recently, he worked as an antiquarian bookseller.

CPSIA information can be obtained
at www.ICGtesting.com
Printed in the USA
JSHW061749250822
29762JS00001B/1

9 781771 964562